2

ScottForesman

Accelerating English Language Learning

Authors

Anna Uhl Chamot

Jim Cummins

Carolyn Kessler

J. Michael O'Malley

Lily Wong Fillmore

Consultant

George González

ScottForesman

A Division of HarperCollins*Publishers*

Editorial Offices: Glenview, Illinois
Regional Offices: Sunnyvale, California • Atlanta, Georgia
Glenview, Illinois • Oakland, New Jersey • Dallas, Texas

Visit ScottForesman's Home Page at http://www.scottforesman.com

ISBN 0-673-19678-X
ISBN 0-673-19686-0 [Texas]
Copyright © 1997 Scott, Foresman and Company, Glenview, Illinois
All Rights Reserved. Printed in the United States of America.

Scott, Foresman and Company,
1900 East Lake Avenue, Glenview, Illinois 60025.

1.800.554.4411
http://www.scottforesman.com

1 2 3 4 5 6 7 8 9 10 BB 05 04 03 02 01 00 99 98 97 96

CONTENTS

ANNA UHL CHAMOT is an associate professor in the area of ESL teacher preparation at George Washington University. Previously Associate Director of the Georgetown University/Center for Applied Linguistics National Foreign Language Resource Center, she also managed two Title VII Special Alternative Instructional Projects in the Arlington, Virginia, Public Schools. She has co-authored two books with J. Michael O'Malley, *Learning Strategies in Second Language Acquisition* and *The CALLA Handbook: How to Implement the Cognitive Academic Language Learning Approach.* Other publications include content-ESL books in history and mathematics and a textbook series based on the CALLA model, *Building Bridges: Content and Learning Strategies for ESL.* Dr. Chamot holds a Ph.D. in ESL and applied linguistics from the University of Texas at Austin, and a Master's degree in foreign language education from Teachers College, Columbia University.

JIM CUMMINS is a professor in the Modern Language Centre and Curriculum Department of the Ontario Institute for Studies in Education. He has published several books related to bilingual education and ESL student achievement including: *Bilingualism and Special Education: Issues in Assessment and Pedagogy; Bilingualism in Education: Aspects of Theory, Research and Policy* (with Merrill Swain); *Minority Education: From Shame to Struggle* (with Tove Skutnabb-Kangas); and *Empowering Minority Students.* His latest and highly acclaimed work is *Brave New Schools: Challenging Cultural Illiteracy Through Global Learning Networks* (with Dennis Sayers). His current research focuses on the challenges educators face in adjusting to classrooms where cultural and linguistic diversity is the norm. Dr. Cummins received his Ph.D. from the University of Alberta, Canada.

CAROLYN KESSLER is a professor of ESL and Applied Linguistics at the University of Texas at San Antonio. She has extensive experience in teacher education for meeting the needs of linguistically and culturally diverse populations. Among recent books and monographs authored or co-authored are: *Cooperative Language Learning: A Teacher's Resource Book; Literacy con Cariño: A Story of Migrant Children's Success; Making Connections: An Integrated Approach to ESL* (a secondary program), *Parade* (a K-6 EFL program), and *Teaching Science to English Learners, Grades 4-8.* Her research interests include the integration of content area learning with second language and literacy development, adult and family literacy and language learning, and second language acquisition for both children and adults. Dr. Kessler holds both an M.S. and a Ph.D. from Georgetown University.

J. MICHAEL O'MALLEY is Supervisor of Assessment and Evaluation in Prince William County Public Schools in Virginia, where he is establishing a performance assessment program in grades K-12. He was previously Senior Researcher in the National Foreign Language Resource Center at Georgetown University and for six years was Director of the Evaluation Assistance Center at Georgetown University. Dr. O'Malley is co-developer with Anna Uhl Chamot of the Cognitive Academic Language Learning Approach (CALLA). CALLA was introduced by O'Malley and Chamot in 1986 and was the subject of both their 1994 work *The CALLA Handbook* and their earlier book on the research and theory underlying the approach. Dr. O'Malley is noted for his research on learning strategies in second language acquisition and for his work on assessment of language minority students. He received his Ph.D. in psychology from George Peabody College.

LILY WONG FILLMORE is a professor in the Graduate School of Education at the University of California, Berkeley. Her specializations are in the areas of second language learning and teaching, the education of language minority students, and socialization for learning across cultures. She is project director and principal investigator for the Family, Community, and the University Partnership, which prepares professionals to work in educational institutions in American Indian communities in the Southwest. She is also a major advisor to the Council of Chief State School Officer's LEP SCASS initiative, in which representatives from several states are working to develop ways to assess the conditions under which LEP students acquire English language skills at school. Dr. Wong Fillmore received her Ph.D. in linguistics from Stanford University.

CRITIC READERS

Sandra H. Bible
Elementary ESL Teacher
Shawnee Mission School District
Shawnee Mission, Kansas

Betty A. Billups
Dallas Independent School District
Dallas, Texas

María G. Cano
BIL/ESL Specialist
Pasadena Independent School District
Pasadena, Texas

Anaida Colón-Muñiz, Ed.D.
Director of English Language
Development
and Bilingual Education
Santa Ana Unified School District
Santa Ana, California

Debbie Corkey-Corber
Educational Consultant
Williamsburg, Virginia

Lily Pham Dam
Instructional Specialist
Dallas Independent School District
Dallas, Texas

María Delgado
Milwaukee Public Schools
Milwaukee, Wisconsin

Dr. María Viramontes de Marín
Chair, Department of Education and
Liberal Studies at the National
Hispanic University
San Jose, California

Tim Hart
Supervisor of English as a Second
Language
Wake County
Raleigh, North Carolina

Lilian I. Jezik
Bilingual Resource Teacher
Colorna-Norco Unified School District
Norco, California

Helen L. Lin
Chairman, Education Program
Multicultural Arts Council of Orange
County, California
Formerly ESL Lab Director, Kansas
City, Kansas Schools

Teresa Montaña
United Teachers Los Angeles
Los Angeles, California

Loriana M. Novoa, Ed.D.
Research and Evaluation Consultants
Miami, Florida

Rosa María Peña
Austin Independent School District
Austin, Texas

Thuy Pham-Remmele
ESL/Bilingual K-12 Specialist
Madison Metropolitan School District
Madison, Wisconsin

Roberto San Miguel
Kennedy-Zapata Elementary School
El Cenizo, Texas

Jacqueline J. Servi Margis
ESL and Foreign Language
Curriculum Specialist
Milwaukee Public Schools
Milwaukee, Wisconsin

Elizabeth Streightoff
ESL Magnet Teacher, Lamar
Elementary School
Conroe Independent School District
The Woodlands, Texas

Susan C. VanLeuven
Poudre R-1 School District
Fort Collins, Colorado

Rosaura Villaseñor
(Educator)
Norwalk, California

Sharon Weiss
ESL Consultant
Glenview, Illinois

Cheryl Wilkinson
J.O. Davis Elementary School
Irving Independent School District
Irving, Texas

Phyllis I. Ziegler
ESL/Bilingual Consultant
New York, New York

PROGRAM PHILOSOPHY

The Philosophy of *ScottForesman ESL*

ScottForesman ESL accelerates English language learning through the use and application of the following principles.

Thematic Units

In theme- or topic-based lessons, curriculum content is presented thematically to provide the basis for language learning. Topic-related language and concepts are recycled over a period of time, ensuring their conceptualization and making students increasingly able to communicate their ideas on the topic. Each level of *ScottForesman ESL* contains six thematic units; each unit contains two related chapters. In each unit students are exposed to a rich array of language and activities based on the major topic. As students work through each unit, the variety of text types, formats, and activities enables them to master both the language and the concepts.

Balanced Skills

In each chapter of *ScottForesman ESL,* students develop all of the four language skills—listening, speaking, reading, and writing. This balanced approach ensures communicative proficiency. Authentic texts, both fiction and nonfiction, give ample reading practice. "Talk About It" and "Write About It" sections in each chapter offer practice in listening, speaking, and writing. The "Writer's Workshop" in Books 2-8 leads students through the writing process. These sections, along with the abundant optional activities, give students the time and opportunity to achieve communicative competence.

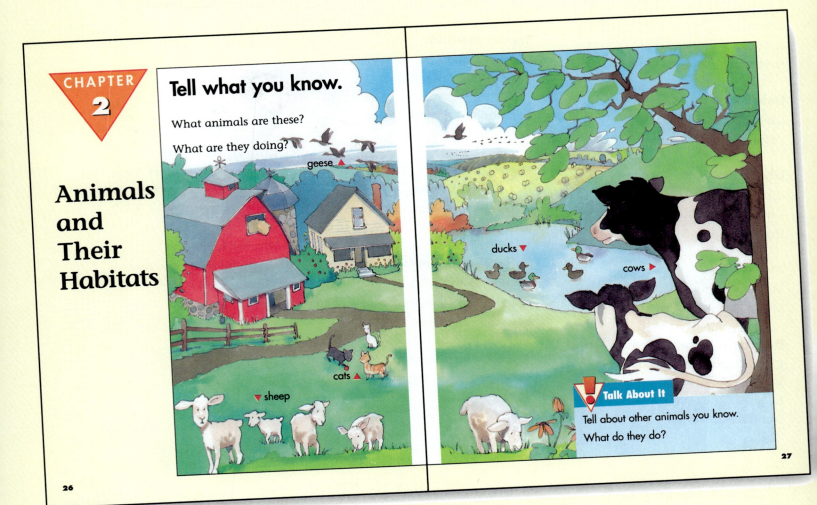

The Cognitive Academic Language Learning Approach (CALLA)

ScottForesman ESL follows the principles of CALLA: it teaches grade-level topics from the major curriculum areas; it develops academic language skills; and it provides explicit instruction in learning strategies for both content and language acquisition.

Learning Strategies

Learning strategies are actions or thoughts that students can apply to challenging tasks. *ScottForesman ESL* integrates learning strategies instruction into each part of the learning process by providing guidelines for teaching the strategies and for helping students develop an awareness of their own learning processes.

Cooperative Learning

Throughout *ScottForesman ESL,* cooperative learning activities give students opportunities to work in groups to share what they know and to learn new information and skills. For a cooperative group to be successful, there should be a common, agreed upon goal and assigned individual roles for achieving that goal. In fact, cooperative learning activities are characterized by three components: (1) Positive interdependence—members rely on each other to achieve the end product; (2) Individual accountability—each member is responsible for information that is used to achieve the group's goal; (3) Face-to-face interaction—members work and talk together. In addition, cooperative learning may entail (4) Group processing—the group reviews what they did in terms of the group process or group mechanics; and (5) Development of social skills—members use group maintenance skills to keep the process going and task skills to perform what is required.

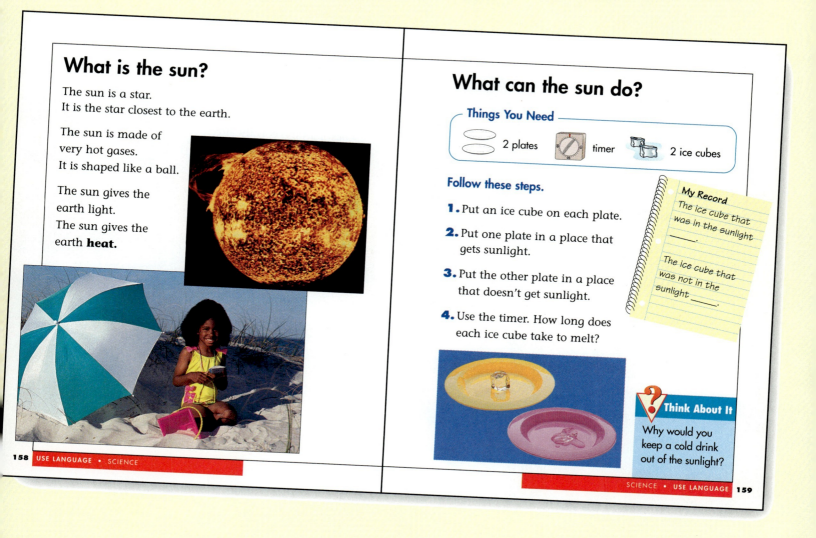

What is the sun?

The sun is a star.
It is the star closest to the earth.

The sun is made of very hot gases.
It is shaped like a ball.

The sun gives the earth light.
The sun gives the earth **heat.**

What can the sun do?

Things You Need

2 plates   timer   2 ice cubes

Follow these steps.

1. Put an ice cube on each plate.

2. Put one plate in a place that gets sunlight.

3. Put the other plate in a place that doesn't get sunlight.

4. Use the timer. How long does each ice cube take to melt?

My Record
The ice cube that was in the sunlight _____.

The ice cube that was not in the sunlight _____.

Think About It

Why would you keep a cold drink out of the sunlight?

PROGRAM PHILOSOPHY

Integrated Curriculum

Each chapter in *ScottForesman ESL* develops language, concepts, and strategies related to a particular area of the curriculum. As students gain control over new material, it is vital that they understand how to transfer this knowledge and understanding to other areas of the curriculum and to "real life." In the Connect section of every chapter, students apply what they have learned to a new curriculum area and to the reading of authentic literature. Throughout the program, students learn how language and ideas cross the curriculum and how they can be applied in their content area classes.

Home/School Connections

ScottForesman ESL fosters a "community building" approach to education so teachers and parents can work together collaboratively as co-educators of children. In this approach, families are key participants in the academic success of children learning English, so learning communities develop in which the culture of hope, possibility, and promise can flourish.

Multicultural Understanding

Americans are a multicultural people. *ScottForesman ESL* recognizes the need to respect and preserve each group's culture, while at the same time acknowledging the interdependence of these cultures, the unity of our nation, and respect for others. Throughout the program, the variety of activities take into consideration students' different learning styles and backgrounds. And by presenting topics that are interesting and relevant to students, it helps them understand their different backgrounds and facilitates communication among them, their families, and the rest of society.

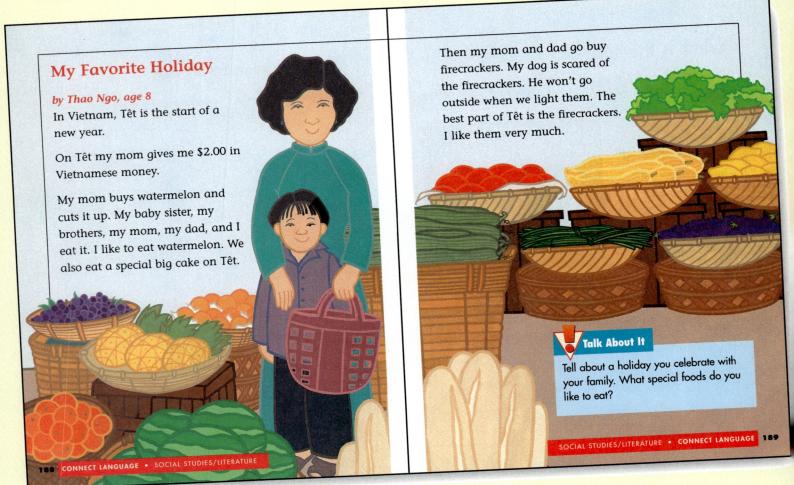

My Favorite Holiday

by Thao Ngo, age 8

In Vietnam, Tết is the start of a new year.

On Tết my mom gives me $2.00 in Vietnamese money.

My mom buys watermelon and cuts it up. My baby sister, my brothers, my mom, my dad, and I eat it. I like to eat watermelon. We also eat a special big cake on Tết.

Then my mom and dad go buy firecrackers. My dog is scared of the firecrackers. He won't go outside when we light them. The best part of Tết is the firecrackers. I like them very much.

Talk About It

Tell about a holiday you celebrate with your family. What special foods do you like to eat?

188 CONNECT LANGUAGE • SOCIAL STUDIES/LITERATURE

SOCIAL STUDIES/LITERATURE • CONNECT LANGUAGE 189

Authentic Literature

Authentic children's literature such as that which appears in *ScottForesman ESL* is perhaps the most reliable and consistent source of academic English input children can have. By using such texts, teachers can help children develop the vocabulary, structures, and background knowledge they need to comprehend the intellectually challenging language of the classroom.

Authentic Assessment

Assessment is authentic when it enables students to communicate successfully their strengths and educational needs and when the results can be used to improve instruction based on accurate knowledge of students' progress. Authentic assessment activities in *ScottForesman ESL* include teacher observation, self assessment, peer assessment, performance assessment, and portfolio assessment. Traditional language and listening assessments are also included, as are standardized test instruction and practice.

Self Esteem

Children thrive in an atmosphere in which their language, culture, and values are acknowledged and respected and in which they can succeed. *ScottForesman ESL* encourages students to affirm their heritages and to celebrate them in the classroom. Activities are suggested throughout in which students demonstrate and explain aspects of their own and their families' lives and cultures. Optional activities provide opportunities for all students—from beginners through advanced—to be successful by demonstrating their accomplishments both individually and in cooperative groups.

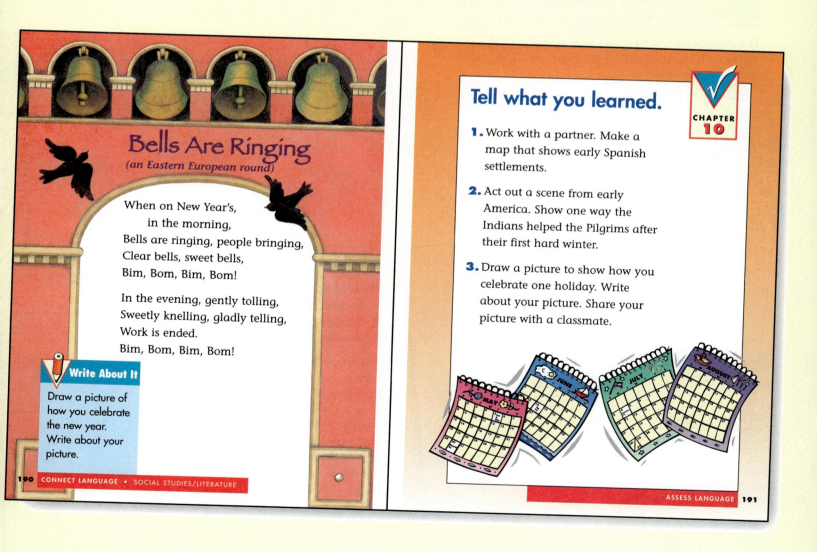

Bells Are Ringing
(an Eastern European round)

When on New Year's,
  in the morning,
Bells are ringing, people bringing,
Clear bells, sweet bells,
Bim, Bom, Bim, Bom!

In the evening, gently tolling,
Sweetly knelling, gladly telling,
Work is ended.
Bim, Bom, Bim, Bom!

Write About It

Draw a picture of how you celebrate the new year. Write about your picture.

Tell what you learned.

CHAPTER 10

1. Work with a partner. Make a map that shows early Spanish settlements.

2. Act out a scene from early America. Show one way the Indians helped the Pilgrims after their first hard winter.

3. Draw a picture to show how you celebrate one holiday. Write about your picture. Share your picture with a classmate.

COMPONENTS

Student Book

The 240-page, hard-cover *Student Book* contains six curriculum-based, thematic units of two chapters each. Each unit contains a full-length piece of authentic literature plus poems, songs, and other shorter literature pieces. Book 1 contains a Children's Reference Section. Books 2-8 contain a Writer's Workshop which leads students through the writing process.

Teacher's Edition

The spiral-bound *Teacher's Edition* contains reproduced student pages with complete instructions for presenting each page along with Options for Reaching All Students. Each unit features a planning guide, a list of resources, suggestions for a unit project, *Activity Book* and test answers, and wrap-up activities.

Language Development Activity Book with Standardized Test Practice

The *Activity Book* contains a variety of language practice along with instructions for and practice in taking standardized tests.

Teacher's Resource Book

BLACKLINE MASTER

The reproducible pages in the *Teacher's Resource Book* contain scoring rubrics, checklists, and rating scales; graphic organizers; letters to families in Cambodian, Cantonese, English, Hmong, Spanish, and Vietnamese; and language and listening assessments for each chapter of the program.

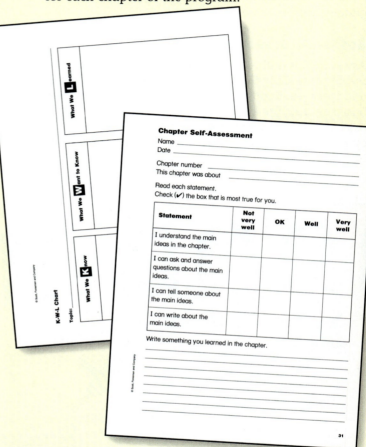

Newcomer Books

A (Grades 1-2),
B (Grades 3-5),
C (Grades 6-8)

These books, which contain age-appropriate lessons in survival English, were designed to ease new students into English and the American school system.

Audio Tapes

Eight audio tapes per level contain all the stories, songs, poems, and rhymes for that book plus a listening assessment for every chapter.

Videos

The video for each level contains a theme-related sequence that reinforces the language and concepts of each unit in the book.

Picture Cards

Seventy-two full-color, labeled cards with 144 pictures can be used to

introduce and reinforce vocabulary in a variety of games and exercises.

Little Celebrations Library

Twenty-four small, thematically related books (two per chapter) that children can read on their own.

Big Pig, Little Pig

The Bus Ride

Busy People

Covers

Down by the Swamp

Farm Day

Gobble Gobble Gone

Grandfather Horned Toad

Little Zoot

Look Up

Max's Box

Mr. Sun and Mr. Sea

Mrs. Sato's Hens

Noggin and Bobbin in the Garden

The Ocean by the Lake

Patchwork Patterns

Potatoes on Tuesday

Something New

A Tasty Bug

Tee-Ball

This Is the Seed

Water

We Can Share It!

Where's Little Mole?

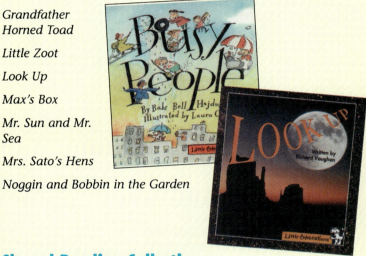

Shared Reading Collection

Six thematically related trade books (one per unit) for reading aloud and reading along.

Agua Agua Agua

The Cake That Mack Ate

Down by the Bay

Hi-De-Hi

On the Go

Through Moon and Stars and Night Skies

ORGANIZATION

The Teacher's Edition

Each level of *ScottForesman ESL* contains six thematic units; each unit contains two related chapters. Each unit of the *Teacher's Edition* contains these features.

Planning Guide

The Planning Guide lists the objectives and the vocabulary focus for each chapter. A chart for each chapter shows the content focus, language awareness objectives, and learning strategies for each lesson in the *Student Book*.

Resources

A list of Resources for each chapter includes Support Materials, Assessment Materials, the Little Celebrations Library and Shared Reading Collection titles for the unit, and a bibliography of books for extended reading and of related technology products.

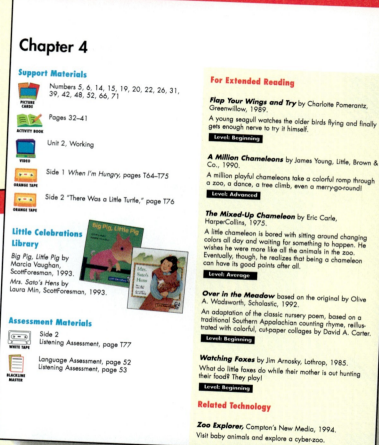

Chapter 4

Support Materials

PICTURE CARDS — Numbers 5, 6, 14, 15, 19, 20, 22, 26, 31, 39, 42, 48, 52, 66, 71

ACTIVITY BOOK — Pages 32–41

VIDEO — Unit 2, Working

ORANGE TAPE — Side 1 *When I'm Hungry*, pages T64–T75

ORANGE TAPE — Side 2 "There Was a Little Turtle," page T76

Little Celebrations Library

Big Pig, Little Pig by Marcia Vaughan, ScottForesman, 1993.

Mrs. Sato's Hens by Laura Min, ScottForesman, 1993.

Assessment Materials

WHITE TAPE — Side 2 Listening Assessment, page T77

BLACKLINE MASTER — Language Assessment, page 52 Listening Assessment, page 53

For Extended Reading

Flap Your Wings and Try by Charlotte Pomerantz, Greenwillow, 1989.

A young seagull watches the older birds flying and finally gets enough nerve to try it himself.

Level: Beginning

A Million Chameleons by James Young, Little, Brown & Co., 1990.

A million playful chameleons take a colorful romp through a zoo, a dance, a tree climb, even a merry-go-round!

Level: Advanced

The Mixed-Up Chameleon by Eric Carle, HarperCollins, 1975.

A little chameleon is bored with sitting around changing colors all day and waiting for something to happen. He wishes he were more like all the animals in the zoo. Eventually, though, he realizes that being a chameleon can have its good points after all.

Level: Average

Over in the Meadow based on the original by Olive A. Wadsworth, Scholastic, 1992.

An adaptation of the classic nursery poem, based on a traditional Southern Appalachian counting rhyme, reillustrated with colorful, cut-paper collages by David A. Carter.

Level: Beginning

Watching Foxes by Jim Arnosky, Lothrop, 1985.

What do little foxes do while their mother is out hunting their food? They play!

Level: Beginning

Related Technology

Zoo Explorer, Compton's New Media, 1994.
Visit baby animals and explore a cyber-zoo.

CHAPTER 4

What Animals Do

Objectives

Tell ways animals work to meet their needs.

Tell how animals protect themselves.

Tell how protective coloration works.

Vocabulary Focus

Animals, such as *rabbit, spider, beaver, woodchuck, armadillo*.

Things animals build, such as *web, dam, honeycomb, tunnel*.

Ways animals protect themselves, such as *spray, hide, run, change colors*.

Lesson	Content Focus	Language Awareness Objectives	Learning Strategies
Preview pages 54–55 Tell what you know.			
Present pages 56–57 How do some animals work?	Science	**Grammar** Subject/ Verb Agreement	Recognize main idea.
Practice pages 58–59 What do animals do to protect themselves?	Science	**Phonics** Blends *sm, sk, spr*	Recognize sentence patterns.
Practice pages 60–61 Color can make things hard to see.	Science	**Language Functions** Giving Directions	Follow directions.
Connect pages 62–63 How many are there now?	Science/Math	**Spelling** Punctuation	Understand specialized language.
Connect pages 64–75 When I'm Hungry	Science/ Literature	**Grammar** Contractions **Grammar** Verbs **Language Functions** Describing	Use prior knowledge. Use pictures to get meaning. Summarize.
Connect page 76 "There Was a Little Turtle"	Science/ Literature	**Phonics** Rhyming Words	
Assess page 77 Tell what you learned.			

Unit Project

This optional project is designed to be completed over the two chapters of the unit. Typically, this is a hands-on, cooperative project that results in a product students can share with friends and family. Letters to invite family participation in each project are provided in Cambodian, Cantonese, English, Hmong, Spanish, and Vietnamese. At the end of the project, family and friends are invited to school to share the results.

Activity Book Answers

The *Activity Book* pages for every chapter of the book are reproduced in mini format with the answers in place. Answers to the practice standardized tests can be found on the *Assess* page of each chapter.

Page-by-Page Teaching Suggestions

Student Book pages are reproduced in the *Teacher's Edition* with complete instructions for presenting each page, for developing language awareness, and for modeling learning strategies. *Options for Reaching All Students* suggest activities for beginning and advanced students and mixed-ability groups, as well as ideas for peer tutoring, cooperative learning, and home connections. Complete lesson plans for the books in the Shared Reading Collections are included as well as suggestions for when to introduce the books in the Little Celebrations Libraries.

Wrap-Up

Following the page-by-page teaching, the Unit Wrap-Up contains suggestions for individual, small group, and class activities based on the unit theme. Suggestions are given for discussing what the children have learned in the unit and for sharing the unit project with family and friends. Signs of Success, a unit checklist, provides a quick way to assess students' progress.

Themes and Topics

The themes and topics for Book 2 of *ScottForesman ESL* are the following.

Unit 1:	**Groups and Their Places**
Chapter 1:	People and Places
Chapter 2:	Animals and Their Habitats
Unit 2:	**Working**
Chapter 3:	How People Work
Chapter 4:	What Animals Do
Unit 3:	**Fun with Motion**
Chapter 5:	How We Have Fun
Chapter 6:	How Things Move
Unit 4:	**Plants**
Chapter 7:	Plants We Eat
Chapter 8:	Where We Buy Food
Unit 5:	**How Time Changes**
Chapter 9:	Day and Night
Chapter 10:	Long Ago and Today
Unit 6:	**Water All Around Us**
Chapter 11:	Where We Find Water
Chapter 12:	Water and the Weather

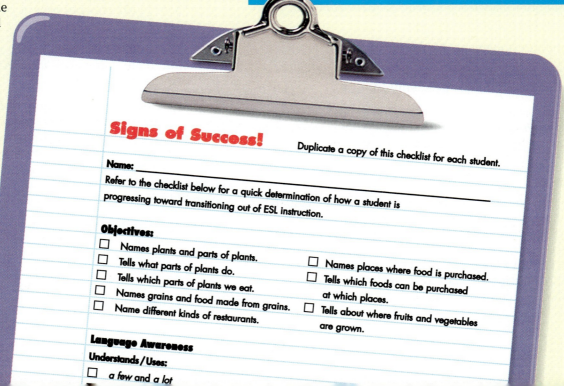

Signs of Success!

Duplicate a copy of this checklist for each student.

Name: _____

Refer to the checklist below for a quick determination of how a student is progressing toward transitioning out of ESL instruction.

Objectives:
☐ Names plants and parts of plants.
☐ Tells what parts of plants do.
☐ Tells which parts of plants we eat.
☐ Names grains and food made from grains.
☐ Name different kinds of restaurants.

☐ Names places where food is purchased.
☐ Tells which foods can be purchased at which places.
☐ Tells about where fruits and vegetables are grown.

Language Awareness
Understands / Uses:
☐ a few and a lot

THE LESSON PLAN

The Lesson Plan

JIM CUMMINS

The five step instructional sequence of each chapter in *ScottForesman ESL* provides the means for teachers to implement effective instructional strategies in ways that affirm ESL students' developing sense of self.

Preview

There is general agreement among cognitive psychologists that we learn by integrating new input into our existing cognitive structures, or schemata. Our prior knowledge and experience provide the foundation for interpreting new information.

In a classroom of English language learners from diverse backgrounds, prior knowledge about a particular topic may vary widely. Simple transmission of the information or skill may fail to connect with the prior knowledge and experience of some students. Other students may have relevant information in their first language but not realize that there is any connection with what they are learning in English.

Every chapter in *ScottForesman ESL* begins with a *Preview* section, designed to activate students' prior knowledge through pictures and brainstorming as a whole class or in small groups or pairs. Finding out what students know about a particular topic allows the teacher to supply relevant concepts or vocabulary that some or all of the students may be lacking but which will be important for understanding the chapter. Building this context permits students to understand more complex language and to pursue more cognitively demanding activities.

In addition to making the learning process more efficient, activating prior knowledge also accelerates academic progress in other significant ways:

- It stimulates students to use the target language.

- It permits teachers to get to know their students as individuals with unique personal histories.

- It creates a classroom in which students' cultural knowledge is expressed, shared, and validated—thereby motivating students to participate more actively in the learning process.

Present

Input in English can be presented orally or through written text. In either case, comprehension can be facilitated through the use of photographs, illustrations, maps, graphs, diagrams, and other graphic organizers such as Venn diagrams, semantic webs, and time lines. This kind of scaffolding enables ESL students to participate effectively in instruction even when their knowledge of the language is still quite limited.

The *Present* section of every chapter in *ScottForesman ESL* introduces language and concepts through a wide variety of scaffolding devices and learning strategies. This linguistic and contextual support gives students access to the language of text, a language very different from the language of interpersonal conversation. In the language of text, the vocabulary usually consists of words that are less frequent than those in everyday conversation; grammatical constructions are more complex because meanings must be made more explicit; and meaning is not supported by the immediacy of context and interpersonal cues (e.g., gestures, intonation). A wide variety of learning strategies is presented to help students become independent interpreters of this language. (See pp. xxi-xxii.)

Academic success depends on students gaining access to and comprehending the language of books and school discourse. *ScottForesman ESL* provides the support students need as they learn school English as a source of comprehensible input.

Practice

Active language use in both oral and written modalities is important for both cognitive and linguistic growth. At a cognitive level, writing about or discussion of complex issues with the teacher and peers encourages students to reflect critically and refine their ideas.

Linguistic growth is stimulated by active language use in at least three ways.

- Students must try to figure out sophisticated aspects of the target language to express what they want to communicate.

- The effort to use language brings home to students (and their teachers) what aspects of language they need assistance with.

- Teachers are given the opportunity to provide corrective feedback to build language awareness and help students see how the language works.

The *Practice* section of every chapter in *ScottForesman ESL* gives students the active language use they need to develop both cognitive and linguistic competencies. Students are also encouraged to express *themselves*; in other words, to explore their own feelings, ideas, and experiences in a supportive context and thereby become more aware of their goals, values, and aspirations.

Among the instructional strategies that encourage this active language use are cooperative learning, drama and role playing, and peer tutoring. All of these strategies are used to promote creative writing and publishing of student work, which are of central importance in accelerating ESL students' academic growth.

Connect

An integrated curriculum crosses subject areas and connects various curriculum components into a meaningful whole. This leads students to a deeper understanding of both the concepts they are learning and the language used to describe those concepts.

The *Connect* section of every chapter in *ScottForesman ESL* gives students practice in applying the language and strategies they are learning to a new area of the curriculum. It also provides the opportunity for students to apply their expanding understanding of language and concepts to the reading of authentic literature. (See pp. xviii-xx.)

Assess

Instruction and assessment are closely linked. Assessment involves monitoring of students' content learning and oral and written language use in order to provide appropriate guidance and feedback to the students.

The *Assess* section of every chapter in *ScottForesman ESL* provides a wide variety of assessment tools. In the Student Book, "Tell What You Learned" checks understanding of content and provides self-assessment. In the Teacher's Edition, "Options for Assessment" provides ideas for language and writing assessment. The Audiotapes and *Teacher's Resource Book* contain a listening assessment for every chapter; the *Teacher's Resource Book* contains additional language assessment; and the *Activity Book* for each chapter contains instructions and practice for standardized tests.

In addition, the *Teachers Resource Book* contains a wide variety of rubrics, rating sheets, checklists, and forms for teacher, peer, and self assessment. (See pp. xxiii-xxv.)

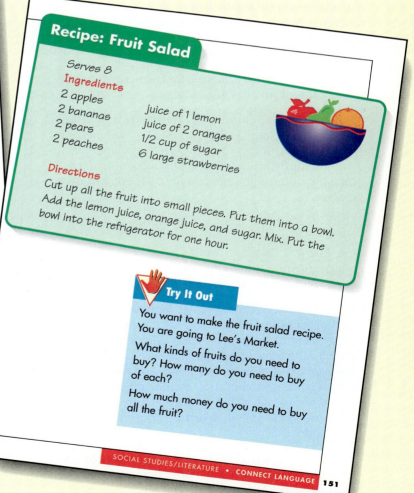

Cognitive Academic Language in ESL Instruction

ANNA UHL CHAMOT & J. MICHAEL O'MALLEY

The Cognitive Academic Language Learning Approach (CALLA) is an instructional model for meeting the academic needs of ESL students in American schools. It is designed to assist ESL students to succeed by providing beginning or transitional instruction in either standard ESL programs or bilingual programs.

The CALLA model includes three components and instructional objectives in its curricular and instructional design:

- topics from the major school subjects,

- the development of academic language skills,

- explicit instruction in learning strategies for both content and language acquisition.

Content subjects are the primary focus of instruction in CALLA. Content, rather than language, drives the curriculum. Language modalities (e.g., listening, speaking, reading, writing) are developed for content-area activities as they are needed, rather than being taught sequentially. Academic language skills can be developed as the need for them emerges from the content. Language skills will be most meaningful when students perceive that they are needed in order to accomplish a communicative or academic task.

There are at least four reasons for incorporating curricular content into the ESL class.

- Students develop important knowledge in all subject areas. Throughout *ScottForesman ESL,* students learn grade level concepts and processes in science, social studies, mathematics, and other academic areas, thus providing a foundation for their content-area classes.

- Students learn the language functions and skills needed for success in content areas. Every lesson of the *Teacher's Edition* of *ScottForesman ESL* suggests language awareness activities designed to strengthen students' abilities to practice these functions and skills.

- Many students exhibit greater motivation when learning content than when they are learning language only. Students in *ScottForesman ESL* are motivated not only by the topics presented but also by knowing that they are developing the concepts and skills associated with science, mathematics, social studies, and literature. They perceive that they are doing "real" schoolwork instead of merely learning English.

- Students learn the strategies necessary for success in curriculum areas. These learning strategies are the mental processes and behaviors students use to access their learning. Extensive suggestions throughout

ScottForesman ESL provide guidelines for learning strategy instruction. *Academic language* is the language that is used by teachers and students for the purpose of acquiring new knowledge and skills. This kind of language differs in many ways from social language, the language that is used for interaction in social settings. Academic language is more difficult and takes longer to learn than social language. It may be less interactive than social language and may provide fewer context clues, such as gestures, to assist comprehension. Academic language has very specific purposes, including imparting new information, describing abstract ideas, and developing conceptual understanding. These purposes are cognitively demanding, thus increasing the comprehension difficulties students experience.

Academic language consists primarily of the functions needed for authentic academic content. These functions include explaining, informing, justifying, comparing, describing, proving, debating, persuading, and evaluating. To accomplish these functions requires the use of both lower-order and higher-order thinking skills. *ScottForesman ESL* enables students to practice the functions and thinking skills needed to engage in specific content activities. Discrete language elements such as vocabulary, grammatical structures, spelling, and pronunciation are integrated into this practice.

Use force to move things.

Things You Need

toy trucks   masking tape

Find out about it.

1. Put 2 trucks at the starting line.

2. Use a gentle push to make the first truck go.

3. Use a hard push to make the second truck go.

4. Use tape. Mark the place where each truck stopped.

My Record
When I gave the truck a gentle push

When I gave the truck a hard push

Talk About It

Which truck went farther? Why?

SCIENCE • USE LANGUAGE **107**

There are at least five reasons for focusing on academic language skills in the ESL classroom.

- For ESL students, the ability to use academic language effectively is a key to success in grade-level classrooms.

- Academic language is not usually learned outside of the classroom setting.

- Grade-level teachers may assume that all of their students already know appropriate academic language, when, in fact, ESL students in their classes have often acquired only social language skills.

- Academic language provides students with practice in using English as a medium of thought.

- Students may need assistance in using learning strategies with academic language, just as they do with content knowledge and skills.

ScottForesman ESL responds to each of these reasons. In its content-based lessons, both teachers and students use academic language to communicate, analyze, and explain. It provides the exposure students need to develop academic language functions and thinking skills. It prepares students for transition into grade-level classrooms. Throughout the program, guidelines are given for:

- modeling academic language appropriate to content topic;

- providing practice in listening to information and answering higher level questions;

- creating opportunities for using academic language through cooperative activities;

- having students describe, explain, justify, evaluate, and express understanding of and feelings about topics and processes;

- having students read and write in every major curriculum area.

Learning Strategies, the third key element in CALLA instruction, are important for language learning and for learning academic content. Learning strategies are the mental processes and overt behaviors students use to assist their learning. Strategies are taught explicitly in CALLA to help students develop metacognitive awareness of their own learning and to become self-directed learners. Knowing how and when to use learning strategies is especially important for ESL students who are learning both a new language and challenging academic content.

In *ScottForesman ESL,* learning strategies are taught in every lesson. Students are prompted to use various learning strategies for language and content activities. The Teacher's Edition contains suggestions for introducing, modeling, practicing, extending, and assessing learning strategies. (See pp. xxi-xxii.)

ScottForesman ESL incorporates the major principles from CALLA, which are based on cognitive research and learning theory. The CALLA model has been successful in accelerating ESL students' academic achievements in school districts nationwide.

Having fun can help you stay healthy.

Do you get **exercise** while you play?

You need exercise to make you **strong**. Exercise can be fun.

▲ swimming

hopping ▶

running ▶

Running, hopping, and swimming are good for your heart and lungs.

lungs

heart

Authentic Literature in ESL Instruction

LILY WONG FILLMORE

How do children acquire those aspects of language knowledge and proficiency that figure in intellectual demanding communication? Few children, whether native speakers of English or learners of English, are fully proficient in this type of language when they first enter school. Children who have had books read to them at home, or who have learned to read in their primary languages, will have some familiarity with the language of written texts. But all will need to develop it further to handle the language demands of school. For most, authentic children's literature such as that appearing in *ScottForesman ESL* is a major source of input for academic language, whether in the native or a second language.

Let us look at a piece of literature, "The Night of the Stars" by Douglas Gutierrez. The story tells of a man who did not like the night because there was no light. He goes to the mountain top from which he thinks night comes and tries to get it to stop obscuring the light of day. But the man is told that nothing can be done, because the light is hidden behind the night. The man thinks about this, and eventually comes up with a solution:

> "Once more he went to the mountain. The night was like an immense awning, covering all things. When at last he reached the highest point on the mountain, the man stood on his tiptoes, and with his finger poked a hole in the black sky. A pinprick of light flickered through the hole. The man who did not like the night was delighted. He poked holes all over the sky. Here, there, everywhere, and all over the sky little points of light appeared. Amazed now at what he could do, the man made a fist and punched it through the darkness. A large hole opened up, and a huge round light, almost like a grapefruit, shone through. All the escaping light cast a brilliant glow at the base of the mountain and lit up everything below . . . the fields, the street, the houses. Everything."

Now one might wonder how a piece of literature such as this one, offering a mythic account of how the stars and the moon came to be, might figure in the interpretation of language such as that found in a science text. Isn't an account like this one contradictory to the science materials that the students are reading? The answer is this: texts like this delightful piece of literature give children access to the language itself. The language of stories gives access to vocabulary, structures, phrasings, and discourse processes that children, whether they are native speakers of English or learners of English, must eventually learn. Let us look at what the readers of "The Night of the Stars" will find as input in this passage:

Vocabulary: Among the words the readers will encounter are nouns such as *mountain, awning, point, tiptoes, pinprick, light,* and *glow*; verbs such as *reach, flicker, shine, poke, amaze,* and *delight*; adjectives such as *brilliant, immense, huge, round,* and *highest*; and adverbials such as *everywhere* and *below*. Notice that this vocabulary is specific and precise—-it tells the reader where the man went and what he did and more. It tells the reader about the event in language that evokes images and feelings and qualities.

According to some experts, vocabulary size and breadth are crucial determinants of reading and overall academic performance. School-age children acquire much of the new vocabulary they learn by reading books. Children reading a text such as the one we are looking at may or may not learn all the words that they do not already know. Whether they do or do not understand every word is not usually critical to the understanding of the story. But having read it, they will have encountered the words used in it. This gives them a passing acquaintance with the ones that are new to them, and of how they are used in this particular text. The next time they encounter these words, they will have some usage information available in memory that may just help them figure out what they mean. The point is, it takes a great deal of reading to learn the words that are crucial to the understanding of texts with real meaning payloads.

Structure: Our story has a relatively simple past narrative—all of the events take place in past time. Most of the verbs are in the simple past tense. But the time relations among the parts of this story are not all that simple. The first two sentences might appear to be a simple sequence of events: The man went to the mountain. Once there, he checks out the night-time sky, and likens it to an immense awning. It is somewhat more complex than that, however.

"Once more" indicates that the man has gone to the mountain before, and "he went to the mountain" describes what he was doing in this event, but not necessarily the completion of the activity. The next sentence—"the night was like an immense awning, etc.," is a description of what the man perceived or thought while he was on his way to the mountain, rather than what he saw once he arrived. How do readers know that? Because in the next sentence, the temporal clause, "when at last he reached the highest point on the mountain" tells them that only then was the journey completed. This then suggests that the second sentence describes the man's observations before the completion of the journey. Does this make any difference to the readers? It probably doesn't—at least in terms of their understanding and enjoyment of the story. However, when readers figure out or are helped to see how the events described in this story relate, they pick up a bit more information about how English works with respect to temporal relations.

Background knowledge: Just as readers must apply their linguistic knowledge to the interpretation of the texts they read, so too must they make use of their knowledge of the world and their prior experiences in reading. No text contains every bit of information needed to understand it fully. Writers generally assume a level of prior language knowledge and cultural and real world experience when they write. If they believe that the intended readers are unlikely to be familiar with certain words or concepts, they will define or discuss them. Otherwise, they simply presuppose that the readers will be able to apply their knowledge of language and of how it works to the reading and interpretation of the text, and that they will draw on their knowledge of the world and on their experiences to fill in the gaps in the text. The ideal reader then is one who has the cultural background, experience, and linguistic knowledge to do just what the writer hopes the readers of the text will be able to do when they read it.

That fact presents a special problem to educators who are concerned with finding or preparing appropriate instructional materials and texts for children from diverse cultural and linguistic backgrounds. How can these children deal with texts that are as complex as those used for mainstream students? How can they possibly comprehend materials that presuppose cultural background, knowledge, and experiences that they don't already have? Shouldn't they be given materials that are culturally familiar, that deal with the world as they know and have experienced it?

I will argue that the education of children irrespective of their background would be greatly diminished if educators were to choose materials for them that were in any way narrowed or lowered in level because of putative deficiencies in the children's backgrounds. Such decisions must take into account the role authentic and challenging materials play in building children's background knowledge and in supporting language development. Authentic literature gives

English learners access to the vocabulary, grammar, and discourse conventions of the language they are learning. Children also gain the very kind of background knowledge that they need to have to deal with materials they read in school from the literature and textbooks they have already read. This argument might seem rather circular, at first glance. How do children get the background they need in the first place? And what kind of useful background could they possibly get from a story like "The Night of the Stars"?

Consider the cognitive skills it takes to make sense of such scientific ideas as supernovas or the time it takes light to travel from a star to earth. How does anyone understand concepts like these without actually having experienced them? How do scientists and theorists come up with ideas like brown dwarfs and black holes? I will argue that this kind of thinking begins with the development of the imagination. One way to develop the imagination is by reading and thinking about stories like "The Night of the Stars." The ability to conceptualize possible worlds is not entirely unrelated to the ability to create and consider impossible ones, of the sort involved in that story. There may be nothing in our story that leads directly to knowledge that will enable a reader to understand a newspaper story about the discovery of a new black hole. Yet, the reader who, as a child, was able to imagine someone standing on top of a mountain, poking holes in the nighttime sky thereby creating stars will no doubt find it easier than one without such early experiences.

Authentic texts such as those in *ScottForesman ESL* are perhaps the most reliable and consistent source of academic English input children can have. However, texts do not by themselves reveal how the language in them works, nor do they provide many clues as to what the words that appear in them mean or how they are used. Such materials work as input when teachers do the following:

- provide the support learners need to make sense of the text;

- call attention to the way language is used in the text;

- discuss with learners the meaning and interpretation of sentences and phrases within the text;

- point out that words in one text may have been encountered or used in other places;

- help learners discover the grammatical cues that indicate relationships such as cause and effect, antecedent and consequence, comparison and contrast, and so on.

In short, teachers help written texts become usable input—not only by helping children make sense of the text, but by drawing their attention, focusing it, in fact, on how language is used in the materials they read. Done consistently enough, the learners themselves will soon come to notice the way language is used in the materials they read. When they can do that, everything they read will be input for learning.

PRESENTING STORIES

Presenting Stories in ESL Instruction

GEORGE A GONZÁLEZ

Reading authentic literature presents special challenges to ESL students. Some students may understand details, but not see the big picture. Others may grasp the gist of a story, but not have the language to explain their understanding.

Sentences

Choosing and presenting the important sentences of a story can convey the most significant and salient ideas of the selection and represent critical story elements. These sentences can form a story map that includes related story elements, such as characters, events, problems, feelings and opinions, setting, time, and conclusion. The important sentences can also convey knowledge and information such as linguistic patterns.

Words

Children who cannot understand and use a wide repertoire of words in their oral language often encounter problems with reading comprehension. For these children, idioms and words that represent new concepts or new labels can be especially challenging. Throughout *ScottForesman ESL* are suggestions for words and terms to be presented to these students.

The following six methods for oral teaching of new vocabulary in context help make words meaningful, relevant, and enjoyable.

Personalization

Relate the word to a situation familiar to children.

example: <u>bad mood</u>

The baby is in a <u>bad mood;</u> he is not happy; he has been crying all day.

Demonstration

Demonstrate the action implied by the word, stating what you are doing as you do it.

example: <u>kneel</u>

I <u>will kneel</u> on the floor; I <u>am kneeling</u> on the floor; I <u>have knelt</u> on the floor.

Dramatization

Act out a situation illustrating the meaning of several words.

example: <u>shake</u>, <u>fall</u>, <u>shuffled</u>, <u>collapsed</u>, <u>couch</u>

Exemplification

Recite several examples of sentences in which a particular word or expression could be used.

example: <u>unpleasant</u>

The weather today is <u>unpleasant</u>. It is <u>unpleasant</u> to be scolded. The odor near the garbage cans was <u>unpleasant</u>.

Illustration

Guide children to draw pictures or to manipulate picture cards that depict the objects or concepts.

Definition

Define words or terms through description followed by a repetition of the word.

example: <u>decision</u>

I have decided to go to Nashville to visit friends. It is my <u>decision.</u>

Sounds

Children who cannot perceive, discriminate, or produce the sounds of English may experience difficulties with word attack skills and spelling. Throughout *ScottForesman ESL*, the "Language Awareness" sections contain lessons on pronunciation and sound/letter relationships that are exemplified in the text. As students become acquainted with the sounds in context, they will develop a sensitivity to and an awareness of the English sound system and at the same time improve their comprehension.

The *ScottForesman ESL* Audio Tapes afford the opportunity for children to listen to the sounds of English within the context of authentic literature—over and over again.

Gestures and Body Language

Children who cannot express in English their ideas about a story will often be able to show their understanding by pantomiming elements of the plot or the emotions of the characters. Help them by pointing out the body language and facial expressions of characters in the illustrations. Demonstrate with students the way people in different cultures use gestures and other paralinguistic language. Compare, for example, the ways people wave hello or good-by, the distance people stand from one another when conversing, and the ways people show deference or respect.

Activities throughout *ScottForesman ESL* suggest ideas for helping students use pantomime, gestures, and body language to help convey what they want to get across in English.

Learning Strategies in ESL Instruction

ANNA UHL CHAMOT

Learning strategies are actions or thoughts that students can apply *on their own* to a challenging task. Learning strategies can be applied with language-related tasks, such as listening to or reading a text, speaking, or writing, or with tasks related to subject matter content, such as information and processes in science, mathematics, social studies, literature, art, and music.

ScottForesman ESL integrates learning strategies throughout and provides guidelines for teaching the strategies and helping students develop an awareness of their own learning processes. The intent of the learning strategies instructional component of *ScottForesman ESL* is to help all students develop their ability to learn independently.

ScottForesman ESL teaches students how to apply a number of useful learning strategies for school subjects. Students are encouraged to make use of their own background knowledge through discussions and brainstorming activities. They are taught to make a plan for carrying out an activity, for monitoring themselves as they work, and for evaluating their own achievements. Other learning strategies taught in *ScottForesman ESL* include predicting, making inferences, classifying, summarizing, note-taking, using picture clues, cooperating with classmates, and asking questions for clarification. Each chapter of *ScottForesman ESL* presents learning strategies that assist in preparing for a task (INTO strategies), for working on a task (THROUGH strategies), and for evaluating and extending a task (BEYOND strategies).

ScottForesman ESL integrates learning strategies instruction into each part of the learning process. The *Teacher's Edition* provides specific suggestions for presenting learning strategies throughout the *ScottForesman ESL* instructional sequence.

Preview

The purpose of this step in learning strategies instruction is to help students become more aware of their own learning processes, thus developing their metacognition, or understanding of their own thinking. The teacher begins by helping students identify their prior knowledge about strategies already familiar to them. The types of strategies students are already using can be quite diverse, especially in the case of students whose previous schooling has been in other countries. Most students are quite interested in finding out about their classmates' varying approaches to learning, and teachers can capitalize on this natural interest in suggesting new learning strategies to try.

Ways to identify students' prior knowledge about learning strategies include class or small group discussions in which students compare their individual approaches to working on a particular task, such as reading a story or following directions for a science experiment. More formal ways to identify existing learning strategies are through student interviews, questionnaires, or personal journals.

Present

In presenting a learning strategy, teachers need to be explicit and direct in their explanation, as this helps students develop awareness of strategic thinking. One of the most effective ways to present a strategy is through teacher modeling, in which teachers think aloud about their own use of the strategy. *ScottForesman ESL* provides examples of think-aloud scripts *(Model a Strategy)* which teachers can use or adapt to demonstrate different strategies.

In addition to modeling the strategy, teachers should also name it, tell students how it will help them learn, and explain when to use it. Naming a strategy makes it more concrete for students and helps focus class discussions about strategy use. Posters of learning strategies associated with easily remembered icons are helpful in reminding students about the names and uses of the strategies they are learning.

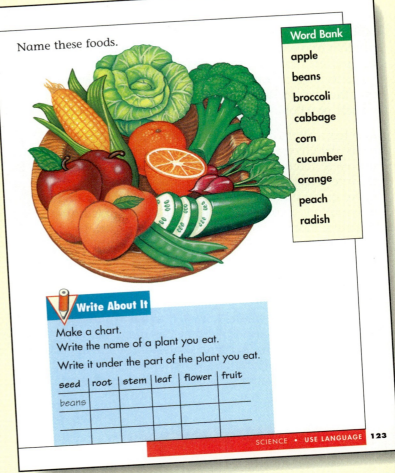

Name these foods.

Word Bank

apple
beans
broccoli
cabbage
corn
cucumber
orange
peach
radish

Write About It

Make a chart.
Write the name of a plant you eat.
Write it under the part of the plant you eat.

seed	root	stem	leaf	flower	fruit
beans					

SCIENCE • USE LANGUAGE **123**

Students also need to understand that the purpose of learning strategies is to provide them with tools that they can use to help themselves in learning. Finally, teachers need to be sure that students understand that knowing *when* to use a strategy is as important as knowing *which* strategy to use.

Practice

As with any type of process or procedure, students need ample practice opportunities in applying learning strategies to their language development and subject matter learning. Learning strategies can be practiced with any task or activity that presents a challenge or a problem to be solved—very easy tasks can be accomplished successfully without consciously using learning strategies!

The rich variety of activities in *ScottForesman ESL* provides extensive opportunities for practicing the learning strategies presented. For example, stories, poems, and informational articles provide opportunities for using different kinds of reading strategies. Projects, reports, experiments, and other hands-on activities can be enhanced with planning, monitoring, and self-assessment strategies. Group discussions and cooperative learning activities are excellent vehicles for developing strategic competence in cooperation and questioning for clarification.

Connect

When students extend a strategy to a new context or connect two or more strategies in a unique approach to a problem, they are well on their way to becoming independent and self-regulated learners. Teachers can assist this process by asking students to brainstorm new ways to use a strategy or combine strategies and by suggesting that they try a strategy in another class or in a setting outside of school.

Another activity that connects learning strategies to students' own lives is to have students interview family members about their learning strategies or teach a favorite learning strategy to a younger sibling. When upper grade students read biographies, they may find it interesting to look for clues about the types of learning strategies that a famous person may have used. Finally, students can learn about strategies used by athletes, artists, dancers, musicians, actors, writers, and other contributors to students' life experiences.

Assess

Students need to evaluate how well different strategies are working for them so that they can build their own repertoire of effective learning strategies. Debriefing discussions after practicing one or more strategies can help students think through their use of strategies and pinpoint moments when a strategy really worked—or did not work—for them.

More formal ways for students to evaluate their own strategy use is through checklists, learning logs, or journals in which they describe their use of different learning strategies. Some teachers have also found that having students compare their performance on similar tasks with and without using a learning strategy is an effective strategy evaluation activity. The most important contribution that teachers can make in student self-evaluation of strategies is to provide many opportunities for students to reflect on, discuss, and write about their insights into their own learning processes.

Learning strategies are fun to teach and fun to learn. Students enjoy talking about their thinking, and teachers gain deeper insights by listening to their students' thoughts. Students who have already developed effective learning strategies should be encouraged to share them with classmates and to continue using them even as they are acquiring additional strategies. Eventually, students will take the responsibility for choosing their own personal repertoire of learning strategies and making their own decisions about when and how to apply the strategies.

The approach to learning strategies instruction in *ScottForesman ESL* helps students deal with challenging tasks, gain an appreciation of their own learning process, and develop both their language skills and their knowledge and understanding of content area subjects.

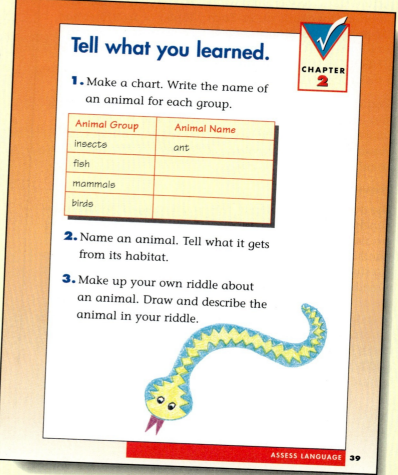

Tell what you learned.

CHAPTER 2

1. Make a chart. Write the name of an animal for each group.

Animal Group	Animal Name
insects	ant
fish	
mammals	
birds	

2. Name an animal. Tell what it gets from its habitat.

3. Make up your own riddle about an animal. Draw and describe the animal in your riddle.

AUTHENTIC ASSESSMENT

Authentic Assessment in ESL Instruction

J. MICHAEL O'MALLEY

Assessment is authentic when it enables students to communicate successfully their strengths and educational needs, and when the results can be used to improve instruction based on accurate knowledge of student progress. Such assessment mirrors good classroom instruction, and it gives students ongoing feedback that enables them to reflect on their accomplishments, identify future learning needs, and develop goals and strategies for attaining them. As a result, this type of assessment empowers students to become self-directed learners and empowers teachers to use assessment information for instructional improvement.

The authentic assessment activities in *ScottForesman ESL* are integrated with and complement instruction. Because the assessment is part of instruction, it should not require significant additional time to prepare and conduct. Students do not need to stop learning for authentic assessment to occur.

The approach to assessment taken in *ScottForesman ESL* addresses four major issues: *who* conducts the assessment, *when* assessment occurs, *what* is assessed, and *how* assessment is accomplished. Each of these is important to ensure that assessment is authentic:

- Who—Assessment is conducted by students, teachers, and parents working in partnership to improve instruction and learning.

- When—Assessment is ongoing and enables both teachers and students to maintain a continuous record of student progress.

- What—The processes and strategies involved in learning as well as the products of learning are assessed.

- How—The assessment is designed to assist students with all levels of proficiency in English to communicate what they know and can do.

Three critical components of authentic assessment in *ScottForesman ESL* are the use of *scoring rubrics, benchmark standards,* and *informed judgment.*

Scoring rubrics are holistic scoring scales that identify what students know and can do at different levels of performance on classroom tasks. Typically, there may be four or five levels of proficiency or achievement defined on a scoring rubric.

Benchmark standards identify clearly for students and teachers the expected levels of performance based on specific tasks. That is, you might determine that all students should be performing at level 4 or 5, the highest levels of performance, on oral proficiency. With rubrics and benchmarks, students understand the nature of the performance expected as they progress through each level of proficiency and achievement toward mastery.

Informed judgment is based on scoring rubrics and benchmark standards. The judgment may be expressed by the teacher, the student, peers, or parents. This aspect of authentic assessment assures that responsibility for educational judgments about students is assumed by those in the classroom and others most closely associated with the child.

The assessment procedures in *ScottForesman ESL* assess students' knowledge through all four language skills—listening, speaking, reading, and writing. And because *ScottForesman ESL* integrates language development with literature and other academic content—including math, science, and social studies—the assessment provides information on the knowledge and procedural skills students use in all subjects.

Assessment activities in *ScottForesman ESL* are contained in the *Student Book,* the *Teacher's Edition,* the *Activity Book,* and the *Teacher's Resource Book. ScottForesman ESL* also provides sample forms, checklists, rubrics, and other guidelines to be used or adapted for assessment. (For additional forms, checklists, and rubrics, see *Authentic Assessment for English Language Learners: Practical Applications for Classroom Teachers* by J.M. O'Malley & L. Valdez Pierce, Addison-Wesley [forthcoming].)

A key element in authentic assessment is the use of multiple assessments, providing students with varied opportunities to demonstrate their learning and accomplishments. *ScottForesman ESL* includes all of the following: *teacher observation, self-assessment, peer assessment, performance assessment,* and *portfolio assessment.*

AUTHENTIC ASSESSMENT

Teacher Observation

Teachers often make daily classroom observations to check on a student's progress or to plan for instruction. *ScottForesman ESL* provides suggestions on how to conduct observations through sample checklists, rating scales, and forms on which to note student behaviors that are directly relevant to the lesson.

Checklists identify specific behaviors to be observed and provide a form on which to indicate that the behavior occurred or how frequently it occurred. Examples of behaviors that might appear on a checklist are: scanning to find information while reading, using various cues for word meaning in context, making an outline or graphic organizer to plan an essay, or explaining successfully a problem-solving approach to a peer. A checklist of unit objectives appears at the end of each unit of *ScottForesman ESL*.

Rating scales are similar to checklists but provide an opportunity to indicate the degree to which a particular behavior occurred. For example, you can use a 3-point scale to indicate the level of control the student exhibited over specific aspects of writing, such as sentence formation—consistent control, reasonable control, or little or no control. A rating scale might also enable you to indicate if the student behavior occurred independently or with peer or adult support. Several examples of rating scales appear in the *ScottForesman ESL Teacher's Resource Book.*

Anecdotal records are notes describing behaviors that provide a rich indication of student progress when reviewed over the course of a school year. You can describe a specific behavior along with the learning materials, setting, student grouping, and time and place the behavior occurred. An example of a form for an anecdotal record appears in the *ScottForesman ESL Teacher's Resource Book.*

ScottForesman ESL provides varied procedures to observe student learning and performance as learning is taking place. You can identify individual students to observe in advance and plan the occasion when you will conduct the observation. In this way, you can manage the observations efficiently.

Self-assessment

The importance of self-assessment cannot be overstated. Self-assessment is the key to student empowerment because it gives students an opportunity to reflect on their own progress toward instructional objectives, to determine the learning strategies that are effective for them, and to develop plans for their future learning. With self-assessment, students are active participants in deciding what and how much to learn and in setting the criteria by which their learning is evaluated.

To encourage self-assessment, you should share scoring rubrics with students and elicit their input on improving the rubrics. You can also share *anchor papers,* i.e., samples of student work that represent each point on the scoring rubric. After students review the anchor papers, they can then rate their own work or the work of their peers. Additional ways to encourage self-assessment include *K-W-L Charts, Reading Logs, Journals,* and *Self Ratings.*

K-W-L Charts are charts students complete using three columns to reflect what they *Know* about a topic before an instructional activity, what they *Want* to know from the lesson, and what they *Learned* from the lesson after its completion. The rows on the chart can reflect specific topics covered. For example, a lesson on Plants We Eat might cover Parts of the Plant, Types of Plants, and How Plants Grow. Suggestions for K-W-L Charts appear throughout *ScottForesman ESL.*

Reading Logs are records students keep of the reading they have completed. These might be categorized by genre and include the title, author, topics, and date on which the reading was completed, as well as the student's personal response to the reading and important concepts or information to remember. A Reading Log form appears in the *ScottForesman ESL Teacher's Resource Book.*

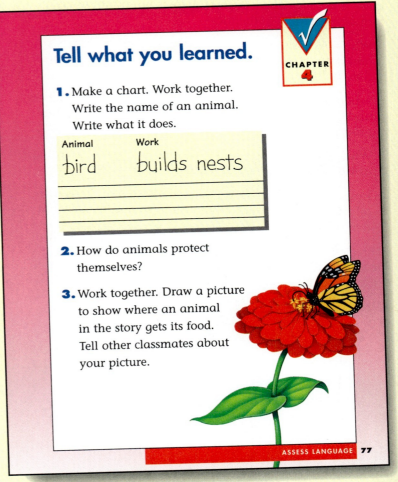

Tell what you learned.

CHAPTER 4

1. Make a chart. Work together. Write the name of an animal. Write what it does.

Animal	Work
bird	builds nests

2. How do animals protect themselves?

3. Work together. Draw a picture to show where an animal in the story gets its food. Tell other classmates about your picture.

ASSESS LANGUAGE **77**

Journals are students' narrative diaries of what they have learned in each subject area. The journal may be kept daily and might mention the topics, what was difficult, what was easy, what strategies helped in learning, and what the student wants to know next.

Self Ratings are the students' use of a scoring rubric to rate their own performance. For example, the use of a rubric for writing might include composing, style, sentence formation, word usage, and mechanics (spelling, capitalization, and punctuation).

ScottForesman ESL provides opportunity for self assessment at the end of each chapter in the *Student Book* (page 35 in the *Teacher's Resource Book*). In addition, the *Teacher's Resource Book* contains a variety of forms and logs that students can use to monitor their own progress (pages 10-14).

Peer Assessment

In addition to rating their own products and learning processes, students can rate the work of their peers as readers, writers, and learners. Students can rate the oral and written work of their peers, identifying areas that can be improved as well as areas that are presented effectively. These ratings can be based on scoring rubrics that students develop themselves or on rubrics provided by teachers. Students may need both guidance and assurance that peer feedback will be stated positively. One of the main advantages of self and peer assessment is that students internalize the standards for learning more readily than they would from teacher assessment alone. Another advantage concerns time management for teachers, who need only spot-check student performance rather than spend time rating every single product from each student. See page 18 in the *ScottForesman ESL Teacher's Resource Book* for a sample peer assessment form.

Performance Assessment

This type of assessment includes exhibitions of student-constructed work such as written products, science demonstrations, oral presentations, retellings, pair interactions, discussions, drawings, and graphic organizers. Some student products can be exhibited in the classroom, presented and described by the student or by groups that worked together, or documented by video or audio recorder. The student work can be evaluated by the teacher, the student, and by peers using a scoring rubric that reflects different levels of performance. Rubrics used in performance assessment typically integrate language and content in a holistic scoring procedure that may also reflect the processes used in solving problems or in reaching conclusions.

Portfolio Assessment

A portfolio is a collection of student work that shows growth over time. The portfolio may contain written products, worksheets, self-assessments, or audio tapes. It is useful to document learning, to identify student strengths and needs, to help in making instructional decisions, and to provide evidence of student progress in student and parent conferences. The keys to a successful portfolio are student involvement and self-assessment. Students should play a major role in deciding what goes into the portfolio and how the work is evaluated, so they can feel ownership over their learning.

There are at least three different types of portfolios: a *collections portfolio,* containing virtually everything the student has produced; a *showcase portfolio,* focusing on the student's best work; and an *assessment portfolio,* illustrating growth with respect to specific instructional objectives. *ScottForesman ESL* encourages the use of assessment portfolios, a type which is efficient for assisting students and teachers in planning for future learning activities. For all portfolios, we suggest using a *portfolio cover sheet* that identifies specific portfolio entries, the date of each entry, and the type of each entry (e. g., written product, tape, peer assessment, checklist). A variety of forms and checklists are provided in the *Teacher's Resource Book* for teacher, self, and peer portfolio assessment (pages 15-20).

The multiple forms of assessment included in *ScottForesman ESL* provide students with varied opportunities to communicate what they know and can do, what learning processes work effectively for them, and what progress they have made over time. Such opportunities put students in a better position to manage their learning and to become self-directed learners.

To take advantage of assessment information, you need to periodically review the student portfolios, your own anecdotal records and ratings, and other evidence of student progress in light of goals established for instruction. The scoring rubrics and benchmark standards are essential parts of authentic assessment that give you indications of how successful students have been in learning and what worked and did not work in your own instruction. Use this information in planning your instructional activities, in student conferences, and in communicating with parents. You can also use it to assist in placement decisions, to communicate with other teachers, to report to administrators, and to anticipate the results of end-of-year testing. By using the assessment information in *ScottForesman ESL* effectively, you can help to ensure that all your students enjoy maximum learning success!

Home/School Connections in ESL Instruction

CAROLYN KESSLER

Parents are children's first teachers; the home the first learning community. Here children acquire their first language and develop a world view shaped by the community of which they are a part. Their experiences as they grow in this community provide a wealth of knowledge about what they believe, value, do in daily encounters, and what they perceive about how the world around them works. As children whose home language is other than English enter the schooling process, they not only meet new teachers and a different community, but often a new world view. Connecting home and school in light of this linguistic and cultural diversity is a challenge for both parents and teachers.

ScottForesman ESL provides the means for teachers and parents to work together collaboratively as co-educators of their children. Educating children so that they can succeed academically in an English-speaking environment is the goal of this collaboration.

Home-school partnerships as developed in *ScottForesman ESL* integrate life at home with that of the school in a "community-building" approach. In this approach, collaborative work between children and parents at home finds an audience at school. The teacher's role is to draw on the funds of knowledge that children have from their home and life experiences and to connect what happens inside the classroom to what happens outside. Under these conditions learning English takes on real meaning.

This community-building approach encourages students to develop their own voices as they interact with others, including family and community members. The home-school connection draws extensively on resources from the home. Among them are the support and encouragement parents give for their children's educational undertakings, frequent parent-child conversations, the exchange of ideas and information about concrete situations or problems children experience, and taking action to solve problems.

Because of the power of family stories in transmitting cultural values and attitudes that can contribute to school success, *ScottForesman ESL* encourages the telling of family stories. In this participatory approach, teachers learn about the community with which their students are identified and work towards building communities of learners in their classrooms where cultural and linguistic differences brought from home are understood and valued.

In the *ScottForesman ESL* community-building approach, the many dimensions of a student's life, including culture and the social context of the home and community, are viewed as rich resources for learning. Teachers value, use, and build on children's prior knowledge through tapping into the funds of knowledge that learners bring to school.

Children from diverse backgrounds have a wealth of cultural capital—experiences, knowledge, attitudes, beliefs, aspirations, and skills that are passed from one generation to another. Activities designed to incorporate children's cultural capital in the classroom validate the home culture. Approaches and strategies, however, that recognize and build on culturally different ways of learning and seeing the world rely on teachers making efforts to know about and understand the socio-cultural contexts of their students' lives. When efforts are made, teachers are in a much stronger position to join parents as full partners in their children's schooling.

ScottForesman ESL provides many opportunities for the development of this partnership. Each unit of the program suggests a unit project to be carried out by the students as a class. Letters to family members inviting their participation in the project are provided in six different languages (Cambodian, Cantonese, English, Hmong, Spanish, and Vietnamese). At the completion of each project families are invited to visit the classroom to see what the children have accomplished.

In addition, *ScottForesman ESL* provides suggestions throughout each chapter for ways to build community. These suggestions include:

- children reading aloud at home to parents in either the home language or English;

- children carrying out research with family members on their family's social history through interviews of parents, grandparents, and other family members;

- parents and children collaborating on writing projects, such as publishing books about their family history, making timelines of family history, making a map of family migrations, keeping portfolios of their work together;

- families telling stories that transmit family beliefs, cultural values, attitudes, aspirations, self-images;

- children telling their stories at school, sometimes in their first language with explanations given in English by the children or a bilingual staff member or volunteer;

- teachers inviting parents to school to read a book in their home language or provide a presentation drawing on some particular area of interest or expertise.

Families are key participants in the academic success of children learning English. When families join in a partnership with the school, learning communities can develop in which the culture of hope, possibility, and promise can flourish.

BIBLIOGRAPHY

Anderson, R.C., and P. Freebody. "Vocabulary Knowledge" in J. T. Guthrie, ed. *Comprehension and Teaching: Research Reviews*. International Reading Association, 1981.

Auerbach, Elsa R. *Making Meaning, Making Change*. Delta Systems, 1992.

Bachman, L.F., & A.S. Palmer. "The Construct Validation of Self-ratings of Communicative Language Ability." *Language Testing 6* (1), 1989.

Bartlett, F. *Remembering*. Cambridge University Press, 1932.

Brown, J.D. "Classroom-centered Language Testing." *TESOL Journal* 1(4), 1992.

Chamot, A.U., & J.M. O'Malley. *The CALLA Handbook: Implementing the Cognitive Academic Language Learning Approach*. Addison-Wesley, 1994.

Clemmons, J., et al. *Portfolios in the Classroom, Grades 1-6*. Scholastic Professional Books, 1993.

Cummins, Jim, & Dennis Sayers. *Brave New Schools: Challenging Cultural Illiteracy Through Global Learning Networks*. St. Martin's Press, 1995.

Cummins, Jim. *Negotiating Identities: Education for Empowerment in a Diverse Society*. California Association for Bilingual Education, 1996.

Cummins, Jim. "Linguistic Interdependence and the Educational Development of Bilingual Children." *Review of Educational Research,* 49 (2), 1979.

El-Dinary, P.B. "Framework for Strategies Instruction." Available from Language Research Projects, Georgetown University, Washington, DC.

Enright, D. Scott, & Mary Lou McCloskey. *Integrating English: Developing English Language and Literacy in the Multilingual Classroom*. Addison-Wesley, 1988.

Fathman, A.K., M.E. Quinn, & C. Kessler. *Teaching Science to English Learners, Grades 4-8*. National Clearinghouse for Bilingual Education, 1992.

Fillmore, C.J. "Ideal Readers and Real Readers" in D. Tannen, ed. *Analyzing Discourse: Text and Talk. Georgetown Round Table on Languages and Linguistics 1981*. Georgetown University Press, 1982.

Freeman, David E., & Yvonne S. Freeman. *Between Worlds: Access to Second Language Acquisition*. Heinemann, 1994.

Gándara, P. *Over the Ivy Walls: The Educational Mobility of Low Income Chicanos*. State University of New York Press, 1995.

Genesee, Fred, ed. *Educating Second Language Children: The Whole Child, the Whole Curriculum, the Whole Community*. Cambridge University Press, 1994.

Glazer, S.M., & C.S. Brown. *Portfolios and Beyond: Collaborative Assessment in Reading and Writing*. Christopher-Gordon, 1993.

Hays, C.W., R. Bahruth, & C. Kessler. *Literacy con cariño: A Story of Migrant Children's Success*. Heinemann, 1991.

Hudelson, Sarah. *Write On: Children Writing in ESL*. Prentice Hall Regents, 1989.

Kessler, Carolyn, ed. *Cooperative Language Learning: A Teacher's Resource Book*. Prentice Hall Regents, 1992.

Larsen-Freeman, Diane, & Michael H. Long. *An Introduction to Second Language Acquisition Research*. Longman, 1991.

Lightbown, Patsy, & Nina Spada. *How Languages Are Learned*. Oxford University Press, 1993.

McCaleb, Sudia P. *Building Communities of Learners: A Collaboration Among Teachers, Students, Families, and Community*. St. Martin's Press, 1994.

Miller, G. "How School Children Learn Words" in F. Marshall, ed. *Proceedings of the Third Eastern States Conference on Linguistics*. The Ohio State University, 1987.

Ogle, D. "K-W-L Group Instruction Strategy" in A.S. Palincsar, et al., eds. *Teaching Reading as Thinking*. Association for Supervision and Curriculum Development, 1986.

O'Malley, J.M., & A.U. Chamot. *Learning Strategies in Second Language Acquisition*. Cambridge University Press, 1990.

O'Malley, J.M., & L. Valdez Pierce. *Authentic Assessment for English Language Learners: Practical Applications for Classroom Teachers*. Addison-Wesley, (forthcoming).

Pressley, M., V. Woloshy, & Associates. *Cognitive Strategy Instruction That Really Improves Children's Academic Performance,* 2nd ed. Brookline Books, 1995.

Richard-Amato, Patricia A., & Marguerite Ann Snow. *The Multicultural Classroom: Readings for Content-area Teachers*. Longman, 1992.

Rigg, Patt, & Virginia G. Allen, eds. *When They Don't All Speak English: Integrating the ESL Student into the Regular Classroom*. National Council of Teachers of English, 1989.

Routman, R. *Invitations: Changing as Teachers and Learners K-12*. Heinemann, 1994.

Rumelhart, De.E. "Schemata: The Building Blocks of Cognition" in Spiro, R.J., B.C. Bruce, & W.J. Brewer, eds. *Theoretical Issues in Reading Comprehension*. Erlbaum, 1980.

Scarcella, Robin. *Teaching Language Minority Students in the Multicultural Classroom*. Prentice Hall Regents, 1990.

Short, D.J. "Assessing Integrated Language and Content Instruction." *TESOL Quarterly,* 27 (4),1993.

Spangenberg-Urbschat, Karen, & Robert Pritchard, eds. *Kids Come in All Languages: Reading Instruction for ESL Students*. International Reading Association, 1994.

Sternberg, R.J., and J.S. Powell. "Comprehending Verbal Comprehension." *American Psychologist* 8, 1983.

Tierney, R.J., M.A. Carter, & L.E. Desai. *Portfolio Assessment in the Reading-Writing Classroom*. Christopher-Gordon, 1991.

Yancey, K. B. *Portfolios in the Writing Classroom*. National Council of Teachers of English, 1992.

Professional Associations

National Association for Bilingual Education, 1220 L Street NW, Suite 605, Washington, DC 20005

National Center for Research on Cultural Diversity and Second Language Learning, Center for Applied Linguistics, 1118 22nd Street NW, Washington, DC 20037

Teachers of English to Speakers of Other Languages, 1600 Cameron Street, Suite 300, Alexandria, VA 22314-2751

USING THE NEWCOMER BOOK

Newcomer Book A was specifically designed for children in grades 1 and 2 who are new to the English language. The activities in this book represent real-life situations centered around school themes that are age- and grade-level appropriate. Pictures, chants, rhymes, games, and opportunities for artistic creativity stimulate communication and motivate children to use language and vocabulary in a variety of settings. The activities provide many opportunities for children to work in small groups or with partners to facilitate cooperation and establish a community atmosphere.

Each lesson is divided into four types of activities: The *Preview/Present* section allows children to see situations they are already familiar with that will activate prior knowledge of words, concepts, and language to be presented. Prior to using this book, model how to find the correct page and how to use a crayon/pencil when necessary. Then begin the lesson by focusing the children's attention on the illustration and by reading the lesson title aloud to them. Have children say all they can about each picture on the first page of each lesson using as many words as they know. Each illustration builds on the previous lessons and provides a context to build on for the next. Model the new words and language by showing the children pictures or real items. Use TPR to model new vocabulary by saying sentences such as "Point to the (pencil)."

The *Present/Practice* and *Practice* sections give children the opportunity to practice the new language. Model the directions and the activities, then have children complete the activities with partners.

Use the *Assess* section to check understanding and to review or reteach any material children may have found difficult. These activities review key vocabulary as well as provide opportunities for children to write about themselves. Self-evaluation objectives give children opportunities to checkmark the objectives they feel they have successfully mastered.

Build on the children's language development by allowing the children to practice conversations and vocabulary words. The following activities will keep children interested and motivated through meaningful play; they can be adapted or expanded to fit any theme or topic within the book.

The Surprise Bag

Place objects representing the target vocabulary in a bag. Have each child feel an object and try to guess what it is.

What's Missing?

Place real objects or picture cards on a chalk ledge or table. Have children close their eyes. Take one item away. Ask "What's missing?" Continue, taking more than one item away.

Use a Puppet

Encourage children to use puppets or pictures when practicing conversations.

Simon Says

Have children act out only the commands preceded by "Simon says." "Point to the chair, Pick up the pen," and so on. Whenever a child carries out a command that is not preceded by "Simon says," that child is eliminated and must sit down. Continue until the winner is left standing.

Lesson 1   *My Class*

Preview/Present page 1

Tell what you know and *Look. Say.* Encourage children to talk about the picture. Introduce the new vocabulary by using realia or picture cards.

Present/Practice page 2

Look. Count. Write. Present the numerals 0–10 and have children practice counting the crayons and tracing numerals on the board. Then have them work in groups to identify and count items in the classroom.

Count. Circle. Read the sample answer and have the children work with partners to complete the activity.

Practice page 3 and page 21

Write numbers. Play Bingo. Have children write any numerals from 0–10 on the lines and cut out nine game pieces. Read off numbers and vocabulary words randomly.

Tell what you have. Have children cut out the cards on page 21 and work with partners to tell what they have.

Make a name tag. (page 21) Model the activity by making and wearing a name tag. Help children write their names on name tags for themselves. Have them share their work with partners.

Assess page 4

Circle. Help children read the words and identify the items before they complete the activity independently.

Write the number. Help children read and complete the sentences orally. Have them complete the activity independently.

Lesson 2   *About Me*

Preview/Present page 5

Tell what you know and *Look. Say.* Encourage children to talk about the picture. Encourage them to talk about their homes by asking "What do you have?" "I have (a phone)." Model and practice the conversations. Have children act out the conversations in groups, then have them say and identify the items at the bottom of the page.

Present/Practice page 6

Say the letters. Present the letters of the alphabet with flash cards, picture cards, "The Alphabet Song," and so on. Have children point to each letter and say its name. If children need additional help recognizing and writing the alphabet, use the Blackline Masters on pages xxx and xxxi as practice.

Write. Say your phone number and *Write your name. Spell it.* Model the activities. Have children work in small groups saying and spelling their phone numbers and names.

Write a word you know. Have children look at the illustration and spell *book.* Encourage them to say and spell words they have learned. Have children complete the activity in small groups.

Practice page 7 and page 23

Write the letters. Chant. Complete the activity orally; then have children work in groups, filling in the missing letters. Model the chant; then have children take turns saying the chant for each other.

Make an address book. Show children a completed address book form from page 23. Read the directions with the children, then have them work in groups.

Assess page 8

Read and model the activities. Have children complete them independently.

Lesson 3   On Time
Preview/Present page 9

Tell what you know and *Look. Say.* Encourage children to talk about the picture. Introduce the new vocabulary by using a toy clock, or use the clock on page 25. Have children practice setting the clock. Model and practice the conversations.

Present/Practice page 10

Say the colors. Have children practice saying the colors using as many items as possible. Have them identify colors in the classroom. Use TPR to model "Point to (red)."

Say the shapes. Have children practice saying the names of the shapes. Use TPR to model "Point to the (circle)."

Color the shapes and *Match. Say the times.* Model the activities. Have children complete them in groups.

Practice page 11 and page 25

Draw a picture. Show the children a completed project.

Make the clock. Have children practice the rhyme with a partner using the clock from page 25, changing the time on the clock each time.

Assess page 12

Read and model the activities. Have children complete them independently.

Lesson 4   My Week
Preview/Present page 13

Tell what you know and *Say the days.* Encourage children to talk about the picture. Introduce the new vocabulary by using a calendar. Have children work in groups to act out the conversations.

Present/Practice page 14

Count. Have children practice saying the numerals by counting items in the classroom.

Look at the pictures. Say. Have children work in groups to act out the conversations.

Practice page 15 and page 27

Circle the word. Have children complete the activity with partners.

Say the chant. Have children practice the chant with partners.

Make a calendar. Show children a completed calendar from page 27. Have them work in groups to make a weekly calendar.

Assess page 16

Read and model the activities. Have children complete them independently.

Lesson 5   My School
Preview/Present page 17

Tell what you know and *What time is it?* Say the times. Have children talk about their school personnel. Have them work in groups, acting out the conversations. Have them practice saying the times.

Present/Practice page 18

Who is this? Say the words. Present the names of the school personnel. Have children practice them with a partner.

Draw the times and *Match. Circle.* Model the activities. Have children complete them with a partner.

Practice page 19 and page 29

Read the story and *Write about you.* Model the activities for the children. Have them work in groups.

Make a book about you. Show children the completed book from page 29. Have them work in groups to complete the activity.

Assess page 20

Read and model the activities. Have children complete them independently.

A A   a a

B B   b b

C C   c c

D D   d d

E E   e e

F F   f f

G G   g g

H H   h h

I I   i i

J J   j j

K K   k k

L L   l l

M M   m m

Name: ______________________________

N N

n n

O O

o o

P P

p p

Q Q

q q

R R

r r

S S

s s

T T

t t

U U

u u

V V

v v

W W

w w

X X

x x

Y Y

y y

Z Z

z z

Planning Guide

CHAPTER 1

People and Places

Objectives

Name different kinds of groups.

Tell what people in different groups can do.

Name places in a community.

Give reasons why people go to each place.

Name states in the United States.

Begin recognizing animal groups and their places.

Vocabulary Focus

Groups of people, such as, *chorus, family, friends, team.*

Places in the community, such as *bakery, library, park, post office, store.*

Environmental words, such as *animals, forest, pond, trees, water.*

Lesson	Content Focus	Language Awareness Objectives	Learning Strategies
Preview pages 2–3 Tell what you know.			
Present pages 4–5 What can these groups do?	Social Studies	**Grammar** Present Tense	Use picture details.
Practice pages 6–7 What is a community?	Social Studies	**Grammar** Sentence Patterns	
Practice pages 8–9 The United States of America	Social Studies	**Spelling** Capitalization	Read maps.
Connect pages 10–11 Where do animals live?	Social Studies/ Science	**Grammar** Irregular Plurals	
Connect pages 12–23 *My Perfect Neighborhood*	Social Studies/ Literature	**Phonics** Rhyming Words with Long *a, e, i* **Vocabulary** Informal English **Language Functions** Approval	Use pictures for meaning. Recognize fact and fantasy. Summarize.
Connect page 24 "The More We Get Together"	Social Studies/ Literature	**Grammar** Verbs	
Assess page 25 Tell what you learned.			

CHAPTER 2

Animals and Their Habitats

Objectives

Name animals and some of their attributes.

Understand what animals get from their habitats.

Tell about groups animals belong to.

Tell about pets and their habitats.

Vocabulary Focus

Animals, such as *sheep, cat, cow, butterfly, lion, polar bear.*

Animal needs words, such as *habitat, food, water, air.*

Pet words, such as *hamster, fish, parakeet, cage, tank.*

Math language, such as *how many, count, in all, number sentence.*

Lesson	Content Focus	Language Awareness Objectives	Learning Strategies
Preview pages 26–27 Tell what you know.			
Present pages 28–29 What animals are there?	Science	**Grammar** Subject/Verb Agreement	Use pictures for meaning.
Practice pages 30–31 What does an animal get from its habitat?	Science	**Phonics** Short *a*	Understand patterns.
Practice pages 32–33 A Pet and Its Habitat	Science	**Language Functions** Explaining Choices	Understand main idea.
Connect pages 34–35 How many in all?	Science/Math	**Grammar** Comparative Adjective	Count how many.
Connect pages 36–37 "An Animal Riddle"	Science/ Literature	**Language Functions** Similes	Remember details.
Connect page 38 "Polar Bear"	Science/ Literature	**Phonics** Rhyme	
Assess page 39 Tell what you learned.			

Resources

Chapter 1

Support Materials

PICTURE CARDS
Numbers 6, 28, 44, 46, 68

ACTIVITY BOOK
Pages 2–11

VIDEO
Unit 1, Groups and Their Places

RED TAPE
Side 1
My Perfect Neighborhood, pages T12–T23

RED TAPE
Side 2
"The More We Get Together," page T24

Little Celebrations Library

Gobble Gobble Gone by Andrea Butler, ScottForesman, 1993.

Tee-Ball by Barry Gordon, ScottForesman, 1993.

Assessment Materials

WHITE TAPE
Side 1
Listening Assessment, page T25

BLACKLINE MASTER
Language Assessment, page 40
Listening Assessment, page 41

Newcomer Book A

Survival Book for absolute beginners. For overview, see pages xxviii–xxxi.

For Extended Reading

A Chair for My Mother by Vera B. Williams, Greenwillow Books, 1982.

After Rosa, her mother, and her grandmother lose their home and belongings in a fire, they save up, bit by bit, to buy a comfortable armchair they can all share.

Level: Advanced

A Country Far Away by Nigel Gray, Orchard Books, 1988.

On opposite sides of the world, in very different societies, two boys, one African, one Western, live their surprisingly similar lives.

Level: Beginning

Frog and Toad Together by Arnold Lobel, HarperCollins, 1971.

Frog and Toad are good friends who have wonderful adventures together.

Level: Average

Look by Michael Grejniec, North-South Books, 1993.

A child discovers that if he really looks carefully, he can see an interesting variety of changes in the world outside his windows.

Level: Beginning

Nobody's Mother Is in Second Grade by Robin Pulver, Dial, 1992.

A story telling how second graders learn a lot about plants when Cassandra's mother disguises herself as a plant to visit school.

Level: Advanced

Related Technology

Trudy's Time and Place House, Edmark, 1995.

Orbit the earth, become a stockbroker, and learn about the earth and its people.

Chapter 2

Support Materials

PICTURE CARDS
Numbers 5, 6, 9, 12, 14, 15, 19, 20, 22, 24, 26, 28, 30, 31, 35, 39, 43, 45, 46, 49, 50, 51, 61, 64, 66, 71

ACTIVITY BOOK
Pages 12–21

VIDEO
Unit 1, Groups and Their Places

RED TAPE
Side 2
"Polar Bear," page T38

Shared Reading Collection

Hi-De-Hi by Martha Vaughn, CelebrationPress, 1996.

Little Celebrations Library

Down by the Swamp by Charlotte Armajo, ScottForesman, 1993.

Where's Little Mole? by Inez Greene, ScottForesman, 1993.

Assessment Materials

WHITE TAPE
Side 1
Listening Assessment, page T39

BLACKLINE MASTER
Language Assessment, page 42
Listening Assessment, page 43

For Extended Reading

Animals Live Here by Muriel Batherman, Greenwillow Books, 1979.

While reading this book, children will come to recognize many animals' homes under, on, and above the ground.

Level: Advanced

Life in the Sea by María Rius and J. M. Parramón, Children's Press Choice, 1987.

As they travel from river to sea, a young fish gets lessons from his teacher about all sorts of living things.

Level: Average

Otters Under Water by Jim Arnosky, Putnam, 1992.

Follow two young otter pups as they explore their underwater world, a world they are more at home in than any other mammal.

Level: Beginning

Over in the Meadow based on the original by Olive A. Wadsworth, Scholastic, 1992.

An adaptation of the classic nursery poem, based on a traditional Southern Appalachian counting rhyme, reillustrated with colorful, cut-paper collages by David A. Carter.

Level: Average

Raccoons and Ripe Corn by Jim Arnosky, Lothrop, 1987.

A mother raccoon and her two kits don't mind when a farm crowds their habitat, not when the corn is ripe.

Level: Beginning

Related Technology

Zurk's Rainforest Lab, Soliel, 1995.

Interact with rainforest animals and learn about their habitats.

Project

A Model of Our School Community

This optional project can be completed over the next two chapters. See the Unit Wrap-Up, page T39a, for more ideas on sharing the project with family members.

What You'll Need

Collect the following sorts of items to make a model of your community:

Art Supplies
- large pieces of drawing paper
- crayons
- markers
- paint
- brushes
- construction paper
- scissors
- pipe cleaners
- clay
- tape
- staples
- drinking straws
- empty toilet paper or paper towel rolls

Containers
- cardboard cartons
- shoe boxes
- cereal boxes
- milk cartons

Beginning the Project

Explain to children that while they study the next two chapters they will be working on a big project that they will share with others. Tell them that the project is to build a model of the community around your school. Encourage them to talk about the school community. Suggest that they be especially observant whenever they are in the neighborhood near the school.

Home Involvement

Send Letter Home, Blackline Masters 34–39 in the Teacher's Resource Book to families to solicit their participation in collecting the containers needed for the community model.

Planning and Building the Model

Encourage children to work in cooperative groups. Assign an adult volunteer to each group for trips outside the classroom. Ask each group to choose a block or area near your school. Have the groups observe the environment, including people, buildings, signs, and animals. Help children make a list of what they saw. Lead children in discussing the procedures involved in making a replica of the area they studied.

Have children decide what the major buildings will be. Then have them sketch their part of the model. You may have to suggest modifications so that the various parts fit together into the community. Let groups determine which members will make the replicas of specific groups, buildings, signs, and animals.

Daily Discussion

Take a few minutes each day for discussion. Encourage children to practice vocabulary learned in conjunction with the community model. At the end of the unit, have children discuss their community model in detail. See page T39a for ideas about sharing their community with families and friends when the unit is completed.

Large Buildings
- Choose a large carton for large buildings.
- If a building is very large, you can attach two cartons to make the building.
- Paint the buildings using tempera paint.
- After the paint is dry, paint windows and doors on the buildings using a different color of paint.

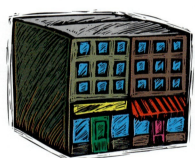

Small Buildings
- Use shoe boxes and milk cartons to represent small buildings and houses.
- Paint the boxes with tempera paint or cover them with construction paper.
- Add doors, windows, or other features.
- Place the small buildings and houses in the community.

Street Signs
- On a piece of drawing paper, write the name of each street in your area. Cut out the name to make a sign.
- Tape the sign to a bathroom tissue or paper towel roll.
- Place the sign in the correct place in your community model.

People
- Draw and cut out people for your community.
- Punch a hole at the top and bottom of each person and place the person on a drinking straw or pipe cleaner.
- Tape the people into the community.

Animals
- Make animals out of clay.
- Place the animals in the community.

Activity Book

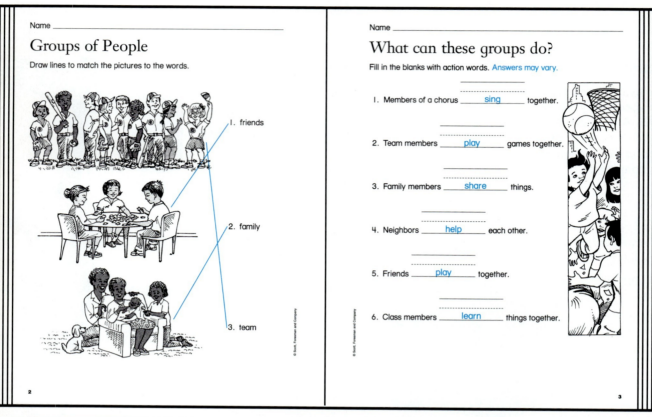

Name _____

Groups of People

Draw lines to match the pictures to the words.

1. friends

2. family

3. team

Name _____

What can these groups do?

Fill in the blanks with action words. Answers may vary.

1. Members of a chorus _____sing_____ together.

2. Team members _____play_____ games together.

3. Family members _____share_____ things.

4. Neighbors _____help_____ each other.

5. Friends _____play_____ together.

6. Class members _____learn_____ things together.

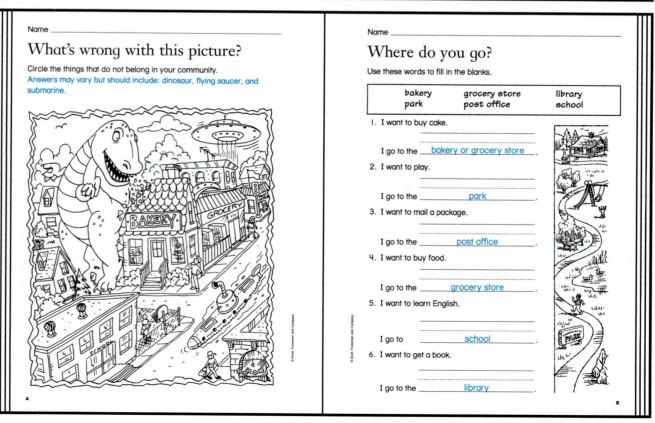

Name _____

What's wrong with this picture?

Circle the things that do not belong in your community.
Answers may vary but should include: dinosaur, flying saucer, and submarine.

Name _____

Where do you go?

Use these words to fill in the blanks.

bakery	grocery store	library
park	post office	school

1. I want to buy cake.

   I go to the ___bakery or grocery store___

2. I want to play.

   I go to the _____park_____

3. I want to mail a package.

   I go to the _____post office_____

4. I want to buy food.

   I go to the _____grocery store_____

5. I want to learn English.

   I go to _____school_____

6. I want to get a book.

   I go to the _____library_____

Special Places

Names of special places start with a capital letter.

1. Write the name of the state where you live.

   _____
   Answers will vary.

2. Write the name of this country.

   _____
   United States

3. Write the name of your school.

   _____
   Answers will vary.

4. Write the name of your city.

   _____
   Answers will vary.

Time for a Rhyme

Circle the word to make the two lines rhyme.

1. I went out for a walk today.
   My neighborhood she looked _____.   happy   (okay)

2. My grandmother was lifting weights,
   And dishwashers were juggling _____.   (plates)   cups

3. The dentist shaved someone's head.
   The baker was baking sweet-tooth _____.   cake   (bread)

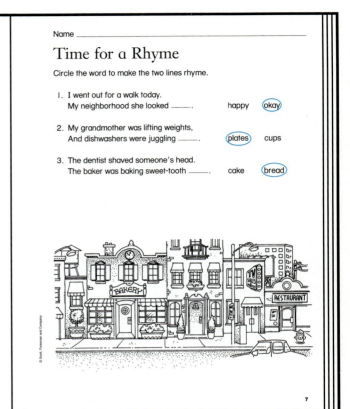

Tell what you like.

Circle the sentences that tell about someone liking something.

1. "My house is special," said the girl.

2. Grown-ups don't like to line up for recess.

3. "My school is great," said the boy.

4. The man did not want his head shaved.

5. Red is my favorite color.

6. I love to eat apples.

7. I like to see my friends.

8. The dogs like to wave at the cats.

Work with a partner. Write a sentence showing you like something.
Use the sentences above for help.

_____
_____
_____

People or Places?

Use these words to complete the word webs below.

class	team	family	school
friends	bakery	park	library

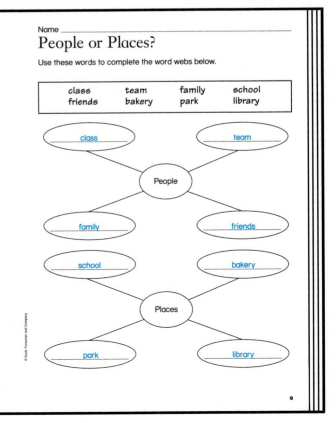

class   team

People

family   friends

school   bakery

Places

park   library

Activity Book

Chapter 2

Which one does not belong?

Circle the animal that does not belong.

1. These animals live in the water.

2. These animals have six legs.

3. These animals have feathers.

4. These animals have hair or fur.

12

Has or Have?

Write **has** or **have** on the line.

1. Insects __have__ six legs.

2. A butterfly __has__ six legs.

3. Mammals __have__ hair or fur.

4. A lion __has__ hair or fur.

5. A dog __has__ hair or fur.

13

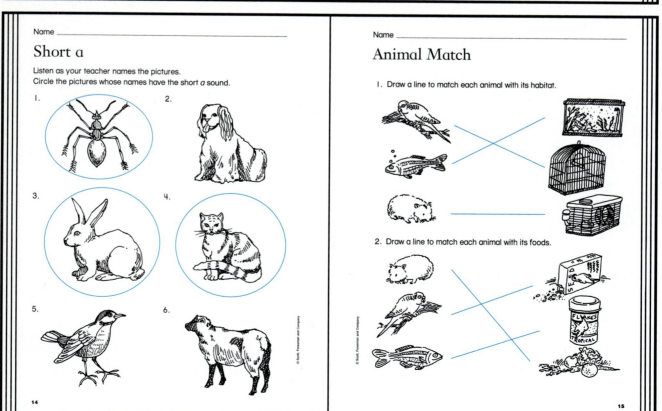

Short a

Listen as your teacher names the pictures.
Circle the pictures whose names have the short *a* sound.

1.

2.

3.

4.

5.

6.

14

Animal Match

1. Draw a line to match each animal with its habitat.

2. Draw a line to match each animal with its foods.

15

Name _____

Animals, Animals

Write the names of animals.
List the name under the correct heading. Answers will vary.

Fish	Birds	Insects	Mammals

Look at the animal names in your chart.

How many are fish? _____

How many are birds? _____

How many are insects? _____

How many are mammals? _____

16

Name _____

I Am . . .

Use animal names to fill in the blanks. Answers will vary.

_____

1. I am as smart as a _____.

_____

2. I am as funny as a _____.

3. I am as friendly as a _____.

_____

4. I am as happy as a _____.

17

Name _____

Rhyme Time

Listen to your teacher say the words.
Circle the word that rhymes with the first word.

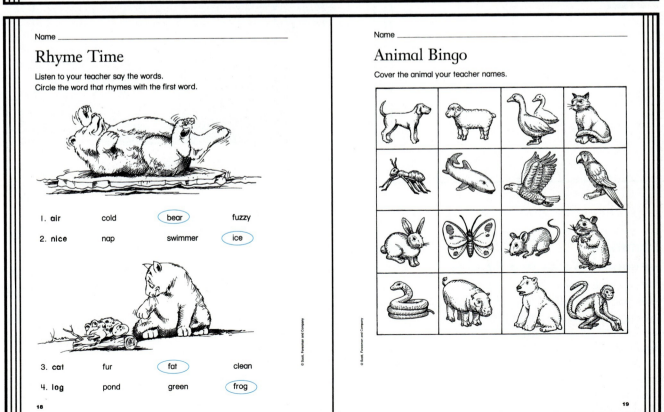

1. air   cold   (bear)   fuzzy

2. nice   nap   swimmer   (ice)

3. cat   fur   (fat)   clean

4. log   pond   green   (frog)

18

Name _____

Animal Bingo

Cover the animal your teacher names.

19

T1j

Preview

Activate Prior Knowledge
Use Pictures

PICTURE CARDS

Start a discussion of "people and places" by showing pictures of different kinds of groups and helping children name them. Have children answer the first question in Tell What You Know. Use Picture Cards 6, 28, 44, 46, 68.

For the second question, ask children to tell what kinds of groups of people they see in the pictures on the page.

Develop Language and Concepts
Present pages 2 and 3.

Ask children to brainstorm names for groups of people. Refer to the Talk About It section. Model pointing to yourself and saying *I'm in a group of teachers.* Encourage children to name groups they are a part of. For example, children may suggest a class, a family, or speakers of a particular language. Write children's suggestions on chart paper. Add to the list during the chapter.

ACTIVITY BOOK

For practice with vocabulary for groups, use Activity Book page 2.

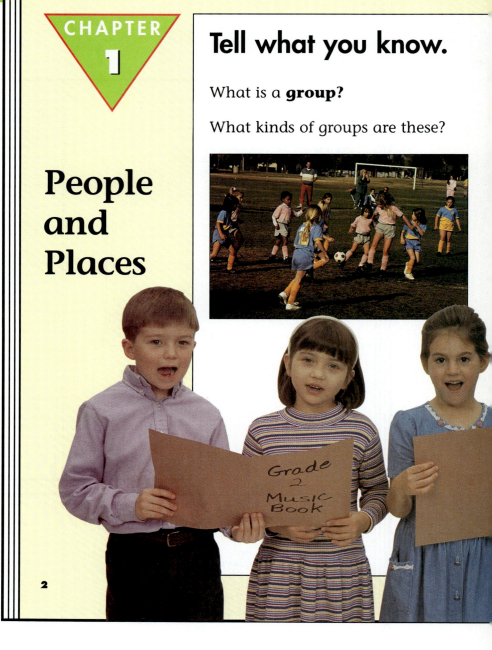

CHAPTER 1

People and Places

Tell what you know.

What is a **group**?

What kinds of groups are these?

Grade 2 Music Book

2

Options for Reaching All Students

Beginning
Language: Words and Pictures

Divide children into five teams and have each team draw one of the following groups: class, team, family, chorus, and friends. Have children label their drawings. Refer children to the chart for writing models. Have team members choose one member to present the illustration to the class and tell about it.

Advanced
Language: Make a Book

List these group names on the board: *class, family, team, chorus.* Assign children to small groups. Ask them to choose one kind of group and talk about the ways in which members work together. Have children create picture books showing how the members of the group work together.

Peer Tutoring
Language: Guessing Game

Have pairs of mixed ability sequence word strips to form a clue and a question about a group. For example:

I sing. What group am I in?

I am the son. What group am I in?

Pairs can exchange word strips with other pairs and compare answers.

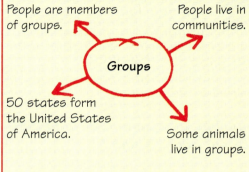

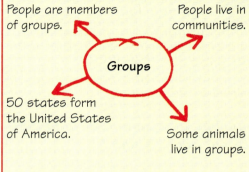

Talk About It

Tell about a group you are part of.

Name other groups you know.

3

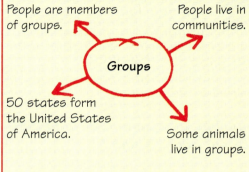

KEY CONCEPTS

In this chapter, children will learn the language connected with different kinds of groups, such as family, community, and country.

Use pages 2 and 3 to assess children's knowledge of the concept of groups.

People are members of groups.

People live in communities.

Groups

50 states form the United States of America.

Some animals live in groups.

Mixed Ability

Video: Groups and Their Places

Show children the video to help build background knowledge on the unit theme. You may also choose to use the video in other ways that are appropriate during the unit.

Present

Activate Prior Knowledge
Review Vocabulary

Display Picture Card 28 that shows a family and have it identified. Then recall the groups of people children talked about in the previous lesson. Invite children to read each group name from the chart. Encourage volunteers to name some groups which they are a part of.

Develop Language and Concepts
Present pages 4 and 5.

Help children identify the groups shown. Read each sentence aloud. Ask children what else these groups do together. Record their answers on the board.

Then name some actions, such as share things or play a game, and ask children to respond with an appropriate group name.

Model a Strategy
Use Picture Details for Meaning

Model using details in pictures for meaning:

When I look at pictures, I look at the details. I look to see who is in the picture and what they are doing. In the first picture I see a family sharing food at dinner. This helps me understand what the sentence says. How can you use picture details?

What can these groups do?

Family **members** share things.

Class members make things together.

4 LEARN LANGUAGE • SOCIAL STUDIES

Options for Reaching All Students

Beginning
Singing

TPR

Sing the song below to the tune of "Row, Row, Row Your Boat".

*Our class is a group.
We like to be together,
Reading, writing, singing, playing,
No matter what the weather.*

Then have children create motions for *reading, writing, singing,* and *playing.*

Advanced
Language: Writing

Ask children to think about what group they would join if they could join any group at all. Children may decide to be with a group of firefighters, a group of detectives, or a rock group. Have children draw pictures of themselves in the group they selected. At the bottom of the picture, have them write a sentence about their illustration.

Cooperative Language Experience
Recalling Details

Have children recall something interesting or funny that happened to the class recently. As children recall the incident, write pertinent words on chart paper. As a class, use the words to write a language experience story about the incident. Children can draw and caption pictures to go with the story.

Team members play a game together.

Neighbors help each other.

Talk About It

What do you do with a group?

How do people in your group help each other?

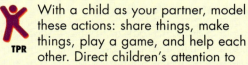

Grammar: Present Tense

TPR

With a child as your partner, model these actions: share things, make things, play a game, and help each other. Direct children's attention to the page. Locate the action word in each sentence and explain that the action word tells what each group of people does. Say the word with children and choose volunteers to pantomime the actions. Continue by having children name other words that name actions and pantomime them.

ACTIVITY BOOK

For practice with words for groups and action words, use Activity Book page 3.

Assess ✓

Use children's responses to Talk About It for assessment. Children should be able to

- say what they do in groups
- tell how the people in a group help each other

LOOK **AHEAD**

Next, children will apply the understanding of small groups they have developed to the understanding of larger groups—communities.

QuickCheck

Letters of the Alphabet

Check whether all children know the alphabet. Invite them to say, spell, and write their first and last names.

Home Connection

Social Studies: Group Photos

Ask children to enlist the aid of relatives or family friends in finding photographs of different groups and explaining what the groups are doing. Have children bring the photographs to class for "Show and Tell."

Practice

Activate Prior Knowledge
Brainstorm Vocabulary

Invite children to look at the illustration on page 6. Tell them that the picture shows a community. Point out the word *community* on the page. Model an example of a place in the school community. Then ask children to tell about places they know about in their community.

Develop Language and Concepts
Present pages 6 and 7.

Read the words in the Word Bank with children. Let them talk about each of the places listed.

Then read the sentences with children. Encourage them to name each place in the illustration and to talk about a similar place in their community.

ACTIVITY BOOK For practice with the concept of community, use Activity Book page 4.

Read the sentences with the class. Then divide the class in half. Let half the class read the sentences beginning *My community has....* Let the other half read the sentences beginning *I go there....*

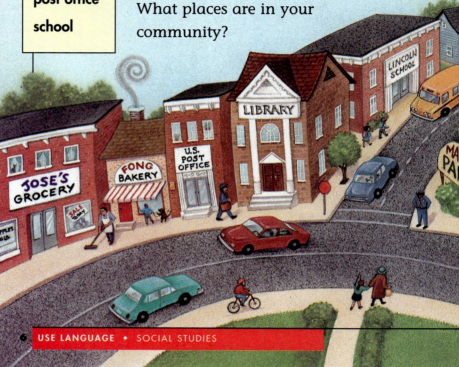

What is a community?

Word Bank
bakery
grocery store
library
park
post office
school

Groups of people live and work in a **community.**

A community has homes and other buildings.

What places do you see in this community?

What places are in your community?

6   USE LANGUAGE • SOCIAL STUDIES

Options for Reaching All Students

Beginning
Language: Sentence Patterns

Have children work with partners and practice the sentence patterns with each other. One child can point to a community location and say *My community has....* The other child can reply *I go there to....* Then have the partners switch roles.

Advanced
Social Studies: Understanding Community Workers

Have children draw or list places in the community. Help them name the people who work at these places.

bakery - baker
library - librarian
post office - mail carrier

Encourage children to write sentences about workers.

My community has a grocery store. I go there to buy food.

My community has a post office. I go there to mail letters.

My community has a park. I go there to play.

Write About It

What places do you go to in your community?

Why do you go there?

Grammar: Sentence Patterns

On the board, write the sentence *My community has a grocery store.* Have children look at the text and find other sentences with *My community has....* Use the same procedure with the sentences beginning *I go there to....* Let children brainstorm other sentences with these beginnings.

 ACTIVITY BOOK For further practice with sentence patterns, use Activity Book page 5.

Assess ✔

Use children's responses to Write About It for assessment. Children should be able to

- name places in their community
- talk about why they visit these

LOOK**AHEAD**

In the next section, children will expand their knowledge of communities to include information about our country and its fifty states.

Gestures and Body Language

Model some gestures. Say: *People are waving. She is smiling.* Walk around the school or your school's community. Ask children to remember examples of gestures or body language that they see. Have children work in small groups to role play what they saw. Elicit from the others what the gestures or body language may mean. Begin a discussion of cultural differences.

Little Celebrations
Tee-Ball

Tee-Ball
Written by BARRY CORDON
Illustrated by GAIL PIAZZA
Little Celebrations

In this story, children get themselves ready for a game of tee-ball in the park.

Level: Beginning

Home Connecttion
Social Studies:
Community Walks

Encourage children to walk with family members around their community. Have children point out to their families the names of places they've studied. On the walk, you may want children to write something they see in environmental print such as a street sign, a store's advertisement or hours, and so on.

Practice

Activate Prior Knowledge
Use Maps

Make a rough map of the classroom on chart paper. Show the location of children's seats, your desk, and various reading and learning stations throughout the room. Help children name the things on the map and locate them in the classroom. Encourage children to point to a part of the map, then walk to the corresponding place.

Develop Language and Concepts
Present pages 8 and 9.

Show children the map and tell them that this map is of our country, The United States of America.

Read the pages with children. Point out the words *country* and *states*. Make sure children understand the difference between the two.

Call attention to the compass rose and have children say the direction words. Help children find north, south, east, and west on the map. Then have them answer the questions.

Model a Strategy
Read Maps

Model locating place on a map.

When I want to find a place on a map I look at one area at a time. I might go across the top and then the bottom, or I might look from left to right. I try not to look at the same area of the map over and over again.

The United States of America

This **country** is the United States of America.

The United States has 50 **states**. A state is an area with many communities.

The United States

8 USE LANGUAGE • SOCIAL STUDIES

Options for Reaching All Students

Beginning
Social Studies: Find Your State

Provide an outline map of the United States. Have children color the map lightly and help them add a few labels on the map. Help children put an *X* on their state.

Advanced
Social Studies: State Names

Challenge children to study the map of the United States to see how many states and locations they can memorize. Let children start by memorizing three or four state names. Help them say the name of each of the states they are learning.

Mixed Ability
Listening and Speaking

Start a game by asking children to look at the map. Say: *I am thinking of a state that is near Kentucky.* Ask children to guess the name of the state you are thinking of. Children will first have to locate Kentucky and then guess which of the surrounding states you had in mind. Children can continue the game by taking turns posing the question.

Point to Indiana on the map.
Which states are next to Indiana?

Point to Colorado on the map.
Which states are next to Colorado?

Try It Out

Point to your state on the map.

Which states are next to your state?

Language Awareness

Spelling: Capitalization

Have children find the place names in the text. As they read aloud each name, write it on chart paper or the board. After all the place names have been written, ask children to tell you what they notice about all the place names. Children should reply that all the names of the places begin with capital letters. Tell them that these words are capitalized because they name special places.

For practice with place names, use Activity Book, page 6.

ACTIVITY BOOK

Assess

Use children's responses to Try It Out for assessment. Children should be able to

- find their state
- name the states near their state

LOOK **AHEAD**

In the next section, children will study animals and where they live.

Multicultural Connection
Social Studies:
Places Around the World

Show a world map. Ask children where they're from. Find, say, and write on the board the places you hear. Have children walk around the room asking each other *Where are you from?* Have them write down the other child's name and response. If necessary, model the question *What's your name?* and *Will you spell it for me, please?*

Writer's Workshop
Write About Places

Refer children to the Writer's Workshop on pages 230–236 of the Student Book. Ask children to write the name of a place they like and something they know about it. Suggest they begin with *The name of a place I like is. . . .*

Connect

Activate Prior Knowledge
Use Pictures

Ask children to look at the pictures and help them identify the animals. Tell children that today they will find out more about where these animals and other animals live.

Develop Language and Concepts
Present pages 10 and 11.

Read the questions at the top of page 10 with children. Help children read the labels. Then read the labels again and ask children to point to each animal as it is named.

Identify the forest on page 10. Encourage children to think of other animals that might live in a forest. Point out that a forest is like a neighborhood for the animals that live there.

Have children read about the pond and use the illustration to discuss animals that live there.

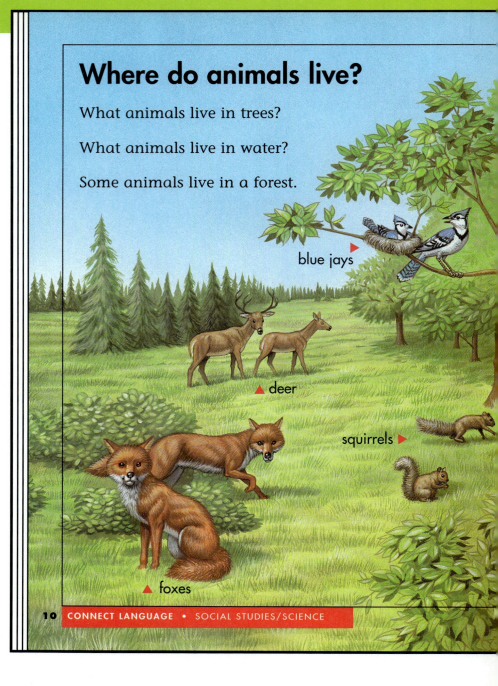

Where do animals live?

What animals live in trees?

What animals live in water?

Some animals live in a forest.

blue jays

▲ deer

squirrels ▶

▲ foxes

10 CONNECT LANGUAGE • SOCIAL STUDIES/SCIENCE

Options for Reaching All Students

Beginning
Language: Identifying Animals

Have each child bring in a picture of a favorite animal—cut from magazines, chosen from the Picture Cards, or in a snapshot. Ask each child to name their animal and tell something about it. Then use the pictures as flash cards for practice in identifying animals.

Advanced
Science: Classifying Animals

Encourage children to work in groups of two to four, looking through magazines and cutting out pictures of animals. Have children tape or paste each picture they find onto a piece of paper and label the picture. Then have the children sort the animals according to habitat, putting all the animals who live in a land habitat in one pile, and those who live in a water habitat in another.

Have them choose one picture to use as a book cover. Have one child write the titles *Land Habitats* and *Water Habitats*. On a separate sheet of paper have one child write the authors' names. On another sheet have the children compile a table of contents. Have the children punch all the pages and use brads to fasten the book together.

Some animals live in a pond.

frogs ▲

▼ ducks

▼ turtles

fish ▼

? Think About It

Why is a pond a good place for a frog to live?

Tell about another animal and where it lives.

Grammar: Irregular Plurals

Write the following on the chalkboard and read them aloud:

2 cat<u>s</u>   2 dog<u>s</u>   2 bird<u>s</u>

Help children see that the words name more than one animal and end with -s. Then write:

2 deer   2 fish

Explain that although these words name more than one animal, they do not end with -s. Other examples of words that name more than one animal but do not end with -s are *sheep* and *geese*.

Assess ✔

Use children's responses to Think About It for assessment. Children should be able to

- give a reason why a pond is a good place for a frog to live
- tell about an animal they have seen and where it lives

LOOK AHEAD ➡

In the next section, children will use what they have learned about groups of people and animals to read a story about a very surprising neighborhood.

Peer Tutoring

Critical Thinking: Summarizing

Have children work in pairs of mixed ability. Ask each child to tell a partner one thing he or she has learned from the article.

Little Celebrations

Gobble Gobble Gone

In this story, a boy who doesn't share his fruit with his friend gets his just desserts—a stomach ache.

GOBBLE GOBBLE GONE

Written by Andrea Butler
Illustrated by Brian Karas

Little Celebrations

Level: Average

Connect

Activate Prior Knowledge

Use Pictures to Predict

Have children look at the pictures in the story. Ask questions such as these

- What do you think this story is about? Why do you think that?
- Name the animals you see in the pictures. What are some things the animals are doing?

Develop Language and Concepts

As children look at the pages, elicit from them examples of the people and places they see. Introduce or review *workers, neighbors,* and *neighborhood.*

Introduce the Selection

Help children find and read the title of the story and the author's name.

Read the Selection

 Read the story to children twice. Then play Side 1 of the Red Tape. Use the suggested activities appropriate to meet children's needs.

Model a Strategy

Use Pictures to Get Meaning

Model using pictures to figure out the meaning of words.

When I look at the picture on page 12, I see a girl tipping her hat to a man selling hot dogs. I see people looking out the windows of an apartment building. Everyone looks happy. I can guess that this story is going to take place in a friendly neighborhood and that the words will tell about the picture.

Continue to discuss the things pictured as you and the children work through the story. For example, you can use the picture on the next page to elicit the meaning of *The dogs waved when the cats marched by.*

Language Awareness

Phonics: Rhyming Words with Long *a, e, i*

After reading the story, point out the rhyming word families:

today	skates	see	by	high
okay	weights	be	pie	thigh
way	plates		dry	eye
	rates		try	

Let children practice saying the words in the word families. Help them make up a sentence that uses at least two of the words in a word family. Encourage them to illustrate the sentence they made up. You may want to call attention to the various spelling patterns for some sounds.

 For practice with rhyming words, use page 7 in the Activity Book.

Options for Reaching All Students

Beginning

Language: Reading Sentences

Ask children to find a picture in the book that shows something silly. Help children learn to say the rhyme for the picture and point to the characters as they read.

Advanced

Language: Writing Poetry

Encourage children to make up a poem about their neighborhood. Let children share their poem with others.

Home Connection

Critical Thinking: Visualization

Have children walk down their block with a family member. Encourage them to look, listen, and smell. Ask children to draw a picture of something from their walk and write whatever they can about it. Have them present to their families their pictures and read what they wrote.

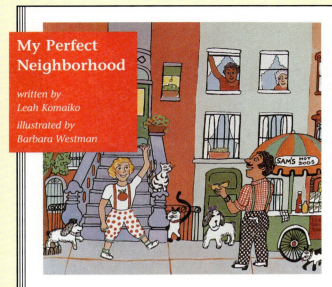

My Perfect Neighborhood

written by
Leah Komaiko

illustrated by
Barbara Westman

I went out for a walk today.
My neighborhood she looked okay.

The dogs waved when
the cats marched by.

The builders built a brick-cream pie

And clothes hung in the trees to dry.
My neighborhood's the place to try.

Connect

Develop Language and Concepts

Ask children to turn to pages 16 and 17. Help them reread the sentences. Ask children why they never see grown-ups lined up for recess. Children should respond that grown-ups don't have recess. Also ask them to tell where they think the poodle found a wedding dress.

Model a Strategy

Recognize Fact and Fantasy

Model recognizing the difference between fact and fantasy.

When I read a sentence such as The horse was out on roller skates, I realize that what I am reading is not a fact. It is a make-believe story. I also know this because when I look at the pictures I see all sorts of things that can't really happen. Do you ever think about the difference between fact and fantasy as you read?

Teachable Moment

Story Elements: Details

As children read the story, encourage them to look at and talk about the funny details in the pictures. Elicit from them how the details in the pictures enrich the story.

Options for Reaching All Students

Beginning

Language: Choral Reading

Have children do a choral reading of the story. Have different groups read the story. One group can read the refrain I went out for my walk today. My neighborhood she looked okay. The other group can read the text that falls between this predictable element. Then the groups can read the story again, changing parts.

Advanced

Language: Personal Word Bank

Have children choose five words from the story to put into their personal word bank. They should write the word on the front of an index card and illustrate it or write a context sentence for it on the back of the card. Have children work in pairs to share their cards.

Home Connection

Critical Thinking: Comparing and Contrasting

Ask children to talk to their families about the neighborhoods they came from. How are they similar to their neighborhoods in the United States? How are they different? Have children share and compare their results in small groups.

I went out for a walk today.
My neighborhood she looked okay.
The grown-ups lined up for recess.

The poodles found a wedding dress

And birds played bongos, more or less.
This neighborhood's the best address.

I went out for my walk today.
My neighborhood she looked okay.
A horse was out on roller skates.

Connect

Develop Language and Concepts

Help children reread pages 20–22 and look at the pictures. Ask children to tell the things that were silly to them. Invite children to draw an illustration showing something silly.

Model a Strategy

Summarize

Model summarizing a story:

After I finish a story, I like to ask myself what the story is about. I try to put everything that happens in the story in a few sentences. For this story, I say to myself This story is about a girl who likes her neighborhood. Everywhere she goes, there are funny and exciting things to be seen. *When I can tell a story in a few sentences like this, I know that I understand what the story is about.*

Teachable Moment

Story Elements: Personification

Direct children's attention to the sentence repeated throughout the story *My neighborhood she looked okay.* Point out that in English we normally refer to *neighborhood* as *it*. Elicit from children why they think the author refers to *neighborhood* as *she*. Explain that authors can use *he* or *she* to make things seem alive like people.

Language Awareness

Language Functions: Approval

 ACTIVITY BOOK Point out that there are many language clues that tell us that the girl in the story loves her neighborhood. First, the title of the story is *My Perfect Neighborhood.* Second, when the girl says *My neighborhood she is okay* she means that it is more than okay; the girl loves living where she does. She later says *This place is special, like I said* and *Things are just as they should be.* For practice with affirmative statements, use page 8 in the Activity Book.

Respond to the Selection

Personal Response: Ask, *Would you like to live in this neighborhood? What do you like best about the neighborhood? What do you like least?*

Critical Response: Let children form groups. Have them look back at the story. Ask, *What are some things we know about animals in this neighborhood?* (Dogs wave, cats march by; poodles find a wedding dress; birds play bongos; a horse roller skates.)

Creative Response: Let children draw a picture of another funny sight that might be seen in *My Perfect Neighborhood.* Encourage children to tell the class about their pictures.

Options for Reaching All Students

Beginning

Language: Reading

 RED TAPE Encourage children to read along with the recording for this story on the Red Tape, Side 1. After reading with the tape, encourage children to find pages they can read on their own.

Advanced

Language: Oral Reading

Let children rehearse reading the story so that they can read it to a group of kindergartners or first-graders in your school. Let children practice showing others the pictures while reading as they rehearse.

Cooperative Learning

Language: Writing

Let children form groups of five or six. Let children discuss what they like about their neighborhood. Have one child copy *I went out for a walk today. My neighborhood she looked okay.* from the book onto art paper. Let the others each draw a picture showing why their neighborhood is okay. Help children label their pictures.

My grandmother was lifting weights
And dishwashers were juggling plates.
I told you, this place really rates.

I went out for my walk today
And saw the sights that came my way:
The dentist shaving someone's head,

The baker baking sweet-tooth bread,
And bed salesmen, asleep in bed.
This place is special, like I said.

I went out for my walk today
And saw . . . *myself* . . . I looked okay.

My legs were each a half arm high.
My elbow almost touched my thigh
And half my nose was in my eye.
Oh, what a gorgeous girl am I!

I love my walks, for then I see
That things are just as they should be.

Connect

Activate Prior Knowledge

Review Vocabulary

Tell children that they will learn a song about people getting together in groups. Ask children to recall a time when they were together with a group of friends. Ask them to tell about what the friends did together. Ask if being together with friends makes them happy.

Develop Language and Concepts

Present page 24.

RED TAPE

Play Side 1 of the Red Tape several times and encourage children to join in singing the song.

Language Awareness

Grammar: Verbs

TPR

After children have worked to make a list of things they might like to do together, ask a volunteer to underline each action word in the list. Then have children pantomime one or two items from their list and let others in the group guess what they are doing.

The More We Get Together

The more we get together,
Together, together,
The more we get together
The happier we'll be.

For your friends are my friends,
And my friends are your friends,
The more we get together
The happier we'll be.

24 CONNECT LANGUAGE • SOCIAL STUDIES/LITERATURE

Options for Reaching All Students

Beginning

Art: Collage

Have groups of three or four children look through magazines to find pictures of groups of people. Let children fasten the pictures to a piece of brown wrapping paper to create a collage entitled "Getting Together."

Advanced

Writing: Being Part of a Group

Ask children to think about things they do in groups. Have them identify the group, write its name, and draw a picture to illustrate one activity the group does together. Then ask them to write about things the group does together.

Home Connection

Music: Group Songs

Encourage children to teach their families "The More We Get Together." Ask children to find out from their families if they know of a similar song about groups or a song in which people hold hands as they sing. Have volunteers tell the class about their experiences teaching and learning about songs.

Tell what you learned.

1. What groups are you part of?

2. Write a list. Put a check next to each place you see in your community. Add other places you see.

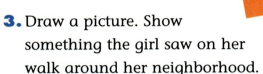

In My Community
library
park
✓school

3. Draw a picture. Show something the girl saw on her walk around her neighborhood.

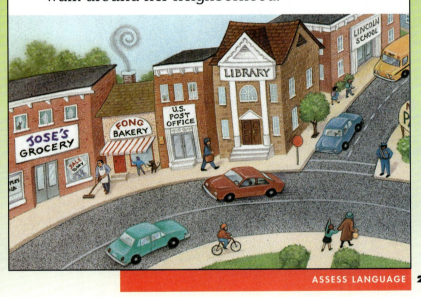

ASSESS LANGUAGE **25**

Assess ✓

Activity 1: Evaluate whether children can name groups they are part of.

Activity 2: Have children write their list on a separate piece of paper. Evaluate number and accuracy of responses.

Activity 3: Check that children draw a girl seeing something mentioned in the literature.

Have children complete the Chapter Self - Assessment, BLM 31. Have them choose products from the activities to place in their portfolios. Add the results of any rubrics, checklists, self-assessments, or portfolio assessments, BLM 2–18.

Listening Assessment

BLACKLINE MASTER

Make sure that each child has copy of Blackline Master 41 and crayons or markers. Play Side 1 of the White Tape several times stopping the tape for children to answer.

TAPESCRIPT

WHITE TAPE

Listen carefully to these directions.

Miguel and Linda are friends. Draw a circle around the friends.

(pause) They have just come from school. Draw a circle around the school. (pause) Now they are in the park. Draw a squirrel in the park. (pause) Draw a bird in the park.

Options for Assessment

Vocabulary Asessment

Write the following headings on the chalkboard: People, Places.

Then say these words: *neighbor, bakery, pond, team, friends, post office, park, family, frogs, library*. As you say each word, ask a volunteer to name the heading under which it belongs.

ACTIVITY BOOK

For further practice with vocabulary, use Activity Book page 8.

Writing Assessment

Have children make personal lists of groups they know.

Language Assessment

BLACKLINE MASTER

Use Blackline Master 40 in the Teacher's Resource Book.

Standardized Test Practice

ACTIVITY BOOK

Use pages 10 and 11 in the Activity Book. Answers: Animals and people do strange things; Poodles wear wedding dresses; Grown-ups stand in a line to play at school.

T25

Preview

Activate Prior Knowledge

Use Pictures

Start discussion of "animals we know" by showing pictures of animals and helping children name them. Encourage children to say whatever they can about the animals—what color they are, where they live, what they eat, what they can do, and so on. Ask which animal they've seen, either in the United States or in their native country.

Use Picture Cards 5, 6, 9, 12, 14, 15, 19, 20, 22, 24, 26, 28, 30, 31, 35, 39, 43, 45, 46, 49, 50, 51, 61, 64, 66, 71.

Develop Language and Concepts

Present pages 26 and 27.

Invite children to look at the pictures on pages 26 and 27. Read the questions aloud. Help children identify the farm, barn, pond, grass, tree, and so on. Help children name the animals. Point to each label and read it for children to repeat. Ask children what each group of animals is doing. Model answers as necessary—*The geese are flying. The ducks are swimming.*

(Continued on page T27)

CHAPTER 2

Animals and Their Habitats

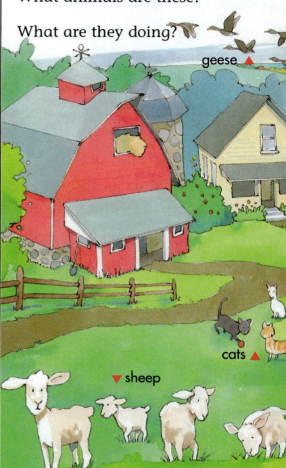

Tell what you know.

What animals are these?

What are they doing?

geese ▲

cats ▲

▼ sheep

26

Options for Reaching All Students

Beginning

Role Playing

TPR

Play the game Who Am I? Pretend to be an animal on page 26 or 27. Say the action words as you imitate the animal's movements and the sounds it makes. Then have children do the actions as you say the words. Have children name the animal in their native language.

Advanced

Language: Vocabulary

Have children draw animals not shown on these pages. Have children label each of their animals and write as much as they can to tell what the animal does.

Then have children work as partners and talk to each other about the animals they have drawn.

Cooperative Language Experience

Field Trip

Take the class to a neighborhood park or to the zoo to observe animals. Help children identify the animals. Elicit from children what the animals are doing.

As a class, write a language experience story about the trip. Children can draw and write about what they saw.

ducks ▼

cows ▶

Talk About It

Tell about other animals you know.

What do they do?

27

In this chapter, children will learn the language for discussing animals and their habitats.

Use pages 26 and 27 to assess children's knowledge of animals and what they do.

Animals live in habitats.

There are many different animals.

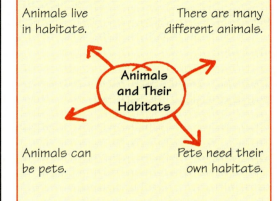

Animals and Their Habitats

Animals can be pets.

Pets need their own habitats.

Help children say what the animals on the Picture Cards can do.

With the class, answer the questions in Talk About It. Explain to children that they are going to be learning about all kinds of animals and about the places where they live.

Mixed Ability
Music: Animal Song

TPR
Teach children the words to "Little White Duck". Use TPR to model the actions. In small groups help children create new verses with animals and actions they know. Invite volunteers to lead the class in saying the new verses and doing the actions.

Home Connection
Ask children to find out about an animal picture book or song in their native language. If possible, have them bring the book or song to class to explain in English.

Present

Activate Prior Knowledge
Brainstorm Vocabulary

Brainstorm a list of animals that children know to assess their knowledge of the varieties of animals. Write the animals children name on chart paper. Add to the list during the chapter.

Develop Language and Concepts
Present pages 28 and 29.

Read the title and directions. Have children identify the animals they know. Read the sentences with children. Then introduce the words in the Word Bank. Help children associate each animal name with the picture of the animal. Then help them form sentences to describe the animals; for example, *Goldfish live in the water.*

Talk about pets. Ask children who have ever had pets to tell the class about them. Have children answer the questions in Think About It. Children could also tell which animals shown on the Picture Cards would or wouldn't make good pets.

Determine comprehension with questions such as these:

- What animals live in water?
- What animals have feathers?
- What animals have six legs?

ACTIVITY BOOK

For practice categorizing animals, use Activity Book page 12.

What animals are there?

Word Bank

- ants
- bear
- butterfly
- dog
- eagle
- goldfish
- lion
- parrot
- shark

Name these animals.

Fish live in the water.

Birds have feathers.

28 LEARN LANGUAGE • SCIENCE

Options for Reaching All Students

Beginning
Science: Studying Where Animals Live

Invite children to pick one of the animals listed in the Word Bank and draw a picture of it, showing where the animal lives. Help children label their pictures.

Advanced
Language: Speaking

Work with children to make statements telling other things they know about the animals pictured, contrasting or comparing the animals.

A goldfish lives in a bowl, but a shark lives in the ocean.
Parrots and eagles are both birds.

Cooperative Learning
Critical Thinking: Classifying

Give each child a sentence strip about an animal. For example, *I have fur.* Have each child draw an appropriate picture and copy the sentence. Then have children form four groups, one for each group of animals listed on the pages. Let each child talk about his or her picture to the others in the group. Fasten each group's pictures together to form a book.

Insects have six legs.

Mammals have hair or fur.

 Think About It

Which animals can be pets?

Would a lion make a good pet? Why? Why not?

Grammar: Subject/Verb Agreement

ACTIVITY BOOK

Help children reread the sentence *Birds have feathers.* Point out that *Birds* ends in *-s.* Show children that *have* is used with plural words. Then on chart paper write *The parrot has feathers.* Help children determine that *parrot* is singular and that *has* is used with it. Let children practice, using other sentences. For practice with *have* and *has,* use Activity Book page 13.

Model a Strategy
Use Pictures for Meaning

Model using pictures for meaning:

When I read sentences near a picture, I can use the ideas in the picture to help me understand what I read.

Assess
Children should be able to

• name and classify animals

• give opinions about animals as pets

LOOK AHEAD ➡

Next, children will use their knowledge of animals to explore how animals benefit from their habitats.

Mixed Ability
Science: Animals Around Us

Help children capture small insects from the school grounds. Place each insect in a vented glass jar. Discuss each insect's size and name, if known. Also let children talk about where they found the insects and how the insects behave. When children are finished with their study, have them release the insects into their natural habitats.

QuickCheck

Plural Forms

Check whether all children are forming regular plurals correctly. Help those who need practice form the plurals of the names of animals. Have children see how many plural words ending in *–s* they can find on pages 28–29.

T29

Practice

Activate Prior Knowledge

Start a K-W-L chart

PICTURE CARDS

See what children know about animals' habitats by showing children the Picture Cards of ducks, a turtle, and fish. Use Picture Cards 26, 30, 71. Ask questions such as these:

- Have you ever seen a turtle? Where was it? How did it live?.

BLACKLINE MASTER

Use the information and Blackline Master 21 in the Teacher's Resource Book to make a K-W-L chart.

K: What We Know	Animals live in many places. Some animals live in the water.
W: What We Want to Find Out	What do different animals eat?
L: What We Learned	

Develop Language and Concepts

Present pages 30 and 31.

Ask children to talk about the picture of the meadow habitat and to name the animals. Read the labels with them. Then read the pages with children. Encourage them to talk about the animals in their habitat and how they might get food and water.

With the children answer the Talk About It question.

What does an animal get from its habitat?

A **habitat** is a place where plants and animals live.

An animal gets food and water from its habitat.

An animal gets air from its habitat.

butterfly

▲ cats

30 USE LANGUAGE • SCIENCE

Options for Reaching All Students

Beginning
Art: Painting

Have children choose an animal to finger paint. After the finger paintings are done, encourage children to label their animals. Each child can also tell the name of the animal in his or her native language.

Advanced
Science: Researching Animals

Let children visit the library to find out about other animals and their habitats. Encourage children to share their findings with others.

Cooperative Language Experience
Bird Watching

Take children on a walk around the block or on the playground to observe birds. When they return to the classroom, help them write a language experience story about the birds they saw.

An animal raises its family in its habitat.

What animals do you see in this habitat?

rabbits

 quail

Talk About It

What do these birds get from their habitat?

SCIENCE • USE LANGUAGE **31**

Language Awareness

Phonics: Short *a*

TPR Write *cat* and *animal* on the board and pronounce them. Have children listen for the short *a* sound. Then have children listen for the short *a* sound in this chant:

Clap your hands: Clap, Clap, Clap.
Stand and pat your back: Pat, Pat, Pat.
Sit and tap your lap: Tap, Tap, Tap.

ACTIVITY BOOK Ask children to follow and give the commands. For practice, use Activity Book page 14.

Model a Strategy
Understand Patterns

Model using patterns:

When I see sentences that begin and end with the same words, I can guess that they will be about the same topic. Since I know the topic, I can think carefully about what the rest of the sentence says.

Assess ✓

Children should be able to

- say what animals get from their habitat

LOOK AHEAD ➡

Next, children will use their general knowledge of animals to find out more about pets and their needs.

Peer Tutoring
Science: Habitats

Let children work as partners. Using paper strips, twigs, string, and so on, have children build birds' nests.

Writer's Workshop
Write About Animals

Refer children to the Writer's Workshop on pages 230–236 of the Student Book. Ask children to write the name of an animal they like and something they know about it. Suggest they begin with *The name of an animal I like is . . .*

Home Connection
Habitats Worldwide

Have children talk to their families about animal habitats found in their native country. Encourage children to report their findings to the class.

Practice

Activate Prior Knowledge
Brainstorm Vocabulary

PICTURE CARDS

Tell children that they are going to find out more about animals that can be pets. Show children Picture Card 46 and ask them to tell where the mouse would live if it were a pet. What would it eat?

Then help children name other animals that can be pets. As children say the names of the animals, write them on the chart.

Develop Language and Concepts
Present pages 32 and 33.

Read the top of page 32 with children. Invite children to look at the first set of illustrations and to name the pets. Read the labels with children. Have them choose which pet they would like to have.

Then read the sentence in the middle of the page and the labels for the pictures below with children. Let children match the habitats to the pets.

For page 33, read each question and the labels for the pictures with children. Let children use the illustrations to help them answer the questions.

ACTIVITY BOOK

For practice with animals and their habitats, use Activity Book page 15.

Help children do Write About It.

A Pet and Its Habitat

A habitat for a pet should have food, water, and air.

Choose a pet you would like to have.

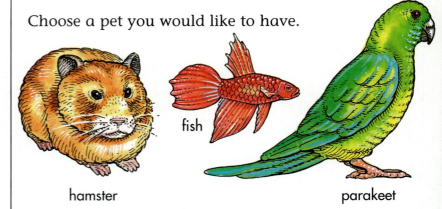

hamster   fish   parakeet

Which habitat would be good for your pet?

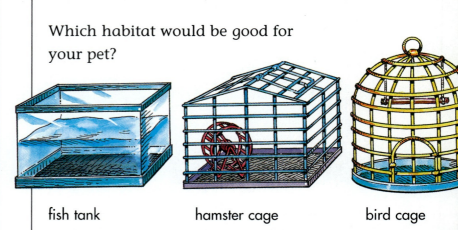

fish tank   hamster cage   bird cage

32 USE LANGUAGE • SCIENCE

Options for Reaching All Students

Beginning
Language: Speaking

Working in pairs, let children take turns talking about the pet they drew in Write About it on page 33. Children should say the pet's name, then say whatever they can about the pet's habitat and the food it eats.

Advanced
Language: Brainstorming

Divide the class into groups of "pet experts." Let children in each group brainstorm everything they know about pets and take notes.

Then let a spokesperson for each group report on everything that the group knows about that pet. When the spokesperson is finished, let others in the group add any additional information.

Cooperative Language Experience
Visit a Pet Store

Arrange to take children to a local pet store. Have a store employee talk about pet care. Encourage children to ask questions.

As a class, write a language experience story about the trip. Children can draw and caption pictures of what they saw.

Which food would be good for your pet?

fruits and vegetables

fish food

bird seed

Does each habitat have the food, water, and air the pet needs?

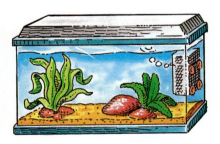

 Write About It

Draw the pet you chose and its habitat. Write how the pet will get what it needs from its habitat.

SCIENCE • USE LANGUAGE **33**

Language Awareness

Language Functions: Explaining Choices

Write *because* on the chalkboard and pronounce it. Then model its use: *The bird cage is the best habitat for the bird, because a bird can perch on the swing.*

Have pairs of children work together to use *because* in sentences explaining another choice from pages 32 or 33.

Model a Strategy
Understanding the Main Idea

Model understanding the main idea:

When I read, I first read the title. This tells me what the reading is about. When I read the sentences, I think about what they have to do with the title. When I look at the pictures, I think about what they have to do with the title and the sentences. This helps me understand what I'm reading.

Assess

Children should be able to

• talk about a pet's habitat and needs

LOOK AHEAD

Next, children will apply the animal vocabulary they learned here to count animals.

Mixed Ability
Writing: Pet Riddles

Have children work in pairs of mixed abilities. Have each pair choose a pet or other animal they have studied and write a riddle for it on the front of a piece of paper and the answer on the back. Have children work in small groups to try to solve one another's riddles.

I live in the water. I swim. I eat fish food. What am I? (a fish)

Multicultural Connection
Pet Stories

Have children investigate the different kinds of pets found in different cultures. Invite them to talk about how different cultures treat pets.

Little Celebrations
Where's Little Mole?

In this story, Mrs. Mole searches through an underground tunnel habitat, looking for Little Mole. Along the way, she meets all the other animals who live in the tunnel.

Level: Beginning

Connect

Activate Prior Knowledge
Use Pictures to Review Number Words Orally

PICTURE CARDS

Show children Picture Cards with different numbers of animals shown on them. Have children say the name and number of each type of animal. For example, show the cow Picture Card. Ask, *What are these animals?* Children should answer, *Cows.* Then ask, *How many cows are there?* Children should answer, *Three.* Continue with other Picture Cards. Use Picture Cards 6, 19, 26, 45, 50, 51, 64.

Develop Language and Concepts
Present pages 34 and 35.

Let children discuss the illustration before you begin. Help them name the animals, read the labels, and describe the habitat.

Read the questions, one by one, with children. As children answer the questions, encourage them to point to the animals as they count them.

Model several number sentences about animals. Write them on the board. Then have each child make up a number sentence about the animals; for example, there are 4 monkeys and 2 birds in the trees: $4 + 2 = 6$

With the children, do the Talk About It.

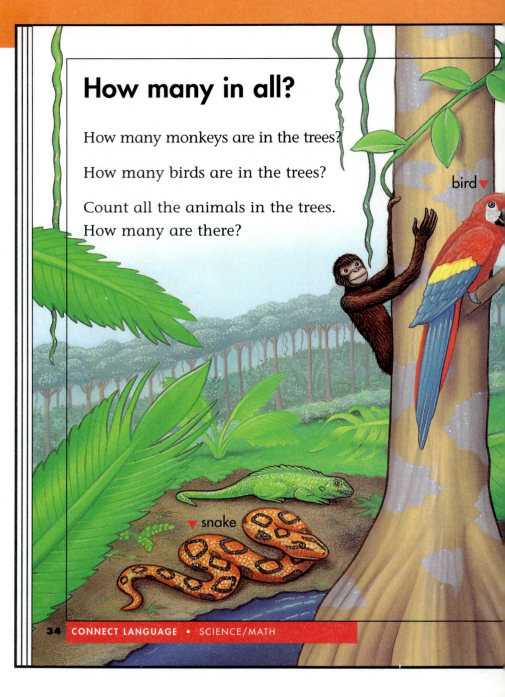

How many in all?

How many monkeys are in the trees?

How many birds are in the trees?

Count all the animals in the trees. How many are there?

bird ▼

▼ snake

34   CONNECT LANGUAGE • SCIENCE/MATH

Options for Reaching All Students

Beginning
Art: Hand Puppets

Help children decorate brown-paper lunch bags to look like animals in the text.

Let children introduce their puppet by having the puppet say, *I'm a/an (animal name).* Then children can make the puppet act like the animal.

Advanced
Language: Talk About Animals

Write a list of number words (two–ten) on the board. Then write a list of animal names (plural forms). Read the two lists with the children. Then ask volunteers say a sentence about a group of animals using a number word and an animal name. For example: *I see four monkeys on a tree.*

Cooperative Learning
Language: Practice Vocabulary

Divide the class into groups of four or five and provide each group with a large piece of brown paper and crayons. Review the jungle animals. Help children create a jungle mural that contains several of the jungle animals studied. Display murals one by one in front of the class and ask children to tell how many of each animal is in the mural.

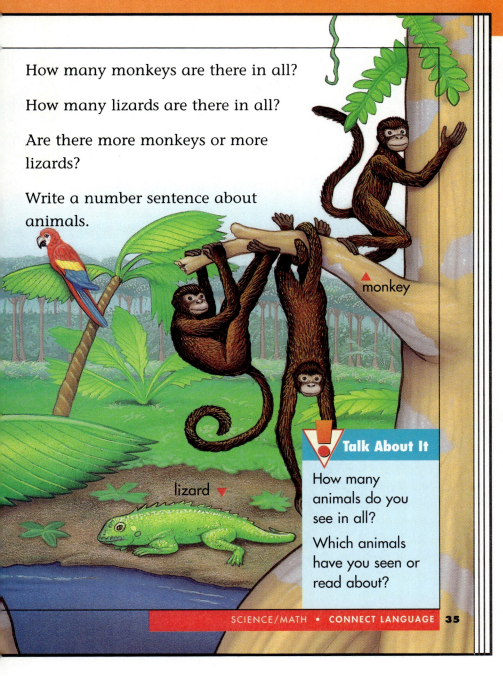

How many monkeys are there in all?

How many lizards are there in all?

Are there more monkeys or more lizards?

Write a number sentence about animals.

monkey

lizard

Talk About It

How many animals do you see in all?

Which animals have you seen or read about?

SCIENCE/MATH • **CONNECT LANGUAGE** **35**

Language Awareness

Grammar: Comparative Adjective

Point to the question *Are there more monkeys or more lizards?* Tell children that this question asks them to count the monkeys and the lizards to tell which animal is greater in number. Let children practice sentences using this pattern. Ask questions, such as: *Are there more boys or more girls?*

Model a Strategy
Counting How Many

Model counting *how many?*

When I see a question with the words *how many,* I know that I will need to count, so I read the question carefully to find out what I should count.

ACTIVITY BOOK

For practice with *how many,* use Activity Book page 16.

Assess ✔
Children should be able to

• identify animals in the jungle and write number sentences

LOOK **AHEAD**

In the next section, children will use their knowledge of the characteristics of animals to guess riddles about animals.

After children count the animals, they can label the mural with the number of animals at the bottom; for example: *3 monkeys, 2 snakes, 5 lizards, 1 bird.*

Peer Tutoring
Math: Counting

Have children work in pairs. Give each pair five or ten counters, depending upon children's ability. Have children take turns setting out various numbers of counters and asking, *How many counters?* Let the other partner count them aloud.

Little Celebrations
Down by the Swamp

This story is about the insects and spiders down by the swamp . . . and the frog who ruins their dance.

Level: Beginning

T35

Connect

Activate Prior Knowledge
Review Vocabulary

Ask children a riddle about an animal they already know: *I have feathers. I can fly. I can build a nest. Who am I?* Children should respond with *bird.* Ask similar riddles for other animals children learned about in this chapter.

Develop Language and Concepts
Present pages 36 and 37.

PICTURE CARDS

Read the first riddle with children. Then reread it, having volunteers act out or explain each line. Use pictures and pantomime actions to clarify vocabulary as necessary. When you ask children to tell what animal the riddle refers to, they should respond with *snake.* Show children the snake Picture Card. Invite them to tell how the snake has some of the attributes listed in the riddle. Use Picture Card 64. Follow the same procedure for the hippopotamus riddle on page 37. Use Picture Card 35.

FYI Children's Riddles
The children who wrote these riddles live in Kuwait. When they wrote these riddles, their teacher was Alison Henderson.

An Animal Riddle

by Faisal Al Shatti, age 10

I am as sneaky as a fox.
I am as long as the neck of a giraffe.
I am as brown as a grizzly bear.
I am as lazy as a snail.
I am as tricky as a wolf.
I am as slow as a turtle.
I am as slimy as a frog.
I am as quiet as an ant.
I live in somewhere green.
. . . I am a "SNAKE."

36 CONNECT LANGUAGE • SCIENCE/LITERATURE

Options for Reaching All Students

Beginning
Language: Role-Playing

PICTURE CARDS

Have children review the animal Picture Cards they have studied—Picture Cards 6, 14, 19, 24, 26, 30, 45, 46, 50.

Let children role-play one of the animals. Have others guess the animal. Help children write the name of their animal on the board.

Advanced
Language: Writing Poetry

Let children think about all the animals they studied. Then have them choose one of the animals to write a riddle about. Help children think about the way the animal looks or how it acts to write the riddle. For example:

I am brown.
I am very small.
I have fur.
I am a MOUSE.

Mixed Ability
Critical Thinking: Using Context Clues

Give children descriptions of objects in the classroom and let them guess the object. For example:

You use them for drawing.

An Animal Riddle

by Abdulla Al Kulaib, age 10

I am as fast as an elephant.
I am as gray as a mouse.
I am lazy as a bear in winter.
I am as large as a log.
I am as smooth as a snake.
My mouth is as wide as a football.
My ears are as small as an egg.
My legs are as small as a shoe.
My head is as tall as a bottle.
My eyes are as round as a knot.
I am a hippopotamus.

SCIENCE/LITERATURE • **CONNECT LANGUAGE** 37

Language Awareness

Language Function: Similes

Point out that most sentences in the riddles compare things. Point out the pattern *as ___ as a ___*. Help children tell what is being compared. Help children make up similar sentences about other animals.

I am as pretty as a butterfly.
I am as small as an ant.

ACTIVITY BOOK
For practice with similes, use Activity Book page 17.

Model a Strategy
Remembering Details

Model remembering details:

To solve a riddle, I read each clue carefully. On page 36, I remember that the animal is sneaky, long, brown, lazy, tricky, slow, slimy, and quiet. Then I think of all the animals I know and decide which one fits the clues.

Assess

Children should be able to

• use adjectives to talk about animals
• make up and solve animal riddles

LOOK **AHEAD**

Next, children will learn about another animal through poetry.

Home Connection
Language: Similes

Have children ask their parents for a simile used in their cultures. Have children tell their simile to the rest of the class. Write the similes on the board. Note the similarities and differences across cultures.

Cooperative Learning
Language: Using Adjectives

Divide the class into groups. Have each group draw an animal on a piece of brown paper. Then encourage children to brainstorm words to describe the animal. Help children write these words on their picture. When all the pictures are complete, let each group display its picture and read the describing words. Let others name the animal.

Hi-De-Hi

written by Marcia Vaughan
illustrated by Kim Howard

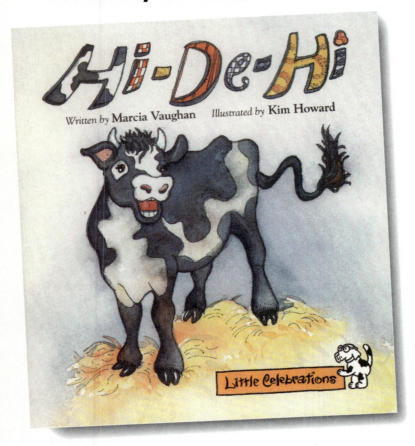

Hi-De-Hi

On this cheery tour of Uncle Marcos's farm, readers will see Uncle Marcos and many of his farm animals.

Shared Reading

1. Introduce

Display the book and read the title. Ask children to describe and name the animal on the cover. Present the word *cow* if necessary. Ask if children have ever seen a cow. If so, invite them to share their personal experiences. Ask children to tell where cows usually live. Encourage them to look at the illustrations for clues. Have children name other animals they know that live on a farm. Ask children to use the picture and their background knowledge to predict what the book will be about.

2. Read

As you read aloud, have children point to the animals in the illustrations as you read about them in the text. Invite children to join in when they see the words *Hi-de-hi, hi-de-ho.*

3. Reread

Invite children to reread the book with you. Pause after each phrase *Out in the _____* (pause) and encourage children to complete the sentence by saying *you'll see _____.* Discuss the book by asking questions such as the following:

- *Which animals live on Uncle Marcos's farm?*
- *Which animal is your favorite? Why?*
- *Where would you find a cow on Uncle Marcos's farm?*

Options for Reaching All Students

Beginning

Art: Animal Masks

Divide children into small groups. Invite each group to choose an animal in the story: hog, cat, dog, duck, hen, sheep, chick, cow, or donkey. Give each child a paper plate. Put art supplies on a table or counter. For example, you may want to provide paints, crayons, markers, cotton balls, string, feathers, and construction paper, tape, and glue. Let children draw the face of the animal they chose on their paper plate and choose which art supplies they want to use. Have them tape a tongue depressor to the back to create a mask. Reread the story. Whenever an animal is mentioned, have the appropriate group hold up their masks and say the sentence about the animal.

Advanced

Language: Books About Farm Life

Have children think about and write down questions they'd like answered about life on a farm. Ask them to find and read a book on this topic.

Encourage children to take turns reporting on their book and sharing information from the book with their classmates.

Grammar: Adjectives

As you reread the story with children, help them spot adjectives that describe nouns. List the adjectives and nouns as they are discovered.

Adjectives	Nouns
old gray	donkey
big, red	barn
orange	cat
yellow	dog
three red	hens
spotted	chicks

Help children name the other nouns in the story and suggest adjectives to describe them.

Model a Strategy
Draw Conclusions

Model using illustrations to draw conclusions:

As I read a story, I look at the pictures. I think about what different characters in the story might be thinking or feeling. In this story, when I look at pictures of Uncle Marcos, I see that he is very busy. He looks looks like he's smiling or laughing while he is taking care of his animals. Near the end of the story, I see musical notes over his head, so I know he is singing as he works. Although Uncle Marcos doesn't talk in the story, I think he must really like his farm, the work he does, and his animals. Drawing conclusions helps me better understand what I am reading. How do you draw conclusions as you read?

Response Activities

Tell About Animal Sounds

Elicit from children the sounds each animal in the story makes. Then give groups of children an index card with the name of an animal from the story. Tell children to listen for their animal as you reread the story. When they hear the animal on their card, invite them to make the sound their animal makes.

Look at Picture Details

To help children understand more about the animals on Uncle Marcos's farm, encourage them to look carefully at the pictures. Where on the farm do the animals live? How does each animal look? Help children tell what they know about each animal. Ask children why they think each animal is kept on the farm.

Create a New Story

Have children work in groups to brainstorm a list of animals they might find on a farm. Using the list of nouns and adjectives from the Language Awareness section as a model, encourage children to think of descriptive words for animals on their list. Then have children write and illustrate their own version of *Hi-De-Hi*. Children may want to pretend it's their farm instead of Uncle Marcos's.

Cooperative Learning
Crtitical Thinking: Classifying

Have children work in groups. Ask them to list as many farm animals as they can. Then invite them to think about the different foods farm animals provide. Have them make a collage from magazine pictures or their drawings. Have them group the food products around the appropriate animals. Invite them to give a "show and tell" presentation to the class.

Peer Tutoring
Language: Favorite Animals

Have children work in pairs. Encourage each partner to name a favorite animal from the story and draw a picture of the animal. Have them take turns showing their pictures, describing their animal, and explaining what they like about that animal. Invite them to caption their pictures together.

Mixed Ability
Language: Guessing Game

Encourage a volunteer to pantomime the actions of one of the animals. Let classmates guess which animal is being pantomimed. The person who correctly guesses the animal gets to take the next turn. You can play a variation of the game by having children give oral clues such as *I'm black and white. I say, "Moo."*

Connect

Activate Prior Knowledge

Use Pictures

Show children the picture on the page. Ask them to name the animal. Children should say that this is a polar bear. Encourage children to tell what they know about this animal.

Develop Language and Concepts

Present page 38.

Read the poem with children and encourage them to notice its rhythm. You may even want to have children clap to the rhythm of the poem.

Do Try It Out. Encourage children to take turns pretending they are a polar bear. Have others in the class guess what the polar bear is doing.

Language Awareness

Phonics: Rhyme

ACTIVITY BOOK After children have heard the poem several times, read it again and have children listen for the words that rhyme. They should name the words *air, bear, nice,* and *ice.* For practice with rhyme, use Activity Book page 18.

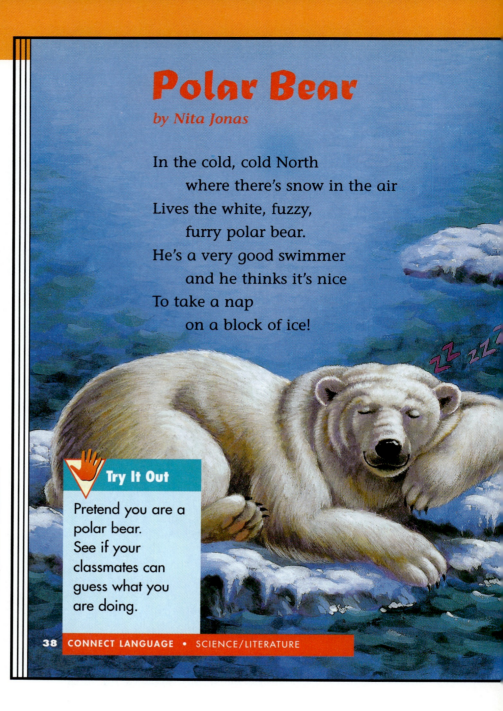

Polar Bear
by Nita Jonas

In the cold, cold North
    where there's snow in the air
Lives the white, fuzzy,
    furry polar bear.
He's a very good swimmer
    and he thinks it's nice
To take a nap
    on a block of ice!

Try It Out

Pretend you are a polar bear. See if your classmates can guess what you are doing.

Options for Reaching All Students

Beginning

Music: Singing

Help children sing the following song to the tune of "Twinkle, Twinkle, Little Star." Have children sing along with you.

Polar bears, polar bears
On the ice,
Playing in snow
Must be nice.

Polar bears, polar bears
Swimming there,
Floating, splashing
Everywhere.

Polar bears, polar bears
On the ice,
Playing in snow
Must be nice.

Advanced

Writing: Poem Variations

Have children write and illustrate alternative versions of the poem, using different animals.

Tell what you learned.

1. Make a chart. Write the name of an animal for each group.

Animal Group	Animal Name
insects	ant
fish	
mammals	
birds	

2. Name an animal. Tell what it gets from its habitat.

3. Make up your own riddle about an animal. Draw and describe the animal in your riddle.

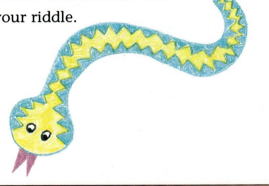

ASSESS LANGUAGE 39

Assess

Activity 1: Have children make a chart on a separate piece of paper. Evaluate their work on number and accuracy of responses.

Activity 2: See if children can talk about the habitat and needs of an animal of their choice.

Activity 3: Check that children can use adjectives.

Have children complete the Chapter Self Assessment, BLM 31. Have them choose products to for their portfolios. Add the results of any rubrics, checklists, self assessments, or portfolio assessments, BLMs 2–18.

Listening Assessment

BLACKLINE MASTER

Make sure that each child has Blackline Master 43 and a pencil. Play Side 1 of the White tape several times stopping the tape to allow children to answer.

TAPESCRIPT

WHITE TAPE

Listen carefully. Circle the correct objects.

Look at the parrot. Circle the food that would be good for the parrot. (pause)

Look at the goldfish. Circle the food that would be good for the goldfish. (pause)

Look at the hamster. Circle the food that would be good for the hamster. (pause)

Look at the cat. Circle the food that would be good for the cat.

Options for Assessment

Vocabulary Assessment

ACTIVITY BOOK

Have children use Activity Book page 19 to play Bingo. Call out the animal names on the page at random. Have children use markers to cover pictures of the animal you call. As children work, check to see that they are covering the correct names. As they cover four animals in a row—either horizontally, vertically or diagonally—encourage them all to say Bingo!

Writing Assessment

Have children make personal picture books in which they illustrate and write about their favorite animals.

Language Assessment

BLACKLINE MASTER

Use Blackline Master 42 in the Teacher's Resource Book.

Standardized Test Practice

ACTIVITY BOOK

Use pages 20 and 21 in the Activity Book. Answers: 1.9, 2.3, 3.10, 4.2.

Wrap-Up

Activities

Role Play

Have children role-play their parents either at work in the community or interacting, as customers, for example, with community workers. Encourage other children to tell what work the child is role playing.

Collect Environmental Print

Encourage children to start a collection of advertisements and sales flyers from their area. Let children discuss the advertising materials to figure out what is being sold and how much it costs. Let children explain where the stores are located. In addition, on a walk with the class around the community, together you can take pictures of street signs with symbols such as school crossing or text such as *One Way, Lincoln Street, Hours: 9:00–5:00*, and so on.

Group Book

Have each child make a page for a Group Book. Suggest that a page should show a group working and the name of the group. It might also contain words that the child would use to tell about the group. Fasten the pages together to make the Group Book. Have each child present his or her page to the class.

Discussing the Theme

Have children work in groups of 2 or 3 to discuss their progress during this unit about the community. Choose from the following activities that will demonstrate to them how much they have learned and how useful that information is.

- Tape-record a list of new words learned.
- Draw or find pictures to create a picture dictionary of words learned. Have children label the pictures.
- Put unit words on the chalkboard or display Picture Cards.
- Ask children to tell when they might use the words they have learned, for example in science class, talking with friends, at school, and so on.
- Play a game in which one child identifies a word that is displayed and another child says a word that goes with it. For example, *forest—trees; pond—water; library—books.*

Sharing the Unit Project

Use the invitation form, Blackline Master 32 or 33, to invite family members to school to see the community model.

Set up the classroom with stations representing each section of the community. Encourage family members to visit each station.

You might want to assign a pair of children to each station. They can tell the area of the community that is being represented and describe its components.

As visitors arrive, a volunteer can read them a short, prepared "Welcome to our Community" speech.

As a concluding activity, help children teach family members the songs they have learned in this unit. Put up a sign that children can read to their family members: *We like living in our community.*

Signs of Success!

Duplicate a copy of this checklist for each child.

Name: _____

Refer to the checklist below for a quick determination of how a child is progressing toward transitioning out of ESL instruction:

Objectives:

- ☐ Names different kinds of groups.
- ☐ Tells what different groups do.
- ☐ Names places in a community.
- ☐ Gives reasons why people go to each place.

- ☐ Names states in the United States.
- ☐ Tells about where some animal groups live.
- ☐ Names and tells about different animals.
- ☐ Tells about groups animals belong to.
- ☐ Tells what animals get from their habitats.

Language Awareness:

Understands/Uses:

- ☐ present tense
- ☐ sentence patterns
- ☐ irregular plural nouns
- ☐ informal English word *okay*

- ☐ statements showing approval
- ☐ subject/verb agreement
- ☐ comparative adjective *more* for counting
- ☐ similes

Hears/Pronounces/Reads:

- ☐ rhyming words with long *a, e, i*
- ☐ commands with short *a*

- ☐ rhyming words with short *e*

Learning Strategies:

- ☐ Uses pictures for meaning.
- ☐ Reads maps to get information.
- ☐ Recognizes fact and fantasy.
- ☐ Summarizes information.

- ☐ Uses patterns.
- ☐ Understands the main idea.
- ☐ Uses counting to draw conclusions.
- ☐ Remembers details.

Comments

_____

_____

Planning Guide

CHAPTER 3

How People Work

Objectives

Name community workers.

Tell how workers help us.

Tell where various workers work.

Understand what people's needs are.

Tell the difference between needs and wants.

Tell what animals' needs are.

Vocabulary Focus

Community workers, such as *garbage collector, mail carrier, librarian, paramedic.*
Workplaces, such as *factory, office, bank, farm.*
Needs, such as *food, water, place to live, clothing.*

Lesson	Content Focus	Language Awareness Objectives	Learning Strategies
Preview pages 40–41 Tell what you know.			
Present pages 42–43 How do these workers help us?	Social Studies	**Grammar** Verbs	Use pictures for meaning.
Practice pages 44–45 Where do other workers work?	Social Studies	**Vocabulary** Related Words	Use title to predict.
Practice pages 46–47 What are needs and wants? How do people get things they need and want?	Social Studies	**Vocabulary** *needs* and *wants*	Note repeated words.
Connect pages 48–49 Do animals have the same needs as people?	Social Studies/ Science	**Vocabulary** Contractions	Find a way to classify.
Connect pages 50–51 "What I Want to Do" "My Family Works"	Social Studies/ Literature		Use what you know.
Connect page 52 "A Gardener's Song"	Social Studies/ Literature	**Phonics** Rhyme	
Assess page 53 Tell what you learned.			

CHAPTER 4

What Animals Do

Objectives

Tell ways animals work to meet their needs.

Tell how animals protect themselves.

Tell how protective coloration works.

Vocabulary Focus

Animals, such as *rabbit, spider, beaver, woodchuck, armadillo.*

Things animals build, such as *web, dam, honeycomb, tunnel.*

Ways animals protect themselves, such as *spray, hide, run, change colors.*

Lesson	Content Focus	Language Awareness Objectives	Learning Strategies
Preview pages 54–55 Tell what you know.			
Present pages 56–57 How do some animals work?	Science	**Grammar** Subject/ Verb Agreement	Recognize main idea.
Practice pages 58–59 What do animals do to protect themselves?	Science	**Phonics** Blends *sm, sk, spr*	Recognize sentence patterns.
Practice pages 60–61 Color can make things hard to see.	Science	**Language Functions** Giving Directions	Follow directions.
Connect pages 62–63 How many are there now?	Science/Math	**Spelling** Punctuation	Understand specialized language.
Connect pages 64–75 *When I'm Hungry*	Science/ Literature	**Grammar** Contractions **Grammar** Verbs **Language Functions** Describing	Use prior knowledge. Use pictures to get meaning. Summarize.
Connect page 76 "There Was a Little Turtle"	Science/ Literature	**Phonics** Rhyming Words	
Assess page 77 Tell what you learned.			

Resources

Chapter 3

Support Materials

PICTURE CARDS
Numbers 17, 23, 24, 30, 32, 34, 36, 37, 38, 43, 47, 53, 59, 60, 71

ACTIVITY BOOK
Pages 22–31

VIDEO
Unit 2, Working

ORANGE TAPE
Side 2
"A Gardener's Song," page T52

Shared Reading Collection

Agua Agua Agua by Pat Mora, CelebrationPress, 1996.

Little Celebrations Library

Busy People by Babs Bell Hajdusiewicz, ScottForesman, 1993.

Farm Day by Sarah Tatler, ScottForesman, 1993.

Assessment Materials

WHITE TAPE
Side 1
Listening Assessment, page T53

BLACKLINE MASTER
Language Assessment, page 50
Listening Assessment, page 51

Newcomer Book A

Survival Book for absolute beginners. For overview, see pages xxviii–xxxi.

For Extended Reading

The Cactus Flower Bakery by Harry Allard, HarperCollins, 1991.

Sunny the snake and Stewart the armadillo decide to open a bakery deep in the heart of Texas. Who knows what these two can cook up together?

Level: Average

Frida's Office Day by Thomas P. Lewis, Harper and Row, 1989.

Frida the cat spends a day at work with her father. She learns how to work the office machines and how the people in the office work together.

Level: Beginning

Go Ask Giorgio! by Patricia Wittman, Macmillan,1992.

Hardworking Giorgio is a man who literally wears many hats—a different one for each job. Soon he finds he's doing too much work. Will Giorgio blow all his tops?

Level: Advanced

If I Could Work by Terence Blacker, J. B. Lippincott, 1987.

A little boy pretends he's a grown-up. He has a great time "working" as an astronaut, a bus driver, a firefighter—anything he can imagine. Why, it's much more fun to work than to play!

Level: Average

When We Grow Up by Anne Rockwell, E. P. Dutton, 1981.

A young boy describes what he and all his classmates want to be when they grow up.

Level: Average

Related Technology

The Busy World of Richard Scarry's Busy-Town, Paramount Interactive, 1993.

Work and play with the busy inhabitants of Busy-Town.

Chapter 4

Support Materials

PICTURE CARDS

Numbers 5, 6, 14, 15, 19, 20, 22, 26, 31, 39, 42, 48, 52, 66, 71

ACTIVITY BOOK

Pages 32–41

VIDEO

Unit 2, Working

ORANGE TAPE

Side 1 *When I'm Hungry,* pages T64–T75

ORANGE TAPE

Side 2 "There Was a Little Turtle," page T76

Little Celebrations Library

Big Pig, Little Pig by Marcia Vaughan, ScottForesman, 1993.

Mrs. Sato's Hens by Laura Min, ScottForesman, 1993.

Assessment Materials

WHITE TAPE

Side 2
Listening Assessment, page T77

BLACKLINE MASTER

Language Assessment, page 52
Listening Assessment, page 53

For Extended Reading

Flap Your Wings and Try by Charlotte Pomerantz, Greenwillow, 1989.

A young seagull watches the older birds flying and finally gets enough nerve to try it himself.

Level: Beginning

A Million Chameleons by James Young, Little, Brown & Co., 1990.

A million playful chameleons take a colorful romp through a zoo, a dance, a tree climb, even a merry-go-round!

Level: Advanced

The Mixed-Up Chameleon by Eric Carle, HarperCollins, 1975.

A little chameleon is bored with sitting around changing colors all day and waiting for something to happen. He wishes he were more like all the animals in the zoo. Eventually, though, he realizes that being a chameleon can have its good points after all.

Level: Average

Over in the Meadow based on the original by Olive A. Wadsworth, Scholastic, 1992.

An adaptation of the classic nursery poem, based on a traditional Southern Appalachian counting rhyme, reillustrated with colorful, cut-paper collages by David A. Carter.

Level: Beginning

Watching Foxes by Jim Arnosky, Lothrop, 1985.

What do little foxes do while their mother is out hunting their food? They play!

Level: Beginning

Related Technology

Zoo Explorer, Compton's New Media, 1994.

Visit baby animals and explore a cyber-zoo.

Project

Skits About Work

This optional project can be completed over the next two chapters. See the Unit Wrap-Up, page T77a, for more ideas on sharing the project with family members.

What You'll Need

Collect some of the following items for the players in skits:

For the Workers

- crossing guard—white belts
- teacher—books and chalk
- librarian—books
- doctor or school nurse—toy stethoscope
- firefighter—fire hat
- lifeguard—whistle
- mail carrier—letters and pouch
- factory workers—objects to pack in boxes
- bank teller—play money
- TV repair person—cardboard TV

For the Animals

- a labeled photo, illustration, or children's drawing of several of the following animals: armadillo, beaver, woodchuck, fish, skunk, turtle, squirrel, rabbit, bird, chameleon, bee, spider
- a replica of a bird nest
- nuts
- leaves
- a replica of a spider web
- a replica of or a real honeycomb
- a tree branch

Beginning the Project

Tell children that as they work on the next two chapters they will also be planning and practicing for skits about work that they will perform for their families. Ask children to be thinking about and watching workers that they see every day. Suggest that they also notice what kinds of work they see animals doing. Encourage them to share with classmates what they learn from their observation.

Home Involvement

Send Letter Home, Blackline Masters 34–39 in the Teacher's Resource Book, to families to solicit their participation in collecting the items needed for the skits.

Planning the Skits

Encourage children to bring in items needed for the skits. Have children discuss which person or animal they want to play and why. If possible, have children talk with workers in their community before they choose their roles.

Assign an area of the classroom for each skit. Assign children to small groups. Group workers with similar jobs; group animals that have something in common. Have children decide how to decorate their performance area.

Prepare the Skits

Organize children's efforts around the following tasks: choosing a place to perform, collecting props and/or costumes, planning a simple script, writing out a script for reference, rehearsing (including one dress rehearsal before classmates). Consider the following categories for the skits:

- Workers at School (teacher, librarian, crossing guard, school nurse)
- Workers Who Keep Us Safe (police officer, firefighter, lifeguard)
- Community Workers (mail carrier, factory worker, bank teller, TV repair person)
- Animal Builders (birds, beavers, bees, spiders)
- Animals That Protect Themselves (turtle, skunk, chameleon, rabbit)

Daily Discussion

Allow some time each day for children to plan their skit. Encourage them to practice the vocabulary they have learned in conjunction with their skit. Children can plan what they will say in their skit and prepare backdrops. Discuss progress and problems with the class. At the end of the unit, have children share their feelings about their performances.

Activity Book

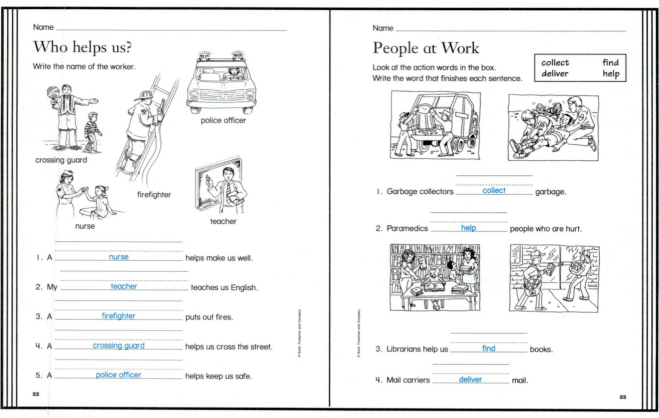

Name _____

Who helps us?

Write the name of the worker.

police officer

crossing guard

firefighter

nurse

teacher

1. A _____nurse_____ helps make us well.

2. My _____teacher_____ teaches us English.

3. A _____firefighter_____ puts out fires.

4. A _____crossing guard_____ helps us cross the street.

5. A _____police officer_____ helps keep us safe.

22

© Scott, Foresman and Company

Name _____

People at Work

Look at the action words in the box.
Write the word that finishes each sentence.

collect	find
deliver	help

1. Garbage collectors _____collect_____ garbage.

2. Paramedics _____help_____ people who are hurt.

3. Librarians help us _____find_____ books.

4. Mail carriers _____deliver_____ mail.

© Scott, Foresman and Company

23

Name _____

Where do I work?

Write the place where each worker works.

bank

factory

farm

office

1. I am a factory worker.

   I work in a _____factory_____.

2. I am a farmer.

   I work on a _____farm_____.

3. I am a bank teller.

   I work in a _____bank_____.

4. I am a office worker.

   I work in an _____office_____.

24

© Scott, Foresman and Company

Name _____

Needs or Wants?

Write **need** or **want** beside each thing.

1. food _____need_____

2. a book _____want_____

3. a TV _____want_____

4. clothing _____need_____

5. water _____need_____

6. a dog _____want_____

On a separate paper draw two things people need to live.

25

© Scott, Foresman and Company

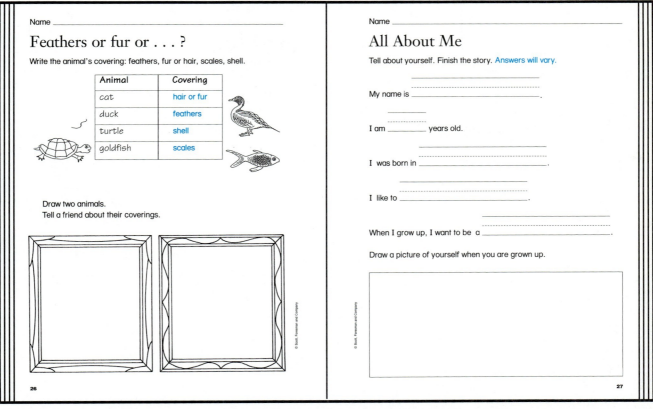

Name _____

Feathers or fur or . . . ?

Write the animal's covering: feathers, fur or hair, scales, shell.

Animal	Covering
cat	hair or fur
duck	feathers
turtle	shell
goldfish	scales

Draw two animals.
Tell a friend about their coverings.

© Scott, Foresman and Company

26

Name _____

All About Me

Tell about yourself. Finish the story. Answers will vary.

My name is _____.

I am _____ years old.

I was born in _____.

I like to _____.

When I grow up, I want to be a _____.

Draw a picture of yourself when you are grown up.

© Scott, Foresman and Company

27

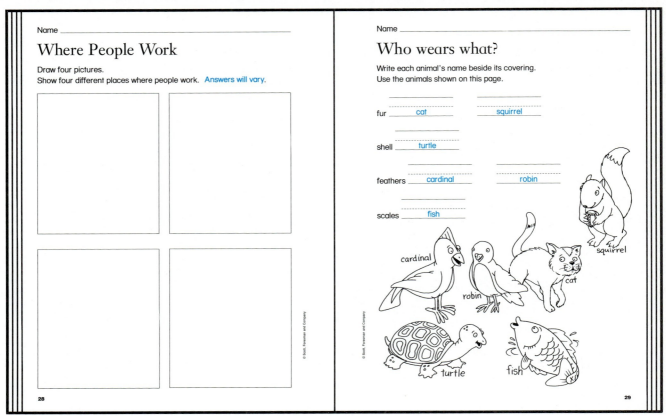

Name _____

Where People Work

Draw four pictures.
Show four different places where people work. Answers will vary.

© Scott, Foresman and Company

28

Name _____

Who wears what?

Write each animal's name beside its covering.
Use the animals shown on this page.

fur _____ cat _____   _____ squirrel _____

shell _____ turtle _____

feathers _____ cardinal _____   _____ robin _____

scales _____ fish _____

cardinal

robin

cat

squirrel

turtle

fish

29

Activity Book

Chapter 4

Animals at Work

Name _____

Draw a line under the action word in each sentence.
Write the action word on the lines.

1. Ants <u>carry</u> pieces of leaves.   _carry_

2. A bird <u>builds</u> a nest.   _builds_

3. A squirrel <u>gathers</u> nuts.   _gathers_

4. Beavers <u>cut</u> down small trees.   _cut_

5. Woodchucks <u>dig</u> tunnels.   _dig_

6. Woodchucks <u>push</u> dirt out with their back feet.   _push_

How Animals Protect Themselves

Name _____

Read the words in the box.
Write an animal name to complete each sentence.

| bird | chameleon | skunk | turtle |

1. A _chameleon_ changes color to protect itself.

2. A _skunk_ smells bad to protect itself.

3. A _bird_ flys away to protect itself.

4. A _turtle_ hides in its shell to protect itself.

Draw a picture of a turtle hiding in its shell.

Scared Rabbits

Name _____

Find the three rabbits that want to hide.
Color them so that they are hard to see.

Ask a Question

Name _____

Write the missing question mark [?] for each question.
Then answer the question.

How many rabbits are there _?_
There are _7_ rabbits.

How many ants are there _?_
There are _9_ ants.

How many turtles are there _?_
There are _5_ turtles.

Write a question about the fish. Then answer the question.
Begin the question with **How many** and end with a [?] .

_____

Contractions

Draw a line to match each contraction
with the words it stands for.

he's   I am

she's   he is

I'm   she is

Write a contraction to finish each sentence.

1. Miguel is my brother. When _____he's_____ hungry,
   he likes to eat fruit.

2. Maria is my sister. When _____she's_____ hungry,
   she likes to drink milk.

3. When _____I'm_____ hungry, I eat anything that's around!

Find the contraction in sentence 3 that stands for **that is** and circle it.

© Scott, Foresman and Company

36

Action Words

Circle the action word in each sentence.

1. A monkey eats food right off the tree.

2. A butterfly sips nectar from a flower.

3. A frog catches food with its tongue.

4. Ducks float on water.

Choose one of the action words you circled. Write it on the line.

_____

Answer will vary.

Draw a picture that shows what **your** word means.

© Scott, Foresman and Company

37

Playful Pets

Write words from the box to complete the poem.

be	me	string	things

I have a little puppy

_____

Who loves to play with _____me_____.

He's as fun to play with

_____

As a little pup can _____be_____.

I have a cat named Pumpkin

_____

Who plays with lots of _____things_____

Like balls, paper, ribbon, yarn,

_____

And she loves to play with _____string_____.

© Scott, Foresman and Company

38

How do some animals work?

Draw a line to match each animal with its work.

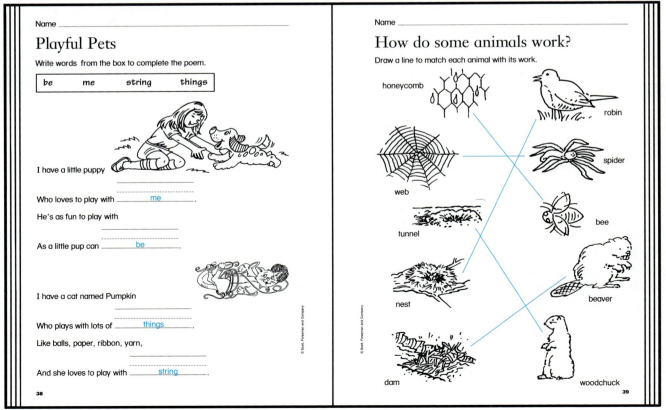

honeycomb

web

tunnel

nest

dam

robin

spider

bee

beaver

woodchuck

© Scott, Foresman and Company

39

Preview

Activate Prior Knowledge
Use Pictures

PICTURE CARDS

Start a discussion of "how people work" by showing pictures of the dentist, doctor, mail carrier, nurse, and police officer. Have children name them and describe the jobs these people do. Use Picture Cards 23, 24, 43, 47, 53.

Develop Language and Concepts
Present pages 40 and 41.

Invite children to look at each picture and help them name each kind of worker. Note places where the work is being done. As children talk, make a chart listing each worker and the job that he or she does. Use the T chart, Blackline Master 22 in the Teacher's Resource Book.

People	What they do to help
crossing guard	helps us cross street
nurse	helps make us well
firefighter	puts out fires
police officer	keeps us safe
teacher	teaches us

Ask children to name other community workers they have seen and add them to the list.

(Continued on page T41)

CHAPTER **3**

How People Work

40

Tell what you know.

Who are these people?

What do they do to help other people?

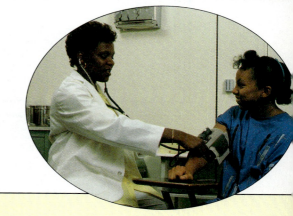

Options for Reaching All Students

Beginning
Language: Words and Pictures

Write the following words on chart paper and read them: *crossing guard, firefighter, police officer, teacher.* Have children fold a paper into four parts. Have children write the name of one worker at the bottom of each of the four sections before they illustrate it.

Advanced
Language: Give Information

Prepare a set of index cards, each marked with the name of a community worker. Ask a volunteer to choose a card from the pile. Help the child identify the worker. Then ask him or her to use the worker's title in a set of sentences, in a pattern like this:

I can help put out fires.
I am a firefighter.

Cooperative Language Experience
Social Studies: Interviews

Ask children which of the following workers they might like to have visit the class to answer questions about the work he or she does: a crossing guard, a nurse, a firefighter, a police officer, another teacher. Help children prepare questions in advance.

Then have children dictate a story containing the information that the visitor

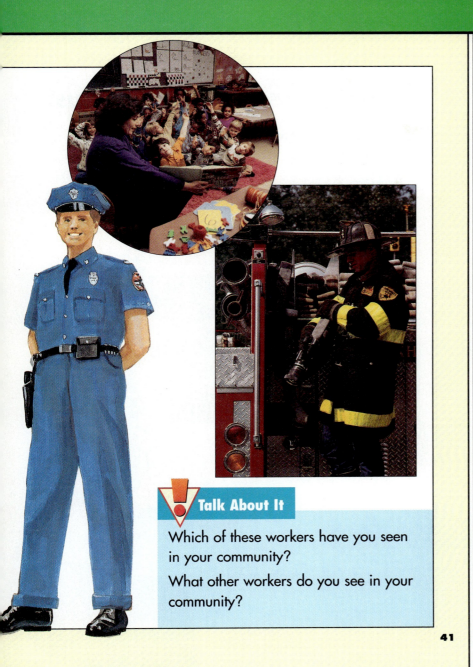

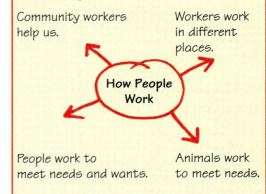

! Talk About It

Which of these workers have you seen in your community?

What other workers do you see in your community?

41

In this unit, children will learn the language connected with how and why people work. They will also discuss the needs of animals.

Use Pages 40 and 41 to assess children's knowledge of people's jobs in a community.

Community workers help us.

Workers work in different places.

How People Work

People work to meet needs and wants.

Animals work to meet needs.

Then have various children act out one kind of work listed on the chart. As they do their actions, encourage children to describe what they are doing in English and in their native language. Let others name the worker being shown. Save the chart for upcoming lessons.

ACTIVITY BOOK

For practice, children can use Activity Book page 22.

With the class, answer the questions in Talk About It. Then have children work in groups of three to share their personal responses.

provided. As you write the sentences children suggest, say the words. Then have children read their sentences aloud with you. Encourage pairs of children to reread the story during free time.

Mixed Ability
Video: Working

Show children the video to provide background information about the unit theme. You may also choose to use the video in other ways that are appropriate during the unit.

VIDEO

Present

Activate Prior Knowledge
Brainstorm Vocabulary

Show children the chart made in the previous lesson and brainstorm additional community workers to build children's knowledge. (Name one yourself to help get the process going.) Write children's additional suggestions on the chart.

Develop Language and Concepts
Present pages 42 and 43.

Have children look at the pages and identify the workers they know. Then help them read the labels for the pictures. Add to the chart any workers not previously named. Invite children to explain what the workers pictured are doing.

Read the sentences with children and have them tell what they know about each worker. Help children make connections between the pictured settings and similar places in your community.

Model a Strategy
Use Pictures for Meaning

Model using pictures for meaning:

When I read, I look at the pictures to help me figure out the meaning of words. When I see the pictures of the workers and the words, I try to match the word, or words, with pictures. This helps me understand what the words mean.

How do these workers help us?

Name these **workers**.
What do they do?

Some workers collect garbage.
Some workers deliver mail.

garbage collector ▲

mail carrier ▶

Options for Reaching All Students

Beginning
Language: Role Play

Invite children to role-play one of the jobs shown on the page and have other children guess which job is being demonstrated. The child who guesses correctly gets to demonstrate another job.

Advanced
Language: Writing Sentences

Have children replace the words *some workers* in each sentence with the name of the workers. For example:

Garbage collectors collect garbage.
Mail carriers deliver mail.

Write the sentences on the board. Then ask children to illustrate one of the sentences and write the appropriate sentence under the illustration.

Home Connection
Social Studies: Interview Parents

Invite children's parents to explain their jobs to the class. Suggest that they bring any gear they use or product they make to show children.

Encourage children to ask questions about the jobs being described.

Some workers help us find books in the library.
Some workers help us when we are hurt.
Some workers keep us safe.

▲ lifeguard

▲ librarian

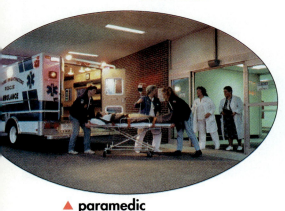
▲ paramedic

 Talk About It

Name some other jobs community workers do.

What community job would you like to do?

Grammar: Verbs

 ACTIVITY BOOK Read each sentence with children. Ask volunteers to act out each kind of work. As each action is demonstrated, write the verb for the action on chart paper.

Point to the action words on the chart at random and have volunteers act out the action. Then have children suggest other actions to demonstrate.

For practice with verbs, children can use Activity Book page 23.

Assess ✓

Use children's responses to Talk About It for assessment. Children should be able to

- name some other jobs community workers do
- tell what community job they would like to do

LOOK **AHEAD** ➤

Next, children will build upon the vocabulary they learned to talk about places where people work and the workers who work there.

Cooperative Language Experience
Painting

Help children plan a mural showing community workers doing their jobs. Discuss the jobs and have each child sketch two or three that interest him or her. Then group children according to their interests and provide each group with paint and brown paper.

Give children in each group time to plan their murals before they paint.

Ask them to decide such things as the kind of work they will show, where the workers will work, and what kinds of equipment they will need.

After you have put the pictures together to form a large mural, invite each group to plan and present a description of the workers they have drawn.

Little Celebrations
Busy People

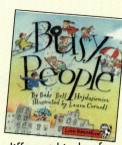

In rhyming couplets, children are introduced to different kinds of work that busy people do.

Level: Beginning

Practice

Activate Prior Knowledge
Review vocabulary

Ask children to look through pages 40–43 and point to the workers as you give clues, such as, *I deliver mail.* Tell children where each worker works. Explain that they will learn about other places where workers work.

Develop Language and Concepts
Present page 44.

Discuss the pictures on page 44 with children. Read aloud and talk about each label. Then help children read the words in the Word Bank. Describe each workplace. Let children practice matching the worker with the workplace in sentences, such as *Factory workers work in factories.*

Language Awareness

Vocabulary: Related Words

ACTIVITY BOOK

Write these word pairs on a chart: *factory worker/factory, office worker/ office, farmer/farm, bank teller/bank*

Point out that the place where a worker works is sometimes a part of a worker's title. Add words to the above list if they are suggested. For practice, use Activity Book page 24.

Where do other workers work?

Word Bank

bank

factory

farm

office

▲ factory workers   ▲ office worker

▲ bank teller   ▲ farmer

Options for Reaching All Students

Beginning
Language: Matching

Let children work in pairs. Have one partner point to a picture on page 44 and say the name of the worker. Ask the other partner to say the name of the place where the worker works. Then have the partners change tasks.

Advanced
Language: Vocabulary Development

Play a *Who Am I?* game with children. Give clues, such as the following:

I drive a bus. Who am I?
I drive a truck. Who am I?
I fix refrigerators. Who am I?

If children are able, let them take turns making up the riddles.

Mixed Ability
Critical Thinking: Classifying

Have children draw two pictures. The first should be of a worker who works in one place. Let children label the picture with the workplace. The second should be of a worker who goes from place to place. Let children label the picture with *goes from place to place.* Have children group their pictures into the two categories

Some people do not work in just one place. This worker goes from place to place to fix TVs.

▲ TV repair person

What other workers go from place to place?

What do you want to be when you grow up?

 Talk About It

Where do people in your family work?

SOCIAL STUDIES • **USE LANGUAGE** **45**

Develop Language and Concepts
Present page 45.

Together look at the picture at the top of the page and read the label for the TV repair person. Ask, *Where does the TV repair person work?* After children reply, help them read the explanation.

Help children read the rest of the page and discuss other workers who go from place to place.

Do the Talk About It activity with children. Point out any similarities in the places family members work with those pictured.

Model a Strategy
Using a Page Title to Predict

Model using a page title to predict:

When I read the title Where do other workers work? I know that these pages will give me information about workers and workplaces.

Assess ✔
Children should be able to

- name both workers who work in one place and name workers who go from place to place

LOOK**AHEAD**

Next, children will use the vocabulary about workers and workplaces to discuss why people work.

Cooperative Language Experience
Field Trip

Take children to a workplace they have studied, such as a bank, factory, or office. If possible, take a picture at each location.

When children return to the classroom, let them dictate a story about the trip. Children can refer to any photos taken to draw and caption pictures of what they saw.

Little Celebrations
Farm Day

In this story, children are introduced to some of the wonderful things children can do, hear, eat, and see on a farm.

FARM DAY
Written by Sarah Tatler
Illustrated by Laura Cornell

Level: Average

Practice

Activate Prior Knowledge

Use Pictures

PICTURE CARDS

Ask children to think about things we need in order to live. Display Picture Cards that show clothing, water glass, food, and housing to help them in their discussion. As children name each of these items, write them on chart paper. Use Picture Cards 17, 32, 34, 36, 37, 38, 59, 60.

Develop Language and Concepts

Present page 46.

Read page 46 with children. Let them point out the clothing, water, food, and housing.

Ask children to name some things they want, and have them compare these things with the things they need. Give several examples to show the difference.

Language Awareness

Vocabulary: Needs and Wants

ACTIVITY BOOK

Review the meanings of *need* and *want*. Give children two pieces of paper. Have them title one page *need* and the other page *want*. Let children draw and label something they need on the paper labeled *need* and something they want on the paper labeled *want*. Let children tell about their drawings. For more practice, children can use Activity Book page 25.

What are needs and wants?

Needs are the things you cannot live without. People need food, water, clothing, and a place to live.

Wants are things you would like to have. You might want a bike or a video game.

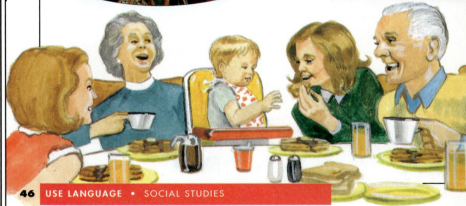

46 USE LANGUAGE • SOCIAL STUDIES

Options for Reaching All Students

Beginning

Language: Chant

TPR

Give each child a card and have him or her draw a picture of something to eat, water to drink, some clothing to wear, or a place to live. Present the following chant. When children hear the word that names what they have drawn on their card, they are to hold it up.

We need
Food, water, clothing,
A place to live.
We need
Food, water, clothing,
A place to live.

Advanced

Social Studies: Meeting Needs

Help children say sentences about where they get things they need.

I *get* food from a grocery store.
I *get* water from a faucet.
I *get* clothing from a clothing store.

Have pairs of children make picture books about where they get the things they need. Have them write sentences like the examples as captions.

How do people get things they need and want?

People earn money for the work they do.

They use the money to buy things they need and want.

They can save some money too.

Develop Language and Concepts
Present page 47.

Read the question at the top of the page with children. Let them discuss answers to the question, then read the rest of the page. Let children examine the illustration and name some things they might get if they saved money. Also at this time, you might want to present different coins and have children identify them.

Do the Think About It Activity with children.

Model a Strategy
Noticing Repeated Words

Model noticing repeated words:

I know that when I read, important words are used more than once. When I read page 47, I'll look to see if any of the words are on the page more than once. On this page, I see the word money several times, so I know that this page probably tells about money.

Assess
Children should be able to

• distinguish between needs and wants

• understand how people get things they need and want

LOOK AHEAD

In the next section, children will use the vocabulary they have developed to discuss the needs of animals.

Mixed Ability
Writing: Draw and Label Wishes

Let children fold a piece of art paper into fourths. In each part, have children draw and label something that they want.

Peer Tutoring
Critical Thinking: Planning a Strategy

Have children work in pairs of mixed abilities. Ask each child to tell a partner about how he or she might save money to get a desired item.

Home Connection
Favorite Foods

Have children ask family members to name their favorite foods and then draw a picture at home to share with the class in school.

Connect

Activate Prior Knowledge

Review Vocabulary

PICTURE CARDS

Tell children that they are going to learn about what animals need to live. Review what people need. List the needs on the chalkboard and read them together. Show examples using Picture Cards 32, 36, 37, 60.

Then point out the picture of the turtle on page 49. Explain that the turtle does not need one of these things to live. Invite children to tell what the turtle and other animals do not need.

Develop Language and Concepts

Present pages 48 and 49.

PICTURE CARDS

Help children read the question at the top of page 49. Then help them read the words in the Word Bank and match each animal name to its picture on page 48. Encourage children to describe what the animals are doing.

ACTIVITY BOOK

Show Picture Card 71, the turtle, and 30, the goldfish. Point out each animal's covering. Then read page 49 with children and help them discuss different animal coverings and why animals don't need clothing. The chart can be found on Activity Book page 26.

Do animals have the same needs as people?

Word Bank

- armadillo
- cardinal
- fish
- robins
- squirrel

People need food, water, and a place to live.

They need clothing too.

People have thin, smooth skin.

48   CONNECT LANGUAGE • SOCIAL STUDIES/SCIENCE

Options for Reaching All Students

Beginning

Critical Thinking: Categorizing

Divide a bulletin board into four parts. Label the parts *Feathers*, *Fur or Hair*, *Scales*, and *Shell* and provide samples or pictures of each. Help each child draw and label an animal that belongs in each category and place it on the bulletin board.

Advanced

Language: Researching

Invite children to go to the library to find more information about one of the animals listed in the Word Bank or the chart. Let children report on their findings.

Mixed Ability

Critical Thinking: Classifying

Provide groups of children with pictures of animals they have studied. Ask each group to discuss how those animals are alike. Then help them chart the information.

Animals	How they are alike
cardinal, robin squirrel, dog, cat	They are birds. They have fur.

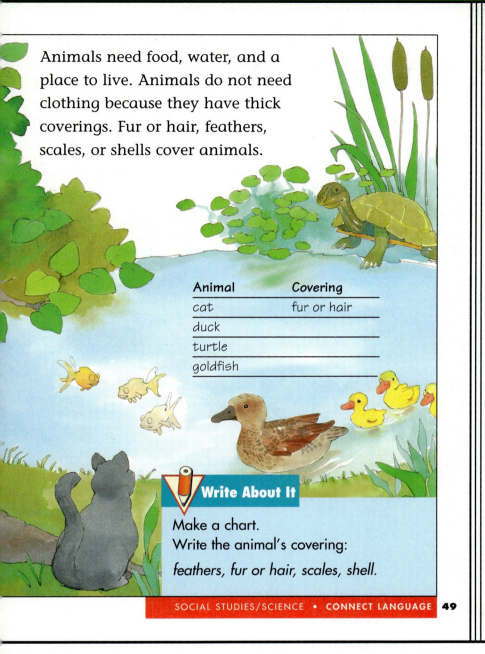

Animals need food, water, and a place to live. Animals do not need clothing because they have thick coverings. Fur or hair, feathers, scales, or shells cover animals.

Animal	Covering
cat	fur or hair
duck	
turtle	
goldfish	

Write About It

Make a chart.
Write the animal's covering:

feathers, fur or hair, scales, shell.

Connect

Activate Prior Knowledge
Share Personal Responses

Ask children to tell what they might like to do when they grow up. Encourage them to give reasons why.

Develop Language and Concepts
Present pages 50 and 51.

Read the title with children and let them discuss what the first story might be about. Then help children read the story. Let them paraphrase why the child wants to learn to speak English, and let them also discuss why they want to learn English.

Then read the title of the second selection with children. Discuss what this story might be about. After helping children read the selection, encourage them to talk about the work their parents do. Again, have them speculate about what work they might like to do.

ACTIVITY BOOK Let children practice writing a personal story using the outline presented on page 27 of the Activity Book.

What I Want to Do

by Cristina Ruiz, age 8

I want to learn English because I want to be a teacher. I like to help children. I like to help my grandmother. I like to help my baby brother.

My Family Works

by Xing Chen Mai, age 7

My name is Xing Chen Mai. I am seven years old. I came to America with my Mom in a big airplane. I come from China.

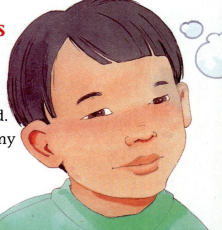

50 CONNECT LANGUAGE • SOCIAL STUDIES/LITERATURE

Options for Reaching All Students

Beginning
Language: Introductions

Let pairs practice the sentence patterns for the first two sentences in "My Family Works" by taking turns saying:

My name is _____.
I am _____ years old.

After children practice with a partner, come together as a group again. Point to individuals and ask each child to answer these questions: *Who are you?, How old are you?*

Advanced
Writing: Creating a Dream Job

Tell children to imagine that they could have any kind of job they want. What would they do? Have children draw a picture of themselves at their dream jobs. Have them label the job, then help them write some words to tell what they would do at this job and why they would like to have the job.

My dad works very hard. He is studying for his doctor's degree in engineering at Cleveland State University. My mom works, too. She works in a Chinese restaurant. She goes to school to learn English.

When I grow up, I want to be a policeman. I want to help people and protect the city.

I love America!

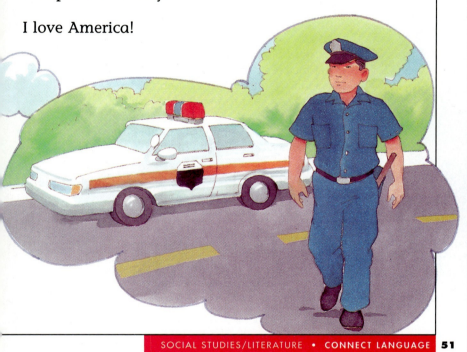

Model a Strategy
Use What You Know

Model using what you know:

When I read a title, such as "My Family Works," I already know something about this topic. I know about my family and the work my family does. When I read the paragraphs, I can compare what I know about the topics to what the author writes. If I use what I already know as I read, I will understand more. Do you think about what you already know as you read?

Assess

Children should be able to

- tell what they want to be when they grow up
- give some reasons why

LOOK AHEAD

In the next section, children will use vocabulary they have learned to discuss a work song.

Home Connection
Where My Family Used to Live

Invite children to talk to their parents about the countries their families come from. If possible, have children bring in photographs, objects, or foods connected with the country. You can also invite parents to talk to the class about the country.

Mixed Ability
Draw: When I Grow Up

Have children work in pairs of mixed abilities. Ask children to sit in a circle and take turns completing the sentence *When I grow up I will be a _____* .

Then distribute drawing paper and have children draw themselves in their grown up roles.

Writer's Workshop
Write About Yourself

Refer children to the Writer's Workshop on pages 230–236 of the Student Book. Have them write something they want to share about their family or about what they want to be when they grow up.

Agua, Agua, Agua

**An Aesop's Fable retold by Pat Mora
illustrated by José Ortega**

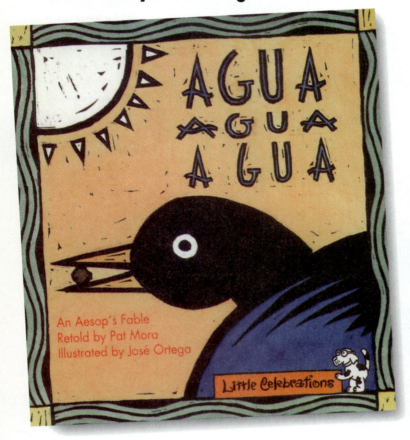

Agua, Agua, Agua
On a hot day in the desert, Crow devises a plan to get the water he needs.

Shared Reading

1. Introduce
Display the book and read the title. Elicit from volunteers what the title means. If no children know, explain that *agua* is the Spanish word for *water*. Ask children to name the animal on the cover. If they say *bird* or *black bird,* tell them this a specific kind of bird called a crow. Ask children to look at the cover, think about the title, and predict what will happen in the story.

2. Read
As you read aloud, invite children to interpret the pictures. Ask questions to help children see that the crow added pebbles to the water to make it rise so that he could drink it. Point out the use of repeated words and invite children to join in when they see: *no, no, no; agua, agua, agua; sí, sí, sí.*

3. Reread
Invite children to reread the book with you. Discuss the book by asking questions such as the following:

- How do you know Crow is thirsty?
- How does Crow get water? What other ways do you think Crow could get water?
- Name things people keep working hard at until they are finished?

Options for Reaching All Students

Beginning
Art/Language: Pictures

Let children use crayons to draw a picture of something they do on a hot, hot day. Help children write and tell about their pictures.

Advanced
Language: Word Meanings

Encourage children who are unfamiliar with the Spanish words used in the story to explain how they could figure out the meanings of the words *agua, una, dos, tres, no,* and *sí.* List the words on the board. Encourage children to add to the list translations of these words into other languages. Ask children to compare the words across languages.

Invite children to brainstorm a list of ways they could figure out the meaning of a word they don't know as they read. For example, rereading the sentence, reading sentences before or after the word, looking at pictures, and so on.

Grammar: Forming Questions with *be*

Model and write on the board a few questions. For example, *Where are your books? What country are you from? Is your teacher sitting at her desk?* Then have children find and read questions formed with *be* in the story (*Where is water hiding on this hot, hot day? Is it on the mountain?*). Ask volunteers to write them on the board. Ask children to work in pairs or small groups and create questions they'd want to ask Crow after reading the story. Invite volunteers to share their questions with the class.

Model a Strategy
Make Predictions

Model using questions in the text as a way of making predictions:

When I see a question in a story, I know that it is important to think about what the answer might be. First, I can ask myself if I know the answer. If I don't, I can make a guess. Sometimes the answer is on the page. Sometimes I can find the answer by looking at the picture. In the story, this question is asked three times: Can he drink the water? Each time I read the question, I predict whether the answer is yes or no. Predicting answers to questions will help me know what is happening in the story. Can you see a way to make predictions as you read?

Response Activities

Answer Questions

Read through the story, pause after each question and invite children to answer. After reading the story, do a question and response exercise in which children respond to a question with *No, there isn't* or *Yes, there is.* For example, ask, *Is there water in the clothes closet? Is there water in the water fountain?* Then encourage volunteers to ask questions of their own.

Explain an Outcome

Invite children to explain in their own words how Crow uses the pebbles to get water. Make sure that children understand that adding pebbles raises the water level.

Put on a Show

Invite children to work in groups and write a story about a person or animal who tries very hard to get something done. Have children decide who will pantomime the actions and who will read aloud the story to the class.

FYI Aesop
Aesop told fables using animals to represent humans. Each fable had a wise lesson for its listeners. There are many versions and translations of these fables as they have been passed down through the years and from country to country.

Mixed Ability
Language: Play "I Am Thirsty"

TPR

Draw a picture of a water fountain on a card and label it. Have a volunteer place the card somewhere in the classroom. Then have children play a directions game using TPR. First model the game with a volunteer. The volunteer can start by saying *I am thirsty. Where can I find water?* You can answer by giving commands, such as *Go to the pencil sharpener. Turn left and walk three steps. Take a drink of water.* The first child should follow the directions to the "fountain" and pretend to get a drink. Continue with other players. As children become familiar with the game, you can make the game more challenging by having children give directions and go to places outside the classroom such as the washrooms, the library, and the cafeteria.

Home Connection
Fables

Invite children to tell family members the fable. Have them discuss what lesson they think Aesop was trying to teach. Ask children to find out what expressions they have in their first language for the moral. Encourage children to ask family members about similar fables from their homeland. Have children share their findings in class.

Connect

Activate Prior Knowledge
Use Illustrations

Have children describe what is happening in the illustration. Ask them if they have ever sung a song as they worked. If so, ask them to sing the song.

Develop Language and Concepts
Present page 52.

ORANGE TAPE

Read the song aloud and clarify any troublesome vocabulary. Then play Side 2 of the Orange Tape several times and encourage children to join in singing the song. Introduce the word *hobby*, and lead children in discussing the fact that all work is not done to make a living.

ACTIVITY BOOK

Use Activity Book page 28 for children to express more ideas about work.

Language Awareness

Phonics: Rhyme

Have children sing the song once again. Point out that the words *grow* and *hoe* rhyme. Explain that they begin with different sounds but they both end with the long *o* sound. Ask children to suggest other words that rhyme, such as *know* and *low*. You may want to point out the different spelling patterns for long *o*.

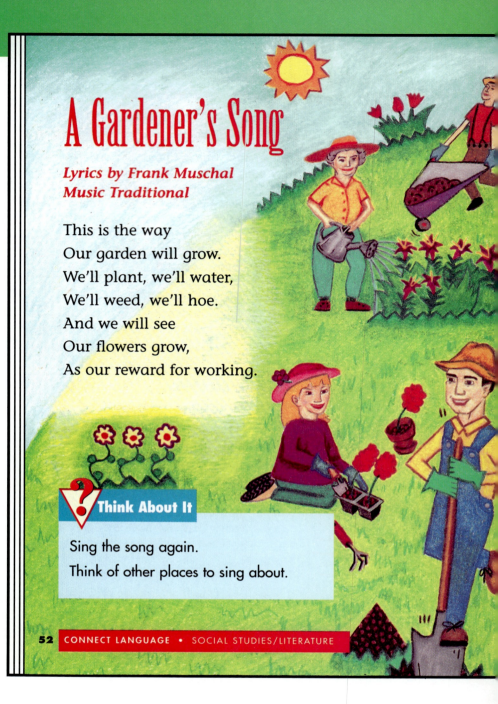

A Gardener's Song

Lyrics by Frank Muschal
Music Traditional

This is the way
Our garden will grow.
We'll plant, we'll water,
We'll weed, we'll hoe.
And we will see
Our flowers grow,
As our reward for working.

? Think About It

Sing the song again.
Think of other places to sing about.

52 CONNECT LANGUAGE • SOCIAL STUDIES/LITERATURE

Options for Reaching All Students

Beginning
Language: Memory Game

Have children orally compose a cumulative sentence by naming places where they can sing, with each child repeating the list and adding an item.

Child A: I sing at school.
Child B: I sing at school and on the bus.

Advanced
Writing: Booklets

Assign children to small groups. Prepare blank books for children to use to create booklets about different kinds of work. Title the booklets "Working" and have children make illustrations and write captions for each of the pages showing people working for a living and working for fun.

Multicultural Awareness
Work Songs

Have children ask family members about work songs from their native country. Encourage children to learn a song and sing it for the class.

Tell what you learned.

1. Make a list of community workers. Put a check next to the ones you have seen.

> Workers
> ✓ police officer
>   garbage collector
>   street cleaner

2. Work with a partner. Take turns naming an animal and saying if it is covered with fur or hair, feathers, scales, or a shell.

3. Draw a picture. Show one of the workers that Xing Chen Mai or Cristina Ruiz wrote about.

ASSESS LANGUAGE **53**

Assess

Activity 1: Have children write their answers on a separate paper. Evaluate on number and accuracy of responses.

Activity 2: Evaluate whether children can name animals and name their coverings.

Activity 3: Check that children draw one of the workers that Xing Chen Mai or Cristina Ruiz wrote about.

Have children complete the Chapter Self Assessment, BLM 33. Have them choose products to place in their portfolios. Add the results of any rubrics, checklists, self-assessments, or portfolio assessments, BLMs 2–18.

Listening Assessment

BLACKLINE MASTER
Make sure that each child has a copy of Blackline Master 51 and crayons or markers for drawing. Play the tape several times stopping the tape to allow children to answer.

TAPESCRIPT

WHITE TAPE
Listen carefully. Follow the directions.

Mr. Turner is a farmer. Mr. Turner grows something that we all need to live. Mr. Turner grows food. Draw a type of food that Mr. Turner can grow in the field. (pause) Under the picture, label the place where Mr. Turner works.

Options for Assessment

Vocabulary Assessment

ACTIVITY BOOK
Have children look at Activity Book page 29 and name the animals. Then give these directions:

Name two animals with feathers.
Name an animal with scales.
Name two animals with hair or fur.
Name an animal with a shell.

Writing Assessment

Have children make personal picture books in which they illustrate workers they have learned about and the places in which they work. Have children label the workers and their workplaces.

Language Assessment

BLACKLINE MASTER
Use Blackline Master 50 in the Teacher's Resource Book.

Standardized Test Practice

ACTIVITY BOOK
Use pages 30 and 31 in the Activity Book. Answers: 4, $5.00 + $5.00 = $10.00, 2.

Preview

Activate Prior Knowledge
Use Pictures

PICTURE CARDS

Begin a discussion of "what animals do." Show children pictures of animals from different environments doing actions such as swimming, flying, and eating. Ask children to say as much as they can about the pictures. Remind them that what they already know is important. For example, did they see the animal in their native country, in the United States, or in both places? What other animals can they talk about?

Develop Language and Concepts
Present pages 54 and 55.

Show children Picture Card 66 of the spider. Name the animal for children. Ask children to tell if and where they have seen a spider. Explain that the spider in the picture is at work building a web and will use that web to catch insects for food.

Ask if anyone has seen a squirrel gathering nuts or a bird building a nest.

Help children answer the questions in Tell What You Know.

(Continued on page T55)

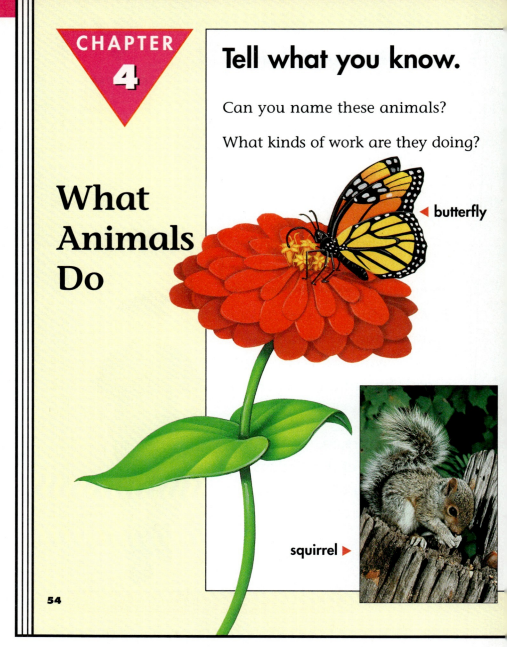

CHAPTER 4

What Animals Do

Tell what you know.

Can you name these animals?

What kinds of work are they doing?

◀ butterfly

squirrel ▶

54

Options for Reaching All Students

Beginning
Language: Words and Pictures

Have children work in pairs. Ask partners to draw an animal working. Encourage children to label both the animals and the objects in the pictures and to share their pictures with the group. Suggest children refer to pages 54 and 55 for ideas.

Advanced
Language: Picture Talk

Have children think of another animal they know and what work it does. Suggest children think of an animal busy at work making a home for itself. Have children draw a picture of the animal at work, label the picture, and tell others about the picture.

Mixed Ability
Language Arts: Role-Playing

Invite volunteers to pantomime the actions of an animal from these pages. Let other children form two teams and guess which animal is being portrayed. When a team gives the name of the animal, encourage team members to tell about the work the animal does.

spider ▼

▼ ants

bird ▲

In this unit, children will learn the language connected with how animals work to get food and shelter and how they protect themselves.

Use pages 54 and 55 to assess children's knowledge of how animals work.

Animals get the food they need.

Some animals build homes.

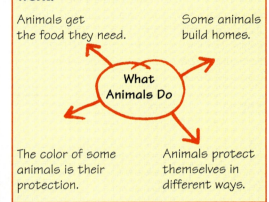

What Animals Do

The color of some animals is their protection.

Animals protect themselves in different ways.

Invite children to look at each picture and help them describe what it shows. Present the following key words and phrases: *bird, building a nest, squirrel, gathering food, butterfly, getting food, ants, carrying bits of leaves, spider, building a web.*

Explain that just as people work to get the things they need to live, animals do the same. Tell children that they will learn more about the ways in which animals get the food and shelter they need. They will also learn how animals protect themselves.

Together answer the Talk About It questions.

! Talk About It

Which animals are getting food?

Which animals are making a home?

55

Cooperative Learning
Art: Clay Sculptures

Have children work in groups. Give each group some modeling clay. Have group members choose an animal to make and an object associated with the animal's work. Have them decide who will work on each task. When they are finished, encourage them to talk about what they did. Have one child take notes on the discussion including the names of the group members and the tasks they did. Provide materials such as string and blunt scissors for the group doing the spider and spider web.

Multicultural Connection
Ask children to think about animals from their native countries. Have children interview each other to find out how these animals get food and make a home.

Present

Activate Prior Knowledge
Review Vocabulary

Review the word *needs*. Elicit from children what some animal needs are. Then review the animals children have discussed. Talk about how each animal takes care of its needs. List the information in a T-Chart, Blackline Master 22 in the Teacher's Resource Book.

Animal	Work
bird	builds a nest
squirrel	gathers nuts
butterfly	gets food from a flower
ant	carries pieces of a leaf
spider	builds a web

Explain that the leaf-cutter ants carry pieces of leaves to their nests.

Develop Language and Concepts
Present pages 56 and 57.

Together read the question at the top of page 56. Elicit possible answers. Then read the introductory paragraph. Help children name each animal group and describe what the animals are doing.

Then read each paragraph together. After using the animal name to refer to a group of animals, use the pronoun *they* and make sure children understand to which animals the word refers.

How do some animals work?

Animals work in different ways. They work to meet their **needs.**

Bees make honeycombs. Then they make honey. They store the honey in their honeycombs.

Beavers cut down small trees. They use some of the wood to build a dam. They use some of the wood to build a home.

▲ honeycomb, honey

▲ dam

Options for Reaching All Students

Beginning
Science: Honeycombs

Bring in a honeycomb containing honey. These can usually be purchased in supermarkets or specialty food shops.

After discussing the honeycomb with children, let each of them try some honey on a small piece of bread and describe the flavor.

Advanced
Social Studies: Groundhog Day

Tell children that another name for *woodchuck* is *groundhog*. Provide sources from the school or classroom library for children to use to find information about Groundhog Day. Have children present the information they learned to their classmates.

Peer Tutoring
Critical Thinking: Summary

Assign partners. Give partners three pieces of paper and crayons. Have them work together to draw bees and a honeycomb on one piece of paper, beavers and a dam on another piece of paper, and woodchucks in underground tunnels on the third piece.

Have children take turns showing the paper, naming the animal, and telling all they know about that animal.

Woodchucks dig tunnels under the ground. They use their front feet to dig the dirt. They use their back feet to push the dirt out. They live inside the tunnels they build.

tunnel

Try It Out

Work with a group. Take turns acting out an animal working. Have others in your group guess the animal.

SCIENCE • LEARN LANGUAGE **57**

Language Awareness

Grammar: Subject/Verb Agreement

ACTIVITY BOOK

Write these action words on the board and read them aloud: *cut, build, dig, push.*

Ask how the words are alike. Children should report that they all show an action. Write sentences such as: *A beaver ____ a dam. Woodchucks ____ tunnels.*
Have children write the sentences with the correct form of the verb. For practice, children can use Activity Book page 32.

Model a Strategy
Recognize the Main Idea

Model recognizing the main idea:

When I read, the first sentence in the paragraph often tells what the paragraph is about—the main idea. For example, when I read Woodchucks dig tunnels under the ground, I know that the rest of the paragraph will tell more about the main idea.

Assess
Children should be able to

• describe how animals meet their needs

LOOK**AHEAD**

Next, children will discuss methods of protection used by several animals.

Cooperative Language Experience

Science: Beekeeping

Invite a beekeeper to visit the classroom wearing the protective clothing used when working with bees. Ask the beekeeper to tell about beekeeping and the kinds of work bees do in hives. After the visit write a language experience story with the class.

Home Connection

Ask children to pantomime an animal at work for family members and see if they can guess what the animal is and what the animal is doing. Then have family members take turns pantomiming other animals at work. In class, ask children to show and talk about what their family members did.

Little Celebrations

Big Pig, Little Pig

Children will enjoy hearing and reciting aloud this rhyming chant about a big and little pig, sheep, and horse.

Level: Beginning

Practice

Activate Prior Knowledge
Use Pictures

Have children look at the Picture Cards for the cat 14, bird 6, and turtle 71. Ask, *What can a cat do if it is scared?* When children answer *run*, say, *Yes. A cat can protect itself by running away.* Use the same model to talk about the bird and the turtle, eliciting the words *fly* and *hide*.

Develop Language and Concepts
Present pages 58 and 59.

Have children look at the pictures on both pages and identify the animals. Talk about what is happening. Read the pages with children. Focus on the corresponding illustration as you read about each animal. Explore the connection between the sentences and the illustrations. Spark discussion by asking questions such as these:

- Why do animals need to protect themselves?
- How does a bad smell protect a skunk?

Together do Talk About It.

Have children work with partners to complete Activity Book page 33.

Review the words in the Word Bank. Ask children to name an animal that uses its claws, uses its teeth, can fly, or can jump away to protect itself.

What do animals do to protect themselves?

Animals need to **protect** themselves from other animals.

A skunk can protect itself from another animal. It sprays the animal with a bad smell.

A turtle can protect itself from another animal. It hides inside its shell.

58 USE LANGUAGE • SCIENCE

Options for Reaching All Students

Beginning
Language: Speaking

Ask children to draw a picture of their favorite animal from these pages. Have them label their animal. Then invite volunteers to tell about their animal. For example:

This is a turtle. It can hide in its shell to protect itself.

Advanced
Critical Thinking: Classifying

Help children make and fill in a chart similar to the one below. Invite children to compare their charts and add additional animals.

Animals	Protects Itself By
lion, crocodile skunk	sharp teeth bad smell hiding running away changing color

Mixed Ability
Music: Singing

TPR Give children cards with the word *runs*. Have them raise their cards each time they hear the word as you sing the song below. Then have them raise their cards as they join in singing these words to the tune of "Old MacDonald Had a Farm."

A rabbit can protect itself, E-I-E-I-O.

A rabbit can protect itself from another animal. It runs very fast.

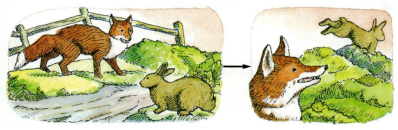

A chameleon can protect itself from another animal. It changes its color.

Can you see the chameleon on the tree?

Talk About It

What animal do you like?

How does it protect itself from other animals?

Model a Strategy

Recognizing Sentence Patterns

Model using sentence patterns:

When I read, I sometimes see sentence patterns that repeat. For example, I read A skunk can protect itself from another animal. Then in the next paragraph A turtle can protect itself from another animal. These repeating sentence patterns make the story easier to understand because I know that each paragraph tells about how one animal protects itself from other animals.

Assess ✔

Use responses to Talk About It for assessment. Children should be able to

- tell how an animal protects itself
- explain why animals need to protect themselves from other animals

LOOK AHEAD

Next, children will use new vocabulary to learn about protective coloration.

It runs away very fast,
E-I-E-I-O.
It runs through here,
It runs through there,
It runs, runs,
Runs, runs, everywhere.
A rabbit can protect itself,
E-I-E-I-O.

Encourage children to make up songs and cards for the other animals they have studied.

Peer Tutoring
Critical Thinking: Summarizing

Have children work in pairs of mixed abilities. Ask one partner to say the name of an animal or draw a picture of an animal discussed on the page, and ask his or her partner to name it and tell how it protects itself. Encourage them to predict what would happen if the animal couldn't protect itself. Then have children reverse roles.

Writer's Workshop

Refer children to the Writer's Workshop on pages 230–236 of the Student Book. Ask children to choose an animal they learned about and use it as the main character in a story. Suggest they begin their story with _One day . . ._

Practice

Activate Prior Knowledge

Use Pictures

Show children the picture of the bear. Ask them why they think this bear might be hard to spot in the wild. Children should respond that the brown bear might be hard to see because its color resembles the ground where it is standing. Explain that the bear is protected from other animals and from hunters by its color. Then show the picture of the kangaroo and discuss how its color helps protect it by making it hard to see. Use Picture Cards 5, 39.

Develop Language and Concepts

Present pages 60 and 61.

Read the activity with children. Children can perform the activity individually or in groups. Have them retell the steps that they need to do to complete the activity. Have children copy the record on page 61 to record the results of the experiment.

Do the Think About It activity with children and help them name other animals with protective coloration.

Color can make things hard to see.

Things You Need

white paper   brown paper   scissors

Follow these steps.

1. Use two small pieces of white paper. Draw and cut out two rabbits.

Options for Reaching All Students

Beginning

Science: Camouflage

Present children with pictures of animals, some being camouflaged in their habitat and some quite visible because of contrasting background colors. Have children decide which animals are hard to see in their habitats because of their color. Use Picture Cards 5, 6, 14, 15, 19, 20, 22, 26, 31.

Advanced

Language: Using Camouflage

Provide children with scenes of different animals in their habitats. Have children work in pairs. Ask partners to find the different animals in the scene. After children find, and if they can name, the animals, have them tell which animals appear to be best camouflaged in each habitat. Children might list the animal's name, its color, and its habitat.

Mixed Ability

Science: Camouflage

Encourage children to visit the library to find books about animals that use camouflage. Assign children to groups of mixed abilities. Give each group paper and crayons to create a mural of animals that use camouflage by blending with their surroundings. Have children work in pairs so that one child gives directions for drawing while the other child draws.

2. Use two small pieces of brown paper. Draw and cut out two rabbits.

3. Put a white rabbit and a brown rabbit on a large piece of brown paper.

4. Put a white rabbit and a brown rabbit on a large piece of white paper.

5. Keep a record. What did you see?

My Record

1. It was harder to see the white rabbit _____.

2. It was harder to see the brown rabbit _____.

Think About It

Name other animals whose colors make them hard to see.

Language Functions: Giving Directions

ACTIVITY BOOK

Have children find the action word in each sentence in the instructions. Tell children that sentences that begin with a verb are often used in directions. Model a sentence such as *Draw three ants.* Encourage volunteers to give other examples. Have children complete Activity Book page 34 independently.

Model a Strategy
Follow Directions

Model following directions:

On this page, there are directions for me to follow. I know I must follow the directions carefully and in order. The first thing I will do is read through the directions. Then I will begin with step 1, and follow the numbers.

Assess

Children should be able to

• follow directions in a given order
• tell what they learned from the activity

LOOK **AHEAD**

In the next section, children will solve story problems involving animals.

Cooperative Learning
Language: Speaking

Have children form groups of four or five. Ask them to imagine they could be anywhere they want to be, but they must wear clothing that makes them invisible. Have children draw a group picture showing where they would want to go and what they would wear. Have volunteers from each group tell the class about the picture.

QuickCheck

Check whether children can recognize and name the colors *brown* and *white* on the page. For children who need practice with naming these colors, use Picture Cards 5, 19, 22. Help children name the animal and its color(s). Review other color names as well.

Home Connection

Ask children to draw with a family member. Have them make a scene with animals that are hard to see because of their color and some animals that are easy to see. Invite volunteers to tell about their pictures.

Connect

Activate Prior Knowledge
Use Pictures

PICTURE CARDS

Show children the picture of pizza, counting the number of slices. Ask, *If two slices were eaten, how many slices would be left?* Continue, showing pictures of lemons and olives and ask children to count them. Then ask a question that requires subtraction. Use Picture Cards 52, 42, 48.

Develop Language and Concepts
Present pages 62 and 63.

Help children read each story problem. Refer them to the illustrations as they study each problem. When children give answers, ask them to explain how they figured them out. Let children work with counters.

Together, do Write About It.

Model a Strategy
Understand Specialized Language

Model understanding specialized language:

When I read a math problem, I may see a sentence that begins how many and ends with a question mark. That question tells me what I should find out. I always read math problems carefully before I try to solve them. I find the numbers in the problem and then I read the problem over to decide whether to add or subtract.

How many are there now?

There were seven birds in the grass. Three flew away. How many are in the grass now?

There were nine fish in the tank. Six fish were sold. How many are in the tank now?

62 CONNECT LANGUAGE • SCIENCE/MATH

Options for Reaching All Students

Beginning
Math: Writing Number Sentences

Let children work in pairs to write a number sentence for each story problem. Ask children to use counters to show the addition or subtraction. For example, for the first problem they would show 7 counters, take away 3 counters, and be left with 4 counters. Children would then write *7–3 = 4.*

Advanced
Math: Creating Subtraction Problems

Have children play a telephone game. Give each child in the group a card to wear with a numeral from 1 to 8. Have children stand in a circle around the Caller, who pretends to have a telephone. The Caller says, *Hello, I'm calling 9 minus 7.* The child wearing numeral 2 should then answer, *Hello, this is Ms. 2.*

Home Connection

Ask children to make up a word problem for a family member and solve it together using any small objects as counters.

There were five bees on a leaf. One flew away. How many are on the leaf now?

There were three armadillos by the road. One ran away. How many are by the road now?

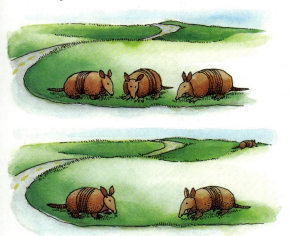

Write About It

Make up a problem about animals. End your problem with this question. How many are there now?

Language Awareness

Spelling: Punctuation

ACTIVITY BOOK Tell children that sentences that tell something end with periods. Help children locate and read aloud the two telling sentences in the first word problem.

Then read aloud the last sentence in the word problem. Ask children to name the punctuation mark at the end of the sentence. Explain that a question mark was used because the sentence asks something. Model the intonation used to ask a question. For practice, children can use Activity Book page 35.

Assess ✔

Children should be able to

• make up a story problem of their own

LOOK **AHEAD** ➡

In the next section, children will use what they have learned about animals to read a story about how they eat.

Peer Tutoring
Math: Using Counters to Subtract

Assign partners of mixed abilities. Give partners a handful of counters and ask each partner to count them. Then have one partner say a subtraction problem while the other partner uses the counters to represent numbers and demonstrates the word problem. For example:

There were 9 rabbits in the park. 3 rabbits ran away. How many rabbits were left?

Little Celebrations
Mrs. Sato's Hens

This is a counting story about Mrs. Sato's hens and her white, brown, and speckled eggs.

Level: Beginning

Connect

Activate Prior Knowledge

Talk about Food Sources

Show children a carton of milk and some fruit, such as a banana and an apple. Have children name each food, then tell where it comes from. Children should know that milk comes from cows and fruit grows on trees.

Introduce the Selection

Help children find and read the title of the story and the author's name.

Read the Selection

ORANGE TAPE

Read the story with children several times. Provide opportunities for children to listen to the story on Side 1 of the Orange Tape as often as they like. Use the suggested activities appropriate to meet children's needs.

Model a Strategy

Activate Prior Knowledge

Model activating prior knowledge while reading.

When I read through this story and see the boy doing things like eating food right off the tree and storing food in his cheeks, I remember that bananas really do come from trees and squirrels really do store food in their cheeks. This helps me understand the story and to enjoy it more.

Teachable Moment

Story Elements: Plot

Discuss the plot of the story with children by asking them what happens in the story. Children should tell you that a boy wishes he could get and eat food like the animals do, although he's also happy to share a meal with his family. Encourage children to share the plots of other stories they have read or TV programs or movies they have seen.

Options for Reaching All Students

Beginning

Language: Speaking

Have children draw a picture of a way they might like to get food as shown in the story. Encourage children to talk about their pictures.

Advanced

Science: Animal Behavior

Let children pick one animal from the story and do research to find out more about the animal's diet and behavior.

Peer Tutoring

Critical Thinking: Summarizing

Let children work in pairs of mixed abilities. Have one child go through the story and name all the animals, while the other child names the food the animal is eating.

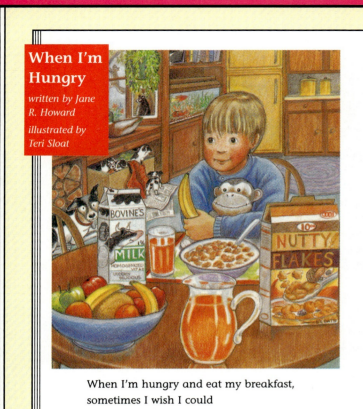

When I'm Hungry

written by Jane R. Howard

illustrated by Teri Sloat

When I'm hungry and eat my breakfast, sometimes I wish I could

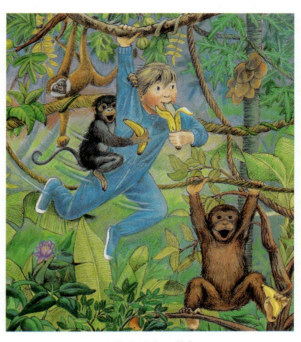

eat my fruit right off the tree

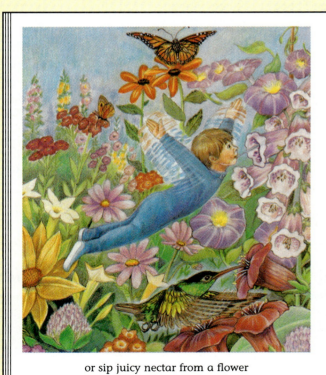

or sip juicy nectar from a flower

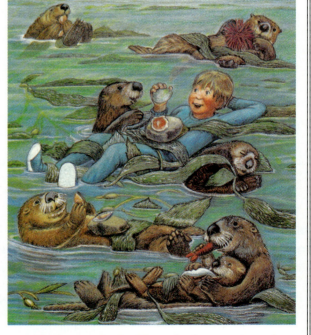

or float on my back with my food on my stomach

Connect

Develop Language and Concepts

Have children look at the pages where the boy is eating underwater. Ask children to name the other animals that are getting food this way. Children should name the fish. Encourage children to discuss places they would go to swim if they were the boy.

Model a Strategy

Use Pictures to Get Meaning

Model using pictures to figure out the meaning of words.

When I read page 70, I see what the boy means when he says, I wonder how it would feel to lap with my tongue. Looking at the picture gives me a lot more information about what the boy is talking about than just reading the words. Have you ever used pictures for help with the meaning of words?

Grammar: Verbs

Point out to children that the boy must do many different actions to get the different kinds of food. As children reread the story, have them name the words that tell an action that the boy is doing. As children name the words, make a list: *eat, wish, sip, float, store, wonder, use, think, dive, dig, get*. Encourage various children to act out one of these words and to have others name the word that is being pantomimed.

 Use page 37 in the Activity Book.

Teachable Moment

Story Elements: Theme

Tell children that the theme of a story tells an important message that the author wants to give the reader. Explain that the theme of *When I'm Hungry* is that different animals eat different foods in different ways. Invite children to give some examples from the story.

Options for Reaching All Students

Beginning

Language: Choral Reading

Have children do a choral reading of the story. Have them read the story as you leaf through it and show them the pictures so that they can read the correct pages.

Advanced

Language: Personal Word Bank

Have children choose five words from the story to put into their personal word bank. They should write each word on the front of an index card and illustrate it or write a context sentence for it on the back of the card. Have children work in pairs to share their cards.

Peer Tutoring

Critical Thinking: Story Retelling

Have children work in pairs of mixed abilities to retell the story up to this point.

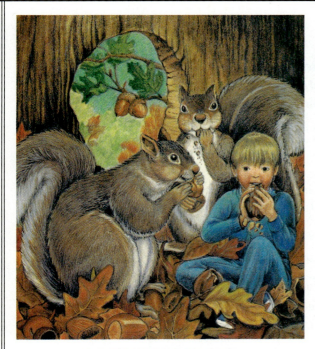

or maybe store it in my cheeks

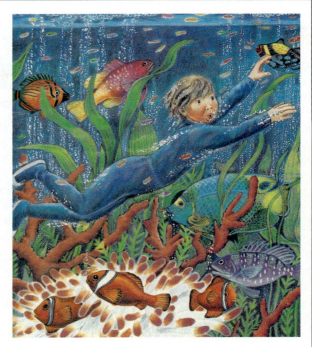

or eat it underwater.

When I'm hungry for my morning snack, I wonder
how it would feel to lap with my tongue or use it to
catch my food.

When I'm hungry, I sometimes think
I'd like to eat my lunch in the mud

Connect

Develop Language and Concepts

Direct children's attention to pages 73. Let them pantomime diving for food and digging for wiggly worms. Also let children identify the animals on these pages. Encourage them to discuss whether they would enjoy having to dive for food or dig for worms.

Model a Strategy

Summarize

Model summarizing a story.

After I finish a story, I ask myself what the story is about. For example, the story When I'm Hungry is about a boy who wishes he could eat the foods that other animals eat in the ways that the animals eat them. Then he realizes that he's happy to eat with his own family. When I can retell the story in this way, using just a few sentences, I know that I understand what the story is about.

Language Awareness

Language Functions: Describing

Point out to children that throughout the story, the boy is describing what he wishes he could do. Have children leaf through the pages and notice that the words and pictures describe in detail what the boy would like to do.

Teachable Moment

Evaluating Information: Distinguish Fact from Nonfact

BLACKLINE MASTER

Invite children to revisit the story to list the facts in the story and to point out the things that couldn't really happen. Make a T-chart to record their findings. Use the T-chart on Blackline Master 22 in the Teacher's Resource Book. Your chart may begin similar to this:

FACT	NONFACT
Monkeys really live in jungles and eat bananas.	Most boys can't pick their bananas in the jungle with the monkeys.

Response to Reading

Personal Response: Ask children, *Did you like this book? What did you like about it most? What did you like least?*

Critical Response: Let children form small groups. Ask each group to name three animals from the story and the food they eat.

Creative Response: Have children draw a picture of a cat or dog they know dressed and sitting at the table eating human food. Have children explain exactly what kind of human food the animal is eating.

Options for Reaching All Students

Beginning

Language: Reading

ORANGE TAPE

Encourage children to read the story while listening to it on the Orange Tape, Side 1. Then invite children to read aloud parts of the story that they feel comfortable with on their own.

Advanced

Language: Speaking and Writing

Remind children that the boy in the story wished that he could eat with the animals. Have children brainstorm wishes that they have. After discussion, have each child draw a picture of his or her wish. Help children write a sentence about the wish at the bottom of the page. Bind the pages together to make *Our Wish Book.*

Cooperative Learning

Critical Thinking: Imagining

If children could be any animal in the story for a day, which one would they be? Encourage children to exchange ideas and to explain their choices. Then let children who want to be the same animal form groups and plan to pantomime that animal for the others.

or with my mouth wide open.

When I'm hungry in the afternoon, I'm glad I don't have to dive for my food or dig for wiggly worms or get my honey from a tree.

And I'm glad I don't have to eat eucalyptus leaves or bamboo shoots.

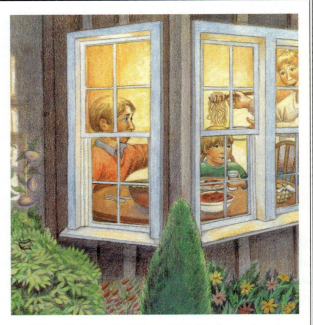

When I'm hungry at dinnertime, I'm happy to eat from my very own plate and drink from my very own glass, right in the middle of my very own family.

Connect

Activate Prior Knowledge

Review Vocabulary

PICTURE CARDS

Show children Picture Card 71 of the turtle and have them name the animal. Then ask questions such as: *Where do turtles live? How do they protect themselves?*

Develop Language and Concepts

Present page 76.

ORANGE TAPE

Play Side 2 of the Orange tape several times and encourage children to join in saying the poem.

Language Awareness

Phonics: Rhyming Words

After children have said the rhyme several times, ask them to name the rhyming words that come at the end of each even-numbered line in the poem. List them on a chart. Point out that *box* and *rocks* end with the same sound. Write the words on the chalkboard. Underline the *x* in *box* and the *-cks* in *rocks*. Explain that *x* and *-cks* both spell the sound they hear at the end of *box* and *rocks*.

ACTIVITY BOOK

For practice with rhymes, children can use Activity Book page 38.

There Was a Little Turtle
by Vachel Lindsay

There was a little turtle.
He lived in a box.
He swam in a puddle.
He climbed on the rocks.

He snapped at a mosquito.
He snapped at a flea.
He snapped at a minnow.
And he snapped at me.

He caught the mosquito.
He caught the flea.
He caught the minnow.
But he didn't catch me!

▽ Try It Out

Use hand motions to act out the poem. Show the little turtle, the box, and what the turtle did.

76 CONNECT LANGUAGE • *SCIENCE/LITERATURE*

Options for Reaching All Students

Beginning
Art: Box Sculpture

Invite children to work in small groups and use a box to make a turtle sculpture. A box can represent the turtle's shell. Children can paint the shell or cover it with construction paper. Provide construction paper and/or pipe cleaners for the head, legs, and tail. Help children cut holes and attach the appendages.

Advanced
Writing: Writing Rhymes

Invite children to complete a two-line rhyme about an animal. Write several choices on the chalkboard for children to copy and complete with an animal name. Do the first one together.

If you see a baby _____,
Whisper but don't go too near.
The _____ crawls all around,
It walks along the muddy ground.

T76

Tell what you learned.

1. Make a chart. Work together.
   Write the name of an animal.
   Write what it does.

Animal	Work
bird	builds nests

2. How do animals protect themselves?

3. Work together. Draw a picture to show where an animal in the story gets its food. Tell other classmates about your picture.

Assess ✓

Activity 1: Have children make their chart on a separate piece of paper. Evaluate on number and accuracy of responses.

Activity 2: Evaluate whether children understand that animals protect themselves in various ways.

Activity 3: Check that children draw an animal along with the place where the animal gets its food.

Have children complete the Chapter Self-Assessment, BLM 31. Have them choose products to place in their portfolios. Add the results of any rubrics. checklists, self-assessments, or portfolio assessments, BLMs 2–18.

Listening Assessment

BLACKLINE MASTER

Give each child BLM 53 and crayons. Play Side 1 of the White Tape several times stopping the tape to allow children to respond.

TAPESCRIPT

WHITE TAPE

Listen carefully. Draw what Luis saw. Luis likes to watch animals. He saw a bee gather honey for its honeycomb. Draw the bee near the honeycomb. (pause) He saw a woodchuck near its tunnel. Draw the woodchuck's tunnel. (pause) He saw a chameleon on a tree trunk, but it was hard to see. Color the chameleon on the tree trunk.

Options for Assessment

Vocabulary Assessment

ACTIVITY BOOK

Write the following words on the chalkboard: *bird, nest, spider, web, bee, honeycomb, beaver, tree, woodchuck, tunnel.* Have a volunteer say a word and ask children to find the word and its picture on Activity Book page 39. After all the pictures are named, ask children to complete the page independently.

Writing Assessment

Have children make personal picture books in which they illustrate and write about animals and how they protect themselves.

Language Assessment

BLACKLINE MASTER

Use Blackline Masters 52 in the Teacher's Resource Book.

Standardized Test Pratice

ACTIVITY BOOK

Use pages 40 and 41 in the Activity Book. Answers: They need a place to put the honey; It wouldn't have a place to live.

Wrap-Up

Activities

Mural

Have each group of children plan a background mural to use as a backdrop for their skit. Let them make a list of things they will draw on the mural. Then give each group a large piece of paper. Let them first make their drawings in pencil to get everything where they want it, then let them paint over the pencil drawings with poster paint.

Invitations

Give children two sheets of construction paper and crayons and suggest that they each make a cover for the invitations they are going to give their family members (Blackline Master 32 or 33). Some children might want to invite grandparents and might make a special cover for them as well.

Journal

Have children keep a journal listing new words and phrases they have learned as they studied community workers. They can check off each word when they have used it three or more times. You may also want to invite then to write their impressions of these workers and identify which workers they might like to be and why.

Discussing the Theme

Have children work in groups of 2 or 3 to discuss their progress during this unit about working. Choose from the following activities that will demonstrate to them how much they have learned and how useful that information is.

- Help children make a list of new words they have learned.
- Encourage children to draw a picture for as many words as possible. Have them write about their pictures and post the pictures and text on a bulletin board.
- Have groups of children tell when the words learned will be useful, for example, in science class, social studies class, in the neighborhood, and so on.
- Play a game in which you tell children a subject, such as places we go, things we see, or jobs people have. Children then think of a sentence that tells about the subject. For example, if your subject is "jobs people have," a child's response might range from "police officer" and *My father is a firefighter* to *A visiting nurse calls on people who are unable to leave their homes.*

Sharing the Unit Project

Use children's covers and the invitation form, Blackline Master 32 or 33, to invite family members to school to see the skits.

Let children put up their murals at their assigned stations. They can make sure their props are there too.

Invite volunteers to introduce the skits. They could name the skit and give the names of the performers. Encourage children to speak slowly and clearly as they perform the skit.

As visitors arrive, you can provide name tags for parents. Suggest that parents write the job they do after their name, if they wish.

Signs of Success!

Duplicate a copy of this checklist for each child.

Name: _____

Refer to the checklist below for a quick determination of how a child is progressing toward transitioning out of ESL instruction:

Objectives:

- ☐ Names community workers.
- ☐ Tells how workers help others.
- ☐ Names workplaces.
- ☐ Tells the difference between *needs* and *wants*.

- ☐ Tells about animals' needs.
- ☐ Tells how animals work to meet their needs.
- ☐ Tells how animals protect themselves.
- ☐ Tells how protective coloration works.

Language Awareness:

Understands/Uses:

- ☐ verbs
- ☐ related words for workers/workplaces
- ☐ *needs* and *wants*
- ☐ contractions *don't, I'm, he's, she's*

- ☐ subject/verb agreement
- ☐ giving directions
- ☐ end punctuation (period, question mark)
- ☐ descriptive words

Hears/Pronounces/Reads:

- ☐ rhyming words
- ☐ *sm, sk,* and *spr* consonant blends

Learning Strategies:

- ☐ Uses pictures for help with meaning.
- ☐ Uses title to predict.
- ☐ Notes repeated words.
- ☐ Finds ways to classify.
- ☐ Recognizes main idea.

- ☐ Recognizes sentence patterns.
- ☐ Follows directions.
- ☐ Understands specialized language.
- ☐ Activates prior knowledge.
- ☐ Summarizes information.

Comments

_____

_____

Planning Guide

CHAPTER 5

How We Have Fun

Objectives

Name toys and games.

Name ways to play alone and to play with friends.

Tell how to get exercise while playing.

Name ways that exercise is good for you.

Tell what parts of the body are used with different exercises.

Vocabulary Focus

Toys, such as *drum, ball, blocks, doll, car, train.*

Games, such as *checkers, jump rope, puzzle, soccer.*

Exercise, such as *swimming, hopping, running, stretching.*

Parts of the body, such as *heart, lungs, muscles, arms, legs, hands.*

Lesson	Content Focus	Language Awareness Objectives	Learning Strategies
Preview pages 78–79 Tell what you know.			
Present pages 80–81 Playing Alone Playing with Friends	Health	**Phonics** Final Consonant *s* /z/	
Practice pages 82–83 Having fun can help you stay healthy.	Health	**Phonics** Long *i*	
Practice pages 84–85 You use your body when you play. Use your eyes and hands.	Health	**Grammar** Number and Present Progressive	
Connect pages 86–87 How many?	Health/Math	**Grammar** Irregular Past Tense	Visualize.
Connect pages 88–99 *When We All Go Out to Play*	Health/ Literature	**Grammar** Future Tense **Grammar** Pronouns **Grammar** Contractions	Use imagery. Recognize cause and effect. Use pictures for meaning.
Connect page 100 "Play the Drum"	Health/ Literature	**Language Functions** Addressing Family Members and Friends	
Assess page 101 Tell what you learned.			

CHAPTER 6

How Things Move

Objectives

Tell what things can be pushed or pulled.

Understand what force is.

Tell what magnets can do.

Name things involving pushing and pulling that are fun to do.

Vocabulary Focus

Things that move, such as *bike, canoe, sailboat, wheelchair*.

Position phrases, *on the ground, in the air, on the water*.

Playthings, such as *toy truck, wagon, merry-go-round, swing*.

Words for science experiments, such as *force, hard push, gentle push, magnet*.

Lesson	Content Focus	Language Awareness Objectives	Learning Strategies
Preview pages 102–103 Tell what you know.			
Present pages 104–105 What can you push and pull?	Science	**Phonics** Consonant Blend *tr*	Use picture clues.
Practice pages 106–107 What makes things move? Use force to move things.	Science	**Grammar** Adjectives	Ask questions for information.
Practice pages 108–109 What do magnets do?	Science	**Grammar** Prepositions	
Connect pages 110–111 Push and Pull for Fun	Science/ Social Studies	**Grammar** Present Progressive	Use word structure.
Connect pages 112–113 "My Eighth Birthday"	Science/ Literature	**Grammar** Future Tense	Use context clues.
Connect page 114 "Pulling and Pushing"	Science/ Literature	**Grammar** Imperatives	
Assess page 115 Tell what you learned.			

Resources

Chapter 5

Support Materials

PICTURE CARDS
Numbers 4, 5, 23, 25, 40, 58, 63, 68

ACTIVITY BOOK
Pages 42–51

VIDEO
Unit 3, Fun With Motion

YELLOW TAPE
Side 1
When We All Go Out to Play, pages T88–T99

YELLOW TAPE
Side 2
"Play the Drum," page T100

Little Celebrations Library

Max's Box by Kristen Avery, ScottForesman, 1993.

We Can Share It! by Sarah Tatler, ScottForesman, 1993.

Assessment Materials

WHITE TAPE
Side 2
Listening Assessment, page T101

BLACKLINE MASTER
Language Assessment, page 60
Listening Assessment, page 61

Newcomer Book A

Survival Book for absolute beginners. For overview, see pages xxviii–xxxi.

For Extended Reading

Keep Running, Allen by Clyde Robert Bulla, Crowell, 1978.

Allen is the youngest of four children and he has a hard time keeping up with his older brothers and sisters. In the end they see that there's something to be said about not hurrying so much.

Level: Advanced

Max, the Music-Maker by Miriam B. Stecher, Lothrop, 1980.

Photographs accompany this story about Max, who likes to make music using all sorts of everyday objects.

Level: Beginning

My Ballet Class by Rachel Isadora, Greenwillow, 1980.

A young girl describes her ballet class—the teacher, students, and the movements they learn.

Level: Average

Playgrounds by Gail Gibbons, Holiday House, 1985.

This simple book describes the various equipment and activities that children can find at playgrounds.

Level: Beginning

Rex and Lilly Playtime by Laurie Krasny Brown, Little, Brown and Company, 1995.

Three stories about brother and sister dinosaurs who just want to have fun.

Level: Beginning

Related Technology

Mixed-up Mother Goose Deluxe, *Sierra,* 1994.

Have fun learning nursery rhymes and develop language skills.

Chapter 6

Support Materials

PICTURE CARDS
Numbers 1, 5, 10, 13, 19, 29, 40, 68

ACTIVITY BOOK
Pages 52–61

VIDEO
Unit 3, Fun With Motion

YELLOW TAPE
Side 2 "Pulling and Pushing," page T114

Shared Reading Collection

On the Go by Ann Morris, ScottForesman, 1993.

Little Celebrations Library

The Bus Ride by Anne Mclean, ScottForesman, 1993.

Something New by Marcia Vaughan, ScottForesman, 1993.

Assessment Materials

WHITE TAPE
Side 2
Listening Assessment, page T115

BLACKLINE MASTER
Language Assessment, page 62
Listening Assessment, page 63

For Extended Reading

Bikes by Anne Rockwell, Dutton, 1987.
Simple book that describes different types of bikes and how they are used for different purposes.

Level: Beginning

Emmett's Snowball by Ned Miller, Holt, 1990.
When Emmett began rolling his snowball, he had no idea how big it could grow, or how much trouble it could cause.

Level: Advanced

Experiment With Movement by Bryan Murphy, Lerner, 1991.
Pulleys, rollers, levers, and gears are some of the devices this book discusses and uses in experiments.

Level: Average

Machines at Work by Byron Barton, Crowell, 1987.
A very simple book which describes how construction equipment is used to do different tasks on a job site.

Level: Beginning

Sliding and Rolling by Terry Jennings, Gloucester Press, 1989.
This simple book contains easy-to-do experiments that demonstrate how friction can be overcome by force and by using wheels.

Level: Beginning

Related Technology

Adventures with Oslo: Tools and Gadgets, Science for Kids, 1994.
Learn all about tools and what they can do.

Project

Folk Dance Festival

This optional project can be completed over the next two chapters. See the Unit Wrap-Up, page T115a, for more ideas on sharing the project with family members.

What You'll Need

Collect the following sorts of items for the folk dance festival:

Music:
- tapes, CDs, or records with music from different countries
- tape recorder, record player, or CD player
- musical instruments

Costumes:
- typical clothing from countries represented
- any props needed for particular dances

Decorations:
- construction paper
- markers
- pictures of the countries represented
- globe

Beginning the Project

Tell children that they will be working on a folk dancing project for the next few weeks. As an introduction to the project, you might demonstrate a simple folk dance from your own cultural background. Talk to the group about folk dancing. Encourage them to share their knowledge and ideas. Explain that they will be putting on a show for friends and family at the end of the project.

Home Involvement

Send Letter Home, Blackline Masters 54–59, to families to let them know what their child will be studying next and to solicit their participation in collecting items needed for the festival.

Planning and Performing the Dances

Find out what dances children know and encourage them to teach each other the steps to folk dances from their native countries. Have children work in groups to select the music for the dances and to plan costumes. Help children write out a list showing the order of dances. Consider the length of each piece to plan the length of the entire performance. Invite children to bring in clothing and props appropriate for their dances.

Learning the Dances

- Invite parents or other adults to come to class and demonstrate dances.

- If children are interested and able, encourage them to learn more than one dance.

- To increase diversity in representation, you may want to show a video or film of folk dances not otherwise represented in your program.

Rehearse for the Festival

- Have children try the costumes on.

- Encourage children to practice the dances frequently to build their confidence.

- Plan a rehearsal with children wearing their costumes and using their props.

Decorations

- Invite children to share drawings or photographs of their native countries.

- Help them make flags from construction paper to represent each country.

- Have children set up a globe with streamers from each country represented in the festival to a picture of that place or to the country's flag.

- Display any costumes, props, or musical instruments not needed for the program.

Masters of Ceremonies

Have children choose a master of ceremonies or have different children introduce the different dances. To introduce each dance, children can name the country of origin, give a brief description of the dance, and name the dancers participating.

Write a Program

Help children create a program that includes all of the staged events, listing participants. Include a list of people to be thanked for their help. Have children make copies of the program and illustrate them. Assign children to welcome visitors and hand out programs at the time of the performance.

Daily Discussion

Take a few minutes each day to discuss the project. Encourage children to practice vocabulary learned in conjunction with the folk dance festival. You may want to relate the festival to chapter topics by asking questions such as

- Does dancing provide exercise?

- What parts of the body are used for each dance?

- Do any of the dances involve pushing or pulling?

- Which of the dances are done alone? in groups?

- How do you feel when dancing?

At the end of the unit have children discuss what they learned from the project. See page T115a for ideas about sharing the festival with families and friends when the presentation is ready.

Activity Book

Chapter 5

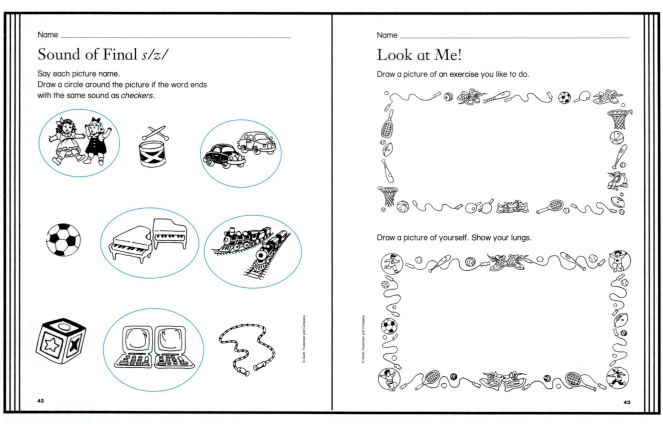

Name _____

Sound of Final *s/z/*

Say each picture name.
Draw a circle around the picture if the word ends
with the same sound as *checkers*.

Name _____

Look at Me!

Draw a picture of an exercise you like to do.

Draw a picture of yourself. Show your lungs.

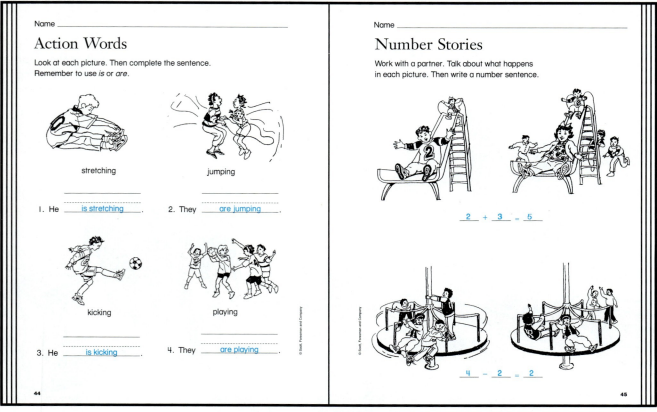

Name _____

Action Words

Look at each picture. Then complete the sentence.
Remember to use *is* or *are*.

stretching

jumping

1. He _____ is stretching _____.

2. They _____ are jumping _____.

kicking

playing

3. He _____ is kicking _____.

4. They _____ are playing _____.

Name _____

Number Stories

Work with a partner. Talk about what happens
in each picture. Then write a number sentence.

__2__ + __3__ = __5__

__4__ − __2__ = __2__

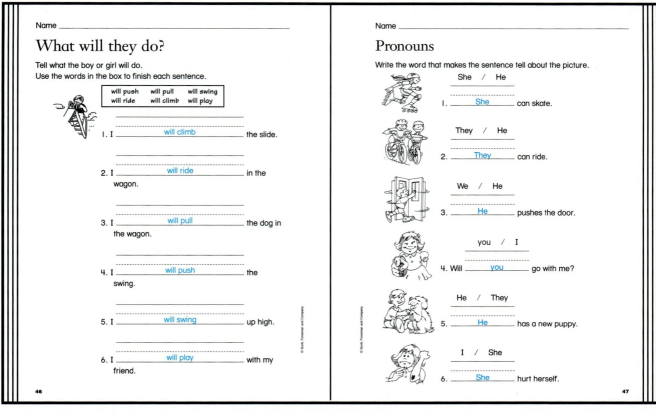

Name _____

What will they do?

Tell what the boy or girl will do.
Use the words in the box to finish each sentence.

will push	will pull	will swing
will ride	will climb	will play

1. I _____ will climb _____ the slide.

2. I _____ will ride _____ in the wagon.

3. I _____ will pull _____ the dog in the wagon.

4. I _____ will push _____ the swing.

5. I _____ will swing _____ up high.

6. I _____ will play _____ with my friend.

© Scott, Foresman and Company

46

Name _____

Pronouns

Write the word that makes the sentence tell about the picture.

She / He

1. _____ She _____ can skate.

They / He

2. _____ They _____ can ride.

We / He

3. _____ He _____ pushes the door.

you / I

4. Will _____ you _____ go with me?

He / They

5. _____ He _____ has a new puppy.

I / She

6. _____ She _____ hurt herself.

© Scott, Foresman and Company

47

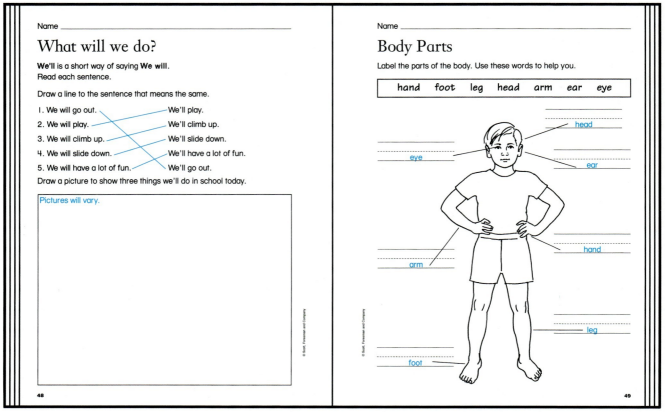

Name _____

What will we do?

We'll is a short way of saying **We will**.
Read each sentence.

Draw a line to the sentence that means the same.

1. We will go out. — We'll play.
2. We will play. — We'll climb up.
3. We will climb up. — We'll slide down.
4. We will slide down. — We'll have a lot of fun.
5. We will have a lot of fun. — We'll go out.

Draw a picture to show three things we'll do in school today.

Pictures will vary.

© Scott, Foresman and Company

48

Name _____

Body Parts

Label the parts of the body. Use these words to help you.

hand	foot	leg	head	arm	ear	eye

head

eye

ear

arm

hand

leg

foot

© Scott, Foresman and Company

49

T78h

Activity Book

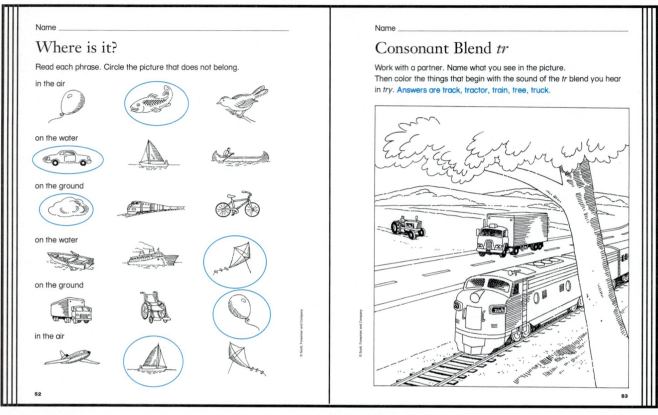

Chapter 6

Name _____

Where is it?

Read each phrase. Circle the picture that does not belong.

in the air

on the water

on the ground

on the water

on the ground

in the air

52

Name _____

Consonant Blend *tr*

Work with a partner. Name what you see in the picture.
Then color the things that begin with the sound of the *tr* blend you hear in *try*. **Answers are track, tractor, train, tree, truck.**

53

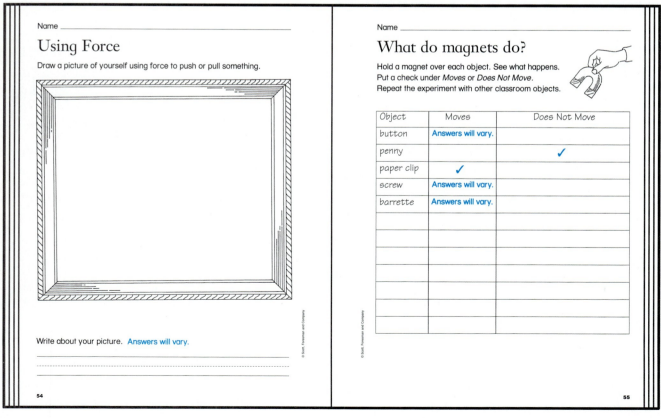

Name _____

Using Force

Draw a picture of yourself using force to push or pull something.

Write about your picture. **Answers will vary.**

_____

54

Name _____

What do magnets do?

Hold a magnet over each object. See what happens.
Put a check under *Moves* or *Does Not Move*.
Repeat the experiment with other classroom objects.

Object	Moves	Does Not Move
button	Answers will vary.	
penny		✓
paper clip	✓	
screw	Answers will vary.	
barrette	Answers will vary.	

55

Pulling or Pushing?

Who is pulling? Who is pushing?
Write **pulling** or **pushing** under each picture.

pushing

pulling

pulling

pushing

On another paper draw a picture of you and your friends having fun.
Show some of you pushing or pulling.

56

It's a match!

Draw a line to match each picture with the correct word.

chicken

mom

friends

piñata

candy

57

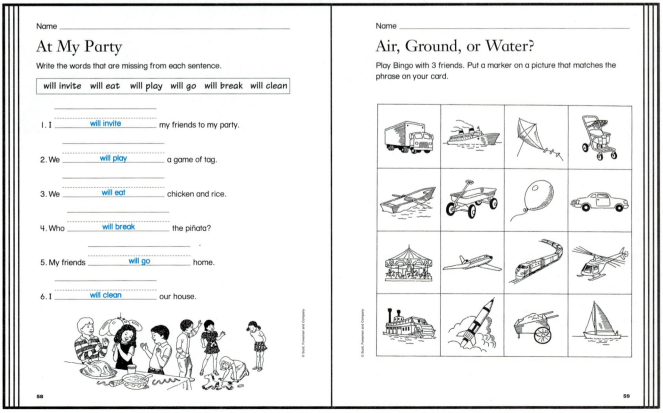

At My Party

Write the words that are missing from each sentence.

| will invite   will eat   will play   will go   will break   will clean |

1. I _will invite_ my friends to my party.

2. We _will play_ a game of tag.

3. We _will eat_ chicken and rice.

4. Who _will break_ the piñata?

5. My friends _will go_ home.

6. I _will clean_ our house.

58

Air, Ground, or Water?

Play Bingo with 3 friends. Put a marker on a picture that matches the phrase on your card.

59

Preview

Activate Prior Knowledge
Use Realia

Display favorite playthings from the classroom as well as toys from other countries. Have volunteers identify the toys and demonstrate how to play with them.

Ask children to sit in a circle. Talk about how we have fun. Elicit the names of toys children like best from their native countries. List the names of the toys on chart paper, then have volunteers illustrate the toys right next to the words. Continue adding to the list throughout the chapter.

Invite children to share with the group what they like about their toys. Also, you may want to have children compare how their toy preferences have changed since they were babies.

Develop Language and Concepts
Present pages 78 and 79.

TPR Display several of the toys shown on pages 78 and 79. Read aloud the labels. Ask children to brainstorm ways in which they would use these toys to play. Encourage them to show different actions following commands, such as *Bounce the ball, Roll the ball,* and so on.

Have children answer the questions in Talk About It. Suggest they think about their toys as well as the toys pictured. Have children

(Continued on page T79)

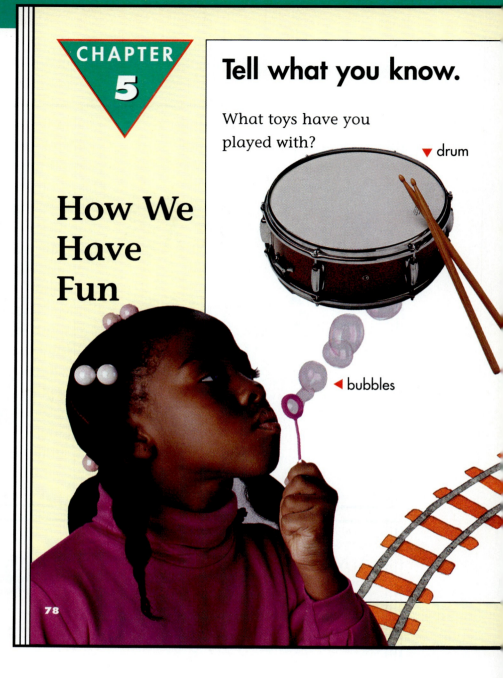

CHAPTER 5

How We Have Fun

Tell what you know.

What toys have you played with?

▼ drum

◀ bubbles

78

Options for Reaching All Students

Beginning
Language: Words and Pictures

Give children two index cards each. Ask them to use crayons to draw and label two of their favorite toys. After children write their own names on their cards, collect the cards so they can be used later in the chapter for independent activities.

Advanced
Language: Making Books

Show children a Table of Contents in a book. Elicit that it tells the reader what the book will be about. Tell children that they will be writing books about toys they like. Have children work in small groups. Ask them to brainstorm ideas and develop a Table of Contents for their book. Then have them work together to complete the pages of the book.

Mixed Ability
Video: Fun with Motion

VIDEO Show children the video to help build background knowledge on the unit theme. You may also choose to use the video in other ways that are appropriate during the unit.

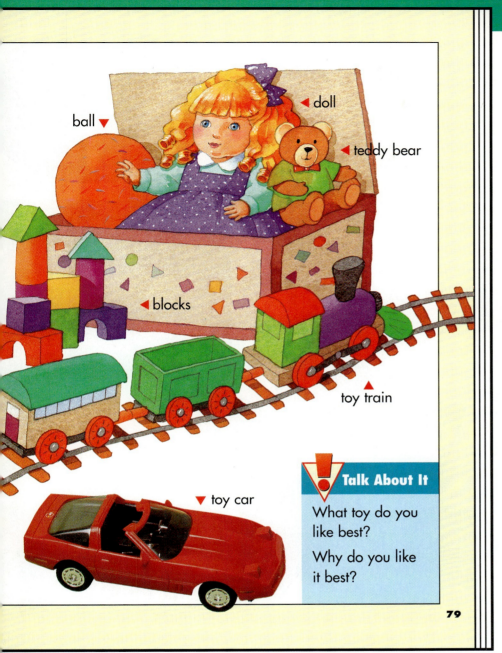

ball ▼

◄ doll

◄ teddy bear

◄ blocks

▲ toy train

▼ toy car

! Talk About It

What toy do you like best?

Why do you like it best?

79

In this chapter, children will learn the language connected with fun and motion.

Use pages 78 and 79 to assess children's knowledge of the concepts related to using movement to have fun.

Playing with toys is fun.

We can have fun playing alone or with others.

How We Have Fun

We can have fun exercising.

Exercise can help you stay healthy.

answer the question in Tell What You Know. Encourage children to explain their choices as much as possible, using sentences such as *I like to play with* ____. The toy I like best is ____. *I like* ____ *because* ____.

Peer Tutoring
Language: Identifying Toys

PICTURE CARDS

Give pairs of children pictures of toys including Picture Cards of the ball, the dinosaurs, the dolls, and the kite. Use Picture Cards 4, 23, 25, 40. Children work together until both can identify all the toys in English.

Mixed Ability
Math: Making a Bar Graph

Use chart paper and colored markers to make a bar graph with children about their toy preferences. Each child can mark his or her own preference on the graph. Then have children use the bar graph to tell which are the most popular toys in the classroom. Display the bar graph on a wall.

Little Celebrations
Max's Box

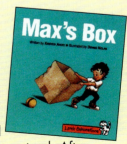

Max uses an empty carton and his imagination to pretend. After trying different roles, he ends up as "Max in a box."

Level: Beginning

Present

Activate Prior Knowledge
Use Realia

Refer to the toys listed on the chart. Display an assortment of these toys. Elicit from children which of these might be played with alone. Then ask for which activity you need a friend. Summarize by saying that children sometimes play alone and sometimes play with friends.

Develop Language and Concepts
Present pages 80 and 81.

Read the text on page 80 with children. Help children identify what each child pictured is doing. Initiate discussion of the pictures using words from the Word Bank and say sentences such as *The boy plays with _____. He plays alone.* Discuss with children whether they sometimes play alone and what kinds of things they play with when they play alone.

Read the text on page 81 with children. Invite children to describe the activities shown. Brainstorm as a group several activities they can do with one or more friends to have fun. Do the Talk About It activity. Lead a discussion about why they might like to play with a friend sometimes and how it might help to have a partner.

Playing Alone

You can play alone.
It can be fun to play alone.

80 LEARN LANGUAGE • HEALTH

Options for Reaching All Students

Beginning
Language: Chant

TPR Have children form two groups. Use a ball. Model the actions while presenting the chant. Ask children to say or do only their part. If possible, distribute balls to Group B. Otherwise have Group B pantomime the actions. Change the key words to cover other actions, and have the groups switch roles.

Group A:	Can you play with a ball?
Group B:	Yes, I can!
Group A:	Bounce the ball.
Group B:	(Children do the action.)
Group A:	Roll the ball.
Group B:	(Children do the action.)
Group A:	Pass the ball.
Group B:	(Children do the action.)
Group A:	Toss the ball.
Group B:	(Children do the action.)

Advanced
Social Studies: Survey

Have children interview other teachers about their favorite childhood toys. In small groups ask them to prepare questions for the interview. After the interviews, have children discuss their findings with the class.

Playing with Friends

To play some games you need one friend.

To play other games you need more than one friend.

Word Bank

ball

blocks

checkers

computer

jump ropes

piano

puzzle

Talk About It

What do you like to do alone?

What do you like to do with friends?

Phonics: Final Consonant s /z/

ACTIVITY BOOK

Say these words as you write them on the board: *pianos, checkers*. Point to and say each word emphasizing the final sound, /z/. Ask children to find the letter that stands for /z/ and underline it. Say the words again, emphasizing the final sound /z/. Point out that the letter s stands for /z/ in these words. For practice, children can use Activity Book page 42.

Assess ✔

Children should be able to

• name ways to have fun alone

• name ways to have fun with friends

LOOK **AHEAD**

In the next section, children will apply their understanding of having fun by moving their bodies to understanding how exercising can be healthy.

Cooperative Language Experience
Field Trip

In groups have children prepare questions for a salesperson in the toy department of a local store. During the visit, encourage children to ask their questions. Help children identify the toys they see. Discuss toys children could play with alone or with friends. Together write a language experience story about the visit.

Home Connection
My Favorite Things

Ask children to interview a family member about his or her favorite childhood activities. Ask children to jot down notes to share in class the next day. Have children compare the favorites and see which old favorites are still favorites today.

Little Celebrations
We Can Share It!

Instead of sharing his new-found rope by cutting it to pieces, Parrot suggests, Monkey and friends share the rope by using it to play jump rope.

Level: Average

Practice

Activate Prior Knowledge
Make an Idea Web

Invite children to join you in a brief exercise. Then ask them to feel how their bodies have changed. Elicit responses such as *Our hearts beat faster when we exercise.*

Brainstorm with children different types of exercise. Construct a web using the ideas you discuss. Use the Idea Web, Blackline Master 20 in the Teacher's Resource Book.

Develop Language and Concepts
Present pages 82 and 83.

TPR Demonstrate actions such as running, hopping, and swimming and name the exercise you are doing. Add new words to the idea web as they are named. Then say the action words and ask children to do the actions.

ACTIVITY BOOK Read page 82 with children and identify the exercises shown. Invite children to do the exercises without moving from their own places. Then have children point to where

(Continued on page T83)

Having fun can help you stay healthy.

Do you get **exercise** while you play?

You need exercise to make you **strong**. Exercise can be fun.

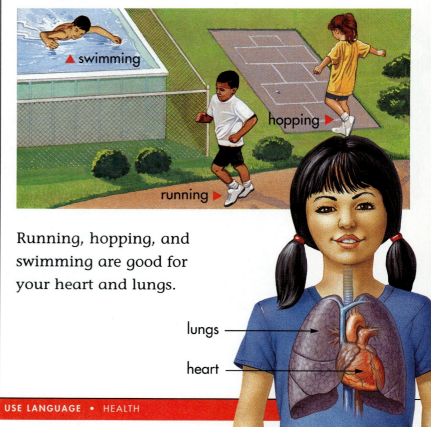

▲ swimming

hopping ▶

running ▶

Running, hopping, and swimming are good for your heart and lungs.

lungs

heart

82 USE LANGUAGE • HEALTH

Options for Reaching All Students

Beginning
Language: Chant

TPR Give children cards and have them write an action word or phrase from page 82 or 83. Repeat the following chant until children can join in with you. When they hear the word or phrase on their card, they are to do the action.

I can stay healthy. Yes, I can.
Running, hopping, swimming too.

There are so many things I can do!
My strong muscles really rate.
Stretching and standing up very straight.
All these things are great, great, great!

Advanced
Art: Body Diagrams

Have children work in pairs to make human body diagrams for posters. Provide chart paper and a variety of art materials. Ask partners to make diagrams in which they show the heart, the lungs, and the muscles. They may use different materials, such as yarn, for the muscles. Encourage children to label body parts.

standing ▸
up straight

stretching ▸

Stretching and standing up straight as you walk are good for your **muscles**.

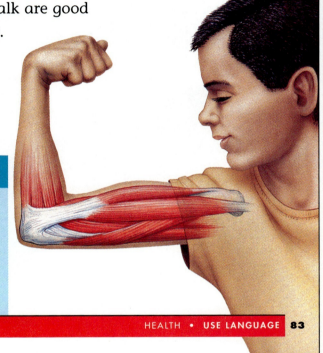

! **Talk About It**

How do you get exercise?

Tell how your exercise is good for you.

HEALTH • USE LANGUAGE 83

Phonics: Long *i*

Write while *and* exercise *on the board. Read the words aloud with children. Help them see what is alike about the two words. Note the consonant-vowel-consonant-e pattern. Point out that the silent e is a clue that the vowel has the long i sound. Brainstorm with children other examples and add them to the list.*

their heart and lungs are in their bodies as you point to the diagram on the page. Elicit from children that exercise makes their heart and lungs stronger. For practice, use page 43 in the Activity book.

Help the class describe what the children in the picture on page 83 are doing. Help them read the labels and the sentence.

Together do the Talk About It activity.

Assess ✓

Children should be able to

• name or do some exercises

• say that exercise is good for their heart, lungs, and muscles

LOOK **AHEAD** ➡

Next, children will identify the different parts of the body used for different movements.

Mixed Ability
Gestures and Body Language

Take children to observe a sporting event such as a Little League game or a team sport played in a physical education class in the school gym or on the playground. Children should note how team members and spectators act. Encourage children to compare and contrast across cultures how people cheer, show disappointment, and so on.

QuickCheck

Gerunds

Check whether children can form gerunds. Help those who need practice form the gerunds of action verbs and use them in sentences.

Writer's Workshop
Write About Exercise

Refer children to the Writer's Workshop on pages 230–236 of the Student Book. Have them write about exercise using the information they learned in this lesson.

Practice

Activate Prior Knowledge
Say a Chant About Body Parts

Invite children to point to different parts of the body while they say the chant below:

Head and shoulders, knees and toes,
Knees and toes.
Head and shoulders, knees and toes,
Knees and toes.
Eyes, nose, mouth and ears too,
Head and shoulders, knees and toes,
Knees and toes.

Then present or review more parts of the body.

Develop Language and Concepts
Present page 84.

Have children look at the page and identify the sports they know. Read the labels with children. Then read the words in the Word Bank and have children point to the parts of the body. Help children associate the words with the people in the pictures to form sentences; for example, *The boy is using his feet.*

Present page 85.

Read the activity on the page with children. Have children read the directions as you model how to play the game. Explain that they need to pay attention to the parts of the body they should or should not move.

Do the Think About It activity.

You use your body when you play.

Which parts of the body are these children using?

Word Bank
arms
ears
eyes
feet
hands
legs

soccer ▲

tennis ▲

swimming ▲

84 USE LANGUAGE • HEALTH

Options for Reaching All Students

Beginning
Oral Language: Sentences

Prepare word cards for actions such as *running, hopping,* and *swimming.* Invite a volunteer to choose a card and demonstrate the action. Then invite another volunteer to tell about the action saying, for example, *He is hopping.* Help by modeling the sentence pattern.

Advanced
Writing: Sentences

Ask children to choose an activity from pages 82, 83, or 84. Have each child draw a picture of himself or herself doing the activity. Guide children to write sentences that describe their picture. Write the following example on the board as a model.

I am playing tennis.
I am using my arms to swing the racket.

Home Connection
Make a List

Ask children, when they are at home, to think of and list five things they did that involved using their hands, arms, and eyes all at the same time. Tell children to work on the list with a family member.

Use your eyes and hands.

Play "Follow the Leader" with a friend.

1. Be the Leader. Do not speak. Show these hand motions.
    clap, clap, snap, snap,
    wave, wave, knock, knock

2. Your friend should do what you do.

3. Take turns being the Leader. Make up motions of your own.

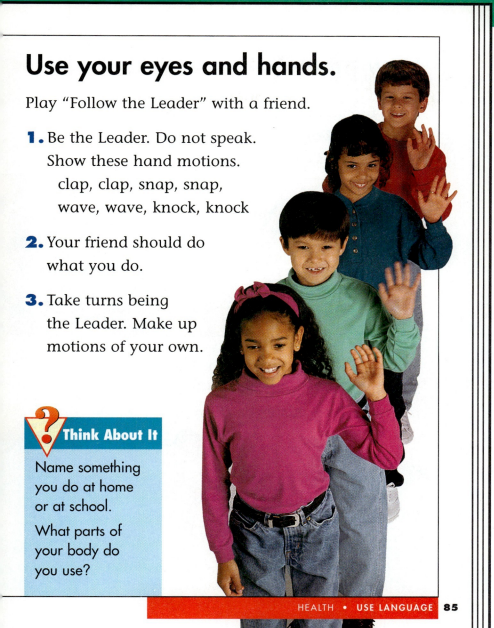

? Think About It

Name something you do at home or at school.

What parts of your body do you use?

HEALTH • **USE LANGUAGE** **85**

Language Awareness

Grammar: Number and Present Progressive

Write these sentences on the board: *He is playing soccer. They are playing tennis.*

 ACTIVITY BOOK Ask a volunteer to name the action in each sentence. Explain that *is playing* names the action in the first sentence and *are playing* names the action in the second. Ask children to look at the picture at the bottom of page 84 and tell what the girls are doing. Write *They are swimming.* Emphasize *are swimming.* For more practice, use Activity Book page 44.

Assess ✓

Children should be able to

• tell the parts of the body used for a specific activity

LOOK **AHEAD** ➡

Next, children will do story problems involving toys.

Multicultural Connection
Sports Festival

Encourage children to share and compare with the class what they know about sports played in different countries. For example, children might tell about soccer or about a time when they or someone they know played it. With the class, plan a festival in which they learn and enjoy the games.

Mixed Ability
Music: Singing in a Circle

Have the class stand in a circle and join in singing "The Hokey Pokey." Children are to move parts of the body as indicated in the song. They can continue the song by using verses for right foot, left foot, and so on.

I put my right hand in,
I put my right hand out,
I put my right hand in,
And shake it all about.

I do the Hokey Pokey
And I turn myself around,
That's what it's all about.
Hokey Pokey!
I put my left hand in,
I put my left hand out,
I put my left hand in,
And shake it all about.
I do the Hokey Pokey
And I turn myself around,
That's what it's all about.
Hokey Pokey!

Connect

Activate Prior Knowledge
Use Role-Playing

Have volunteers role-play addition and subtraction problems, using familiar toys. Provide several toys of the same kind. Ask volunteers to act out a word problem, such as *Luisa puts 3 blocks on the table. Peter puts 2 blocks. How many blocks are there in all?*

Discuss with children how they can figure out the answer by using addition.

Develop Language and Concepts
Present pages 86 and 87.

Direct children's attention to the first picture on page 86. Ask volunteers to describe it. Then read the word problem aloud. Draw the toys on the board. Write the plus sign and the equal sign to make an addition sentence. Say the words. Help children solve the problem. Then write the addition sentence with numerals for children to solve. Read with children the completed sentence.

If possible, provide manipulatives for children to use to represent the other word problems on pages 86 and 87 as you read. As children solve each problem, emphasize how to read +, −, and =.

ACTIVITY BOOK

For more practice, use page 45 in the Activity Book.

Do the Write About It with children. Lead them through making up the subtraction problem.

How many?

Hilda brought 2 toy cars to the birthday party. Marc brought 1 toy car. How many toy cars were there in all?

Pablo and Rosa played catch. Then Su came to play with them. How many children played catch in all?

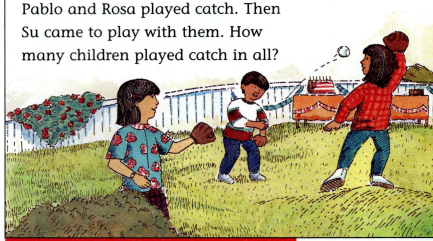

86 CONNECT LANGUAGE • HEALTH/MATH

Options for Reaching All Students

Beginning
Math: Illustrate Word Problems

To help children visualize word problems, have them draw with you as you illustrate the first word problem on page 86. Then ask a volunteer to come up and count the cars to see how many there are in all. Repeat for each of the problems on pages 86 and 87.

Advanced
Language: Use Past Tense

Have children work in pairs. Give each pair a sheet with these sentences:

She <u>comes</u> to the birthday party.
He <u>gives</u> me a toy car.
She <u>brings</u> red checkers.
He <u>takes</u> some balloons home.

Have pairs take turns reading each sentence and changing the underlined word to the past tense form using *came, gave, brought,* and *took.*

Leah had 9 red checkers. She gave
3 red checkers to her sister.
How many were left?

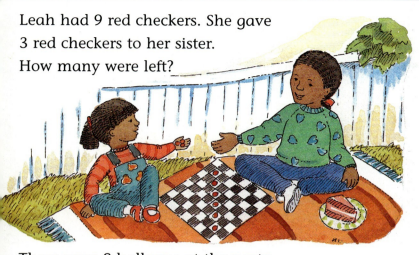

There were 8 balloons at the party.
Lee took 2 balloons home.
How many were left?

 Write About It

Make up a problem. End your problem with this question. How many were left?

Grammar: Irregular Past Tense

Write on the board: *Marc brings one toy car. Marc brought one toy car.*

Elicit from children what is different about the sentences. Point out that *brings* tells the action is happening now and *brought* tells that the action happened in the past. Continue with *comes/came; gives/gave,* and *takes/took.* Remind children that regular past-tense words end with *-ed;* give several examples.

Model a Strategy
Visualize

Model visualizing text for meaning:

When I read, I try to see a picture in my head of what I am reading on the page. This helps me figure out word problems. For example, when I read 9 red checkers, I see 9 red checkers in my head.

Assess ✔
Children should be able to

• solve addition and subtraction problems

LOOK AHEAD

Next, children will build on vocabulary they have learned when they read a Mother Goose rhyme about going out to play.

Mixed Ability
Hopscotch

TPR Take children to the playground, and use colored chalk to draw an outline for playing hopscotch. Ask volunteers to write, in sequence, one numeral per box. Draw several outlines so that all children can play. Have those children who know how to play hopscotch teach the others how to play.

Multicultural Connection
Sidewalk Games

Invite volunteers to show the rest of the class games from different cultures that are commonly played on sidewalk drawings. For example, children might share a game from Latin America similar to hopscotch, in which the drawing is an airplane, or *avión*.

Connect

Activate Prior Knowledge
Use Pictures to Predict

Have children look at the pictures in the selection. Ask questions such as these:

- What do you think the selection is about? How do you know?

Review with children what they know about playgrounds. Ask children to say what they like to do on a playground.

Introduce the Selection

Help children read the title of the rhyme and the byline. Explain that this is a variation of the traditional Mother Goose rhyme they may be familiar with.

Read the Selection

 Read through the rhyme with children several times. Point out the repetitive patterns. During each rereading, encourage children to join in. Also play Side 1 of the Yellow Tape.

Use the suggested activities appropriate to meet children's needs.

Model a Strategy
Use Imagery

Model using mental images to aid understanding:

This rhyme asks what kinds of things we can do at a playground. First I picture a playground. I picture the different things I might see there and name them. When I read, I use the pictures in my mind to give me clues to the meaning of the words on the page.

Teachable Moment
Oral History

Explain to children that this rhyme, like many others they have heard, has been told from generation to generation. Have volunteers give examples of rhymes they know. Discuss with children the importance of preserving traditional rhymes and stories for future generations.

Options for Reaching All Students

Beginning
Language: Words and Sentences

PICTURE CARDS

Show Picture Cards of ball, bike, run, slide, and swing. Invite children to describe the pictures. Then give children word strips and encourage them to form sentences about the Picture Cards. Use Picture Cards 4, 5, 58, 63, 68.

Advanced
Math: Time for Play

Direct children's attention to a class clock. Ask what time is a good time to play outdoors. They may say their recess time or an after-school time. Help children draw clock faces showing one suggested time. Then have children copy and complete the following sentences: It is ___ o'clock. It is time to _____. Encourage volunteers to describe what they do at their chosen time.

Home Connection
Traditional Tales

Invite children to bring from home a book of traditional tales or rhymes from their native countries to share with the class. Or, they can tell a traditional story or rhyme they know.

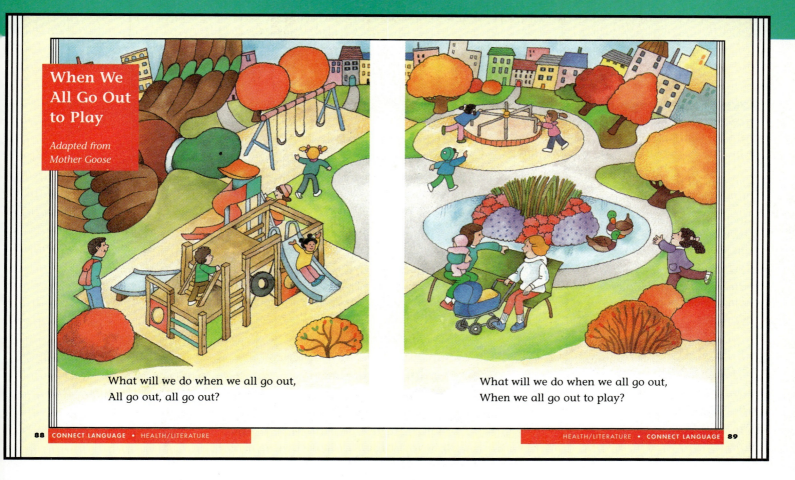

When We All Go Out to Play

Adapted from Mother Goose

What will we do when we all go out,
All go out, all go out?

What will we do when we all go out,
When we all go out to play?

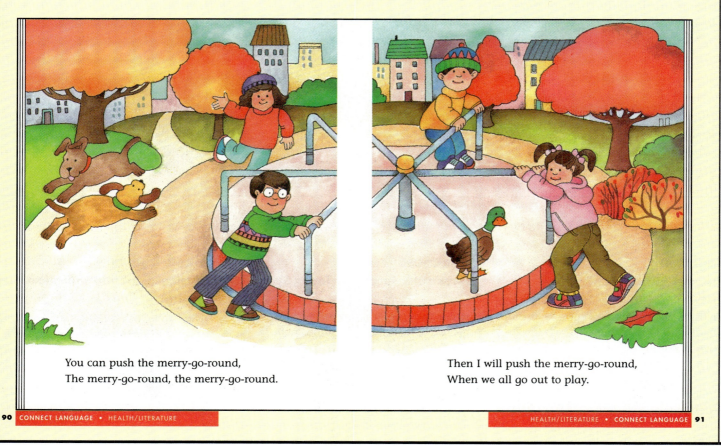

You can push the merry-go-round,
The merry-go-round, the merry-go-round.

Then I will push the merry-go-round,
When we all go out to play.

Connect

Develop Language and Concepts

In advance, prepare a medium-sized box and fill it with heavy objects, such as books or blocks. Ask volunteers to try to move the box. Elicit *push* and *pull* to describe the actions used to move it. Ask children what things they usually push or pull.

Direct children's attention to the actions shown on pages 92–95 and have them pantomime as they reread the text with you.

Have children note how the people in the pictures take turns helping each other. Elicit examples of cooperation when they play with others.

Model a Strategy
Recognize Cause and Effect

Model recognizing cause and effect to get meaning:

When I read I think about what happens and why. On page 94, I read I will push and you can swing. *I know that if I push a swing, the person on the seat swings forward. As I read the rhyme, I understand as one person pushes, the other person swings. How can you use cause and effect as you read?*

Teachable Moment
Realism and Fantasy

Have children look at the pictures throughout the poem and decide whether they show real people or make-believe characters. Encourage them to think about whether details in the pictures show things that can happen in real life.

Options for Reaching All Students

Beginning
Science: Experiment

Find a small cart or wagon. Invite each child to move several objects with and without the help of the cart/wagon. Have children describe how the wheels make a difference. Children can record their observations by making pictures and writing down what they experienced.

Advanced
Physical Education: Team Sports

Brainstorm with children examples of sports that require cooperation. Have groups talk about why a team effort is important. Then have each group choose a sport to illustrate. Allow time for groups to prepare a talk and present it to the class along with the illustration. Encourage them to tell what they know about their sport.

Mixed Ability
Physical Education: Motion and Rhythm

Divide the class into two groups. Lead a group in acting out the verses of "When We all Go Out to Play" as the other group reads the rhyme. Alternate groups, and encourage children to vary the tempo and styles to include different beats.

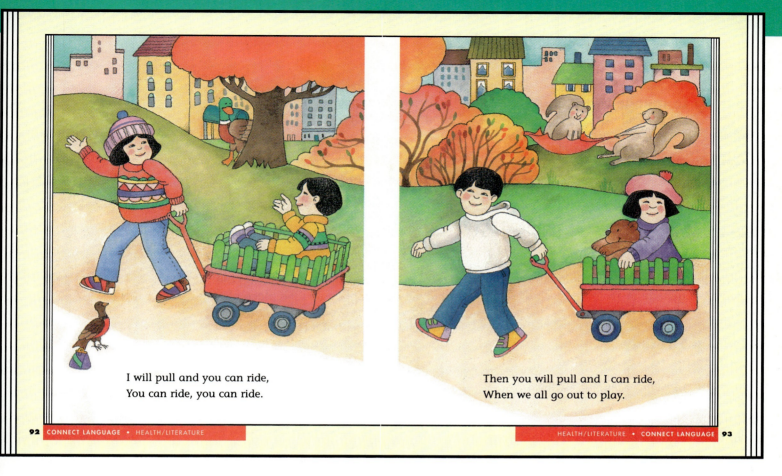

I will pull and you can ride,
You can ride, you can ride.

Then you will pull and I can ride,
When we all go out to play.

I will push and you can swing,
You can swing, you can swing.

You will push and I can swing,
When we all go out to play.

Connect

Develop Language and Concepts

PICTURE CARDS

Display Picture Card 63 of a slide to initiate a discussion about the fun of sliding down a slide. Encourage children to tell what else they do before they slide. Ask children to describe what it feels like to go down the slide.

Reread the pages with the class. Explore what activities can be most fun to play at a playground. Invite children to share their favorite thing to play at a playground or outdoors in general in sentences such as, *I like ___. It's a lot of fun.*

Model a Strategy

Use Pictures to Get Meaning

Model using pictures to figure out the meaning of words:

When I read, the pictures help me understand the words. The picture on pages 98 and 99 show children sliding. I imagine that the words tell what the children are doing or saying. I look for the words slide down on these pages. Looking at pictures helps me better understand what I read.

Teachable Moment

Repetition

Have children look for repeated phrases throughout the rhyme. Then encourage them to reread the rhyme, paying attention to the repeated phrases. Children can brainstorm examples of other rhymes or songs in which repeated phrases are found.

Language Awareness

Grammar: Contractions

ACTIVITY BOOK

Call attention to the use of the contraction *we'll* in the rhyme on pages 96 and 97. Tell children that *we'll* is a short way of saying *we will.* Write both on the chalkboard and compare the spellings, pointing out that the apostrophe takes the place of *wi.* Ask to whom the word *we'll* refers and help children see that it refers to the children pictured. Ask a volunteer to use *we'll* in a sentence that tells what the class will do that day. For practice, children can use Activity Book page 48.

Response to the Selection

Personal Response: Ask, *How did the rhyme make you feel?* and *Which part did you like best?*

Critical Response: Have children work with a group of classmates to choose the one thing pictured that they think is the most fun to do.

Creative Response: Have children draw a picture of something they would do for fun that might be added to the rhyme. Help them write their own verse about the picture.

Options for Reaching All Students

Beginning

Language: Mother Goose Show

Children can select some Mother Goose rhymes they know, or learn some new ones, to act out in front of the class. They can bring props from home and also make a poster to announce the performance.

Advanced

Social Studies: Maps

Invite children to design their own playgrounds and make maps representing all their favorite activities and equipment. Guide them in making a map key that includes symbols for what they show on their maps.

Home Connection

Places to Play

Encourage children to interview family members about favorite places they played in their native country. Invite children to bring in photographs or drawings of these places they make with their families. Ask volunteers to describe these places and the things their family memebers did there.

We'll climb up and then slide down,
Then slide down, then slide down.

We'll climb up and then slide down,
When we all go out to play.

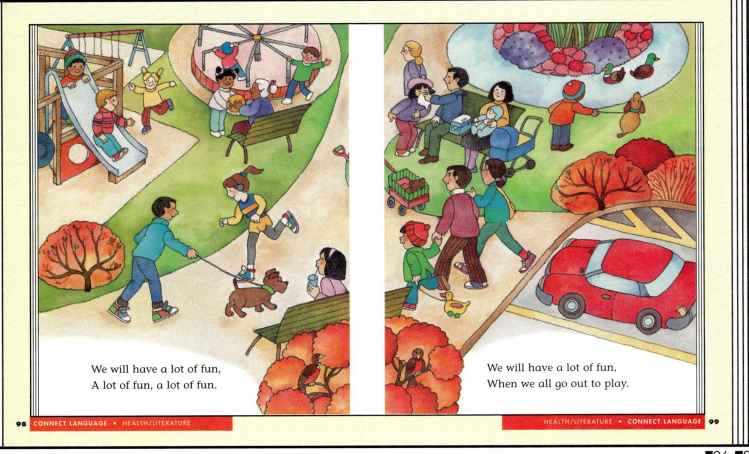

We will have a lot of fun,
A lot of fun, a lot of fun.

We will have a lot of fun,
When we all go out to play.

Connect

Activate Prior Knowledge
Use a Globe

Help children locate the United States and their state on a globe. Discuss the location of other countries and oceans. Show children where Panama is located in Central America. Tell them that they will learn a song from Panama. Read the title of the song with children. Ask children to share any information that they might have about drums and maracas.

Develop Language and Concepts
Present page 100.

YELLOW TAPE

Read through the lyrics on the page with children to help them understand the words. Then play Side 2 of the Yellow Tape several times and encourage children to join in singing the song. Children can clap their hands, shake a cup of paper clips, or the like in time with the song.

Together, do the Try It Out activity.

Language Awareness

Language Functions: Addressing Family Members and Friends

Focus on the words *dear Maria* in the song. Elicit from children the meaning of *dear* in the context of the song. Ask children how they address or refer to family members and friends in their native language.

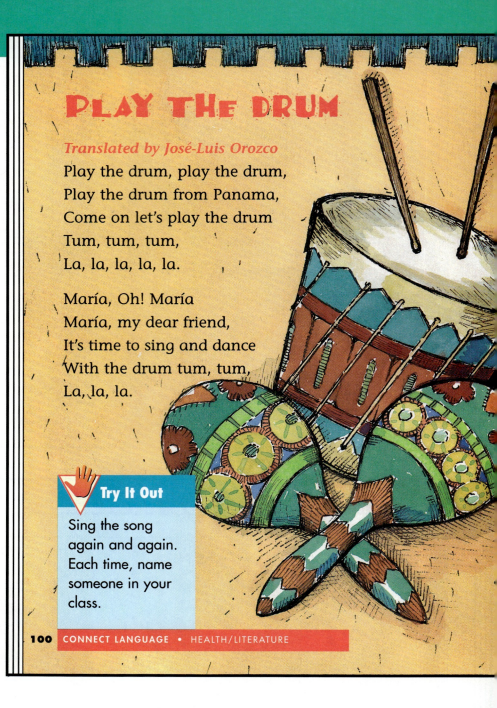

PLAY THE DRUM

Translated by José-Luis Orozco

Play the drum, play the drum,
Play the drum from Panama,
Come on let's play the drum
Tum, tum, tum,
La, la, la, la, la.

María, Oh! María
María, my dear friend,
It's time to sing and dance
With the drum tum, tum,
La, la, la.

Try It Out

Sing the song again and again. Each time, name someone in your class.

100 CONNECT LANGUAGE • HEALTH/LITERATURE

Options for Reaching All Students

Beginning
Music: Musical Instruments

Invite children to bring a musical instrument from home. Let children show and/or play their instruments.

Advanced
Writing: Advertisement

As a group, have children write and illustrate a poster advertising a performance of "Play the Drum." They are to include the time when they will perform, as well as each of their names. Then encourage the group to practice a performance that includes some dance movements.

Tell What You Learned.

1. Name something you like to do alone. Name something you like to do with a friend.

2. Draw a picture of yourself getting exercise. Label the parts of your body you are using.

3. Work in groups. Make a book of things you like to do on the playground. Tell other groups about your book.

ASSESS LANGUAGE 101

Assess

Activity 1: Evaluate whether children can name activities that they do by themselves and activities that they do with others.

Activity 2: Have children work on a piece of art paper. Evaluate whether children can identify the parts of the body they use while they get exercise.

Activity 3: Evaluate whether children can describe what they like to do on the playground.

Have children complete the Chapter Self-Assessment, BLM 31. Have them choose products to place in their portfolios. Add the results of any rubrics, checklists, self-assessments, or portfolio assessments, BLMs 2–18.

Listening Assessment

 BLACKLINE MASTER Make sure that each child has a copy of Blackline Master 61 and a pencil. Play Side 1 of the White Tape several times stopping the tape to allow children to write. Have children listen to the dictation and write what they hear.

TAPESCRIPT

 WHITE TAPE Listen carefully. Write what you hear.

You need exercise to make you strong. (pause)

Excercise can be fun. (pause)

Running, hopping, and swimming are good for your heart and lungs.

Options for Assessment

Vocabulary Assessment

 ACTIVITY BOOK Have pairs copy onto index cards the words in the box from Activity Book page 49. Then have the pairs use the cards as prompts to identify parts of the body on pictures of people. For more practice with vocabulary about parts of the body, have children complete Activity Book page 49.

Writing Assessment

 BLACKLINE MASTER Have each child fill in a T-Chart to show exercises in the left column and the body parts used in the right column. You may wish to use Blackline Master 22 in the Teacher's Resource Book.

Language Assessment

 BLACKLINE MASTER Use Blackline Master 60 in the Teacher's Resource Book.

Standardized Test Practice

 ACTIVITY BOOK Use pages 50 and 51 in the Activity Book. Answers: Everyone has more fun; You stay healthy.

Preview

Activate Prior Knowledge

Use TPR

Model actions as you say *Swim. Hop. Fly.* Then have children pantomime the actions in response to your commands. Ask them what parts of their body they used to show each movement.

Then point to the canoe on page 102. Ask children to pretend they are in a canoe, trying to cross a river. Elicit from children what people do to make boats move. Then have them pantomime rowing in response to commands, such as Row fast and Row slow. Have children join in singing "Row, Row, Row Your Boat."

Develop Language and Concepts

Present pages 102 and 103.

Explore the concept of things that move by showing real toys and Picture Cards of some things that move (airplane, bike, bus, car, fire engine) and some things that don't (cookies, sweater). Have children talk about each item and whether or not it moves. Use Picture Cards 1, 5, 10, 13, 19, 29, 68.

Help children complete the first question in Tell What You Know. List their responses on chart paper. Add to the list as you complete the chapter together.

Introduce the words in the Word Bank and help children associate the pictures with the

(Continued on page T103)

CHAPTER 6

How Things Move

102

Tell what you know.

Can you name things that move?

Where do you see them?

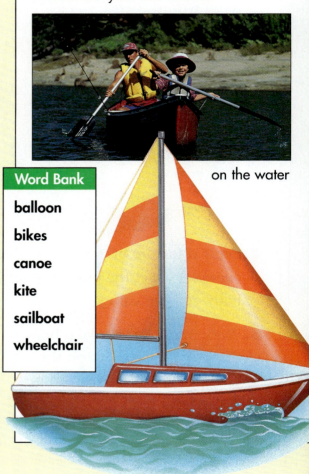

on the water

Word Bank

balloon

bikes

canoe

kite

sailboat

wheelchair

Options for Reaching All Students

Beginning

Language: Words and Pictures

Invite children to make a bulletin-board display entitled "How Things Move." Have them use magazine pictures of things that move. Help children write labels for the pictures on construction paper. Then ask children to group the pictures by air, water, or ground and arrange them on the bulletin board.

Advanced

Language: Finding Facts

Ask children to find information about the objects on the bulletin-board display entitled "How Things Move." The group can ask the school librarian to help them find books with interesting facts about the objects on display. Children can summarize the information on index cards and attach the cards to the pictures on the bulletin board.

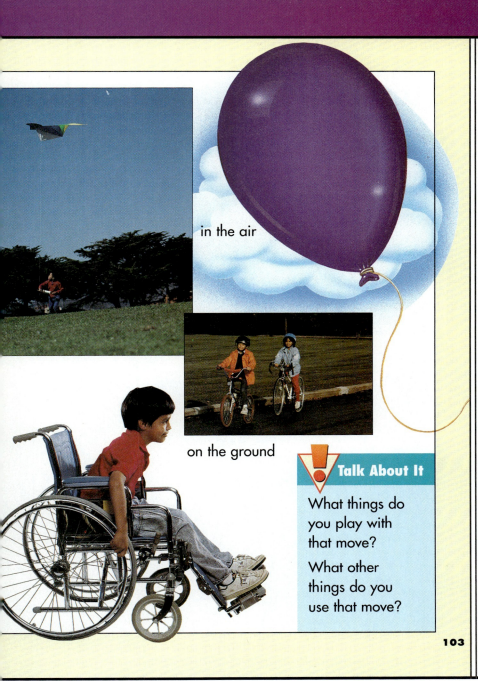

in the air

on the ground

Talk About It

What things do you play with that move?

What other things do you use that move?

In this chapter, children will learn the language connected with force, pushing, pulling, and magnets.

Use pages 102 and 103 to assess children's knowledge of how things move.

Things move in different ways.

We can make things move.

How Things Move

We use force to make things move.

We can use force to have fun.

words. Then read the captions and point to the sky, the ground, and a bowl of water. Help children do the second question in Tell What You Know. Elicit responses based on the page and on the class list.

ACTIVITY BOOK On chart paper, make a three-column chart with these categories: Air, Water, and Ground. Invite children to think of objects, including means of transportation from their countires, for each category. For more practice with phrases use Activity Book page 52.

With the class, answer the questions in Talk About It. Encourage children to describe how the objects mentioned move or which parts of the objects move. For the first question, invite children to tell about the toys they played with in their native countries.

Mixed Ability

Music: Song and Movement

TPR Use TPR to introduce or review commands such as *March. Move your thumb. Tie your shoe. Climb a tree. Close the door.* Then sing the song "The Ants Go Marching One By One." Add verses with two by two . . . tie his shoe, and so on. Encourage children to make the movements named in the lyrics and join in singing. Then invite children to work in groups of

mixed ability to make up new verses with different animals and action words.

The ants go marching one by one
   Hurrah! Hurrah!
The ants go marching one by one
   Hurrah! Hurrah!
When the ants go marching one by one
The little one stops to move his thumb,
And they all go marching down to the earth to get out of the rain—
boom, boom, boom.

Little Celebrations

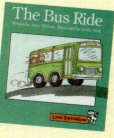

The Bus Ride

In this story, a bus keeps getting more and more crowded . . . until a bee tries to get on board.

Level: Beginning

Present

Activate Prior Knowledge
Use Realia

Place a toy car on a cleared desktop. Ask children to show different ways of moving it. Note if they push or pull it, and, if not, demonstrate push and pull. Then have children take turns using a push and/or a pull to move a pencil, a book, and a ruler.

Develop Language and Concepts
Present pages 104 and 105.

Have children look at the pictures on these pages and identify what each child is doing. Introduce the words in the Word Bank.

Read with children the questions on page 104. Brainstorm examples of familiar objects that children push or pull. Help children express their ideas in sentence form.

Model a Strategy
Use Picture Clues

Model using picture clues:

When I read and come to a question on a page where there is a picture, I look for clues in the picture. For example, when I see the question What can you push? I look at the picture for answers. I see three things I can push—a merry-go-round, a stroller, and a truck. I can name these things as answers. Do you use picture clues to help you answer questions?

What can you push and pull?

Word Bank
merry-go-round
stroller
toy
toy truck
wagon

What can you push?

What can you pull?

104 LEARN LANGUAGE • SCIENCE

Options for Reaching All Students

Beginning
Critical Thinking: Classifying

In advance, prepare magazine cut-outs of people pushing and pulling objects. Help children identify the activities pictured. Have them classify the activities as either pushing or pulling. Then ask them to paste the pictures in separate columns on art paper. Children can label the columns and the activities.

Advanced
Oral Language: Skits

Provide the group with a variety of materials to be pushed or pulled. Ask pairs of children to plan simple skits in which they represent daily life situations. For example, partners can ask each other for help in pulling or pushing heavy objects. Allow children to perform for the class.

Mixed Ability
Music: Old Song, New Words

Invite children to join in singing and pantomiming different actions for the tune of "Here We Go 'Round the Mulberry Bush." Encourage children to invent verses about pushing and pulling for the song.

This is the way we push a door,
Push a door, push a door.
This is the way we push a door,
On a cold and frosty morning.

Try It Out

Look around your classroom.

What things can you push or pull?

Phonics: Consonant Blend tr

ACTIVITY BOOK

Say this sentence as you write it on the board:

Don't trip over the toy truck.

Point to and say the words *trip* and *truck* emphasizing the /tr/. Have children repeat the words after you. Say the words again and point to the letters *tr* at the beginning of each word and explain that the two letters blend together to make *the sound* /tr/. Have a volunteer trace the letters. Introduce *train, track, tractor, tricycle,* and *tree* in same way. For practice, children can use Activity Book page 53.

Assess

Use responses to Try It Out to assess children's understanding. Children should be able to

- name two things that can be pushed
- name two things that can be pulled

LOOK AHEAD

Next, children will apply their understanding of push and pull to learn what force is.

This is the way we pull a chair,
Pull a chair, pull a chair.
This is the way we pull a chair,
On a cold and frosty morning.

This is the way we push a toy truck,
Push a toy truck, push a toy truck.
This is the way we push a toy truck,
On a cold and frosty morning.

This is the way we pull a wagon,
Pull a wagon, pull a wagon.
This is the way we pull a wagon,
On a cold and frosty morning.

Home Connection
A Push or a Pull

Ask children to talk with a family member about actions that are done in a kitchen that involve using a push or using a pull, such as opening the refrigerator, closing a cabinet door, and sweeping the floor. Have children share their findings in class.

Practice

Activate Prior Knowledge

Use Pictures

Start a discussion about what makes things move by showing the following Picture Cards: 40 kick, 68 swing. Have children describe the pictures. Ask if the people in the pictures are pushing or pulling. Introduce the word *force* and tell children that force is what makes both the swing and the ball move.

Develop Language and Concepts

Present page 106.

Ask children to describe what the boy and girl in the illustration are doing, modeling as necessary. Read the page with children. Help them discuss how we use force to push or to pull objects. For more practice, use Activity Book page 54.

Model a Strategy

Ask Questions to Get Information

Model getting information from others:

When I read and come to something I don't understand, I can ask someone for help. For example, I can ask another person in my group. When working in groups, sharing information helps everybody understand what we read. Do you like to ask questions? Why or why not?

What makes things move?

Force makes things move. You use force when you push open a door. You use force when you pull up your sock.

What have you moved today?
How did you move it?

Options for Reaching All Students

Beginning

Language: Push and Pull

Write the following lists on the board and review them. Then give children a paper folded in half. Ask them to label one side *Push* and the other *Pull*. Have children draw and write about one thing from the list for each category.

Push—door, swing, toy car
Pull—socks, wagon, pull-toy

Advanced

Writing: Directions for a Game

Teach children the following rules for a board game entitled "Push and Pull." In the game, the players use a die to advance their markers on a path. When a player lands on a square containing directions, he or she moves to the square with a picture of the action indicated. For example, if a child's marker lands on the square that says "Push a door," the child advances to

the square that shows a hand pushing a door. The player who reaches the exit first wins. When children understand how the game is played, help them to construct a board for playing the game. Have them make or draw pictures and write the corresponding directions. Then have them write game directions so that they can play the game with classmates.

Use force to move things.

Things You Need

 toy trucks masking tape

Find out about it.

1. Put 2 trucks at the starting line.

2. Use a gentle push to make the first truck go.

3. Use a hard push to make the second truck go.

My Record

When I gave the truck a gentle push

_____.

When I gave the truck a hard push

_____.

4. Use tape. Mark the place where each truck stopped.

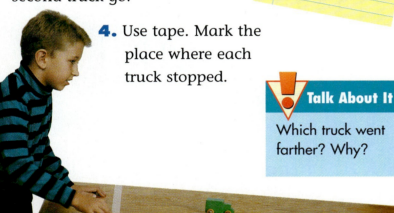

Talk About It

Which truck went farther? Why?

SCIENCE • USE LANGUAGE **107**

Develop Language and Concepts
Present page 107.

Tell children that they will be doing this experiment. Point to the pictures of the materials, and have children identify them. Help children read the page and follow the directions. Have them use the "My Record" page in the Student Book as a model to record results. When they have finished, have them compare their results and answer the questions in Talk About It with a partner.

Assess

Children should be able to

• tell how force makes things move

LOOK **AHEAD**

Next, children will explore what magnets do.

Mixed Ability
Art: Wheels and More Wheels

Have children compare pushing a toy truck and pushing an object without wheels. Help them draw conclusions. Then provide children with colored construction paper, scissors, and glue. Invite children to make the objects with wheels that they commonly push or pull.

Cooperative Learning
Science: Comparing Force and Surface

Divide the class into groups. Provide a shoe box and blocks for each. Each group is to put the blocks in the box and push the box on different surfaces, such as a bare floor, carpet, sand, and grass. Children should compare the force they need to move the box on the different surfaces and make a report.

Writers Workshop
Write About Force

Refer children to the Writer's Workshop on pages 230–236 of the Student Book. Have them write about force, using what they learned in the experiment.

Practice

Activate Prior Knowledge
Start a K-W-L Chart

Hold up a magnet as you say the word *magnet* for children to repeat after you. To find out what children know about magnets, ask questions such as:

- Have you ever used a magnet?
- What happened?

BLACKLINE MASTER Enter the information on a K-W-L chart. Copy the K-W-L chart on BLM 21 in the Teacher's Resource Book.

K: What We Know	Magnets move some things.
W: What We Want to Find Out	What kinds of things do magnets move?
L: What We Learned	

Develop Language and Concepts
Present pages 108 and 109.

Demonstrate how a magnet will move a safety pin. Invite children to take turns using the magnet to pick up the pin and then describing in a sentence what happens.

Tell children that they will experiment with a magnet and other objects. Read aloud the list of materials on page 108.

Then read the directions with children.

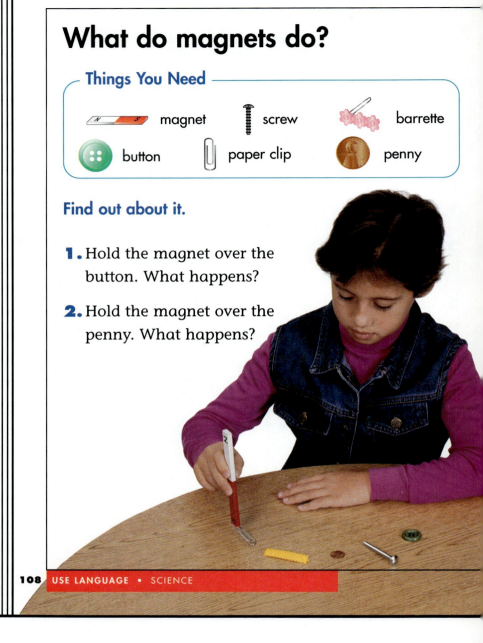

What do magnets do?

Things You Need

magnet screw barrette
button paper clip penny

Find out about it.

1. Hold the magnet over the button. What happens?
2. Hold the magnet over the penny. What happens?

108 USE LANGUAGE • SCIENCE

Options for Reaching All Students

Beginning
Critical Thinking: Categorize

Provide children with a variety of small objects that can be pasted to construction paper. Have children work in groups to make a display showing two sections: objects that magnets move and objects that magnets do not move. Let each group use magnets to sort the objects.

Advanced
Reading: More About Magnets

Invite pairs of children to read easy nonfiction books about magnets. Encourage them to find out how people use magnets in everyday life and what kinds of materials are attracted to magnets. Children can add new information to the class K-W-L chart.

Home Connection
Magnets at Home

Have the class find out how magnets are used at their own homes. Children can get information from parents or relatives and write a list. Then they can illustrate their work. At school, have children share what they learned.

3. Hold the magnet over the paper clip. What happens?

4. Hold the magnet over the screw. What happens?

5. Hold the magnet over the barrette. What happens?

Write About It

Make a chart. Next to each object, put a check under *moves* or *does not move*.

Object	Moves	Does Not Move
button		
penny		
paper clip		
screw		
barrette		

Have volunteers do each step, and let children describe what happens. Have children complete the Write About It chart found on page 55 in the Activity Book.

Then have children help you complete the K-W-L chart.

Language Awareness

Grammar: Prepositions

Set a block, book, paper, and pencil on a cleared desktop. Use TPR to demonstrate the meaning of the prepositions *over* and *under*. Then give commands and ask volunteers to do the actions. Ask other volunteers to describe the locations of objects such as, *The paper is over the book.* Repeat the process with *in* and *on*.

Assess

Assess children's understanding of what magnets do. Children should be able to

- name two objects that a magnet moves
- name two objects that a magnet doesn't move

LOOK **AHEAD**

Next, children will find out about ways in which people push and pull to have fun.

Mixed Ability

Art/Language: Puppet Show

Have two volunteers hold a large sheet of chart paper parallel to the floor. Place some clips on top of the paper. Ask a volunteer to hold a magnet under the paper and move it in different directions. Children will see how the clips move also. Invite the class to make construction-paper puppets and attach clips to them. Volunteers can use the chart paper as a puppet theater.

Children can use the magnets to make the puppets, which face the audience, move. Children can perform familiar stories or invent their own show.

QuickCheck

Negation

Check to find whether all children are using the word *not* or the contracted form *n't* after a form of the verb *do* when it is needed in a sentence. Help those who need practice complete sentences such as the following: *The button _____ move.*

Practice

Activate Prior Knowledge
Use Pantomime

Show a real skateboard or a picture. Invite children to join you on an imaginary ride. Tell them to imagine that they are going through a park with a group of friends. Along the way, model and tell how you push in order to advance. Children can pantomime riding skateboards, using one of their legs to advance. Encourage children to keep a rhythm by saying with you, *One, two, three, push! One, two, three, push!*

Develop Language and Concepts
Present pages 110 and 111.

Have volunteers describe each picture. Then read the sentences and questions on the pages, and let children answer.

Help children discuss how we use different parts of the body to push and pull. Children can share with others how they use force when they play.

Model a Strategy
Using Word Structure

Model using known words to aid decoding:

In some of these sentences, I find words I know, like push and pull. Push helps me read the word pushing, and pull helps me read the word pulling. So when I read, I can use words I know to read new and longer words.

Push and Pull for Fun

These people are having fun.

Which pictures show a push?
Who is pushing?

Which pictures show a pull?
What is pulling?

110 CONNECT LANGUAGE • SCIENCE/SOCIAL STUDIES

Options for Reaching All Students

Beginning
Writing: Repetitive Language

Have children fold art paper in three sections. Write the following sentences on the board: *I am _____. It is so much fun!* Children can copy the sentences on all three sections. Then help them fill the blanks with their favorite activities. Finally, ask children to illustrate their sentences.

Advanced
Math: Measuring Distances

Show children how to build a ramp by placing blocks under a book. Provide groups of children with blocks, books, small boxes, measuring tape, paper, and pencils. Suggest they build ramps with different inclines and push their small boxes down the ramp with the same force. Children are to measure how far each object moves and write their observations.

Multicultural Connection
Play "Tug-of-War" Games

TPR Encourage children to share pushing and pulling games from different cultures. For example, Spanish children play La Soga. In some Latin American countries children play a game similar to tug-of-war in which they "pull onions out." Allow children to teach each other to play the games.

Which picture shows a father pulling a swing?

Which picture shows a father pushing a swing?

 Think About It

Name a game you play.

Tell how you push or pull when you play.

Grammar: Present Progressive

ACTIVITY BOOK

Write the following sentence on the board: *These people are having fun.* Read it with emphasis on *are having.* Explain that these words indicate that the action is happening now. Point to the questions *Who is pushing?* and *What is pulling?* Help children answer with sentences such as *The mother is pushing the boy.* Write the sentences on the board and have volunteers read them. For practice, children can use page 56 in the Activity Book.

Assess

Use responses to Think About It for assessment. Children should be able to

- name a game they play
- tell how they push or pull when they play

LOOK **AHEAD** →

Next, children will use what they have learned about how things move to read a story written by a child about her birthday.

Cooperative Learning
Language/Art: Literature

Read to children a version of the traditional tale "The Big Turnip." In this cumulative tale, a chain of people and animals pull and pull an enormous turnip from the ground. Have children work in groups and create a series of labeled pictures that retell the story. Invite groups to exhange pictures and sequence them.

Cooperative Language Experience
On the Playground

Take children to the playground. Encourage them to note how other children are pushing and pulling the equipment as they play. As a class, write a language experience story using the children's observations.

Little Celebrations
Something New

In this story, Pup is tired of digging and wants to do something new. Pup tries many different things that other animals do, including "pulling," but soon decides that digging is just fine after all.

Level: Beginning

Connect

Activate Prior Knowledge
Brainstorm Birthday Traditions

BLACKLINE MASTER

Invite children to brainstorm what people do on their birthdays. Add the information to a web. Use the Idea Web on Blackline Master 20.

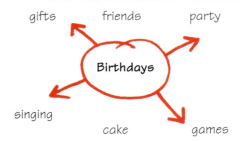

gifts   friends   party

Birthdays

singing

cake   games

Develop Language and Concepts
Present pages 112 and 113.

Ask children to describe the pictures that decorate pages 112 and 113. Ask if anyone knows what piñatas are and how they are used. Volunteers can pantomime how to break a piñata. Explain that you need to use a strong force to break it.

ACTIVITY BOOK

Tell children that they will be reading with you a selection written by a young girl. First, read the entire narration to children. Then, read it with them several times. For practice with the words in this story, children can use page 57 in the Activity Book.

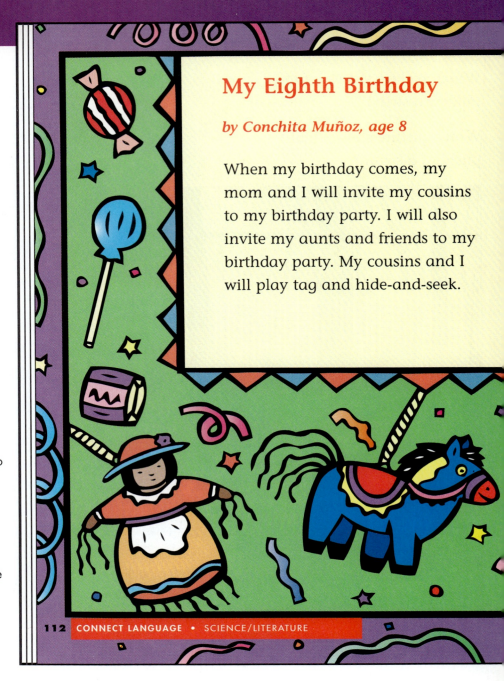

My Eighth Birthday

by Conchita Muñoz, age 8

When my birthday comes, my mom and I will invite my cousins to my birthday party. I will also invite my aunts and friends to my birthday party. My cousins and I will play tag and hide-and-seek.

112 CONNECT LANGUAGE • SCIENCE/LITERATURE

Options for Reaching All Students

Beginning
Music: Happy Birthday Song

Some children may not be familiar with the traditional "Happy Birthday" song. Write the lyrics on the board, and encourage children to sing the song with you. Then have them copy the lyrics and make a picture of their own birthday celebration.

Advanced
Writing/Art: At a Party

Invite children to imagine what an upcoming family celebration might be like. Have them use a web to brainstorm ideas. Have them write and illustrate their stories to share with the class.

Home Connection
Social Studies: Family Traditions

Have children ask their families about family traditions or special occasions that their families celebrate. Invite children to share the information with the class. They can describe who is involved and what they do.

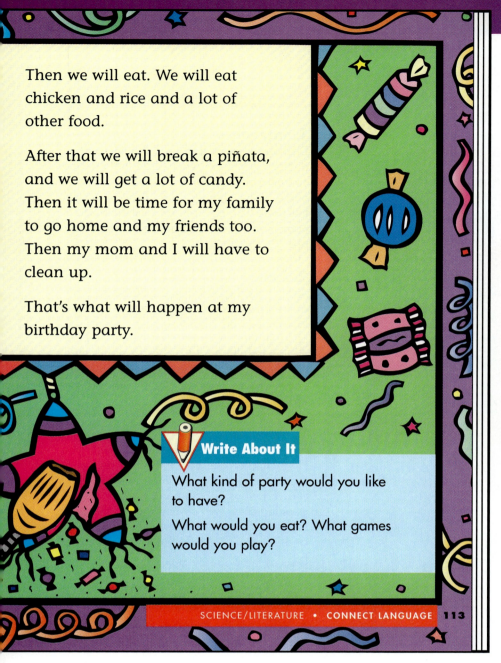

Then we will eat. We will eat chicken and rice and a lot of other food.

After that we will break a piñata, and we will get a lot of candy. Then it will be time for my family to go home and my friends too. Then my mom and I will have to clean up.

That's what will happen at my birthday party.

Write About It

What kind of party would you like to have?

What would you eat? What games would you play?

Model a Strategy

Use Context Clues

Model using context clues:

If I don't know what hide-and-seek means, I look at the other words in the sentence. I know that tag is a game and I see the word play. Hide-and-seek must be a game too. If I don't know a word, I think about the other words in the sentence to figure out what I don't know. How do you use context clues?

Language Awareness

Grammar: Future Tense

ACTIVITY BOOK Point out that some words in the story tell about events or actions that will happen in the future. Help children see that the girl is thinking about her birthday, but it has not come yet. On the board, draw a sketch of Conchita and a large thought-bubble above her head. Write these verbs inside the bubble: *will invite, will play, will eat, will break, will get.* Tell children that the bubble shows that she is thinking what she will do. Use Activity Book page 58 for practice.

Assess ✔

Children should be able to

- tell how they would like to celebrate their birthdays or other occasions
- name foods they would like to eat and games they would like to play

Peer Tutoring

Reading: Rereading the Story

Have children work in pairs of mixed abilities and reread the story together.

Multicultural Connection

Big Book of Birthdays

Have children work in small groups to make pages for a big book. Invite children to use crayons and large sheets of paper to draw a birthday party as celebrated in his or her own culture. Help each child write a brief description of their drawing at the bottom of the paper. Then help children make a cover and table of contents for the book and staple the pages together.

Each group can then share its work with the class. Because some people do not celebrate birthdays, let any child who wishes illustrate any important family event.

On the Go

by Ann Morris
photographs by Ken Heyman

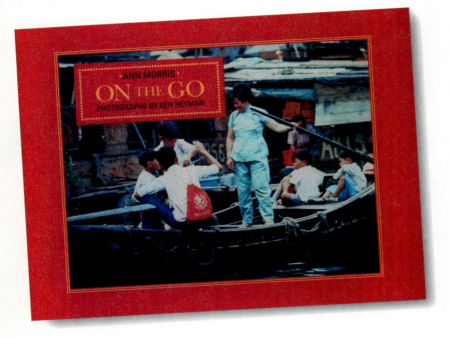

On the Go
People all over the world move from place to place, traveling in different ways.

Shared Reading

1. Introduce
Display the book and read the title and author's name. Show children that the book contains photographs and point out the name of the photographer. Browse through the book with children and ask them to name some ways people travel when they are "on the go."

2. Read
As you read aloud, invite children to look at the photographs. Pause and ask children to comment on what they see. Encourage children who have personal knowledge of the part of the world shown to share what they know. Point out that a sentence may begin on one page and continue over several pages.

3. Reread
Invite children to reread the book with you. Help children see how the writer and photographer grouped the information. They showed ways people carry things, ways people travel, ways wheels make things go faster, and ways people travel on water and in the air.

Discuss the book by asking questions.

- Where do people carry things?
- Which animals do people ride?
- What are the fastest ways people travel?

Options for Reaching All Students

Beginning
Language: Make a Mobile
Children can work in small groups to identify words that name things that go. Distribute index cards and have each child draw a picture of one means of travel. Collect the cards and use them to make a "Ways to Go" mobile.

Advanced
Critical Thinking: Make Judgments
Help children make a separate word card for each means of transportation in the book. Then let them work together to put them in order from slowest to fastest. Because some means of travel are not clearly faster or slower than others, have them tell how they made their judgments.

Mixed Abilities
Language: Tell About Traveling
Write the name of each way to travel shown in the book on a slip of paper and place it in a bag. Have one child pull a paper from the bag and read the word. Ask another child to tell whether the word names a way to travel on land, on water, or in the air. Let volunteers suggest other ways of traveling and tell whether they move on land, on water, or in the air.

Grammar: Prepostional Phrases

Help children locate phrases that tell where. Look at page 5 together and ask which words tell where people move. Help children see that the phrase *from place to place* tells where people move. Then look at page 6 and ask children to tell where people carry their baskets. Help children see that the words *over their shoulders* tells where. Continue on page 7, asking children where else people carry things and locating the words *on their heads*. Remind children to look for words that tell where when they read.

Model a Strategy
Activate Prior Knowledge

Model using what you know:

When I look through the book and read the title *On the Go*, I see that I already know something about the topic. I know how I go from place to place and how people in my family have traveled from place to place. When I read the information on these pages, I think about and compare what I know about travel with what the author writes and what the photographer shows. This helps me better understand what I read. Do you ever use prior knowledge as you read?

Response Activities

Find Action Words

As children reread the story with partners, ask them to find and list the action words. The list may include: *move, travel, ride, go, pedaled, pushed, pulled, hurries, carry, row.* Invite pairs to write new sentences for five words on their list.

Look at Photographs for Information

Look through the book with children and discuss details in the photographs. Help children name ways to travel. Invite children to take turns retelling information they learned using the photographs for help.

Reread the Story

Use a paper to cover a word on each page that names a way to travel. Reread the story and when you come to the word, ask children to predict the word using clues from the sentence and picture. Let children see the initial letter, blend, or digraph first so that they can check to see whether their guess is the word the author used.

FYI Monorails

A monorail is an electric railway whose cars run on a single track. Monorails were first used in Germany at the turn of the century. One advantage to their use is that they are relatively quiet.

Peer Tutoring
Social Studies: Work Animals

Pair children of mixed abilities and invite them to work together to make a list of the different work animals shown in the book. Encourage them to add other work animals they may know about.

Home Connection
Plan a Trip

Ask children to tell a family member about the book *On the Go* and work together to plan a pretend trip. They should decide which way they would travel and make a list of things they would take along on their trip.

Multicultural Awareness
People and Places

Share the index for *On the Go* with children. As you identify each location by reading the text in the index, turn back to the page in the book and ask children what differences and similarities (other than the modes of transportation) they see between places shown. Help volunteers locate the various countries on the map on page 32.

Connect

Activate Prior Knowledge
Review Vocabulary

Review *pulling* and *pushing* by helping children read the title. Ask them to describe what the boys and girls in the picture are doing. Introduce the word *kingdom* as land governed by a king or queen.

Develop Language and Concepts
Present page 114.

YELLOW TAPE

Read through the chant on the page with children. Explain that the word *you* refers to two different people—one person pushes while the other person pulls. Then play Side 2 of the Yellow Tape several times and encourage children to join in. Have children follow the Try It Out suggestion.

Language Awareness

Grammar: Imperatives

TPR

Model the actions as you say these commands: *Brush your teeth. Jump.* Then encourage children to pantomime the actions in response to your commands. Write simple imperative sentences on the board. Ask volunteers to underline the action words in each. Ask who is expected to do each action. Point out that the word *you* is understood and there is no ending such as -s, -ed, or -ing on the verb.

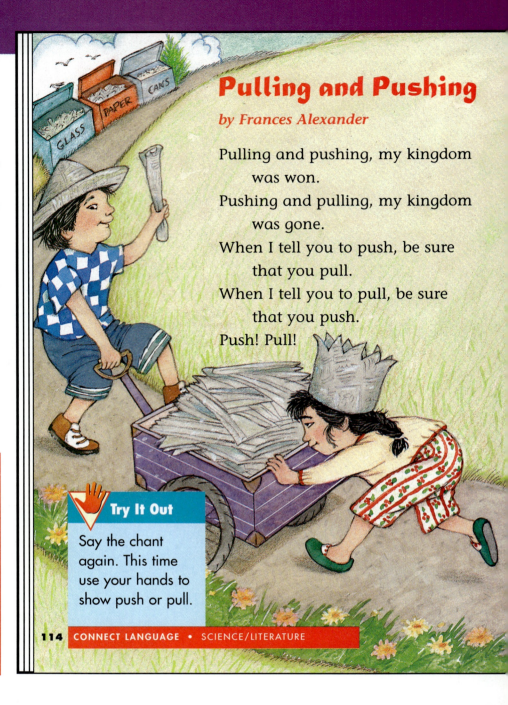

Pulling and Pushing
by Frances Alexander

Pulling and pushing, my kingdom
    was won.
Pushing and pulling, my kingdom
    was gone.
When I tell you to push, be sure
    that you pull.
When I tell you to pull, be sure
    that you push.
Push! Pull!

Try It Out

Say the chant again. This time use your hands to show push or pull.

114   CONNECT LANGUAGE • SCIENCE/LITERATURE

Options for Reaching All Students

Beginning
Art: Crowns for Kings and Queens

Provide children with construction paper, scissors, glitter, and glue. Suggest that children make crowns and pretend they are kings and queens of the kingdom mentioned in the poem. Invite all the "kings" and "queens" to wear their crowns and recite the chant.

Advanced
Phonics: Rhyming in a Song

TPR

Copy the lyrics of the song "Ring-a-Ring O'Roses" on chart paper. Invite children to join in singing this traditional song, holding hands in a circle. They can bow, kneel, and fall down when indicated. Then read through the lyrics with children, and have them listen to and look for rhyming words.

Ring-a-ring o'roses,
A pocket full of posies,
Hush-a! Hush-a! We all fall down.
The king has sent his daughter
To fetch a pail of water,
Hush-a! Hush-a! All bow down.
The bird upon the steeple
Sits high above the people,
Hush-a! Hush-a! All kneel down.

Tell what you learned.

1. Tell a friend about some things you play with that move.

2. Work in groups. Take turns moving things. Have your classmates describe your movements.

3. Draw a picture to show what the children did to break the piñata. Describe your picture.

Assess ✓

Activity 1: Evaluate on number and accuracy of responses.

Activity 2: Evaluate whether children can name objects that they can push and objects that they can pull.

Activity 3: Check that children showed a child hitting the piñata with a stick. They should indicate that children in the story used a strong force.

Have children complete the Chapter Self-Assessment, Blackline Master 31. Have them choose products to place in their portfolios. Add the results of any rubrics, checklists, self-assessments, or portfolio assessments, Blackline Masters 2–18.

Listening Assessment

BLACKLINE MASTER

Make sure that each child has a copy of Blackline Master 63 and crayons. Play Side 1 of the White Tape several times stopping the tape to allow children to answer.

TAPESCRIPT

WHITE TAPE

Listen carefully. Follow the directions.

Anita and Leon are having fun on the swings. Two friends join them. One friend is pushing one swing. Another friend is pulling the other swing. Draw a blue circle around the friend who is pushing a swing. (pause) Draw a red circle around the friend who is pulling a swing.

Options for Assessment

Vocabulary Assessment

ACTIVITY BOOK

Prepare twelve cards, each with one of the following phrases: *in the air, on the water, on the ground.* Have groups of three play the bingo game on Activity Book page 59. Children take turns drawing a card from a face-down pile. If the card reads *in the air,* for example, the child places a marker on any appropriate square. When someone has four markers in a row, that child names the objects he or she has covered.

Writing Assessment

BLACKLINE MASTER

Have groups fill in a Venn Diagram, Blackline Master 23. Have groups label one circle *Push* and the other circle *Pull.* Ask them to write things they push, inside the Push circle. Have them write things they pull, inside the Pull circle. Then ask them to write things they can push or pull inside the overlapping circle area.

Language Assessment

BLACKLINE MASTER

Use Blackline Master 62 in the Teacher's Resource Book.

Standardized Test Practice

ACTIVITY BOOK

Use pages 60 and 61 in the Activity Book. Answers: 33, 13, 28.

Wrap-Up

Activities

Fun With Music

Provide paper streamers and any other props for children to use as they dance. For example, play the songs "Play the Drum," "Yankee Doodle," "Mary Had a Little Lamb," and "Twinkle, Twinkle, Little Star." Encourage children to move around the room following the rhythm in each song. Then have children comment on the different movements and how it felt to move to each song.

Large Body Images

Ask children to work with a partner. On large sheets of chart paper, have partners take turns tracing the other's body with a crayon. Then each child draws his or her face, hands, shoes, clothes, and so on to finish the picture. Children can work together to label different parts of the body. Ask partners to present their work to the class.

Survey and Graph

Have children ask friends and family members what is their favorite way to exercise. Have them list the responses and create a class bar graph. Children can use chart paper and markers to show the data. Let children comment on the results.

Discussing the Theme

Have children work in groups of two or three to discuss their progress during this unit about motion. Choose from the following activities that will demonstrate to them how much they have learned.

- Tape record two lists of words learned (exercises and parts of the body).

- Put drawings or magazine cutouts into boxes labeled "My Toy Box." Have children label the pictures as much as possible. They can indicate how they play with each toy, such as if they push or pull the toy. Use Picture Cards you've used in the unit.

- Play a game in which a child in one group holds up a picture of an object that moves and a child in the other group tells where it moves. For example, a child in Group A holds up a picture of a sailboat, and a child in Group B says, "A sailboat moves on water."

- Have children in groups role-play situations in which they add or subtract numbers of toys. For example, one child makes up a problem such as "I play with one balloon. She plays with two. How many balloons are there in all?" Another child responds, "There are three balloons in all."

Sharing the Unit Project

Use the invitation form, Blackline Master 32 or 33, to invite family members to school to see the folk dance festival.

Set up the classroom so that family members can sit down to enjoy the show. Make sure that the decorations are in place.

You may want to have a few parents arrive early to help children with their costumes. They can also help with playing the music and assisting children as necessary.

As the show begins, you may want to make a brief introduction and then let the master of ceremonies introduce the show.

Suggest to parents that they take pictures or make a video of the dance festival for children to bring to school. Plan time for children to share some of their pictures and make comments about them.

Signs of Success!

Duplicate a copy of this checklist for each child.

Name: _____

Refer to the checklist below for a quick determination of how a child is progressing toward transitioning out of ESL instruction.

Objectives:

- ☐ Names toys and games.
- ☐ Names ways to play alone.
- ☐ Names ways to play with friends.
- ☐ Tells how to get exercise while playing.
- ☐ Tells how exercise is good for you.

- ☐ Tells parts of the body used with exercises.
- ☐ Tells what things can be pushed or pulled.
- ☐ Understands what force is.
- ☐ Tells what magnets can do.

Language Awareness:

Understands/Uses:

- ☐ present progressive tense
- ☐ irregular past tense
- ☐ future tense
- ☐ pronouns
- ☐ adjectives

- ☐ contractions
- ☐ forms of address
- ☐ prepositions
- ☐ imperatives

Hears/Pronounces/Reads:

- ☐ final consonant s /z/
- ☐ consonant blend *tr*

- ☐ long *i*

Learning Strategies:

- ☐ Visualizes text for meaning.
- ☐ Recognizes cause and effect.
- ☐ Uses pictures for meaning.

- ☐ Asks questions for information.
- ☐ Uses word structure for decoding.
- ☐ Uses context clues.

Comments

_____

_____

Planning Guide

CHAPTER 7

Plants We Eat

Objectives

Name the parts of plants.

Tell what each part of a plant does.

Name plants we eat.

Tell which parts of plants we eat.

Name grains and foods made from grains.

Vocabulary Focus

Fruits and vegetables, such as *carrot, celery, peach, strawberry.*

Parts of plants, such as *flower, fruit, leaf, stem.*

Science project words, such as *grow, record, watch.*

Grains and foods from grains, such as *corn, noodles, tortilla, wheat.*

Lesson	Content Focus	Language Awareness Objectives	Learning Strategies
Preview pages 116–117 Tell what you know.			
Present pages 118–119 What are the parts of a plant?	Science	**Phonics** Consonant Blends *st, str*	Use pictures for meaning.
Practice pages 120–121 You can grow a plant.	Science	**Vocabulary** *a few, a lot (of)*	Understand that numerals show sequence.
Practice pages 122–123 What parts of plants do we eat?	Science	**Grammar** Count vs. Noncount Nouns	Find a way to classify.
Connect pages 124–125 Grains Around the World	Science/ Social Studies	**Grammar** Passive Expressions	Locate patterns.
Connect pages 126–137 *Bread Is for Eating*	Science/ Literature	**Grammar** Sentence Patterns **Grammar** Verbs **Grammar** Nouns and Verbs	Understand a process. Explain a process. Summarize.
Connect page 138 "Oats, Peas, Beans, and Barley Grow"	Science/ Literature	**Phonics** Letter-Sound Correspondence *ow, oa*	
Assess page 139 Tell what you learned.			

CHAPTER 8

Where We Buy Food

Objectives

Tell about where fruits and vegetables are raised.

Name places where foods are purchased.

Tell which foods can be purchased at which places.

Name different kinds of restaurants.

Vocabulary Focus

Food stores, such as *bakery, famers' market, grocery store, supermarket.*

Places to eat, such as *restaurant, cafeteria, fast-food restaurant.*

Recipe words, such as *series, ingredients, directions.*

Lesson	Content Focus	Language Awareness Objectives	Learning Strategies
Preview pages 140–141 Tell what you know.			
Present pages 142–143 Food from Farms	Social Studies	**Vocabulary** Phrases	Preview text.
Practice pages 144–145 From Farms to Customers	Social Studies	**Spelling** Capitalization	Monitor meaning.
Practice pages 146–147 Let's Eat	Social Studies	**Language Functions** Making Requests	Plan to read orally.
Connect pages 148–149 Would would you do if. . . ?	Social Studies/ Math	**Vocabulary** Numerals and Number Words	Use pictures and text to predict.
Connect pages 150–151 Lee's Market	Social Studies/ Literature	**Grammar** Possessives	Use context clues.
Connect page 152 Growing Song	Social Studies/ Literature	**Grammar** Pronouns	
Assess page 153 Tell what you learned.			

Resources

Chapter 7

Support Materials

PICTURE CARDS
Numbers 2, 4, 33, 42, 49, 51, 67, 72

ACTIVITY BOOK
Pages 62–71

VIDEO
Unit 4, Plants

GREEN TAPE
Side 1
Bread Is for Eating, pages T126–T137

GREEN TAPE
Side 2
"Oats, Peas, Beans, and Barley Grow," page T138

Little Celebrations Library

Potatoes on Tuesday by Dee Lillegard, ScottForesman, 1993.

This Is the Seed by Alan Trussell-Cullen, ScottForesman, 1993.

Assessment Materials

CREAM TAPE
Side 1
Listening Assessment, page T139

BLACKLINE MASTER
Language Assessment, page 70
Listening Assessment, page 71

Newcomer Book A

Survival language for absolute beginners. For overview, see pages xxviii–xxxi.

For Extended Reading

A Garden Alphabet by Isabel Wilner, Dutton, 1991.
An alphabet book in rhyme telling about gardening. Detailed illustrations good for discussion.
Level: Advanced

Jack's Garden by Henry Cole, Greenwillow Books, 1995.
A rhythmic and cumulative story about a garden with many labeled pictures of tools, insects, flowers, and other gardening-related things.
Level: Average

The Little Red Hen by Byron Barton, HarperCollins, 1993.
A simple telling of the classic tale.
Level: Beginning

Mealtime by Zoë Davenport, Ticknor & Fields, 1995.
A simple vocabulary book for foods and other mealtime items.
Level: Beginning

Potluck by Anne Shelby, Orchard Books, 1991.
A multi-ethnic alphabet book of foods at a potluck supper.
Level: Average

The Tale of Peter Rabbit by Beatrix Potter, Platt & Munk, 1990.
The classic tale about the misbehaving rabbit.
Level: Advanced

Related Technology

Earthcare Interactive, Wayzata Technology, 1994.
Emphasize reading skills and caring for the earth.

Chapter 8

Support Materials

PICTURE CARDS
Numbers 2, 4, 8, 11, 14, 15, 19, 25, 29, 33, 34, 36, 37, 38, 42, 44, 49, 52, 54, 56, 57, 59, 60, 66, 70, 72

ACTIVITY BOOK
Pages 72–81

VIDEO
Unit 4, Plants

GREEN TAPE
Side 2
"Get 'Em Here," page T147
"Growing Song," page T152

Shared Reading Collection

The Cake That Mack Ate by Rose Robart, ScottForesman, 1989.

Little Celebrations Library

A Tasty Bug by Sarah Tatler, ScottForesman, 1993.

Noggin and Bobbin in the Garden by Olivier Dunrea, ScottForesman, 1993.

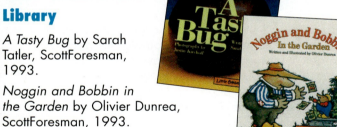

Assessment Materials

CREAM TAPE
Side 1
Listening Assessment, page T153

BLACKLINE MASTER
Language Assessment, page 80
Listening Assessment, page 81

For Extended Reading

A Fruit and Vegetable Man by Roni Schotter, Little, Brown & Co., 1993.

Sun Ho watches Ruby, the fruit and vegetable man, set up his market. The two become friends.

Level: Advanced

Garden by Zoë Davenport, Ticknor & Fields, 1995.

A simple vocabulary book for things found in a garden.

Level: Beginning

The Pumpkin Patch by Elizabeth King, Dutton, 1990.

A photo essay with information about pumpkins from preparing the soil for seeds to making a jack-o-lantern.

Level: Advanced

The Tiny Seed by Eric Carle, Picture Book Studio, 1987.

The reader travels with a tiny seed across the land and through the seasons.

Level: Beginning

Truck Song by Diane Siebert, Harper Trophy, 1986.

Trucks transporting goods journey from place to place.

Level: Average

What It's Like to Be a Farmer by Morgan Matthews, Troll Associates, 1990.

A look at the life of a farmer with labeled pictures of farm buildings, machinery, and the like.

Level: Average

Related Technology

James Discovers Math, Broderbund/Active Mind Series, 1995.

Visit a market and hone math skills.

Project

A Garbage Garden

This optional project can be completed over the next two chapters. See the Unit Wrap Up, page T153a, for more ideas on sharing the project with family members.

What You'll Need

Collect the following kinds of items for your garden:

Containers:
- milk cartons
- shallow frozen food pans
- wide-mouthed glass jars (some with a lid)

Soil:
- dirt
- pebbles
- sand

Plants:
- carrot, pineapple, and beet tops
- avocado pits
- mung beans
- sweet potatoes

Other:
- toothpicks

Beginning the Project

Describe the Garbage Garden project to children. Talk about how they will be planting and caring for plants. Explain that they will be asked to bring things from home to help with the project. They will want to know that at the end of the project their families will be invited to see what they have done.

Home Involvement

Send Letter Home, Blackline Master 64 in the Teacher's Resource Book, to families to solicit their participation in collecting the "garbage" needed for the garden project.

Planting and Caring for the Garden

Encourage children to bring in the plants after containers and soil are collected. Lead children in discussing the procedures and help them label each plant with its name and the date planted.

Have children take turns caring for the plants and monitoring their progress. Some children might enjoy measuring growth and keeping a graph of results.

Daily Discussion

Take a few minutes each day for discussion to practice vocabulary learned in conjunction with the garbage garden. At the end of the unit have children draw conclusions about how plants grow (or why some plants did not grow). See page T153a for ideas about sharing the garden with families and friends when the unit is completed.

Avocado

- Let pit dry for 24 hours.
- Peel off outer brown skin.
- Insert toothpicks to hold pointed end of pit out of water.
- When root appears (in about a week), transplant into a container with at least an inch of dirt over the pit.

Carrots or Beets

- Fill bottom of shallow pan with pebbles.
- Put carrot or beet tops in the pan and cover with water.
- Place in a sunny area.
- Keep well watered. They should sprout in 2 or 3 weeks.

Sweet Potato

- Insert toothpicks to hold sweet potato away from bottom of jar.
- Fill jar 2/3 full of water.
- Keep in dimly lit place until sprouts appear (in about a week).
- Move to stronger light.
- Change water often.

Mung Beans

- Wash beans and soak overnight in cold water.
- Drain and put them in a jar with holes punched in the lid.
- Keep in a dark place.
- Rinse beans twice daily.
- Sprouts should appear in about 5 days.

Pineapple

- Dry the top of a pineapple plant on its side for 3 or 4 days.
- Plant it in sand.
- Keep the sand moist.

Activity Book

Chapter 7

Name ______________________

In the Garden

Finish the words. Use *st* or *str*.
Color the garden.

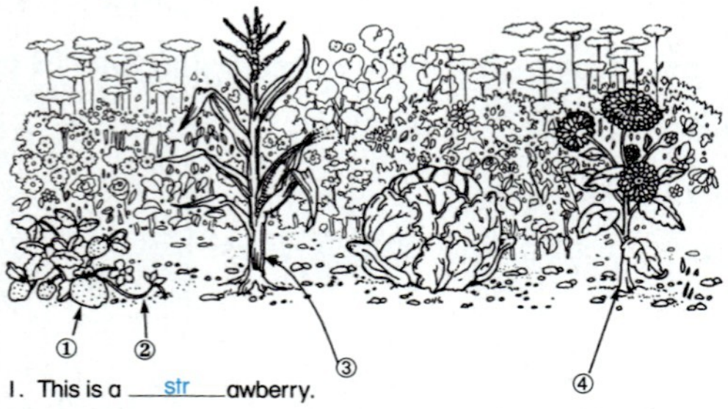

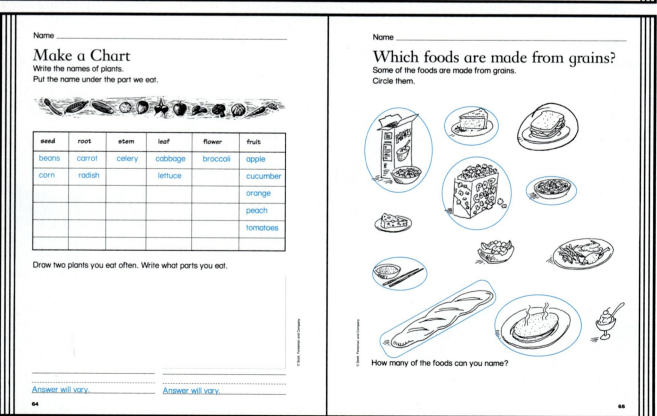

1. This is a __str__awberry.
2. This is the __st__em of the __str__awberry plant.
3. This is the __st__alk of the corn.
4. This is the __st__em of the flower.

What plants do you see in the garden? Make a list. Answers may vary.

flower | cabbage
corn | strawberry

© Scott, Foresman and Company

Name ______________________

How many are there?

Complete the sentences. Use *a few* or *a lot of*.

1. Avi has __a few__ seeds.

2. Magda's plant has __a lot of__ leaves.

3. Iris's cactus has __a few__ flowers.

Draw a plant. Answers will vary.

My plant has ________ leaves.

© Scott, Foresman and Company

Name ______________________

Make a Chart

Write the names of plants.
Put the name under the part we eat.

seed	root	stem	leaf	flower	fruit
beans	carrot	celery	cabbage	broccoli	apple
corn	radish		lettuce		cucumber
					orange
					peach
					tomatoes

Draw two plants you eat often. Write what parts you eat.

Answer will vary. | Answer will vary.

© Scott, Foresman and Company

Name ______________________

Which foods are made from grains?

Some of the foods are made from grains.
Circle them.

How many of the foods can you name?

© Scott, Foresman and Company

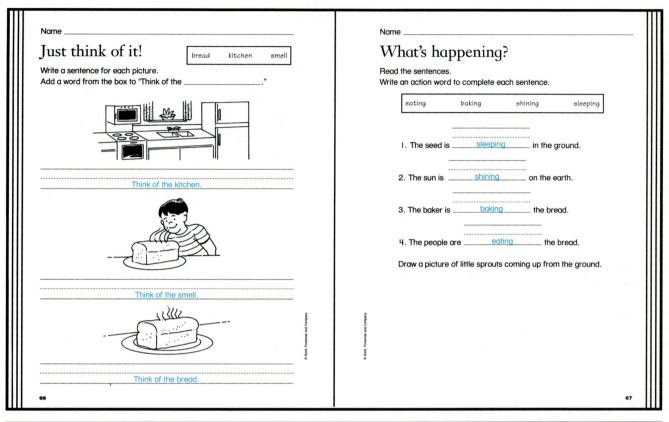

Just think of it!

bread   kitchen   smell

Write a sentence for each picture.
Add a word from the box to "Think of the _____."

Think of the kitchen.

Think of the smell.

Think of the bread.

66

What's happening?

Read the sentences.
Write an action word to complete each sentence.

eating   baking   shining   sleeping

1. The seed is _____ sleeping _____ in the ground.

2. The sun is _____ shining _____ on the earth.

3. The baker is _____ baking _____ the bread.

4. The people are _____ eating _____ the bread.

Draw a picture of little sprouts coming up from the ground.

67

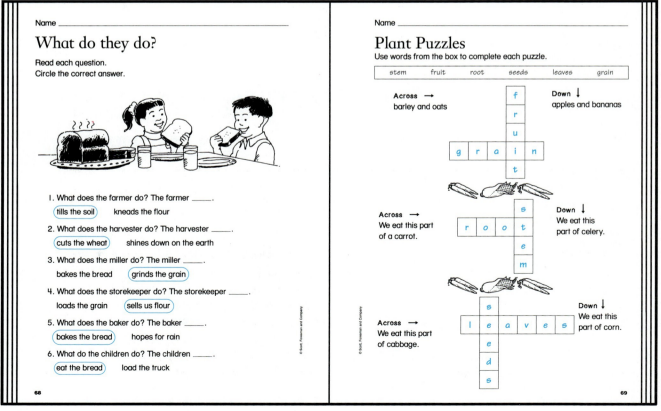

What do they do?

Read each question.
Circle the correct answer.

1. What does the farmer do? The farmer _____.
   (tills the soil)   kneads the flour

2. What does the harvester do? The harvester _____.
   (cuts the wheat)   shines down on the earth

3. What does the miller do? The miller _____.
   bakes the bread   (grinds the grain)

4. What does the storekeeper do? The storekeeper _____.
   loads the grain   (sells us flour)

5. What does the baker do? The baker _____.
   (bakes the bread)   hopes for rain

6. What do the children do? The children _____.
   (eat the bread)   load the truck

68

Plant Puzzles

Use words from the box to complete each puzzle.

stem   fruit   root   seeds   leaves   grain

Across →
barley and oats

Down ↓
apples and bananas

f
r
u
g r a i n
t

Across →
We eat this part of a carrot.

Down ↓
We eat this part of celery.

s
r o o t
e
m

Across →
We eat this part of cabbage.

Down ↓
We eat this part of corn.

s
l e a v e s
e
d
s

69

Activity Book

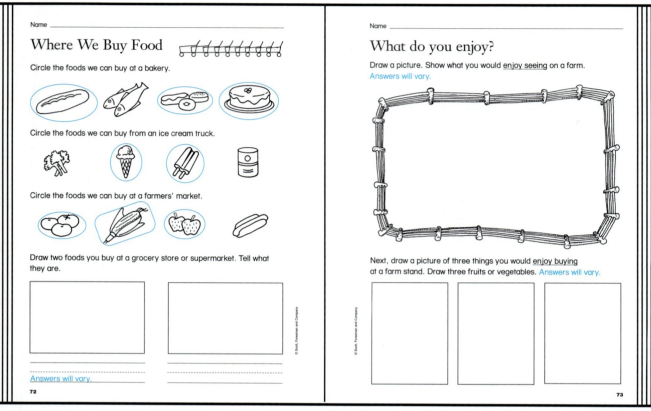

Name _____

Where We Buy Food

Circle the foods we can buy at a bakery.

Circle the foods we can buy from an ice cream truck.

Circle the foods we can buy at a farmers' market.

Draw two foods you buy at a grocery store or supermarket. Tell what they are.

Answers will vary.

72

Name _____

What do you enjoy?

Draw a picture. Show what you would enjoy seeing on a farm.
Answers will vary.

Next, draw a picture of three things you would enjoy buying at a farm stand. Draw three fruits or vegetables. Answers will vary.

73

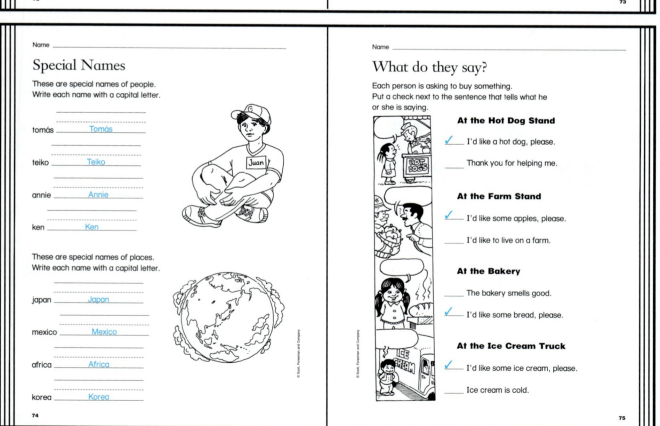

Name _____

Special Names

These are special names of people.
Write each name with a capital letter.

tomás _____ Tomás

teiko _____ Teiko

annie _____ Annie

ken _____ Ken

These are special names of places.
Write each name with a capital letter.

japan _____ Japan

mexico _____ Mexico

africa _____ Africa

korea _____ Korea

74

Name _____

What do they say?

Each person is asking to buy something.
Put a check next to the sentence that tells what he or she is saying.

At the Hot Dog Stand

✓ I'd like a hot dog, please.

___ Thank you for helping me.

At the Farm Stand

✓ I'd like some apples, please.

___ I'd like to live on a farm.

At the Bakery

___ The bakery smells good.

✓ I'd like some bread, please.

At the Ice Cream Truck

✓ I'd like some ice cream, please.

___ Ice cream is cold.

75

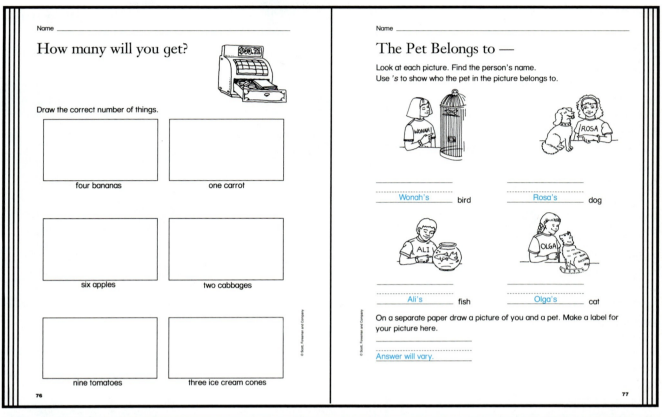

How many will you get?

Draw the correct number of things.

four bananas	one carrot
six apples	two cabbages
nine tomatoes	three ice cream cones

76

© Scott, Foresman and Company

The Pet Belongs to —

Look at each picture. Find the person's name.
Use 's to show who the pet in the picture belongs to.

__Wonah's__ bird

__Rosa's__ dog

__Ali's__ fish

__Olga's__ cat

On a separate paper draw a picture of you and a pet. Make a label for your picture here.

__Answer will vary.__

77

© Scott, Foresman and Company

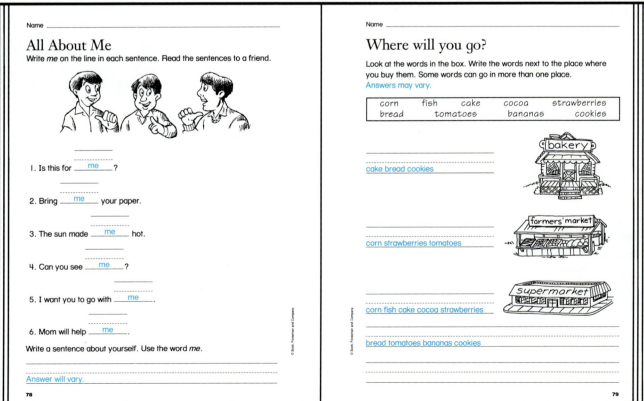

All About Me

Write *me* on the line in each sentence. Read the sentences to a friend.

1. Is this for __me__ ?

2. Bring __me__ your paper.

3. The sun made __me__ hot.

4. Can you see __me__ ?

5. I want you to go with __me__ .

6. Mom will help __me__ .

Write a sentence about yourself. Use the word *me*.

__Answer will vary.__

78

© Scott, Foresman and Company

Where will you go?

Look at the words in the box. Write the words next to the place where you buy them. Some words can go in more than one place.
Answers may vary.

corn	fish	cake	cocoa	strawberries
bread	tomatoes		bananas	cookies

bakery

__cake bread cookies__

farmers' market

__corn strawberries tomatoes__

supermarket

__corn fish cake cocoa strawberries__

__bread tomatoes bananas cookies__

79

© Scott, Foresman and Company

Preview

Activate Prior Knowledge
Use Pictures

Start discussion of "plants we eat" by showing pictures of fruits and helping children name them. Have children answer the first question in Tell What You Know, naming the fruits they like to eat. Use Picture Cards 2, 4, 33, 42, 49, 51, 67, 72.

For the second question, in Tell What You Know, invite children to tell where their families get fruits. Use Picture Cards 29, 31, 33.

Develop Language and Concepts
Present pages 116 and 117.

Invite children to look at each picture and help them describe what it shows. Present key words including *strawberry, plant, farm, pick, store/market, eat.*

Explain the process of how plants get to our tables. Help children understand that the steps happen in a certain order or sequence. You might set up three areas to represent a farm, a market or store, and a table in a home and move a small toy vehicle from area to area, as you explain the process:

1. Farmers plant the strawberries.
2. The strawberries grow in fields.
3. Farmers pick the strawberries.
4. Trucks take the strawberries to a market.

(Continued on page T117)

Plants We Eat

Tell what you know.

Do you like eating fruit?

Where do we get the fruit we eat?

116

Options for Reaching All Students

Beginning
Language: Words and Pictures

Write the following words on the board and read them: *strawberry, farmer, plant, eat.* Have children take a sheet of paper and fold it into four sections. Have them copy one word in each of the four sections and illustrate it.

Advanced
Language: Picture Story

Have children choose another plant and draw pictures to show how it gets to market, using the pictures on pages 116 and 117 as a guide. Help children caption their stories.

Peer Tutoring
Language: Identifying Fruits

Give pairs of children of mixed abilities the following Picture Cards with fruits: 2 apple, 4 bananas, 33 grapes, 42 lemons, 49 orange, 51 pears, 67 strawberries, 72 watermelon. Children use the cards as flashcards and work together until both can identify all the fruits.

In this chapter, children will learn the language connected with plants and growing, as well as investigate the parts of plants people eat.

Use pages 116 and 117 to assess children's knowledge of the process of growing plants and getting them to market.

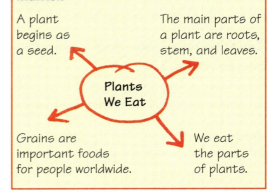

A plant begins as a seed.

The main parts of a plant are roots, stem, and leaves.

Plants We Eat

Grains are important foods for people worldwide.

We eat the parts of plants.

5. People buy the strawberries at the market.

6. People eat the strawberries at home.

Then have children act out the process, taking the various roles: farmer, truck driver, seller in a market, family buying strawberries. Encourage them to use as much English as they can.

With the class, answer the questions in Talk About It. Then have children work in groups of three to share their personal answers.

Strawberries $1.49/pint

Talk About It

How do strawberries get to your table?

What other fruits can you name?

117

Mixed Ability
Video: Plants

Show children the video to help build background knowledge on the unit theme. You may also choose to use the video in other ways that are appropriate during the unit.

Home Connection
From Fields of Wheat to House Plants

Have children interview family members about their experiences with plants of any kind. Children can share the stories with the class.

Cooperative Learning
Talk About Fruit

Have children work in groups to brainstorm a list of fruits they like. Encourage each group to choose a fruit to bring to class. Ask groups to bring enough fruit to share with the rest of the class. Ask groups to prepare a "show and tell" presentation for the class which includes where they got the fruit and a description of the fruit using the senses taste, touch, see, and smell.

Present

Brainstorm Vocabulary

Brainstorm a list of plants that children know to assess their knowledge of plants and plant vocabulary. Write their suggestions on chart paper. Add to the list during the unit.

Develop Language and Concepts

Present Page 118.

Have children look at the page and identify the plants they know. Read the labels with them. Then help children associate the words with the plants. Then help them form sentences to describe the plants.

Language Awareness

Phonics: Consonant Blends *st, str*

TPR

Write these words on the board and model their pronunciation: *stem* and *strawberry*.

Present this TPR activity, having children give and follow the commands that contain examples of the blends:

Stand up straight and tall as a tree.
Stretch your arms as high as can be.
Stop stretching now and stoop down low.
Touch the ground, where strawberries grow.

ACTIVITY BOOK For practice with these blends, children can use Activity Book page 62.

What are the parts of a plant?

Name each plant.

What parts of each plant do you see?

◀ coconut palm

▲ broccoli

◀ corn   ▲ cabbage   ▲ rice

118 LEARN LANGUAGE • SCIENCE

Options for Reaching All Students

Beginning

Language: Chant

TPR

Give children cards and have them write the name of a part of a plant on each one. Present the following chant. When children hear or say the word on their card, they are to hold it up.

Fruit, flowers, leaves.
Stem, trunk.
Fruit, flowers, leaves.

Advanced

Social Studies: Climates

Work with children to identify the climates where the plants pictured on page 118 grow. For example:

Rice grows in wet places.
Coconuts grow in warm places.

Have children work in pairs and make picture books about where plants grow, using sentences like those in the examples as captions.

fruit ▲

leaves ▲

trunk ▶

roots ▼

The parts of plants
do different things.

Plants need water to live.
Roots take water from
the ground.

The trunk of a tree is a stem.
Stems carry water from the roots
to other parts of plants.

Plants need food too.
Leaves make food from sunlight.

? Think About It

Why do plants need roots?

What do the leaves of plants do?

SCIENCE • LEARN LANGUAGE 119

Develop Language and Concepts
Present Page 119.

Help children locate the parts of the tree
(roots, trunk, leaves, fruit) in the picture.
Read the page with them. Check comprehension with questions such as:

- What do the roots of plants do?
- What part of the plant makes food?

Model a Strategy
Use Pictures for Meaning

Model using pictures for meaning:

When I read, I look at the pictures to help me
figure out the meaning of words. I can use
the labels on the picture to understand the
meaning of leaves, fruit, trunk, and roots.
When I read the word leaves, the picture of
leaves helps me see them in my head. When
do you use pictures to help with meaning?

Assess ✓

Use responses to Think About It for assessment. Children should be able to

- name the parts of a plant
- tell what the various plant parts do

LOOK AHEAD

**Next, children will use the vocabulary
they learned here to understand how a
plant grows from a seed.**

Cooperative Language Experience
Field Trip

Take children on a walk through the
neighborhood near the school. Help
them identify plants and parts of
plants.

As a class, write a language experience story about the trip. Children can
draw and label pictures of what they
saw.

Mixed Ability
Writing: Invent a Plant

Have each child invent a plant and
make a drawing of it. Have them label
its parts.

QuickCheck

Plural Forms

Check whether children are forming
plurals correctly. Help those who need
practice form the plurals of the names
of plants and parts of plants. Point out
that corn and rice do not have plural
forms.

Practice

Activate Prior Knowledge
Start a K-W-L Chart

Find out what children know about growing plants. Ask questions such as these:

- Have you ever grown a plant?
- What did you do first?

Use the information and Blackline Master 21 in the Teacher's Resource Book to make a K-W-L chart:

Complete the chart when the lesson is finished.

K: What We Know	Plants grow from seeds. We plant seeds in the ground.
W: What We Want to Find Out	Which part of a plant grows first?
L: What We Learned	

Develop Language and Concepts
Present pages 120 and 121.

Read the activity with children. Then they can perform the activity individually or in groups. Have them retell the steps that they need to do before they begin the activity. Have children use My Record on page 121 in the Student Book as a model to record results.

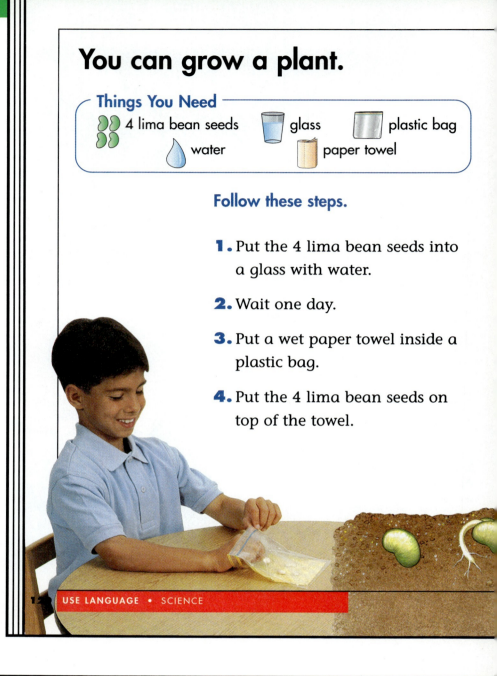

You can grow a plant.

Things You Need

4 lima bean seeds   glass   plastic bag
water   paper towel

Follow these steps.

1. Put the 4 lima bean seeds into a glass with water.

2. Wait one day.

3. Put a wet paper towel inside a plastic bag.

4. Put the 4 lima bean seeds on top of the towel.

USE LANGUAGE • SCIENCE

Options for Reaching All Students

Beginning
Science: Seed Display

Have children work in groups and collect different kinds of seeds. Have them draw or collect pictures of the plant that would grow from the seed. They should paste the seed next to the plant drawing and put the pictures on display.

Advanced
Math: Measuring

Have children work in groups of five. Have each group plant two different kinds of seeds in different pots. Have groups measure the growth of the plants with a ruler over the period of a month and record the data. Have them use the data they collect to draw conclusions about the rate of growth of different plants.

Home Connection
Home-Grown Plants

Suggest that children repeat the plant measuring activity at home with the help of family members. Have them report to the class about their home-grown plants.

5. Watch the seeds for a few days.

6. Keep a record. What happens to your seeds? Write about your plants.

My Record

The parts of the plant that grew first were _____.

I saw roots _____.

I saw leaves _____.

Write About It

Draw your plant. Write the names of the parts of your plant. Tell about your drawing.

Vocabulary: a few, a lot (of)

ACTIVITY BOOK

Explain that *a few* means "not very many." It usually means three or four; for example, three or four seeds. It is the opposite of *a lot (of)*. Ask children how many days *a few* days are (as in step 4). Use page 63 in the Activity Book.

Model a Strategy
Understand That Numerals Show Sequence

Model using numbers in text:

I have seen a number in front of each sentence in other books. These numbers tell the steps I must do to have things come out right. I know I have to do step 1 before I do step 2.

Assess ✔

Use responses to Write About It for assessment. Children should be able to

- tell what they learned from the activity

LOOK AHEAD

Next, children will identify the parts of plants people eat.

Cooperative Language Experience

Science Experiment

Provide three plants of the same kind and about the same size. Have children do the following:

1. Give one plant water but place it in a dark place such as a closet.

2. Place one plant in the sunlight but do not give it any water.

3. Place one plant in the sunlight and give it water.

Have children observe the plants for a period of time. Begin a class chart to record what happens to each plant. Help children draw the conclusion that plants need light and water. With the class, write a language experience story about the experiment.

Writer's Workshop
Write About Plants

Refer children to the Writer's Workshop on pages 230–236 of the Student Book. Have them write about plants using the information in the K-W-L chart or what they learned doing the experiment.

Practice

Activate Prior Knowledge
Review Vocabulary

Brainstorm a list of fruits and vegetables. Write them on chart paper and add to the list throughout the unit.

Develop Language and Concepts
Present page 122.

On the board, list some foods from plants that you ate yesterday. Encourage children to add to the list. Read the text with them. Then add the part of the plant people eat to the list.

FYI Fruit Facts
• Botanically, a fruit is the fleshy part of the plant containing seeds.
• Plants such as tomatoes, often called vegetables, are actually fruits.

Language Awareness

Grammar: Count vs. Noncount Nouns

Point out that some food names do not use the article *a* or *an*. Show children that *celery* and *lettuce* on page 122 do not. Have children identify the objects on the pages, saying, *This is celery. This is a tomato.* Then have them work in pairs using pictures on this and other pages in the chapter as a stimulus to tell about the parts of plants we eat.

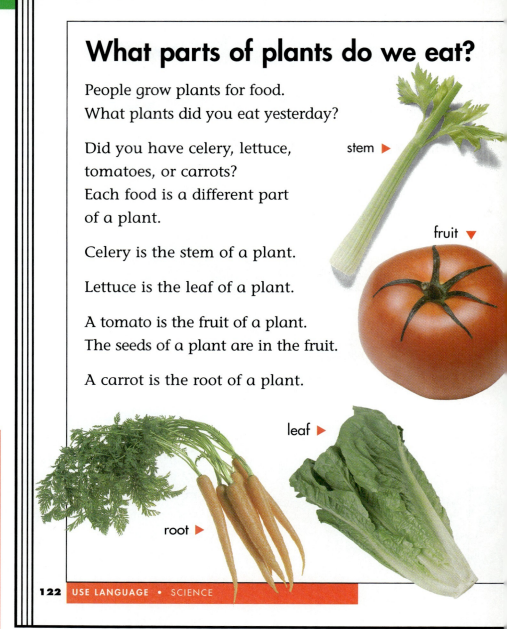

What parts of plants do we eat?

People grow plants for food.
What plants did you eat yesterday?

Did you have celery, lettuce, tomatoes, or carrots?
Each food is a different part of a plant.

Celery is the stem of a plant.

Lettuce is the leaf of a plant.

A tomato is the fruit of a plant.
The seeds of a plant are in the fruit.

A carrot is the root of a plant.

stem ▶

fruit ▼

leaf ▶

root ▶

122 USE LANGUAGE • SCIENCE

Options for Reaching All Students

Beginning
Language: Food Guessing Game

Get a variety of fruits and vegetables, and place each item in a separate bag. Give individual children a bag and have them feel and guess the food in the bag.

Advanced
Critical Thinking: Classifying

Provide groups with pictures of fruits and vegetables. Have them think of various ways to classify the foods and make a chart:

Plants	How they are alike
grape, broccoli	They are green.
apple, peach, grape	They are fruits.

Cooperative Language Experience
Describe Fruits and Vegetables

Bring in fruits and vegetables. Have children examine them and name the various parts of the plants. Cut open fruits such as apples and tomatoes so that the seeds are visible. Together, write a language experience story.

Name these foods.

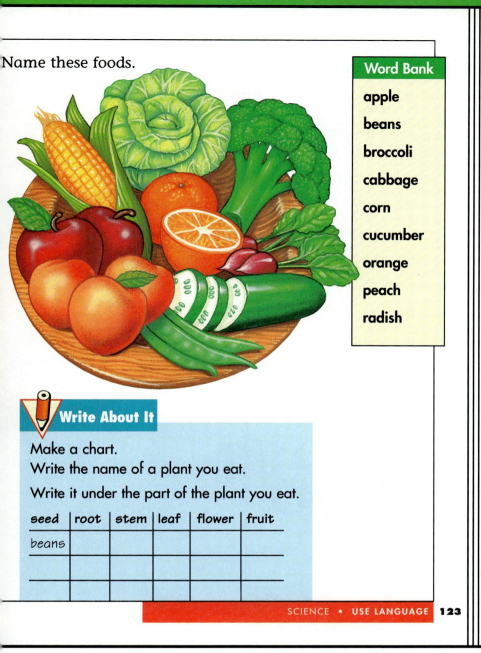

Word Bank

apple

beans

broccoli

cabbage

corn

cucumber

orange

peach

radish

 Write About It

Make a chart.
Write the name of a plant you eat.
Write it under the part of the plant you eat.

seed	root	stem	leaf	flower	fruit
beans					

Develop Language and Concepts
Present page 123.

ACTIVITY BOOK

Read the words in the Word Bank with children. Help them associate the words with the pictures. Have children complete the chart in Write About It. Encourage them to list additional plants. Use page 64 in the Activity Book.

Model a Strategy
Find a Way to Classify

Model one way for classifying plants:

When I write the name of each food in a column, I think about how the plant looks and grows. I see that cabbage looks like a leaf. It must be a leaf like lettuce. Can you think of other ways to classify?

Assess

Children should be able to

• tell the parts we eat of various plants

LOOK AHEAD ➡

Next, children will read about grains, a group of plants that people everywhere eat.

Mixed Ability
Writing: Fruit and Vegetable Riddles

Have children work in pairs of mixed abilities. Have each pair choose a fruit or vegetable and write a riddle for it on the front of a piece of paper and the answer on the back. Have children work in small groups and try to solve one another's riddles. Present this riddle as a model:

I am the fruit of a plant. I have seeds. I grow on trees. My skin is red. What am I? **(apple)**

Little Celebrations
Potatoes on Tuesday

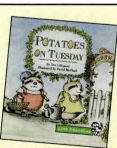

In this story, a family of animals grows vegetables and uses them to make a stew.

Level: Beginning

Connect

Activate Prior Knowledge
Use Illustrations to Predict

Have children look at the pictures and identify any foods that they can. Have them talk about which foods they eat. Finally, ask them to predict what the pages are about.

Develop Language and Concepts
Present pages 124 and 125.

Read the article with children. Spark discussion by asking questions such as these:

- How are oats and rice alike?
- What foods can you name that are made from wheat/corn?

Discuss places where various foods are eaten and locate them on a map.

ACTIVITY BOOK Use Activity Book page 65 to reinforce information and vocabulary learned about grains.

Model a Strategy
Locate Patterns

Model using patterns to aid reading:

In this article, many sentences have the expression is or are made from. The name of a food starts the sentence and the name of a grain ends the sentence. So as I read, I can guess that when a sentence begins with the name of a food and is made from, the sentence will end with the name of a grain.

Grains Around the World

Grains are important plants. Most people in the world eat grain. Wheat, corn, rice, rye, oats, and barley are grains.

Bread is made from grain. Bread is made from wheat, rye, corn, or barley.

Noodles are made from grain. Noodles are made from wheat or rice.

RICE

124 CONNECT LANGUAGE • SCIENCE/SOCIAL STUDIES

Options for Reaching All Students

Beginning
Critical Thinking: Foods from Plants

Provide children with white paper plates. Have them choose a plant and draw different foods made from the plant on the plate. For example, for corn, they could draw corn on the cob, tortillas, and corn bread. Encourage them to label their pictures.

Advanced
Language: Guessing Game

Provide pictures of prepared foods or bring in examples (e.g., cereals such as oat and wheat puffs or tortilla chips) and have children work in pairs to write sentences in which they tell what they think each food is made from. Then provide answers and determine winners.

Peer Tutoring
Critical Thinking: Recalling Details

Have children work in pairs of mixed ability. Ask each child to tell a partner one thing he or she learned from the article.

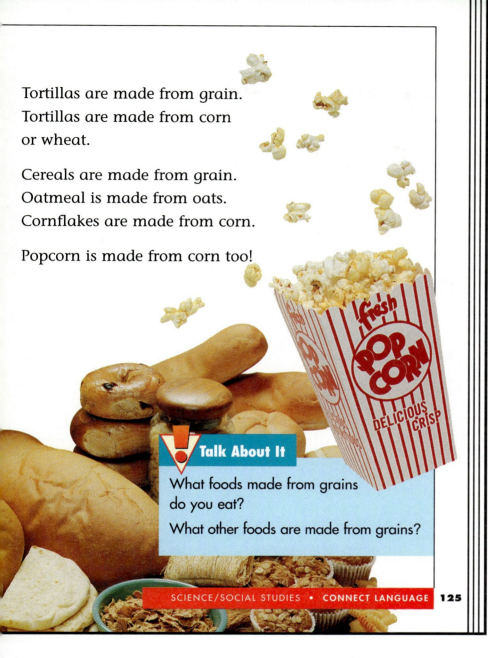

Tortillas are made from grain.
Tortillas are made from corn
or wheat.

Cereals are made from grain.
Oatmeal is made from oats.
Cornflakes are made from corn.

Popcorn is made from corn too!

! Talk About It

What foods made from grains
do you eat?

What other foods are made from grains?

SCIENCE/SOCIAL STUDIES • CONNECT LANGUAGE **125**

Language Awareness

Grammar: Passive Expressions— is/are made from

On the board, write the sentence *Bread is made from wheat.* Have children find sentences with *made from.* Then write sentences such as these on the board and have children complete them:

Noodles are made from _____.

_____ is made from wheat.

FYI Grain Facts
• **In botany, grains are both the fruit and seed of the grain plant.**

• **Wheat is grown around the world. China is the leading producer of wheat.**

Assess ✓

Use responses to Talk About It for assessment. Children should be able to

• name two grains

• name two foods made from grains

LOOK **AHEAD** ➡

Next, children will use what they have learned about plants and grains to read a story about bread.

Home Connection
Breads from Around the World

Bring in various kinds of breads such as rye bread, croissants, and pita bread. Invite children to bring in samples of breads and other foods made from grains that they eat at home. Share the breads.

Mixed Ability
Critical Thinking: Classifying

Have children work in groups of three. They should list the foods they ate for breakfast and supper and then divide them into two groups: foods that are made from grains, foods that are not made from grains.

Little Celebrations
This Is the Seed

This story covers the bread-making process from wheat to flour to bread.

Level: Average

This Is the
Seed

Connect

Activate Prior Knowledge
Use Title and Pictures to Predict

Read the title with children and invite them to look at the pictures in the story. Ask questions such as these:

- What do you think the story is about?
- How do you know?
- What things in the pictures do you recognize?

Introduce the Selection

Help children find and reread the title of the story. Have children find the authors' names and the illustrator's name.

Read the Selection

Read the story with children several times. Encourage them to listen to the story on Side 1 of the Green Tape as often as they like.

Model a Strategy
Understand a Process

Model understanding a process:

As I read this story, I begin to understand where bread comes from. I read carefully to find out how the wheat is grown, harvested, and made into bread. I think about the order in which these things happen. I know that the order is very important to understanding a process.

Teachable Moment
Recognizing Sequence

As children read the story, make a list on the board to show the sequence of events that lead to eating bread.

Options for Reaching All Students

Beginning
Language: Talk About the Story

After reading the story, pass a plate of bread slices that have been quartered. If you wish, you can also provide a topping such as butter or jam. Let children enjoy their bread as they discuss the story.

Advanced
Social Studies: Find Out About Workers

Encourage children to go to the library or interview workers to find out more about a job mentioned in the story: farmer, miller, storekeeper, or cook. Ask children to present their findings in class.

Cooperative Language Experience
Visit a Bakery

Arrange for children to tour a bakery. After the field trip, help children write a language experience story about their trip. Children can draw and caption pictures showing what they saw.

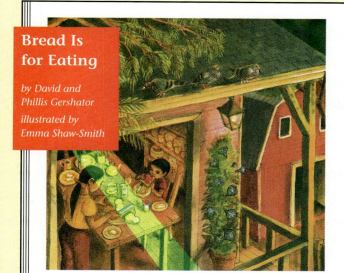

Bread Is for Eating

by David and Phillis Gershator

illustrated by Emma Shaw-Smith

"Bread is for eating," Mamita says when I leave bread on my plate. "Bread is for eating!" And she sings this song to me:

> "El pan es para comer. El pan es para la vida.
> ¡No tires el pan! ¡Ay, ay! Vida mía."

"Think of the seed, asleep in the ground. Think of the earth, a dark, cozy bed."

"Think of the sun, shining down on the earth. Think of the rain, waking the seed from its slumber."

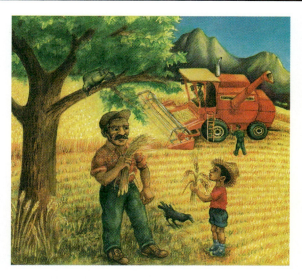

"I'm thinking, Mamita. I'm thinking about the little sprouts coming up from the ground." And Mamita says, "This song is for the sprouting seed:

> "El pan es para comer. El pan es para la vida.
> ¡No tires el pan! ¡Ay, ay! Vida mía."

"Think of the farmer, who tills the soil, hoping the rains will come on time.

Think of the harvester, who cuts the wheat and catches the grain."

Connect

Develop Language and Concepts

Invite children to look at the picture and to reread page 129. Have a volunteer demonstrate what is meant by tilling the soil. Help children discuss why it is important for the rains to come on time. Also use the picture to point out how the grain grows at the tip of the wheat plant.

Model a Strategy

Explain a Process

Model explaining a process:

When I read about growing wheat, I read carefully. Then I see if I can explain the process to myself: The seed is planted in the ground. The sun shines on the seed, and the rain waters it. Then the sprouts come up. The farmer tills the soil around the wheat, and the harvester cuts the wheat and catches the grain. If I can explain it to myself I know that I understand the process.

Teachable Moment

Make Judgments: Authors' Purpose

Invite children to tell why they think the authors, David and Phillis Gershator, wrote this story. Children may say that the authors wrote the story to tell how wheat is grown and how bread is made, or they may say the authors wrote the story to help us appreciate the bread we eat.

Options for Reaching All Students

Beginning
Language: Choral Reading

Have children do a choral reading of the story. Have one group read the main text, and have the other groups sing the song. Then have children switch parts.

Advanced
Language: Use Context Clues

Encourage children who don't speak Spanish to use story context to guess what the words in the song mean. Then let Spanish-speaking children translate.

Bread is for eating. /Bread is for life./ Don't throw bread away! /Oh, oh, my life!

Multicultural Awareness
Breads

Call attention to the illustration on page 133. Ask volunteers to tell what "people around the world" are shown in the picture. Help children discuss what kinds of bread these people may be dreaming about. Then ask children to describe breads eaten in their homelands.

"Is it time for a song—a song for the grains of wheat?"

> *"El pan es para comer. El pan es para la vida.*
> *¡No tires el pan! ¡Ay, ay! Vida mía."*

"Think of the worker, who loads the grain and takes it to town.

Think of the miller, who grinds grain into flour, so soft and fine. Think of the storekeeper, who sells us the flour."

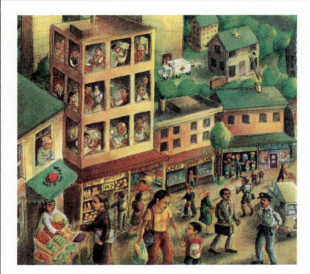

"Yes, I'm thinking, Mamita. I'm thinking about the money we need to buy flour." And Mamita says, "This song is also for the families working all day to put bread on the table:

> *"El pan es para comer. El pan es para la vida.*
> *¡No tires el pan! ¡Ay, ay! Vida mía."*

"Think of the cook, kneading flour with water and yeast. Think of the baker, baking bread before dawn."

"Think of the people around the world, dreaming of bread."

Connect

Develop Language and Concepts

Help children reread page 132. Have them study the picture and name some jobs people do to earn money. Encourage them to tell about different jobs that people in their family do.

Grammar: Nouns and Verbs

ACTIVITY BOOK

Have children go through the story to find the people and things mentioned, such as the farmer, the harvester, and the miller. List the words on the board. Point out to children that these words are all nouns, or naming words. After each noun has been listed, invite children to think of an action word that tells what the person or thing does. Write the action words on the board beside each naming word.

farmer	tills
harvester	cuts and catches
miller	grinds

Then ask for volunteers to make sentences using the listed words. Remind children that the word order in many sentences in English is subject (noun phrase), verb, object (noun phrase). For example, *The farmer tills the soil.* Use Activity Book page 68.

Model a Strategy

Summarize

Model summarizing a story:

When I finish reading a story, I recall what the story is mainly about. This story is about the seeds that sprout into wheat and the grain that comes from the wheat. The story tells about all the workers needed to make bread. It also tells about how people earn money so that they can buy bread. Do you ever summarize a story you've just heard?

Teachable Moment

Identifying Information: Details

Discuss with children the details they learned about the making of bread. Help children find and read the sentences that present various details.

Response to Literature

Personal Response: Did you learn anything new about bread? What was it? What is your favorite part of this story?

Critical Response: Name the different people and what they do to help make bread.

Creative Response: Divide children into groups of four or five. Give each group a large piece of poster paper and have them use crayons to draw a poster for the story *Bread Is for Eating.*

Options for Reaching All Students

Beginning

Language: Listen and Read

GREEN TAPE

Have children read along with Side 1 of the Green Tape. After playing the tape, help children sing the song they heard in the story.

Advanced

Language: Write Poetry

Encourage children to write a short poem about bread or another food they enjoy. Write these rhyming words on the board to get them started:

*eat, beat, heat, meat, neat, wheat
bread, ahead, said
food, mood
best, rest, west*

Home Connection

Cooking with Flour

Encourage children to bring to school a food or dish made with flour that they helped a family member prepare. As classmates sample the food, help the child who brought it explain how it was prepared.

"I'm hungry for bread, Mamita," I say.

"Then toast it and butter it or spread it with jam.
   Eat it cold, eat it hot. Eat a little, eat a lot.
   ¡El pan es bueno!"

"We thank the seed, earth, sun, and rain for the
   grain, the beautiful grain, and sing for the bread
   that gives us life again and again and again."

"Will you sing the song with me?"

"*El pan es para comer.
   El pan es para la vida.
   ¡No tires el pan!
   ¡Ay, ay! Vida mía.*"

Connect

Activate Prior Knowledge
Review Vocabulary

Review the names of grains by helping children read the title. Have them talk about the picture.

Develop Language and Concepts
Present page 138.

GREEN TAPE Read the song to children and clarify meanings of unknown words. Then play Side 2 of the Green Tape several times and encourage children to join in singing the song.

FYI Traditional song
This is a traditional English song. It may have originally been sung by farmers in the belief it would help make the plants in their fields grow better.

Language Awareness

Phonics: Letter-Sound Correspondence—*ow, oa*

Have children listen to the song and clap when they hear the sound /ō/. Have them look at the words and find the words with the sound /ō/ (*oats, grow,* and *know*) and tell the two ways in which the sound is spelled (*oa, ow*). Point out that the sound is often spelled *ow* at the end of words.

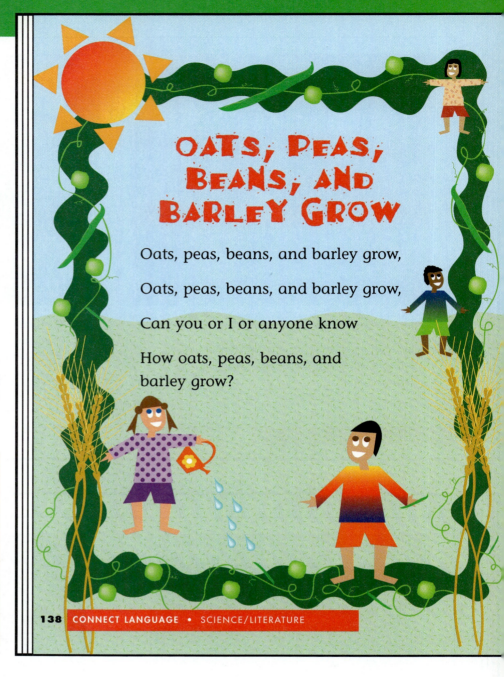

OATS, PEAS, BEANS, AND BARLEY GROW

Oats, peas, beans, and barley grow,

Oats, peas, beans, and barley grow,

Can you or I or anyone know

How oats, peas, beans, and barley grow?

138 CONNECT LANGUAGE • SCIENCE/LITERATURE

Options for Reaching All Students

Beginning
Language: Memory Game

Have children orally compose a cumulative sentence with foods they like, with each child repeating the list and adding an item.

Child A: We like apples, peaches, and bananas.

Child B: We like apples, peaches, bananas, and peas.

Advanced
Writing: Song Variations

Have children write and illustrate alternate versions of the song, with different food names.

Home Connection
Family Sing-Along

Encourage children to teach "Oats, Peas, and Barley Grow" to other family members. Ask children to report to classmates about how the family sing-along went.

Tell what you learned.

1. Make a chart. List each plant you ate last week. Write the part of the plant you ate.

Plants I Ate	Part I Ate

2. What does a plant need to live?

3. Draw one of the workers the story tells about. Put a title on your picture. Tell what that worker does.

ASSESS LANGUAGE **139**

Assess ✓

Activity 1: Have children write their answers on a separate piece of paper. Evaluate number and accuracy of responses.

Activity 2: Evaluate whether children understand that plants need water and sunlight to live.

Activity 3: Check that children label *roots, leaves,* and *trunk.*

Have children complete the Chapter Self-Assessment, Blackline Master 31. Have them choose products to place in their portfolios. Add the results of any rubrics, checklists, self-assessments, or portfolio assessments, Blackline Masters 2–18.

Listening Assessment

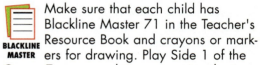

Make sure that each child has Blackline Master 71 in the Teacher's Resource Book and crayons or markers for drawing. Play Side 1 of the Cream Tape several times stopping the tape to allow children to draw.

TAPESCRIPT

CREAM TAPE

Listen carefully. Draw Lisa's plants.

Lisa likes to grow plants. She has three plants. Her first plant has a tall stem and a lot of leaves. It has ten leaves. (pause) Her second plant is small. It has a short stem and only two leaves. (pause) Her third plant is just beginning to grow. It is a sprout.

Options for Reaching All Students

Vocabulary Assessment

ACTIVITY BOOK

Have children complete page 69 of the Activity Book.

Writing Assessment

Have children make personal picture books in which they illustrate and write about the plants they eat.

Strategy Assessment

Have children use the pictures to retell all or part of the story *Bread Is for Eating.*

Language Assessment

BLACKLINE MASTER

Use Blackline Master 70 in the Teacher's Resource Book.

Standardized Test Practice

ACTIVITY BOOK

Use pages 70 and 71 in the Activity Book. Answers: grind grain, happy to have bread.

T139

Preview

Activate Prior Knowledge
Use Pictures and Realia

PICTURE CARDS

Prepare a collection of foods from around the world, including some plants we eat, and display them. Ask children to name as many of these foods as they can. Help children answer the first question in Tell What You Know, naming these and any other foods they like. Start a discussion of "where we buy food" by showing Picture Card 33 of a grocery store and helping children identify it. Repeat with pictures of other food stores. Elicit from children where the foods displayed can be bought. Say, *Tell What You Know is a good strategy. It helps you get ready to learn new things.* Then continue the discussion by showing Picture Cards 8 bread, 11 cake, 36 hot dog, 37 ice cream, and 57 rice.

Develop Language and Concepts
Present pages 140 and 141.

ACTIVITY BOOK

Read aloud the second question in Tell What You Know and direct children's attention to the pictures. Help children identify each place and locate its label. Suggest they look for details in the picture to help answer the questions.

You may model responses with simple sentences, such as *I buy bread at the bakery.*

(Continued on page T141)

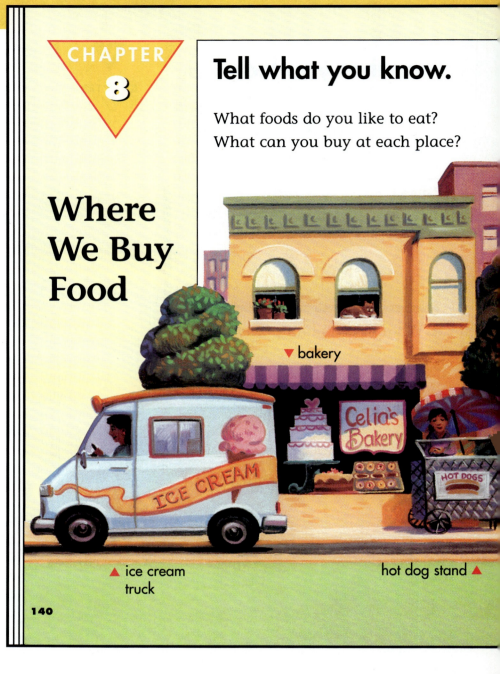

CHAPTER 8

Where We Buy Food

Tell what you know.

What foods do you like to eat?
What can you buy at each place?

▼ bakery

Celia's Bakery

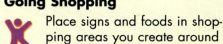
HOT DOGS

▲ ice cream truck

hot dog stand ▲

140

Options for Reaching All Students

Beginning
Social Studies: Workers

Write on the board and then read aloud the following words: *bakery, butcher shop,* and *farmers' market.* Help children name the worker for each place: *baker, butcher, farmer.* Write the words on the board. Help children notice the similarity among the words. Then invite children to copy the list and illustrate it.

Advanced
Language: Classifying Food

Prepare a set of index cards, each printed with the name of a place to buy food as shown on pages 140 and 141. Have children take turns choosing a card, saying the name of the place, and naming two things they might buy there. Model what to say using the following example:

I am going to a hot dog stand. I will buy a hot dog and some juice.

Mixed Ability
Going Shopping

TPR

Place signs and foods in shopping areas you create around the room for places shown on pages 140 and 141. Model directions such as *Go to the bakery. Buy bread.* Encourage children to act out a purchase. Then invite volunteers to repeat or give similar directions to the others in the class.

farmers' market ▶

▼ supermarket

▼ grocery store

Sanchez Grocery

EGGS 49¢   MILK 89¢ ½ gal

▼ butcher shop

SAM'S MEATS

SALE

Talk About It

Where does your family buy food?

Where do people in other countries buy food?

141

KEY CONCEPTS

In this chapter, children will learn language connected with where food is grown and where people can buy food.

Use pages 140 and 141 to assess children's knowledge of food vocabulary and kinds of stores and shops associated with different foods.

Communities need places where people can buy food.

Different places sell different kinds of food.

Where We Buy Food

Most of our food grows on farms.

People can buy food at restaurants and cafeterias.

Help children answer the questions in Talk About It. Encourage children to visualize places in their current community and in their native country. Then invite them to work in small groups to share their personal answers.

Help the class discuss why communities need different places where people can buy food. Use Activity Book page 72 to practice vocabulary.

Cooperative Learning
Art Project

Divide the class into seven groups. Each group is to work on one of the following places: bakery, butcher shop, farmers' market, grocery store, hot dog stand, ice cream truck, and supermarket. Have the groups negotiate among themselves so that each group is working on a different place. Invite children to make a "town" by having each group paint or draw the facade for their "store" on sections of mural paper. Each group is to make a sign with the name of its store. Children can stock the shelves with foods you brought to class. They can work at the different stores in later lessons.

Home Connection
Family Favorites

Invite children to find out what their families consider their favorite foods. Have children ask family members and list their responses to share in class the next day.

Present

Activate Prior Knowledge
Share Experiences

PICTURE CARDS

Show children pictures of farms. Ask if any children have visited or lived on a farm and encourage them to share their experiences. Display pictures of foods that grow on farms to aid children in the discussion. Invite children to identify the foods and read the labels with you. Use Picture Cards 2, 4, 14, 29, 42, 49, 54, 56, 70, 72.

Develop Language and Concepts
Present pages 142 and 143.

Read aloud the title and question on page 142. After children respond, read the second sentence. Call attention to the cornfield, wheat field, citrus orchard, and apple orchard. Help children name the crops.

Help children describe the scene on page 143. Model sentences such as *The boy is running.* Introduce the words in the Word Bank and help children identify the produce shown. Then read the text with children. Elicit from them why customers might enjoy seeing the farm and buying fresh produce.

Do the Write About It activity. Have children share their letters with a partner and give each other feedback.

Food From Farms

Where do stores get the food you buy?

Farmers grow **crops** on **farms.**

142   LEARN LANGUAGE • SOCIAL STUDIES

Options for Reaching All Students

Beginning
Language: Seeking Information

Prepare word strips with the names of stores and food items and sentence strips with the following conversation pattern: *Where are you going? I'm going to the _____. What are you going to buy? I'm going to buy _____.*

Have pairs take turns asking and answering the questions using the word and sentence strips.

Advanced
Writing: Shopping Lists

Brainstorm with children examples of food their families buy regularly. Provide newspaper ads as source material. Have each child write a shopping list that includes the amounts for each item. Children can estimate the amounts their families need during a week. Then have children form small groups and compare lists.

Cooperative Language Experience
Field Trip

Take children on a visit to a nearby farm, farmers' market, or neighborhood grocery store. Help children identify foods. As a class, write a language experience story about the visit. Children can draw and write about what they saw.

Sometimes customers drive to a farm in the country.

They enjoy seeing a farm.

They enjoy buying fresh fruits and vegetables.

What can they buy at this **farm stand?**

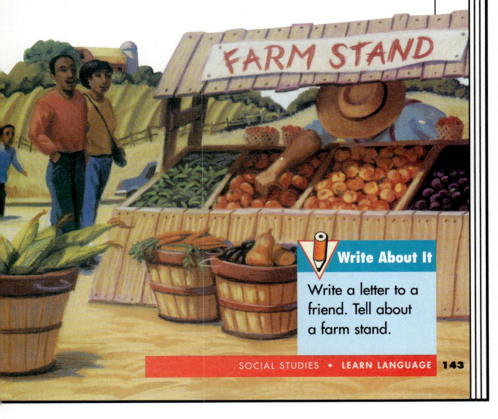

 Write About It

Write a letter to a friend. Tell about a farm stand.

Vocabulary: Phrases

ACTIVITY BOOK

Have children locate the phrases *enjoy seeing* and *enjoy buying* in the second and third sentences on page 143. Ask, *What do you enjoy seeing on a farm? What do you enjoy buying at a farm stand?* Have children use the phrases and Word Bank words in their answers. Use Activity Book page 73.

Model a Strategy
Preview Text

Model locating key words to get meaning:

Before I read, I look for important words in the text. This helps me figure out what the text is mostly about. On page 143, the word farm *is in most sentences. This tells me the text will mostly be about farms.*

Assess ✔

Children should be able to

- name some food grown on farms
- tell something about a farm stand

LOOK AHEAD ➔

Next, children will further explore where food from farms is sold.

Mixed Ability
Music: Farm Song

Sing with children "Old MacDonald." Invite them to make up new verses.

Old MacDonald had a farm
E-i, e-i-o!
And on his farm he had some apples
E-i, e-i-o!
With a crunch, crunch here
And a crunch, crunch there
Here a crunch, there a crunch, every-
where a crunch crunch.

Home Connection
Multicultural Awareness

Write and review the following rhyme on the board: *An apple a day keeps the doctor away.* Explain the meaning of the rhyme and elicit responses reflecting our need for healthy diets. Have children ask family members about sayings in their own language telling how to stay healthy and bring the sayings to school to share.

QuickCheck

Pronouns

Check children's understanding of the pronoun *they* on page 143. See that they know that it replaces the plural noun *customers*. Ask children to write new sentences about the people on pages 143 and 144 using *they* and other pronouns.

Practice

Activate Prior Knowledge
Brainstorm Vocabulary

Brainstorm a list of places in the school community where people buy food. Encourage children to compare the list with the places pictured on pages 140 and 141.

Develop Language and Concepts
Present pages 144 and 145.

Have children look at the illustrations and say what they can about each scene. Then read the text with children. Discuss similarities and differences between the two places.

Show children a globe and help them locate Costa Rica, Ghana, and the Philippines. Invite volunteers to share any information they have about these countries and the foods they produce.

Do the Think About It activity with children. Have them use the globe to locate their native countries. Have volunteers tell what foods are produced there.

Model a Strategy
Monitoring

Model using monitoring:

As I read pages 144 and 145, I check to see if I understand what I'm reading. If I don't understand, I can find ways to solve the problem. I can think about what I already know about this topic and read again. I can

(Continued on page T145)

From Farms to Customers

Most of the time customers buy food near their homes.

This is a **farmers' market** in the city.

Farmers bring food and plants to this market. Customers enjoy buying foods and plants that come directly from a farm.

What can they buy at this farmers' market?

144 USE LANGUAGE • SOCIAL STUDIES

Options for Reaching All Students

Beginning
Critical Thinking: Categorizing

Play a variation of Musical Chairs in which children walk around a row of chairs, each child holding a picture card of a food item. Model the game with volunteers. Play music from different countries as children walk. When the music stops, call out a category such as "Fruits." Children whose food is in that category sit and name their food.

Advanced
Language: Ask for Assistance

Invite children to go to the "stores" set up previously and ask a "salesperson" for assistance. Use the dialogue below.

Child A: *Excuse me, where is the ___?*
Child B: *It's (right here; on that shelf; and so on).*
Child A: *Thank you. How much is the ___?*
Child B: *It's ___.*

Peer Tutoring
Writing: "From Farm to Table" Books

Have pairs of children work on books, showing the steps it takes for two kinds of food to go from the farm to the table. If they wish, they can choose foods grown in their native country. Have partners illustrate and write in their books and share them with the class.

This is a **supermarket.** All food comes to supermarkets on trucks. The trucks get some food from ships, trains, and planes.

Customers can buy food from all over the world. Bananas may come from Costa Rica, cocoa from Ghana, and coconuts from the Philippines.

Supermarkets let customers buy all their food in one place.

 Think About It

What other foods grow outside the United States?

ask for help. I can look back at sentences I have already read or read ahead. Can you use monitoring too? How?

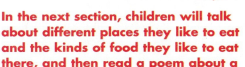

Practice

Activate Prior Knowledge
Use Visualization

Invite children to talk about places where people eat. Name some familiar neighborhood places and encourage children to picture in their minds and then name others they know.

Develop Language and Concepts
Present pages 146 and 147.

Focus on each illustration on pages 146 and 147. Help children name and describe each place where people go to buy food and eat. Have volunteers answer the questions on page 146. Finally, talk about how the places are different.

 Read aloud the poem on page 147, emphasizing the vendor's chant. Play Side 2 of the Green Tape and encourage children to join in saying the poem.

Invite children to share their comments about the poem. Ask how vendors in their native country encourage customers to buy food. Ask comprehension questions such as *Who speaks in the first part of the poem? What is the city's smallest store?*

Explain what sauerkraut is and have children tell what they like to put on their favorite foods. Provide a model, such as *I eat hot dogs with mustard.*

Do the Try It Out activity as a class before children do it themselves.

Let's Eat

Where do you like to eat?

What foods do you like to eat there?

fast-food restaurant ▲

restaurant ▲

▼ cafeteria

146 USE LANGUAGE • SOCIAL STUDIES

Options for Reaching All Students

Beginning
Writing: Make a Book

Brainstorm a list of favorite foods. Display the list on chart paper. Sketch illustrations to help children read the words. Have children work in small groups. Give each group a blank booklet. Have them make a book entitled "Our Favorite Foods." Encourage children to write and draw pictures for the book.

Advanced
Writing: Create an Ad

Locate ads for fast-food restaurants. Present them as models. Have children work in small groups to make up their own ads. Give each group drawing paper. Have them write the name of a restaurant, illustrate the page with pictures of food from the restaurant that would make the reader "hungry," and write some ad copy. Help children name and label the foods.

Cooperative Learning
Writing: Make a Menu

Assign children to small groups. Ask each group to create a special menu for a restaurant. First have children choose a kind of restaurant and think of a name for it. Ask children to decide what items to include on a menu, such as the name of the food and the price. Ask them to also draw pictures to help the customer envision the food.

Get 'Em Here

by Lee Bennett Hopkins

"Hot dogs with sauerkraut
Cold drinks here!
Hot dogs with sauerkraut
Get 'em here!
Hot dogs with sauerkraut
Cold drinks here!"

Shouts the man as he rolls the city's
smallest store
All tucked neatly
under a huge,
blue-and-orange-
striped umbrella.

Try It Out

Use the first 6 lines of the chant. Make up a new chant about your favorite foods and drinks. Share your chant with a partner.

SOCIAL STUDIES • USE LANGUAGE **147**

Model a Strategy
Use Planning

Model planning to read orally:

Before I read a chant aloud to a group, I can do some planning. I can listen to the chant on tape as I read silently. I can read it aloud many times and remember where to pause. I can see what is easy to say and what needs more work. I can practice with a friend.

Language Awareness

Language Functions: Making Requests

ACTIVITY BOOK Have children take turns pretending to sell each other food. Model making a polite request. Say, *I'd like a hot dog with ketchup, please.* Encourage children to say *Thank you* when they receive what they want. Ask children how requests are made in their native language. Use Activity Book page 75.

Assess ✓

Children should be able to
- name places where they like to eat
- name foods they like to eat there

LOOK AHEAD ➡

Next, children will read about sharing.

Peer Tutoring
Language: Identifying Foods

PICTURE CARDS Give pairs of children of mixed abilities the following Picture Cards: 8 bread, 11 cake, 15 cheese, 19 cookies, 25 doughnut, 34 hamburger, 36 hot dog, 37 ice cream, 38 juice, 44 milk, 52 pizza, 59 salad, 60 sandwich, 66 soup. Children can use the cards as flashcards to work with until both can identify the foods.

Mixed Ability
Gestures and Body Language

Explain and act out some typical examples of how customers get a waiter's attention such as making eye contact, waving, and raising an index finger. Then have children give examples about restaurants in their native country. For example, customers may leave an empty, opened teapot in the corner of the table to signal that they want more tea. Children may want to ask family members and report back to class.

Connect

Activate Prior Knowledge
Use Puppets

Use a pair of puppets to tell a story about two friends. One of them has a bag of cheese cubes. When he meets his friend, he asks the audience for advice. Should he eat all the cheese or give some to his friend? Allow children to respond. Invite volunteers to act out a conversation using the puppets.

Develop Language and Concepts
Present pages 148 and 149.

Encourage children to look at the picture on page 148 as you read the text in the first speech balloon. Ask children to predict the answer and then read it. Point out that the words *What if* tell about something that might happen. Point out that the word *I'd* is a short way of saying *I would*. Have children suggest their own responses beginning with *I'd*. Read aloud the questions on page 149 and have children work in pairs to answer them.

Do the Think About It activity together.

Model a Strategy
Use Pictures and Text to Predict

Model making predictions:

On page 148, I see two children talking. They look happy. They look like friends. I see that

(Continued on page T149)

What would you do if . . . ?

What would you do if you had two bananas and your friend didn't have any?

I'd eat one banana and give the other one to my friend.

148 CONNECT LANGUAGE • SOCIAL STUDIES/MATH

Options for Reaching All Students

Beginning
Art: Paper-Plate Collage

Provide children with paper plates, old magazines, scissors, paste, and crayons. Have children cut out magazine pictures to make a collage that shows foods they can share with friends. Children can paste the pictures of their foods on paper plates and share their work with the class.

Advanced
Math: Story Problems

Tell children: *Kim had three plums. Sally didn't have any. Then Kim gave one to Sally. How many plums did Kim have left?* Have a volunteer represent it with a number sentence on the board. (3 – 1 = 2) Invite children to make up story problems about friends sharing food. In small groups, children can write problems in words and then in number sentences.

Mixed Ability
Language: Choral Reading

Write the following rhyme on chart paper, alternating colors so that every other line is written in the same color. Read it aloud a few times. Divide the class into two groups and assign each group one color to read.

I eat my peas with honey.
I've done it all my life.
It makes my peas taste funny,
But it keeps them on the knife.

Work in pairs. Answer the questions.

1. What would you do if you had four cookies and your friend didn't have any?

2. What would you do if you had six strawberries and your friend didn't have any?

 Think About It

What food would you like to share with your class?

How much of it would you need to bring?

one child is asking a question. I think about what I'd do in this situation. This helps me predict what the friend would do. Can you see ways to use predicting?

Language Awareness

Vocabulary: Numerals and Number Words

 ACTIVITY BOOK Read the text again with children and have them find the words that indicate numbers. Write the number words on the board. Ask volunteers to write the corresponding numerals. Then write all the number words from 1 to 10 and invite children to write the corresponding numerals. Use Activity Book page 76.

Assess ✓

Children should be able to

• respond to "what if. . . " questions

LOOK **AHEAD**

In the next section, children will apply what they know about foods to read a supermarket flier and to follow a recipe.

Peer Tutoring
Language: Ways to Share

Prepare cards with pictures of food items for the following list: *four cookies, two carrots, six pretzels, one cupcake, two pears, eight grapes.*

Have children work in pairs of mixed abilities. Ask them to take turns choosing a card, naming the number of food items shown, and telling how they might share them with each other.

Little Celebrations
Noggin and Bobbin In the Garden

There is so much to do to make a garden grow, but when Noggin and Bobbin share the chores, singing, whistling, and working, they can enjoy the "fruits" of their efforts.

Level: Average

Connect

Activate Prior Knowledge

Use Realia

Bring supermarket fliers to class and invite children to describe them. Ask children if they have seen fliers in stores in their native countries or in their present communities. Help children discuss why stores want customers to see fliers.

Develop Language and Concepts

Present page 150.

Have children look at the flier on the page. Elicit what kind of store Lee's Market might be. Let children identify all the items they can. Then read the flier with children. Point out how different kinds of produce are priced differently.

Invite volunteers to create a dialogue about how much a certain item costs. Provide models such as these:

Tomás, how much are the oranges?

The oranges are 40 cents each.

Language Awareness

Grammar: Possessives

ACTIVITY BOOK

Have children read the title of the flier. Write *Lee's* on the board. Ask if anyone knows why *-'s* is used. Model showing possession with a child's name. Have volunteers come to the board and write the name of their own market. Use Activity Book page 77.

Lee's Market

Sale This Week

pears 30¢ each

bananas 10¢ each

oranges 40¢ each

corn 20¢ each

apples 20¢ each

potatoes $1.25 a bag
beans 75¢ a bag
cabbage $1.00 a head
lemons 35¢ each
peas 89¢ a bag
strawberries (large) 5¢ each
peaches 50¢ each

150 CONNECT LANGUAGE • SOCIAL STUDIES/LITERATURE

Options for Reaching All Students

Beginning

Language: Cooking Rhyme

TPR

Model the actions and say this rhyme. Repeat the ryhme, having children do the actions.

> Mix a pancake,
> Stir a pancake,
> Pop it in the pan.
> Fry a pancake,
> Toss a pancake,
> Catch it if you can!

Advanced

Language: Tasting Fruits

Invite volunteers to taste small pieces of fruit, such as apples and lemons. Encourage children to describe what the fruits taste like. Present such words as *sweet, tart,* and *juicy* where apt. Then have children write short sentences describing the fruits. Encourage them to illustrate their sentences.

Mixed Ability

Math/Language: At the Store

Use the flier from Lee's Market. Have children work in pairs. Give play money to each pair. Ask children to take turns buying and selling food using the dialogue below.

Can I help you?

Yes, I'd like ___. How much is it?

It's ___.

Recipe: Fruit Salad

Serves 8

Ingredients

2 apples
2 bananas
2 pears
2 peaches

juice of 1 lemon
juice of 2 oranges
1/2 cup of sugar
6 large strawberries

Directions

Cut up all the fruit into small pieces. Put them into a bowl. Add the lemon juice, orange juice, and sugar. Mix. Put the bowl into the refrigerator for one hour.

 Try It Out

You want to make the fruit salad recipe. You are going to Lee's Market.

What kinds of fruits do you need to buy? How many do you need to buy of each?

How much money do you need to buy all the fruit?

SOCIAL STUDIES/LITERATURE • **CONNECT LANGUAGE** **151**

Develop Language and Concepts
Present page 151.

Read the recipe title. Ask children to predict what things they might need for a fruit salad. Then present the ingredients.

Invite children to share their experiences with recipes. Then read the recipe with children. Elicit from them why measuring ingredients and following the steps are important. Then assign the Try It Out tasks to groups.

Later, help children figure out how much of each ingredient was needed for the class.

Model a Strategy
Use Context Clues

Model using context clues:

In this recipe, I found a word that I didn't know. I read all the words before it and after it. I read *Cut up the fruit into ___ pieces.* I know that fruit for a salad will probably be cut into little pieces, but the word I see begins with *sm.* I think *small* is a word that means little.

Assess

Children should be able to

- get information from a flyer
- follow directions in a recipe

LOOK AHEAD ➡

In the next section, children will read a Navajo poem, "Growing Song."

Home Connection
Food for a Party

Invite children's families to prepare a typical dish from their native countries and come to a class party. Help children label each food and list the ingredients. Encourage children and families to talk about their dishes and to taste the variety of foods.

Little Celebrations
A Tasty Bug

In this recipe book, containing photographs and directions, children can follow to see how to make a tasty "ladybug" using grapes, an apple, peanut butter, raisins, and lettuce.

Level: Beginning

The Cake That Mack Ate

by Rose Robart
Illustrated by Maryann Kovalski

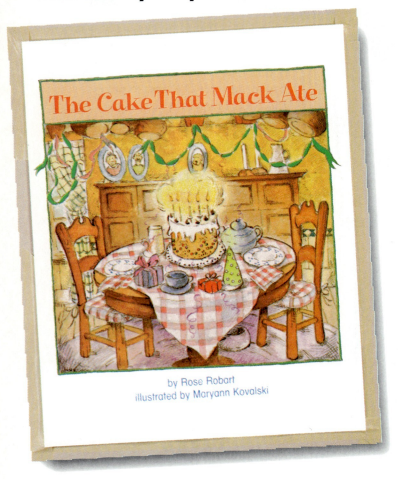

by Rose Robart
illustrated by Maryann Kovalski

Shared Reading

1. Introduce
Display the book and read the title, author, and illustrator. Invite children to look at the picture on the cover and predict what the book will be about. Ask children to name their favorite kind of cake. Then have children name ingredients that go into a cake. Let children speculate about where some of the ingredients in a cake come from.

2. Read
As you read aloud, invite children to say the repeated lines with you as you read them. Call attention to the picture details that support the text for each page.

3. Reread
Invite children to reread the book with you. Discuss the book by asking questions, such as the following

- What were the steps that went into producing the egg for the cake?
- Do you think that Mack was supposed to eat the cake? Why or why not?

The Cake That Mack Ate
How do we get the ingredients that make up our food? In this cumulative story the reader traces an ingredient for the cake that Mack ate.

Options for Reaching All Students

Beginning
Art: Draw Cake Ingredients
Help children discuss other ingredients that may be needed to make a cake. Then have them draw an ingredient. Together chant *This is the ____ that went into the cake that Mack ate.* As you come to the blank have a volunteer hold up his or her ingredient and say what it is—*This is the sugar that went into the cake that Mack ate.*

Advanced
Language: Innovate on the Text
Have children innovate on the text as they suggest other ingredients to add to the cake in a pattern such as this:

This is the cow

That gave the milk

That went into the cake

that Mack ate.

Then read the Mother Goose Rhyme "The House That Jack Built" and compare how it is similar in structure to *The Cake That Mack Ate.*

Phonics: Long and Short *a*

TPR Wave at children and say *long a—wave*. Pat your head and say *short a—pat*. Have them follow these commands noting the vowel sounds until they associate the sound with the action. Then write the words *candles*, *planted*, *cake*, *made*, and *laid* on the chalkboard. Invite children to circle each short *a* word and underline each long *a* word. Then have children respond with the action (wave or pat) as you randomly read the words on the board.

Model a Strategy
Locate Patterns

Model locating patterns in a story:

When I read a story, I look for patterns that the writer uses. In this story, I see that on each page the writer tells more about what came before in the process of making a cake. She begins with the egg and goes back to the hen, the corn, the seed, the farmer, and his wife. When I see a pattern like this, it helps me know what to expect and it helps me be a better reader. Do you look for patterns as you read?

Response Activities

Diagram the Plot
As children reread the story in groups, they can make a list of the things necessary for producing the egg that was used in the cake. Encourage children to illustrate their list.

Read Chorally
Have the book read chorally by assigning a small group of children to read each repeated line. After practicing reading the story one time, you might want each group to decide on an action to perform while reading.

Look at Picture Details
To help children identify the nouns in the story, have them look at each picture and identify it. Have them point to the word for each picture in the story. Then invite the children to retell the story looking only at the pictures.

Cooperative Language Experience
How to Bake a Cake
Take children to a bakery or a middle school cooking class to watch as a cake is made. Help clarify any vocabulary, and encourage children to ask questions. When they return to their own classroom help them write a language experience story about the demonstration.

Mixed Ability
Language: Discuss the Ending
Have small groups discuss the ending of the story. Ask whether they expected Mack to be a dog. Encourage children to tell what or whom they think the cake was really for.

Home Connection
Favorite Recipes
Name some kinds of cake with children, such as chocolate, vanilla, carrot, lemon, and spice. Have them add other flavors that might be favorites in their homelands. Ask children to survey family members to find out what their favorite kinds of cake are. At school the next day, collate the results of their findings to see whether there is a class favorite.

Connect

Activate Prior Knowledge
Review Vocabulary

Read aloud the title and ask children to predict what the poem will tell about. Point out that the specific writer is unknown, but that the words have been passed down through generations of Navajo people.

Develop Language and Concepts
Present page 152.

Read through the poem several times. Elicit from children that the writer talks to plants as if they were human.

GREEN TAPE Play Side 2 of the Green Tape several times and encourage children to join in saying the words.

Have pairs do the Think About It activity.

Language Awareness

Grammar: Pronouns

ACTIVITY BOOK Have children listen to the words of the poem and point to themselves when they hear the pronoun *me*. Then brainstorm examples of sentences in which the pronoun *me* is used, such as *Look at me*. Write the sentences on the board and ask volunteers to underline the pronoun. Use Activity Book page 78.

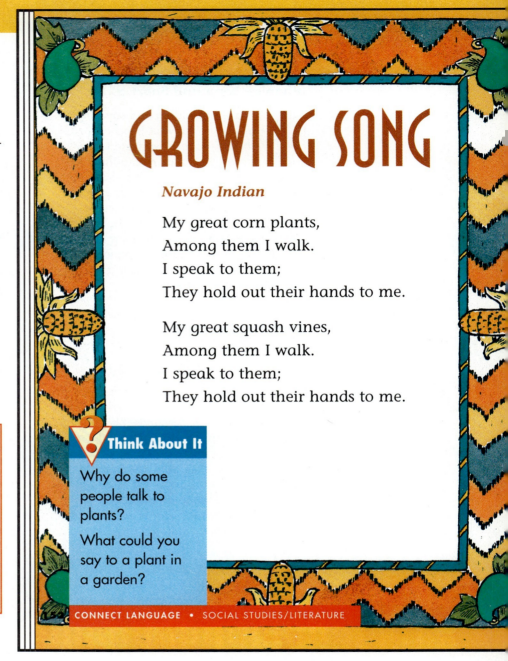

GROWING SONG

Navajo Indian

My great corn plants,
Among them I walk.
I speak to them;
They hold out their hands to me.

My great squash vines,
Among them I walk.
I speak to them;
They hold out their hands to me.

Think About It

Why do some people talk to plants?

What could you say to a plant in a garden?

CONNECT LANGUAGE • SOCIAL STUDIES/LITERATURE

Options for Reaching All Students

Beginning
Science: Plant Illustrations

Write *corn plants* and *squash vines* on the board and read the terms with children. Have each child fold a sheet of paper in half. Invite children to copy one term on each side of the paper and illustrate it. Children can label any plant parts they know.

Advanced
Language: Innovations

Invite children to write and illustrate new versions of "Growing Song," changing the names of the plants. Children can modify the poem further by changing the verb *walk* to another action.

Home Connection
Songs about Growing

Encourage children to ask family members to teach them songs about harvests that have been passed down through generations in their culture. Have volunteers tell about the song before they sing it to the class. Invite volunteers to use a map to show the place where the song originated.

Tell what you learned.

1. Where do you and your family buy food? Make a chart.

Where We Buy Food	What We Buy

2. Draw a picture about a time when you went with your family to buy food. Write about your picture.

3. Make an ad for a grocery store. Draw pictures and write names of foods. Then put prices in your ad.

ASSESS LANGUAGE **153**

Assess ✓

Activity 1: Evaluate whether children can name different kinds of stores and tell what their families buy there.

Activity 2: Check that children draw themselves shopping with their families. Evaluate what children write about their picture.

Activity 3: Evaluate whether children can write names of grocery store items and their prices in a logical format for an advertisement.

Have children complete the Chapter Self-Assessment BLM 33. Have them choose products to place in their portfolios. Add the results of any rubrics, checklists, self-assessments, or portfolio assessments, BLMs 2–18.

Listening Assessment

 BLACKLINE MASTER

Make sure that each child has a copy of Blackline Master 73 and red, blue, and orange crayons or markers. Play Side 1 of the Cream Tape several times, stopping the tape to allow children to answer.

TAPESCRIPT

 CREAM TAPE

Listen carefully to these directions. Carmen and her father are at the supermarket buying food. There are many things on sale this week. Squash is on sale. Draw a red circle around the squash. (pause) Carmen wants some peaches. Draw a blue circle around the peaches. (pause) Carmen's father wants some carrots. Draw some orange carrots in his cart .

Options for Assessment

Vocabulary Assessment

 ACTIVITY BOOK

Have children complete Activity Book page 79.

Writing Assessment

Have children write a diary entry about a day when they went grocery shopping with a family member. Children can illustrate their work.

Language Assessment

 BLACKLINE MASTER

Use Blackline Master 72 in the Teacher's Resource Book.

Standardized Test Practice

 ACTIVITY BOOK

Use pages 80 and 81 in the Activity Book. Answers: 3+3+3=9, 2, 30¢, 90¢.

Wrap-Up

Activities

Mural

Have children collect information for a plant mural. They should investigate the plants where they live—collect samples, take photographs, or make drawings. Then have them work in groups of five. Decide which plants to put in the mural. Complete the mural, and share it with other groups.

Survey

Have children interview people starting with family members. They should collect information about each person's favorite food from plants. A chart like the one that follows would be an easy way to compile the survey information.

Name	Favorite Food from Plants
Mom	grapes, tomatoes, rice
Dad	

Map

Suggest that children draw a map showing places where food can be purchased. It might include a supermarket, a produce store, a fast-food restaurant.

Discussing the Theme

Have children work in groups of two or three to discuss their progress during this unit about plants. Choose from the following activities that will demonstrate to them how much they have learned and how useful that information is.

- Have children tape-record a list of new words learned.
- Have children draw or find pictures to create a picture dictionary of words learned. Have more advanced children label the pictures.
- Have groups discuss situations in which the words learned will be useful, for example, in the cafeteria, in science class, at the supermarket, and so on. Small groups could share the results of their discussions with the class.
- Play a game in which one group makes a statement and another group guesses the situation in which it might be used. For example,

"I want to eat noodles."

— the cafeteria.

"I'll water the tomato plants."

— in a garden.

Sharing the Project

Use the invitation form, Blackline Master 32 or 33, to invite family members to school to see the Garbage Garden.

Set up the classroom with stations family members can visit. Make sure that plant labels made earlier are properly displayed.

You might want to assign a pair of children to each plant. They can tell the name of the plant, how it was started, what kind of care it needs, and so on.

As visitors arrive, write the family name on a slip of paper and put it in a bag or box. Just before guests leave, ask a child to draw the names of families that can take the plants home.

To offer simple refreshments, have children help make popcorn. Using an air popper is probably healthiest and safest. Put up a sign that children can read to their families: *Popcorn is made from corn. Corn is a grain.*

Signs of Success!

Duplicate a copy of this checklist for each child.

Name: _____

Refer to the checklist below for a quick determination of how a child is progressing toward transitioning out of ESL instruction.

Objectives:

- ☐ Names plants and parts of plants.
- ☐ Tells what parts of plants do.
- ☐ Tells which parts of plants we eat.
- ☐ Names grains and food made from grains.
- ☐ Name different kinds of restaurants.
- ☐ Names places where food is purchased.
- ☐ Tells which foods can be purchased at which places.
- ☐ Tells about where fruits and vegetables are grown.

Language Awareness

Understands / Uses:

- ☐ *a few* and *a lot*
- ☐ count / noncount nouns
- ☐ *is / are made from*
- ☐ past tense
- ☐ *enjoy seeing, enjoy buying*
- ☐ proper nouns
- ☐ making requests
- ☐ numerals and number words
- ☐ possessives
- ☐ *me*

Hears / Pronounces / Reads:

- ☐ *st* and *str* blends
- ☐ long *o* spelled *ow* and *oa*

Learning Strategies:

- ☐ Uses pictures for help with meaning.
- ☐ Understands that numerals show sequence.
- ☐ Uses patterns for help with meaning.
- ☐ Finds ways to classify.
- ☐ Looks for key words.
- ☐ Monitors meaning.
- ☐ Prepares for oral reading.
- ☐ Uses context clues.

Comments:

_____

Planning Guide

CHAPTER 9

Day and Night

Objectives

Name things in the sky.

Tell what causes night and day.

Tell about the sun.

Tell about the moon.

Tell why a calendar is important.

Vocabulary Focus

Things in the sky, such as *clouds, moon, stars, sun.*

Words for discussing night and day, such as *earth, day, night, faces, light, dark.*

Words to talk about the sun, such as *gases, heat, melt.*

Words to talk about the moon, such as *rocks, soil, air, month, year.*

Lesson	Content Focus	Language Awareness Objectives	Learning Strategies
Preview pages 154–155 Tell what you know.			
Present pages 156–157 How Day and Night Happen	Science	**Vocabulary** Homophones	Use a diagram.
Practice pages 158–159 What is the sun? What can the sun do?	Science	**Vocabulary** Compound Words	Generalize.
Practice pages 160–161 What is the moon like? "Old Man Moon"	Science	**Language Functions** Express Time	Predict content.
Connect pages 162–163 How did people long ago measure time?	Science/ Social Studies	**Grammar** Irregular Past Tense	Make comparisons.
Connect pages 164–175 *Nine O'Clock Lullaby*	Science/ Literature	**Grammar** Comparatives **Grammar** Similes **Language Functions** Describing	Predict content. Use context. Activate prior knowledge.
Connect page 176 "Out in the Dark and Daylight"	Science/ Literature	**Phonics** Pattern and Rhyme	
Assess page 177 Tell what you learned.			

Long Ago and Today

Objectives

Tell about the first people in North America.

Tell about the early Spanish settlers of North America.

Tell about the Pilgrims.

Name holidays celebrated in this country.

Vocabulary Focus

Timepieces, such as *clock, watch, hourglass, sundial.*

Words for telling time, such as *o'clock, one, two, eleven, twelve.*

Words for discussing early settlers, such as *Indian, Spanish, English, Pilgrims, settlement.*

Words for holidays, such as *celebrate, Thanksgiving, Martin Luther King Day, thankful.*

Months of the year, *January, February, March, April, May, June, July, August, September, October, November, December.*

Lesson	Content Focus	Language Awareness Objectives	Learning Strategies
Preview pages 178–179 Tell what you know.			
Present pages 180–181 What was it like in this country long ago?	Social Studies	**Language Functions** Telling Why	
Practice pages 182–183 Who were the next settlers?	Social Studies	**Vocabulary** Time Expressions	Understand chronology.
Practice pages 184–185 What holidays do people celebrate in this country?	Social Studies	**Vocabulary** Ordinal Numbers	
Connect pages 186–187 A Look at a Calendar	Social Studies/ Math	**Language Functions** Questions/Answers	Use a calendar.
Connect pages 188–189 "My Favorite Holiday"	Social Studies/ Literature	**Grammar** Present Tense	Summarize.
Connect page 190 "Bells Are Ringing"	Social Studies/ Literature	**Vocabulary** Onomatopoeia	
Assess page 191 Tell what you learned.			

Resources

Chapter 9

Support Materials

ACTIVITY BOOK
Pages 82–91

VIDEO
Unit 5, How Time Changes

BLUE TAPE
Side 1
Nine O'Clock Lullaby, pages T164–T175

BLUE TAPE
Side 2
"Star Light, Star Bright," page T155
"Old Man Moon," page T161
"Out in the Dark and Daylight," page T176

Little Celebrations Library

Look Up by Richard Vaughn, ScottForesman, 1993.

Little Zoot, by Bill Hawley, ScottForesman, 1993.

Assessment Materials

CREAM TAPE
Side 1
Listening Assessment, page T177

BLACKLINE MASTER
Language Assessment, page 80
Listening Assessment, page 81

Newcomer Book A

Survival Book for absolute beginners. For overview, see pages xxviii–xxxi.

For Extended Reading

All in a Day by Mitsumasa Anno, *et al,* Philomel Books, 1986.

Beautiful illustrations by ten famous artists plus entertaining text show what children in different countries around the world have in common.

Level: Average

The Big Dipper by Franklyn M. Branley, HarperCollins, 1991.

When you know what to look for, finding patterns in the stars scattered across the night sky can be fun.

Level: Average

Cabbage Moon by Tim Chadwick, Orchard Books, 1993.

Albert was one rabbit who didn't like cabbage. Then one night in a dream (or was it?), He floated up to the moon and helped other bunnies nibble the full moon into a crescent.

Level: Average

Is Anybody Up? by Ellen Kandoian, G. P. Putnam's Sons, 1989.

Molly gets up one quiet morning and wonders who else is awake. This book shows people in Molly's time zone from Quebec to Peru making their different breakfasts just as Molly is making hers.

Level: Beginning

Sun Up by Alvin Tresselt, Lothrop, 1991.

When the sun comes up on a farm, people are already hard at work.

Level: Advanced

Related Technology

Time Town, Steck-Vaughn Interactive Learning, 1996.
Interactive games teach time and other skills.

Chapter 10

Support Materials

PICTURE CARDS
Numbers 1, 6, 10, 13, 59

ACTIVITY BOOK
Pages 92–101

VIDEO
Unit 5, How Time Changes

BLUE TAPE
Side 2 "Bells Are Ringing," page T190

Shared Reading Collection

Through Moon and Stars and Night Skies, by Anne Turner, HarperCollins, 1990.

Little Celebrations Library

Grandfather Horned Toad, by Joe Hayes, CelebrationPress, 1996.

Patchwork Patterns, by Andrea Butler, CelebrationPress, 1996.

Assessment Materials

CREAM TAPE
Side 2
Listening Assessment, page T191

BLACKLINE MASTER
Language Assessment, page 82
Listening Assessment, page 83

For Extended Reading

The Moon Was at a Fiesta by Matthew Gollub, Tambourine Books, 1994.

In this colorful, original folk tale set in Mexico, the people of Oaxaca explain why the moon has lingered in the sky past dawn—the moon was at a fiesta!

Level: Advanced

Northwest Coast Indians by Mira Bartok and Christine Ronan, GoodYearBooks, 1996.

Loaded with fascinating pictures, this book describes customs of Indians who call the Northwest coast home.

Level: Beginning

Pueblo Indians of the Southwest by Mira Bartok and Christine Ronan, GoodYearBooks, 1996.

Children will learn about customs and traditions passed down from generation to generation.

Level: Beginning

Thanksgiving at Our House by Wendy Watson, Clarion, 1991.

It takes a whole week to prepare for Thanksgiving Day. This book combines traditional rhymes with a simple story line to invite the reader to the celebration.

Level: Average

Wheels by Byron Barton, Crowell, 1979.

Using lots of illustrations, this book shows the history of the wheel from round logs to modern tires.

Level: Average

Related Technology

Smithsonian's America, Creative Multimedia, 1994.

Excellent teaching tool for comparing America's past and present.

Project

Our Calendar

This optional project can be completed over the next two chapters. See the Unit Wrap-Up, page T191a, for more ideas on sharing the project with family members.

What You'll Need

Collect the following items for your calendar:

Art Supplies:
- a large piece of paper for drawing a mural
- pencils and crayons or markers
- yardsticks, rulers, or some other kind of straightedge

Other Supplies:
- a current calendar
- photos or pictures of children that show holiday celebrations, in the U.S. or in their native countries

Beginning the Project

Tell children that they will be working on a classroom calendar for the next few weeks. Explain that the next two chapters in their books are about time and a calendar is a very important device for noting time. Ask children to tell what they know about calendars and how they are used.

Home Involvement

Send Letter Home, Blackline Masters 74–79, to families to let them know what their child will be studying and to solicit their participation in collecting materials needed for the calendar project.

Making and Adding to the Calendar

Divide the mural into twelve equal spaces, one for each calendar month. Allow space surrounding each month where children can attach art, photographs, and the like. Encourage children to bring to class pictures or photographs that represent a holiday celebrated in the U.S. or in their native country. The pictures may be cut from magazines or they may be family photos. Write the child's name on each picture he or she brings to ensure it is returned to the correct family.

As the project progresses add other information as decided by the class or as is described on the following pages.

Create Each Month

- Assign children to each month and give them the relevant part of a current calendar.
- Let them copy the basic information of their month onto the mural in pencil and then color over the pencil using crayons or markers.

Record Important Dates

- Tell children to record special days. Let each child choose two dates. For example, they may add their birthday and a holiday their family celebrates.
- Help them add important school dates such as school vacations or special events.

Decorate the Calendar

- Have children attach the pictures they brought from home to the appropriate month.
- On months where there is room, have volunteers decorate the calendar with seasonal drawings; for example, kites for March.

Talk About the Calendar

- Have each "month" group brainstorm ideas about what is most interesting about their month
- Have children plan a talk about the month, using pictures or props. Every child should have some a role in the presentation of his or her month.
- Give children time to practice their presentations. Encourage them to practice their presentations in front of classmates before the presentation to family members.

Daily Discussion

Take a few minutes each day for discussion. Let children practice vocabulary learned in conjunction with the classroom calendar. Talk about how the project is going and how the calendar could be improved. At the end of the unit, have children summarize the information on their calendar and tell how it is useful. See page T191a for ideas about sharing the calendar with families and friends when the unit has been completed.

Activity Book

Chapter 9

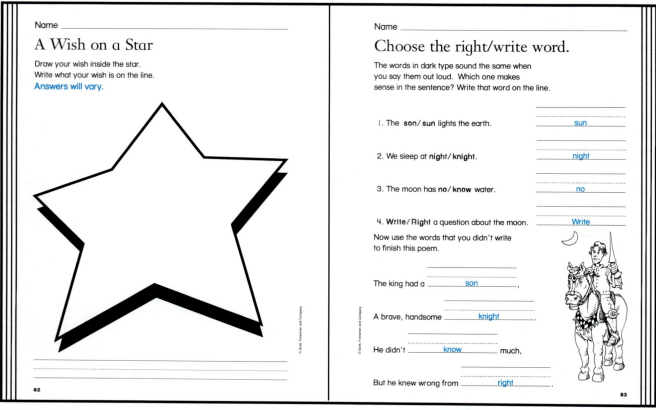

Name _____

A Wish on a Star

Draw your wish inside the star.
Write what your wish is on the line.
Answers will vary.

82

Name _____

Choose the right/write word.

The words in dark type sound the same when
you say them out loud. Which one makes
sense in the sentence? Write that word on the line.

1. The **son**/**sun** lights the earth.   _____ sun

2. We sleep at **night**/**knight**.   _____ night

3. The moon has **no**/**know** water.   _____ no

4. **Write**/**Right** a question about the moon.   _____ Write

Now use the words that you didn't write
to finish this poem.

The king had a _____ son ,

A brave, handsome _____ knight .

He didn't _____ know much,

But he knew wrong from _____ right

83

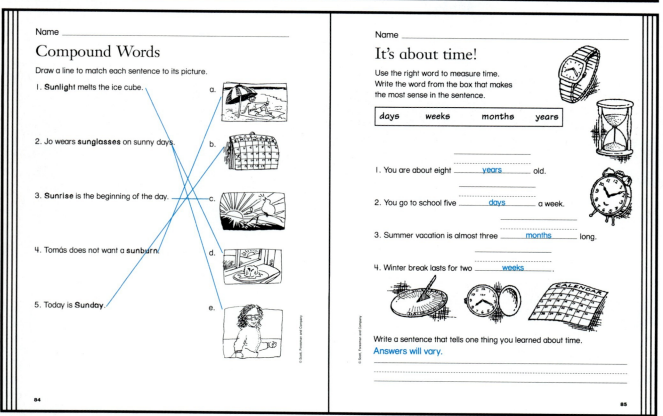

Name _____

Compound Words

Draw a line to match each sentence to its picture.

1. **Sunlight** melts the ice cube.   a.

2. Jo wears **sunglasses** on sunny days.   b.

3. **Sunrise** is the beginning of the day.   c.

4. Tomás does not want a **sunburn**.   d.

5. Today is **Sunday**.   e.

84

Name _____

It's about time!

Use the right word to measure time.
Write the word from the box that makes
the most sense in the sentence.

days	weeks	months	years

1. You are about eight _____ years _____ old.

2. You go to school five _____ days _____ a week.

3. Summer vacation is almost three _____ months _____ long.

4. Winter break lasts for two _____ weeks _____.

Write a sentence that tells one thing you learned about time.
Answers will vary.

85

Today and Long Ago

Change the underlined word to show that
the action happened in the past.
Use the new word to complete the sentence.

Today we <u>write</u> with words.

Long ago people _____ wrote _____
with pictures.

Today we <u>watch</u> sports on T.V.

Long ago people _____ watched _____
sports in the Colisseum.

Today we <u>find</u> new worlds in space.

Long ago people _____ found _____
new worlds across the ocean.

86

Words That Compare

Look for the -**er** ending.
If the sentence has a word that compares,
write the word on the line.

1. The water is dark. _____

2. My dog is darker than the water. _____ darker

3. The sky is wide. _____

4. The sky is wider than the river. _____ wider

5. A turtle is slow. _____

6. A turtle is slower than a rabbit. _____ slower

Choose one of the sentences that compares.
Write the two things that are compared. **Answers will vary.**

_____ _____

87

It's like this.

Tell what is being compared in each sentence.

1. The sky is like a clock, telling us whether it is night or day.

   The sky is being compared to a _____ clock _____.

2. The Big Dipper is like a ladle that could dip a drink out of the sea.

   The Big Dipper is being compared to a _____ ladle _____.

3. The sun hangs in the sky like a big golden plate.

   The sun is being compared to a _____ plate _____.

Describe the moon by comparing it to something else.

The moon is like a _____ Answers will vary. _____.

88

Vocabulary Assessment

Use the words in the box to complete each activity.

hour	day	night	earth	month	year	light	heat

1. Find the words that describe time. Write them on
   the blanks from the longest time to the shortest.

   _____ year
   _____ month
   _____ day
   _____ hour

2. Write the words that have opposite meanings.

   _____ Light _____ is the opposite of dark.

   _____ Night _____ is the opposite of day.

3. Move the letters around to write two words from
   the box.

   thear _____ earth _____

   thae _____ heat _____

89

Activity Book

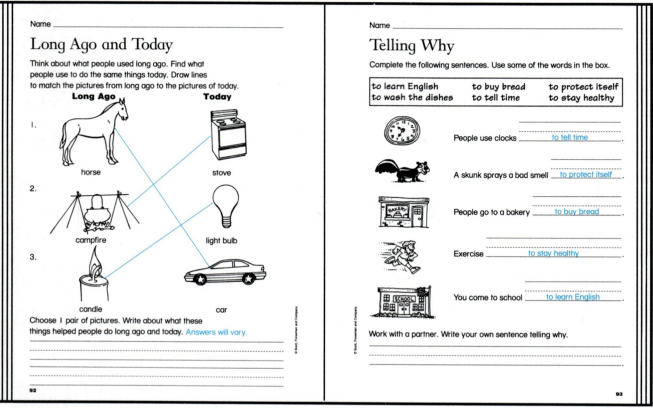

Name _____

Long Ago and Today

Think about what people used long ago. Find what people use to do the same things today. Draw lines to match the pictures from long ago to the pictures of today.

Long Ago   **Today**

1. horse   stove

2. campfire   light bulb

3. candle   car

Choose 1 pair of pictures. Write about what these things helped people do long ago and today. Answers will vary.

_____
_____
_____

92

Name _____

Telling Why

Complete the following sentences. Use some of the words in the box.

to learn English	to buy bread	to protect itself
to wash the dishes	to tell time	to stay healthy

_____
People use clocks ____to tell time____

_____
A skunk sprays a bad smell ____to protect itself____.

_____
People go to a bakery ____to buy bread____.

_____
Exercise ____to stay healthy____.

_____
You come to school ____to learn English____.

Work with a partner. Write your own sentence telling why.

_____
_____

93

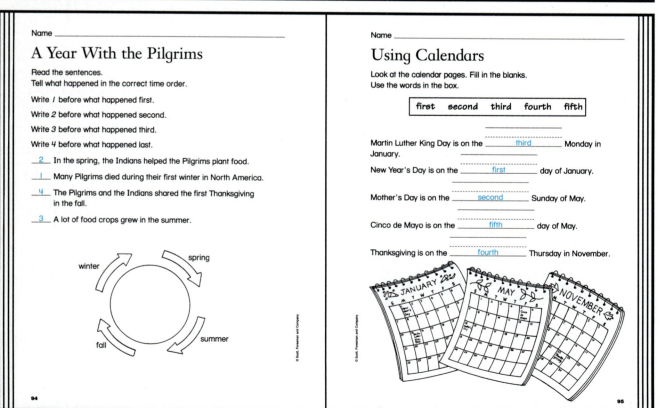

Name _____

A Year With the Pilgrims

Read the sentences.
Tell what happened in the correct time order.

Write *1* before what happened first.

Write *2* before what happened second.

Write *3* before what happened third.

Write *4* before what happened last.

__2__ In the spring, the Indians helped the Pilgrims plant food.

__1__ Many Pilgrims died during their first winter in North America.

__4__ The Pilgrims and the Indians shared the first Thanksgiving in the fall.

__3__ A lot of food crops grew in the summer.

winter   spring   summer   fall

94

Name _____

Using Calendars

Look at the calendar pages. Fill in the blanks.
Use the words in the box.

first	second	third	fourth	fifth

_____
Martin Luther King Day is on the ____third____ Monday in January.

_____
New Year's Day is on the ____first____ day of January.

_____
Mother's Day is on the ____second____ Sunday of May.

_____
Cinco de Mayo is on the ____fifth____ day of May.

_____
Thanksgiving is on the ____fourth____ Thursday in November.

JANUARY   MAY   NOVEMBER

95

Name _____

How Many? Which?

Use the pictures to count how many.
Write your answer.

1. How many flags do you see? __3__

2. How many pumpkins do you see? __5__

Look at the calendar pages below.
Write the day on which the holiday comes.

1. On which day is Columbus Day celebrated? _____ October 13

2. On which day is Halloween celebrated? _____ October 31

October

Sunday	Monday	Tuesday	Wednesday	Thursday	Friday	Saturday
				1	2	3	4
5	6	7	8	9	10	11
12	Columbus Day 13	14	15	16	17	18
19	20	21	22	23	24	25
26	27	28	29	30	Halloween 31	

96

Name _____

My Favorite Holiday

Write the name of your favorite holiday on the line below.
Answers will vary.

1. My favorite holiday is _____

2. Here is a picture of me having fun on that holiday.

3. On that holiday I like to _____

4. The holiday I'd like to learn more about is _____

97

Name _____

Using Verbs

Fill in the blanks with different action words to complete the story.
Answers may vary.

Today is Independence Day. In the afternoon, my

mom _____gives_____ me some money. Then

we _____walk_____ to the store. We

_____buy_____ a lot of fruit. She

_____puts_____ the fruit on a plate. Then she

_____cuts_____ it up. At night, some family and

friends _____come_____ to our house. We

_____go_____ outside. We _____hear_____

firecrackers.

98

Name _____

Vocabulary Assessment

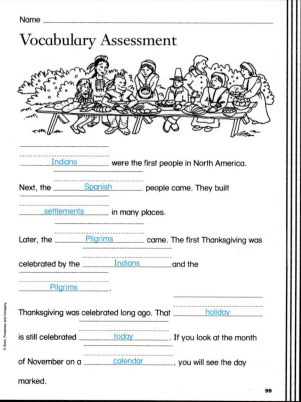

_____Indians_____ were the first people in North America.

Next, the _____Spanish_____ people came. They built

_____settlements_____ in many places.

Later, the _____Pilgrims_____ came. The first Thanksgiving was

celebrated by the _____Indians_____ and the

_____Pilgrims_____.

Thanksgiving was celebrated long ago. That _____holiday_____

is still celebrated _____today_____. If you look at the month

of November on a _____calendar_____, you will see the day

marked.

99

Preview

Activate Prior Knowledge
Introduce Vocabulary

Prepare for a discussion of "day and night" by showing children pictures of daytime and nighttime scenes. You may also want to point out the window, take the class outdoors, and darken the room. Tell children some activities you like to do during the day and at night. Invite volunteers to share their favorite activities with the class. As necessary, give prompts such as *Do you eat lunch during the day?*

Ask children how they can tell when it's daytime and nighttime. Introduce or review the word *sky*.

Develop Language and Concepts
Present page 154.

Give each child a piece of drawing paper. Ask children to fold their paper in half. Read aloud the first question in Tell What You Know. Have children draw a picture on the left side of their paper. Then read aloud the second question. Have children draw a picture on the right side of their paper. Encourage them to compare their pictures with other classmates. Then invite children to look at and describe the pictures on pages 154 and 155. Help them use the words in the Word Bank. Ask children to think about words they used to talk about their drawings and which words are new to them in English.

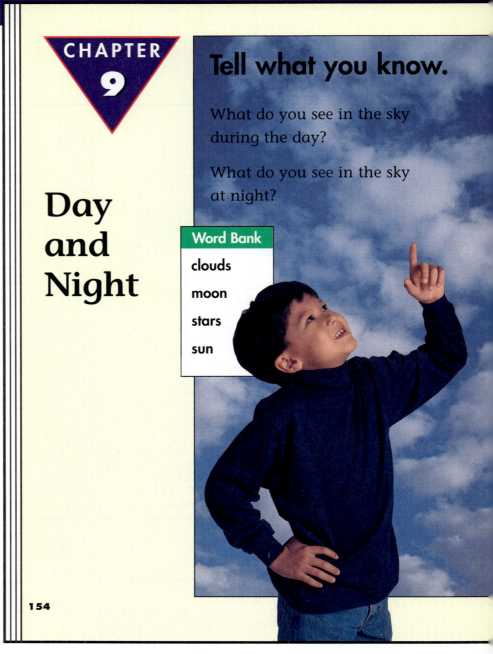

CHAPTER 9

Day and Night

154

Tell what you know.

What do you see in the sky during the day?

What do you see in the sky at night?

Word Bank
- clouds
- moon
- stars
- sun

Options for Reaching All Students

Beginning
Language: Vocabulary

Assign partners. Give each pair a set of word cards with the following words: *sky, night, day, clouds, moon, stars, sun.* Encourage children to take turns saying each word, as well as using it in a sentence or drawing a quick sketch showing what the word means. Invite children to talk about the sketches with their partners.

Advanced
Critical Thinking: Summarizing

Provide simple nonfiction books about the sun and the moon. Encourage children to find information about the sun and the moon and to draw or write to show what they learned. Allow time for children to share information orally.

Ask them to give opinions about the books they saw. Model sentences such as *This book was very helpful. This book was too hard.*

Home Connection
Science: The Big Dipper

Note the part of the night sky where the Big Dipper or Orion is located. On a clear day send home a note, describing the Big Dipper or Orion and asking family members to help their child find it in the night sky. Ask children to draw a picture of the Big Dipper or Orion. When children bring in their pictures, have them share their stargazing experiences.

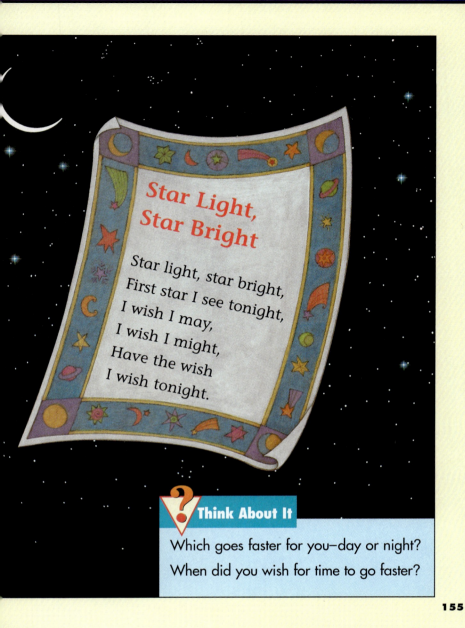

Star Light, Star Bright

Star light, star bright,
First star I see tonight,
I wish I may,
I wish I might,
Have the wish
I wish tonight.

? Think About It

Which goes faster for you—day or night?

When did you wish for time to go faster?

155

In this chapter, children will learn why we have day and night, as well as facts about the sun and the moon.

Use pages 154 and 155 to assess children's knowledge about the daytime and nighttime sky.

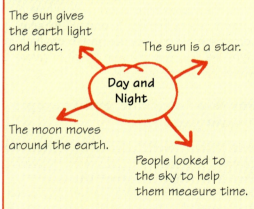

The sun gives the earth light and heat.

The sun is a star.

Day and Night

The moon moves around the earth.

People looked to the sky to help them measure time.

Develop Language and Concepts
Present page 155.

BLUE TAPE

Read aloud the poem. Tell children that some English-speaking people say this poem when they see the first star of the night. Then they make a wish. Invite volunteers to share similar wishing charms in their first languages. Then play Side 2 of the Blue Tape several times and encourage children to join in.

ACTIVITY BOOK

Use Activity Book page 82 to let children express a wish.

With the class, answer the questions in Think About It. Encourage children to explain their responses.

Mixed Ability
Video: How Time Changes

VIDEO

Show children the video to help build background information about the unit theme. You may also choose to use the video in other ways that are appropriate during the unit.

Little Celebrations
Look Up

This story points out the many different things that can be seen in the daytime and nighttime sky.

Level: Average

Present

Activate Prior Knowledge
Review Vocabulary

Elicit a list of objects children see in the sky. Write the words on a chart. Ask volunteers to read one of the words and tell whether it names something they see in the daytime or nighttime sky. Ask children to tell or guess where the sun is at night.

Develop Language and Concepts
Present page 156.

Help children read the question. Have them examine the diagram and predict answers. Then read the text together. Use a yellow paper circle to represent the sun. Have children pretend to be the earth, spining slowly in place to demonstrate "facing the sun" and "facing away from the sun."

Model a Strategy
Use a Diagram

Model using a diagram for information:

In this diagram, I see the sun and the earth. I read the labels to help me understand what I see. I see that the part of the earth labeled day is facing the sun. I see that the part of the earth labeled night is facing away from the sun. I think that whatever part of the earth faces the sun has day and whatever part of the earth faces away from the sun has night. Studying diagrams will help me understand what I am reading.

How do day and night happen?

The sun lights the **earth**.
But the earth is always turning.

The part of the earth that faces the sun has **day**.

The part of the earth that faces away from the sun has **night**.

Earth

night   day

sun

156 LEARN LANGUAGE • SCIENCE

Options for Reaching All Students

Beginning
Language: Demonstrate

Have a volunteer be the earth and turn slowly. Ask another volunteer to be the sun and shine a flashlight on the child who is the earth. Ask the child who is the earth to say "day" when he or she can see the flashlight and "night" when he or she cannot see the flashlight. Encourage volunteers to tell what is happening.

Advanced
Critical Thinking: Predict Outcomes

Put an X of tape on a globe to show your location. Have a child shine a flashlight on the globe while another slowly rotates the globe. Ask the child to stop the globe when the X faces the sun. Then ask what would happen if the earth did not turn. Help children see that if the earth did not turn, we would not have day and night.

Mixed Ability
Art: Chalk Drawing

Distribute white drawing paper, black construction paper, and some colored chalk. Ask children to think of a favorite outdoor place and draw it on the white paper as it looks during the day. Then have them use the black paper and draw the same favorite place as it appears at night. Encourage children to describe the places shown in their drawings.

It takes 24 **hours** for the earth to make one turn. So, there are 24 hours in one day.

It is **light** outside for part of each day. It is **dark** outside for part of each day.

Talk About It

What do you do when it is light outside?

What do you do when it is dark outside?

Develop Language and Concepts
Present page 157.

Help children read the page and study the illustrations. Encourage children to explain the concept in their own words.

Language Awareness

Vocabulary: Homophones

ACTIVITY BOOK

Write these sentences on the board: *"Come here, son,"* a *mother called. The sun is setting in the evening sky.*

Ask children to listen for two words that sound alike as you read the sentences. Point out that *son* and *sun* sound alike but have different spellings and different meanings. Help children explain the meaning of each word. For practice, use Activity Book page 83.

Assess

Use responses to Talk About It for assessment. Children should be able to

- name an activity done during the day
- name an activity done at night

LOOK AHEAD

Next, children will use their new vocabulary to learn more about the sun and to conduct an experiment.

Cooperative Learning
Language: Memory Game

Have children work in groups to compose oral cumulative sentences with activities they do during the day or at night, with each child repeating the list and adding an item.

Child A: *Every day I get up, eat breakfast, and brush my teeth.*

Child B: *Every day I get up, eat breakfast, brush my teeth, and go to school.*

Have groups write out each item on their lists on separate pieces of construction paper. Collect the papers and distribute them to other groups. Have groups sequence the new papers they receive.

QuickCheck

Subject-Verb Agreement

Check whether children are adding *-s* to a verb when the subject of the sentence is third person singular. Help those who need practice add *-s* to each of the following verbs and use each to complete the following sentence. *The earth (turn, move, travel) around the sun.*

Practice

Activate Prior Knowledge

Start a K-W-L Chart

BLACKLINE MASTER

Ask questions such as these to gather information to begin a K-W-L chart:

- Where is the sun?
- Is the sun hot or cold?

Use Blackline Master 21 and children's answers to make the K-W-L chart.

K: What We Know	The sun is hot. It gives us light.
W: What We Want to Find Out	What is the sun made of?
L: What We Learned	

Develop Language and Concepts

Present pages 158 and 159.

Read page 158 with children and discuss the pictures. Elicit what would happen if the earth didn't get the sun's heat and light. Ask children to tell what they learned about the sun and add their ideas to the K-W-L chart.

Then read the activity on page 159. Ask children to repeat the steps that they need to follow before they begin the activity. Have children work individually or in groups. Share the results. Then have children answer the Think About It question.

What is the sun?

The sun is a star.
It is the star closest to the earth.

The sun is made of very hot gases.
It is shaped like a ball.

The sun gives the earth light.
The sun gives the earth **heat.**

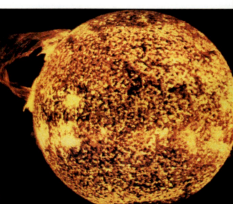

158 USE LANGUAGE • SCIENCE

Options for Reaching All Students

Beginning

Language: Labeling

Ask children to draw a picture of the sun shining on the earth. Help them label the sun and the earth. Encourage them to write about their pictures.

Advanced

Language: Writing

Ask children to say and write original sentences about the sun and the earth. Invite volunteers to share their sentences with the class. Then have classmates draw pictures to illustrate the sentences.

Home Connection

Recording Temperatures

For a weekend activity, ask family members to help children record the temperature in the morning, at midday, and in the evening on both Saturday and Sunday. You might also provide a simple form for recording the temperatures.

Ask children to tell why they think temperatures usually rise during the day and fall at night.

What can the sun do?

Things You Need

 2 plates   timer   2 ice cubes

Follow these steps.

1. Put an ice cube on each plate.

2. Put one plate in a place that gets sunlight.

3. Put the other plate in a place that doesn't get sunlight.

4. Use the timer. How long does each ice cube take to melt?

My Record

The ice cube that was in the sunlight _____.

The ice cube that was not in the sunlight _____.

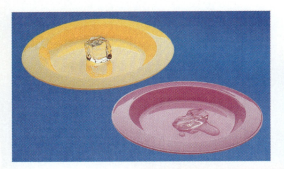

 Think About It

Why would you keep a cold drink out of the sunlight?

Language Awareness

Vocabulary: Compound Words

ACTIVITY BOOK Write *sunlight* on the board. Help children see the two words in *sunlight* and discuss their meanings. Remind children that a compound word is made up of two smaller words. Then use the same procedure with: *sunshine, sunrise, sunglasses, sunburn.* Use page 84 in the Activity Book.

Model a Strategy
Generalize

Model generalizing:

In this experiment I saw that the ice cube in the sunlight melted faster than the ice cube that didn't get sunlight. I know the warm sunlight made the ice cube melt faster. I think that the same thing would happen if I did the experiment with other things that melt, like chocolate or ice cream.

Assess ✓
Children should be able to

• name two things the sun gives the earth

• tell what they learned from the activity

LOOK**AHEAD** ➡

In the next section, children will learn more about the moon.

Cooperative Language Experience
Field Trip

Take children to a planetarium. Arrange for a simple talk to be given about the sun, moon, and stars.

Upon your return to the classroom, work together to write a language experience story about the trip. Children can talk about and draw their favorite things from what they saw.

Writer's Workshop
Write About the Sun

Refer children to the Writer's Workshop on pages 230–236 of the Student Book. Have them write about the sun, using the information in the K-W-L chart or other sources.

Little Celebrations
Little Zoot

In this story set in outer space, Little Zoot "cooks with the sun."

Level: Beginning

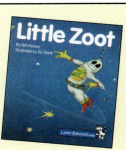

Little Zoot

Practice

Activate Prior Knowledge

Start a Venn Diagram

BLACKLINE MASTER

Compare and contrast the moon and the sun with children by asking questions. Use their answers and Blackline Master 23 to make a Venn diagram.

- How are the sun and the moon alike?
- How are they different?

Add information throughout the lesson.

Develop Language and Concepts

Present page 160.

Read the title question aloud and have children examine the illustration. Elicit responses. Then read the first two paragraphs. Encourage children to answer the second question, using what they know about needs and wants from previous units.

Then read the last two paragraphs aloud. Elicit how the words *moon* and *month* are related.

Model a Strategy

Predict Content

Model using a question to predict content:

When I read the question What is the moon like? I can predict that the answer will be on the page. I look for details about the moon to help me answer the question. Predicting what a page is about can make reading it easier.

What is the moon like?

The moon has no water.
The moon has no air.
The moon has only rocks and soil.

Can people, plants, or animals
live on the moon?

The moon circles the earth.
It takes a **month** for the moon to
move around the earth.

There are 12 months in a **year**.

160 USE LANGUAGE • SCIENCE

Options for Reaching All Students

Beginning

Art/Language: Drawing and Labeling

Distribute black construction paper folded in half. On the first half, have children use white chalk to draw the moon in the sky. Help them label it *Far Away from the Moon*. On the second, have children make a drawing to show details of the moon's surface. Help them label this section *On the Moon*.

Advanced

Science: Study Space Maps

Show a moon map from NASA. Invite children to discuss the need for maps in space travel. For example, astronauts would need a map to locate a good place to land on the moon. If possible, find a picture of the earth that was taken from space and have children compare the picture to a geographic map of the same surface.

Mixed Ability

Language: Vocabulary

On a chart, write sentences similar to the following:

The moon has no _____.

The moon has only _____ and _____.

There are 12 months in a _____.

Ask for volunteers to fill in the missing words.

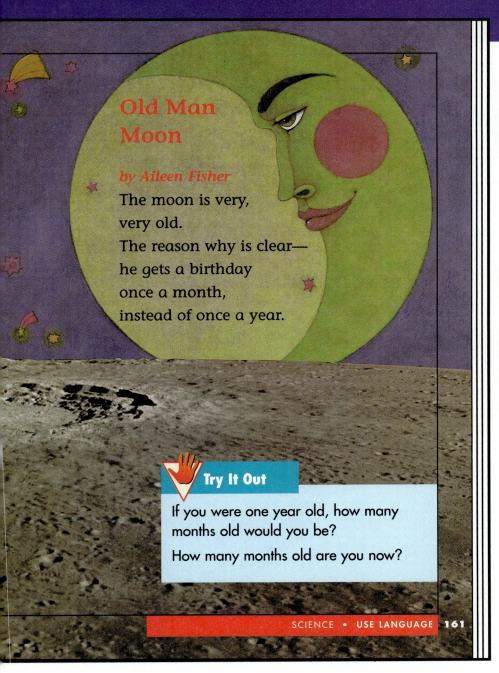

Old Man Moon

by Aileen Fisher

The moon is very,
very old.
The reason why is clear—
he gets a birthday
once a month,
instead of once a year.

Try It Out

If you were one year old, how many months old would you be?

How many months old are you now?

Develop Language and Concepts
Present page 161.

BLUE TAPE

Read aloud the poem title, the author's name, and the poem. Then play Side 2 of the Blue Tape several times and invite children to join in. Help children understand that the moon gets a birthday every time it goes around the earth.

Help children work in small groups to do the Try It Out activity.

Language Awareness

Language Functions: Express Time

ACTIVITY BOOK

Ask children to find two words on page 161 that express time—*month* and *year*. Review the word *day* and introduce *week*. Have children make up sentences expressing time: *There is one more day of school this week.* Use Activity Book page 85.

Assess

Children should be able to
- tell two facts about the moon
- tell the number of months in a year

LOOK **AHEAD**

In the next section, children will learn how people measured time long ago.

Cooperative Learning
Language/Music: Earth and Moon

Sing this song several times to the tune of "Row, Row, Row Your Boat." Encourage children to join in.

I am the moon above
Going round in space
Round and round and round I go.
Space's an awesome place.

I am the grand old earth
I watch the moon in space.
Round and round and round I go.
I see its friendly face.

Have children work in groups to decide who will be the earth and who will be the moon and how the earth and moon should be represented. Invite the "earth" and the "moon" to sing their parts as each moon revolves around its earth.

Multicultural Awareness
Moon Myths

To Americans, the moon's markings conjure up the image of the "man in the moon." In China, it's a banished princess. And in Vietnam, the markings form the outline of a rabbit. Have children share any moon myths they know.

Connect

Show children some calendars. Have them share what they know about calendars. Help children speculate why and how the first calendar was invented.

Develop Language and Concepts
Present pages 162 and 163.

Read the title question with children. Together look at the illustrations on both pages and ask children to predict what they will be reading about.

Then read the pages with children. Use a globe to show where Egypt and Central America are located. Ask children to tell why they think the people of Egypt and the people of Central America came up with similar calendars.

With the class, answer the questions in Think About It. Then have small groups share their personal answers.

Model a Strategy
Make Comparisions

Model making comparisons:

Comparing helps me understand what I read. When I read these pages, I compare how Egyptians and Central Americans measured time. I see that both these groups watched the sun and the moon, wrote about what they saw, and found out the same things.

How did people measure time long ago?

Long, long ago in Egypt, people watched the sun and the moon. They wrote about what they saw.

They found that there are about 365 days in a year. They found that there are about 30 days in a month.

162 CONNECT LANGUAGE • SCIENCE/SOCIAL STUDIES

Options for Reaching All Students

Beginning
Social Studies: The Calendar

Display a calendar. Look through the calendar with children. Help them name the different months of the year. Help them find out how many days are in each month. Reinforce the idea that the 12 months equal a year of 365 days.

Advanced
Language: Time Expressions

Assign partners and have them look at the present month's calendar and name yesterday's date, today's date, and tomorrow's date. Invite children to talk about yesterday, today, and tomorrow and describe things they did, are doing, or plan to do.

Mixed Ability
Social Studies: Understanding Our Calendar

Provide copies of the present month's calendar. Let children put an X on the current date. Model questions about specific dates, such as "What is the date for the first Saturday in the month?" Invite volunteers to answer and then ask questions of their own.

Long, long ago
in Central America,
people watched the
sun and the moon.
They wrote about what they saw.

They found that there are about
365 days in a year.
They found that there are about
30 days in a month.

Today, in the United States, we use
a calendar like these old ones.
It has about 365 days in a year.
It has about 30 days in a month.

 **Think About It**

Why is it
important to have
a calendar?

What other ways
do you tell time?

Grammar: Irregular Past Tense

ACTIVITY BOOK

Call attention to the words *watched, wrote, saw,* and *found* on page 163. Guide children to see that these words show actions that happened in the past. On the board, write these words with their present-tense forms—*watch, write, see,* and *find.* Point out which action words tell about things that happen now. Have children match action words that tell about now with those that tell about the past. Point out the *-ed* ending which helps signal the past tense for regular verbs and the new form for the past tense that irregular verbs have. For further practice, children can use page 86 in the Activity Book.

Assess

Children should be able to

- tell what people of long ago found out
- tell why it is important to have a calendar

LOOK AHEAD

Next, children will use what they have learned about day and night to read a story about what goes on at different times of the day in different parts of the world.

Peer Tutoring
Critical Thinking: Drawing Conclusions

Have children work in pairs of mixed abilities to play a "What Am I?" game. Prepare cards with questions similar to the following:

I have about 365 days. What am I?

I shine during the day. What am I?

Include the answer on the back of each card. Invite partners to take turns asking and answering the questions.

Provide blank index cards and encourage children to make up their own questions and answers. Have pairs exchange cards and continue playing the game.

Home Connection
Calendars Around the World

Encourage children to talk with family members about calendars from their culture. Ask children to bring the calendars to class and talk about what they learned from their families. Invite the class to compare and contrast the calendars.

Connect

Activate Prior Knowledge
Use Pictures to Predict

Have children look at the pictures in the story. Ask questions such as these:

- Where does this story take place?
- What do you think will happen in the story?

Introduce the Selection

Help children find and read the title of the story and the author's name.

Read the Selection

Read the story with children. Then play side 1 of the Blue Tape. Encourage children to listen to the tape as often as they like. Use the suggested activities appropriate to meet children's needs.

Model a Strategy
Predict Content

Model predicting the content of a story.

When I read the title of this book, Nine O'Clock Lullaby, I can guess that this book might have something to do with time, since nine o'clock is a time of day. The pictures on the first two pages make me think about nighttime. As I turn the pages, I see that many pages begin and end with a time of day. This makes me think that the book will have something to do with time. As I read the book I will think about my prediction to see whether I am right. Can you see ways to use prediction as you read?

Teachable Moment
Evaluating Information: Author's Purpose

After reading the book with children, ask them to guess why the author, Marilyn Singer, wrote this book. Children should guess that the book was written to help children find out about time in different parts of the world.

Options for Reaching All Students

Beginning
Critical Thinking: Comparing and Contrasting

Encourage children to point out the place in the story that looks most like their native country. Help children explain how the picture is like their native country and how it is different.

Advanced
Social Studies: Geography

BLUE TAPE

Let children work in groups to mark each place mentioned in the book on a world map. As children listen to the recorded story on the Blue Tape, Side 1, have them point to each place as it is mentioned.

Home Connection
What Time Is It?

Encourage children to ask their parents about the time difference between where they are now and their native land. With the help of their parents, have children draw a picture illustrating what they would be doing in each place. Encourage children to show their pictures and use the map when discussing their findings at school.

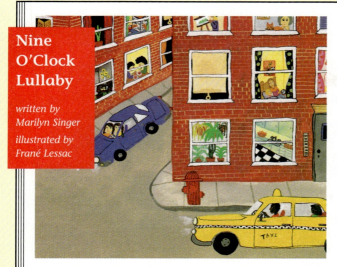

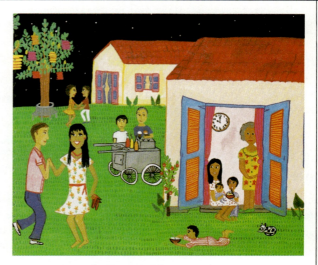

9 P.M. in Brooklyn, New York

The vroom and shush of traffic outside
the bedroom window while Mama turns
the pages of a sleepytime tale.
9 P.M. in Brooklyn, New York, is . . .

10 P.M. in Puerto Rico

Sweet rice, fruit ice, coconut candy. Papa
playing congas, Tío his guitar. Swaying
lanterns in the branches, dancing people
on the grass. Bedtime is forgotten on a
special party night.
10 P.M. in Puerto Rico is . . .

Midnight on the mid-Atlantic

Nothing blacker than the water, nothing
wider than the sky. Pitch and toss, pitch
and toss. The Big Dipper might just ladle
a drink out of the sea.
Midnight on the mid-Atlantic is . . .

2 A.M. in England

Bread in the pantry at nighttime
tastes better than cream cakes at tea.
2 A.M. in England is . . .

3 A.M. in Zaire

Dreaming by the Congo.

Connect

Develop Language and Concepts

Have children review pages 164–167. Then use a globe to find the places already mentioned in the selection. Help them see how the route is basically east.

Model a Strategy

Use Context

Model using total context to get information from a story:

As I read this story, I notice that people have different customs in different places on earth. I read the pages and look at the pictures to find out all I can about the various people and their customs. I realize that I can get information beyond the basic topic by using the pictures and details in the text.

Talk About the Selection

Help children discuss the fact that the time is different in different parts of the world because as the earth turns, half the earth is in light and half in shadow. Our time of day depends on how far into the light or shadow we are, so different places have different times.

Teachable Moment

Interpret Information: Predict Outcome

After children have read this far in the story, have them predict the pattern of the rest of the book. Children should predict that the pages of the rest of the book will tell them what people in other parts of the world are doing at different times.

Options for Reaching All Students

Beginning

Language: Choral Reading

Have children do a choral reading of the story. Let a different group read each page. Make sure children are ready to read when their turn comes.

Advanced

Language: Personal Word Bank

Have children choose five words from the story to put into their personal word bank. They should write the word on the front of an index card and illustrate it or write a context sentence for it on the back of the card. Have children work in pairs to share their cards.

Peer Tutoring

Critical Thinking: Story Retelling

Have students work in pairs of mixed abilities and talk about the different times of day and the places that they have read about up to this point.

3 A.M. in Switzerland

Dreaming in the Alps.
3 A.M. in Zaire and Switzerland is . . .

5 A.M. in Moscow

A crash and a clatter and the samovar on the floor.
The cat has done it again! Papa wakes up with a
laugh. Mama wakes up with a shout. Babushka
doesn't wake at all, but just stays snoring in her bed.
5 A.M. in Moscow, Russia, is . . .

7:30 A.M. in India

All over the village well ropes
squeak, buckets splash, bracelets
jingle, long braids swish. All over
the village morning music.
7:30 A.M. in India is . . .

10 A.M. in Guangzhou, China

On the way to Goat City auntie pedals quickly,
flying like a dragon. On the way to Goat City
elder sister pedals slowly, flapping like a goose.
10 A.M. in Guangzhou, China, is . . .

11 A.M. in Japan

In the pond
  grandfather floats a tulip
    so the fish can greet the spring.
11 A.M. in Japan is . . .

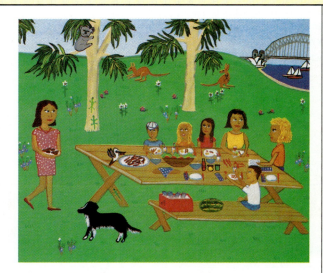

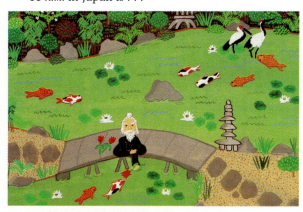

Noon in Sydney, Australia

At the barbie, five cousins, four
uncles, three aunts, two sheepdogs,
six lizards, and one sly kookaburra
stealing sausage right off the plates.
Noon in Sydney, Australia, is . . .

Connect

Develop Language and Concepts

Have children reread page 173. Ask what the children in Alaska seem to be doing. Children should tell you that they are using a blanket to toss a child into the air. Elicit from children that the scene takes place in a cold region. Tell children that tossing children on a blanket is an old Inuit (Eskimo) tradition.

Model a Strategy

Activate Prior Knowledge

Model activating prior knowledge:

When I read, I think about what I already know. I know that the part of the earth that faces the sun has day, while the part of the earth that faces away from the sun has night. Thinking about what I already know helps me understand that the time of day is different in different parts of the world.

Language Awareness

Language Functions: Describing

Point out to children that this book tells about people living in different places all over the world. Help children describe in their own words one of the cultures they have read about.

Teachable Moments

Recognize Logical Relationships: Sequence

Invite children to use a globe and a flashlight to represent the sun to explain in their own words why the time of day is different on different parts of the earth.

Respond to the Selection

Personal Response: Ask children, *What place that you read about is your favorite? Why? Would you like to find out more about this culture? How would you do that?*

Critical Response: Ask, *What do the different people seem to have in common?* Children should reply that people need to sleep, eat, and do a meaningful activity.

Creative Response: Have children each draw a picture of a place that could be used in *Nine O'Clock Lullaby.* Have them choose either the place in which they are living now or the place where they lived in their native country. Help them write a caption telling what time it would be in the place they chose.

Options for Reaching All Students

Beginning

Language: Reading

BLUE TAPE

Have children read along with this story on the Blue Tape, Side 1. After reading, have children find a page they feel confident in reading aloud on their own or with a partner.

Advanced

Language: Researching, Speaking, and Listening

Encourage children to investigate one of the cultures mentioned in the story. They can interview each other or use library resources. Then let children share with others what they found out about the culture.

Mixed Ability

Math: Time Zones

Display a map of the United States showing time zones. Pick a time and location, such as 1 P.M. where you live, and ask children to name the time in the other time zones. Children should add an hour for each time zone to the east, and subtract an hour for each time zone to the west. Continue with various times and locations.

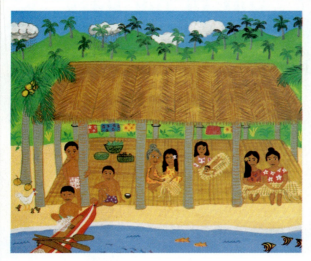

3 P.M. in Samoa

The rain has stopped. The sea is calm.
"Let's weave," say the mothers. "Let's fish,"
say the fathers. "Let's chase the dogs," say
the brothers, "before it rains again."
3 P.M. in Samoa is . . .

5 P.M. in Nome, Alaska

Toss the blanket high. Toss the
blanket higher. Ask her, can
she see the caribou? Ask her,
can she touch the sky?
5 P.M. in Nome, Alaska, is . . .

6 P.M. in Los Angeles

The sun eases down like a big golden dinner
plate at the end of the day on the beach.
6 P.M. in Los Angeles is . . .

8 P.M. in Mexico

Saying good night to the burros

8 P.M. in Wisconsin

Saying good night to the calves
8 P.M. in Mexico and Wisconsin is . . .

9 P.M. in Brooklyn, New York

The vroom and shush of traffic outside the bedroom
window while Mama turns the pages of a sleepytime tale.

Connect

Activate Prior Knowledge

Review Vocabulary

Ask children to look at the illustration on the page and predict what the poem will be about. Then ask children to tell about things they do during the day and things they do at night.

Develop Language and Concepts

Present page 176.

BLUE TAPE

Read aloud the poem title, author's name, and the poem itself. Then play Side 2 of the Blue Tape several times and encourage children to join in saying the poem.

Help children write an answer to the Write About It question. Encourage then to share their personal responses with a classmate.

Language Awareness

Phonics: Pattern and Rhyme

After saying the poem several times, let children read the first line of each couplet only and let them notice the pattern. Then have children find the words in the poem that end each couplet and rhyme. Have children take turns saying this set of rhyming words: *tree, free, see, be.*

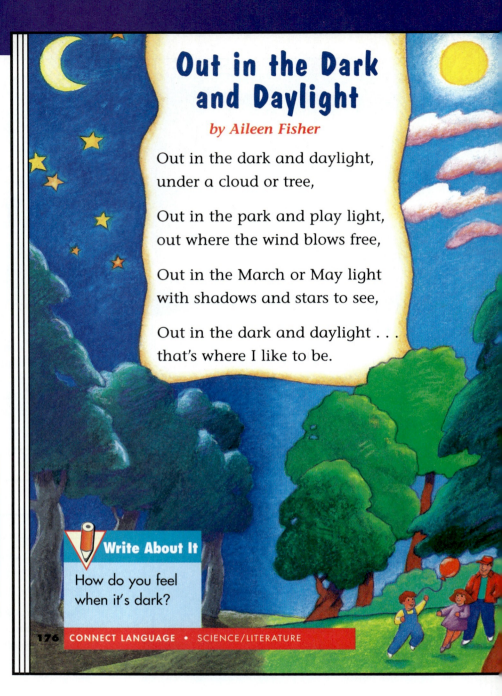

Out in the Dark and Daylight

by Aileen Fisher

Out in the dark and daylight,
under a cloud or tree,

Out in the park and play light,
out where the wind blows free,

Out in the March or May light
with shadows and stars to see,

Out in the dark and daylight . . .
that's where I like to be.

Write About It

How do you feel when it's dark?

176 CONNECT LANGUAGE • SCIENCE/LITERATURE

Options for Reaching All Students

Beginning

Language: Words and Pictures

Invite children to pick one of the couplets in the poem to illustrate. You may want them to write the appropriate couplet at the top of their drawing.

Advanced

Math: List and Tally

Have children work in groups. Have groups brainstorm a list of their favorite daytime activities. Then ask each group to poll its members to determine three favorites. Have children report their findings to the other groups and compare favorites. Together make a composite class graph.

Mixed Ability

Language: Role Play

TPR

Have volunteers say and act out a favorite thing to do during the day or at night. Then have these volunteers say a series of action words for their classmates to act out.

Tell what you learned.

1. Work with a group. List things the sun can do.

2. Work with a partner. Write a question about the moon. Ask the class your question.

3. Choose an hour from the story. Draw a picture. Show something you do at that time. Put a title on your picture. Tell a classmate about your picture.

ASSESS LANGUAGE **177**

Assess

Activity 1: Have children brainstorm answers. Have one group member write the answers on a separate piece of paper. Evaluate the number and accuracy of responses.

Activity 2: Evaluate whether children can write logical questions. Notice which children can answer their classmates' questions.

Activity 3: Check that children draw a picture that shows them doing something at a certain time of day or night.

Have children complete the Chapter Self-Assessment Blackline Master 33. Have them choose products to place in their portfolios. Add the results of any rubrics, checklists, self-assessments, or portfolio assessments, Blackline Masters 2–18.

Listening Assessment

 BLACKLINE MASTER

Make sure that each child has a copy of Blackline Master 81 and a pencil. Play Side 1 of the Cream Tape several times stopping the tape to allow children to write. Have children listen to the dictation and write what they hear.

TAPESCRIPT

CREAM TAPE

Listen carefully and write what you hear.

The sun is a star. (pause) It is the star closest to the earth. (pause) The sun gives the earth light. (pause) The sun gives the earth heat.

Vocabulary Assessment

 ACTIVITY BOOK

Have children complete Activity Book page 89.

Strategy Assessment

Give each child a pencil and a crayon and ask him or her to compare and contrast them.

Writing Assessment

Have children make personal picture books in which they illustrate and write about the sun, earth, and moon.

Language Assessment

 BLACKLINE MASTER

Use Blackline Master 80 in the Teacher's Resource Book.

Standardized Test Practice

 ACTIVITY BOOK

Use pages 90 and 91 in the Activity Book. Answers: 3:30, Wednesday, the moon.

Preview

Activate Prior Knowledge

Use a Clock

Start a discussion of "long ago and today" by bringing in a small clock and helping children name it and tell how and where it is used. You may wish to make a paper-plate clock with moveable hands. Check to see that children can tell time in English. Ask questions such as:

- Long ago, when people did not have clocks, how might people have been able to tell time?

Have children answer the first two questions in Tell What You Know by pointing out the clocks on the page.

For the third question, invite children to tell about clocks they use.

Develop Language and Concepts

Present pages 178 and 179.

Invite children to look at the picture of each timepiece and help them read the labels. Discuss how each one works. Help children talk about which are old and which ones are new. Recall with children what they read about people watching the sun and the moon to measure time.

Read the words in the Word Bank with children. Recite the numbers together and point to each corresponding numeral on a clock

(Continued on page T179)

CHAPTER 10

Long Ago and Today

Tell what you know.

Which clocks were used long ago?

Which clocks are used today?

Which clocks do you use?

hourglass
sundial

Options for Reaching All Students

Beginning

Language: Counting

Read aloud the number words from the Word Bank several times. Then distribute twelve cards, each with a numeral from 1 to 12 and the corresponding word. Say a number and ask children holding that number, the number that comes before, and the number that comes after to stand. Have a volunteer say the numbers in sequence.

Advanced

Language: What Time Is It?

Start a "What Time Is It?" game by saying, *I just woke up and got out of bed. What time is it?* Have children respond, using the sentence pattern *It's ______ o'clock.* Have children talk about what time they get up during the week and weekends and the times they do other things.

Mixed Ability

Math: Telling Time

Give each child a paper plate and show children how to write numerals on the plate to make a clock face. Have children draw the minute hand in the twelve position. Give children brass fasteners and black construction paper to use to make hour hands. Name different times and ask children to show the times on their clocks.

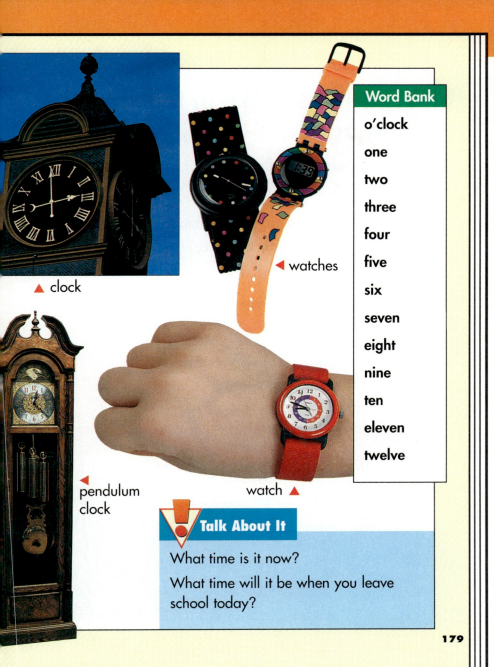

▲ clock

◄ watches

◄ pendulum clock

watch ▲

Word Bank

o'clock
one
two
three
four
five
six
seven
eight
nine
ten
eleven
twelve

In this chapter, children will learn the language connected with measuring time, find out about how our country was settled, and learn how holidays are associated with different events that occurred in the past.

Use pages 178 and 179 to assess children's understanding of the time concepts of long ago and today.

People have used different kinds of clocks to tell time.

Different groups settled in North America.

Long Ago and Today

We celebrate old and new holidays.

Holidays can be shown on a calendar.

face. Ask children to tell time, using the sentence pattern *It's _____ o'clock.*

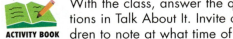

ACTIVITY BOOK

With the class, answer the questions in Talk About It. Invite children to note at what time of day other activities take place. Use Activity Book page 92 to reinforce the concept of long ago and today.

⚠️ **Talk About It**

What time is it now?

What time will it be when you leave school today?

Peer Tutoring
Social Studies: Daily Activities

Have children work in pairs of mixed abilities. Give each pair a set of six large blank index cards. Ask children to draw six pictures of everyday activities, such as getting out of bed, going to school, having lunch, or playing after school. When a set is complete, demonstrate how to sort the cards in time sequence. Have children work

with their partners to sort their sets and talk about them.

First , I wake up and get out of bed. Then, . . .

Home Connection
Clocks

Children might ask family members to describe and help them draw pictures of the different kinds of clocks they have in their home. Or they might just draw pictures of favorite kinds of clocks they have seen. Children might also bring in pictures cut from magazines that show different kinds of time-pieces.

Present

Activate Prior Knowledge
Brainstorm Ideas

Ask children to think about what things might be important for someone who goes to live in another country to learn about his or her new home. Model sharing ideas.

Point out North America and Spain on a globe. Then tell children they will read about people who went from their homes in Spain to settle in North America long ago.

Develop Language and Concepts
Present pages 180 and 181.

Read through the information with children. Encourage them to share ideas about different reasons settlers might have had for coming here.

Together, study the map and help children pronounce the names of some early Spanish settlements. Read through the information with children. Compare what the Spanish settlers had to learn in their new land to the list children brainstormed previously.

Help children answer the Think About It question.

What was it like in this country long ago?

The first people in North America were Indians.

About 500 years ago, people from other countries began to come to North America.

People came from Spain to look for gold.

Later, more Spanish people came to settle the land. The settlers lived in settlements.

180 LEARN LANGUAGE • SOCIAL STUDIES

Options for Reaching All Students

Beginning
Science: How Plants Grow

Recall with children that the Indians taught the Spanish how to grow crops. Have children fold a piece of paper into four sections. Invite them to make drawings to show a seed being planted, the ground being watered, the sun shining on the planted seed, and the plant sprouting. Help children caption their four pictures.

Advanced
Social Studies: Crops

Invite children to point out their native country on a globe and tell what kinds of crops are grown there. Then children can draw and label a picture of the crops.

Mixed Ability
Social Studies: Customs

Ask children who arrived recently enough to remember when they first got to in their new country. Have them tell what things they learned from their new friends. Then have them tell what they have taught or would like to teach their new friends.

Look at the map.
Can you name some early Spanish settlements?

Early Spanish Settlements in North America

- Land claimed by Spain
- Early mission settlements

NORTH AMERICA
PACIFIC OCEAN
ATLANTIC OCEAN
San Diego
Santa Fe
Albuquerque
Tucson
El Paso
San Antonio
St. Augustine
Gulf of Mexico
Havana
San Juan
Santo Domingo
Mexico City
SOUTH AMERICA

The Spanish settlers and the Indians learned new things from each other.

The Indians taught the Spanish about new plants.

Many Indians learned to speak Spanish.

Think About It

Why was it important for the Indians and the Spanish people to learn each other's language?

Language Functions: Telling Why

ACTIVITY BOOK

Write the following sentence on the chalkboard: *People came from Spain to look for gold.*

Ask a volunteer to find the part of the sentence that tells why the people came from Spain. Help children focus on the words *to look for gold.* Point out that these words tell why they came. Then write: *Later, more Spanish people came to settle the land.*

Ask a volunteer to find the part of the sentence that tells why more Spanish people came. Help children focus on the words *to settle the land.* Point out that these words tell why more Spanish people came. For practice, children can use page 93 in the Activity Book.

Assess ✔

Children should be able to

- give facts about Spanish settlers
- tell how the Spanish and Indians helped each other

LOOK **AHEAD**

Next, children will find out about Pilgrims who settled in North America.

Cooperative Language Experience
Guest Speaker

If possible, invite a guest to speak about the Indians' customs and daily life in North America before the time of the settlers. Ask the speaker to bring in artifacts of the Indians' culture. As an alternative, take children to visit your local natural history museum.

As a class, write a language experience story about what children have learned. Children can draw and caption pictures.

Little Celebrations
Grandfather Horned Toad

In this Navajo tale, a little girl named Nanabah is saved from a giant by a horned toad, as well as some helpful ants.

Level: Advanced

GRANDFATHER HORNED TOAD

Practice

Activate Prior Knowledge

Use Pictures

PICTURE CARDS

Show the following Picture Cards: airplane, boat, bus, car, sailboat. As you name each means of transportation, have children raise their hand if they have ever ridden in one. Then ask volunteers to tell how their families came to the U.S. Use Picture Cards 1, 6, 10, 13, 59.

Develop Language and Concepts

Present pages 182 and 183.

Invite children to look at the illustration of people arriving in North America. Point out that this picture shows another group of settlers coming to North America. Explain that they used this smaller kind of boat to get from the ship to the land. Find out if any children have heard of the Pilgrims. Ask volunteers to share any information they may have about the Pilgrims.

Help children read the pages. Encourage them to look at the illustrations as they read. Ask children to tell why they think the Pilgrims asked the Indians to share a meal with them. Then ask them why they think the Indians helped the Pilgrims so much.

With the class, answer the Think About It question. Then have children work in groups of three to share their personal answers.

Who were the next settlers?

About 400 years ago, the Pilgrims came to North America from England. They came on ships. The first ship was called the *Mayflower*.

Their first winter was hard. It was cold. The Pilgrims didn't have enough to eat. Many Pilgrims died.

182 USE LANGUAGE • SOCIAL STUDIES

Options for Reaching All Students

Beginning

Social Studies: Picture Story

Help children understand that the Pilgrims and the Indians were friends because they helped each other. Have children draw a picture of themselves and a friend doing something together. Help children label their pictures.

Advanced

Social Studies: Using a Globe

Explain that the Pilgrims left England, lived in Holland for a time, and then traveled to North America. Have children use a globe to trace a possible route the Pilgrims may have taken. Help children talk about the Pilgrims' route. Then ask them to trace on a globe the routes they took from their native countries to the U.S.

Mixed Ability

Writing: Make a Book

Prepare booklets for children to use. Assign children to groups of four. Ask them to title the booklet "A Year With the Pilgrims." Then ask children to draw a scene from each season of the Pilgrim's first year as discussed in the lesson. Help children label the seasons. Display the booklets for children to share.

In the spring, the Indians helped the Pilgrims plant crops.

During the summer, the crops grew. The Pilgrims had a lot of food that year.

In the fall, the Pilgrims asked the Indians to share a meal with them. They thanked God for their friends and food. This was the first Thanksgiving.

 Think About It

The Indians helped the Pilgrims. Who helps newcomers today?

SOCIAL STUDIES • **USE LANGUAGE** 183

Language Awareness

Vocabulary: Time Expressions

ACTIVITY BOOK

Point out that the names of the seasons can be expressions of time passing. Have volunteers read aloud the sentences that include the seasons. Children should be aware that text about the Pilgrims tells about a full year. Point out that a year's time span can begin with any season. Use page 94 in the Activity Book.

Model a Strategy
Understand Chronology

Model understanding chronology:

When I read about what this country was like long ago, it helps me to think about the order in which things happened. I know that the Indians were in North America when the Spanish people came. I also know that the Pilgrims came after the Spanish settlers.

Assess ✔

Children should be able to
- tell where the Pilgrims came from
- tell why they celebrated Thanksgiving

LOOK AHEAD

Next, children will find out about holidays celebrated in this country.

Cooperative Language Experience

Critical Thinking: Brainstorming

Have children imagine that a time machine could bring some Pilgrims and Indians of long ago into the world of today. Have children form groups to brainstorm questions for their guests. For example:

What would you like to see first?

What would you like to know more about?

Can you tell us about the first Thanksgiving?

Have children take turns role-playing an interview session. Then have the class write together about the interviews.

Little Celebrations
Patchwork Patterns

This story explores different sources of inspiration for design patterns used in patchwork quilts.

Level: Advanced

Practice

Activate Prior Knowledge
Use a Calendar

Browse through a calendar with children, reading the name of each month and saying the names of the holidays celebrated in that month. Invite children to add the names of holidays from their native cultures.

Develop Language and Concepts
Present pages 184 and 185.

Read through the pages with children. Help them find the fourth Thursday in November on a calendar and see where Thanksgiving Day is marked. Recall with them why the first Thanksgiving was celebrated. Introduce the key word *thankful*.

Then help children find the third Monday in January and see where Martin Luther King Day is marked. Introduce the word *fairly*.

Encourage children to discuss the pictures on these pages. Read the holiday names in the Word Bank and invite children to tell what they know about each holiday. Then have children do the Talk About It activity.

What holidays do people celebrate in this country?

We celebrate old **holidays.**

We celebrate Thanksgiving Day on the fourth Thursday in November.

How do people celebrate Thanksgiving today? What do you think people are thankful for today?

184 USE LANGUAGE • SOCIAL STUDIES

Options for Reaching All Students

Beginning
Language: Label a Picture

Make sure that children know what the word *thankful* means. Remind them that Thanksgiving Day is a time to think about what we are thankful for. Have children use crayons to draw something for which they are thankful. Help children label their drawings. Display them on a bulletin board titled "We Are Thankful."

Advanced
Language: Share Information

Have children interview teachers, librarians, or other adults about Martin Luther King, Jr. The interviewers can present their findings. Alternatively, provide sources for children to use to find out more about him. Encourage children to share their information with others.

Cooperative Learning
Invent a Holiday

Ask small groups to invent a brand new holiday. Let children decide what will be celebrated and what the celebration should include. Have children justify the date they choose for their holiday.

We celebrate new holidays.

We celebrate Martin Luther King Day on the third Monday in January.

Dr. Martin Luther King, Jr., helped people. African Americans were not treated fairly. He dreamed that all people would be treated fairly. He told people about his dream. His dream helped change things.

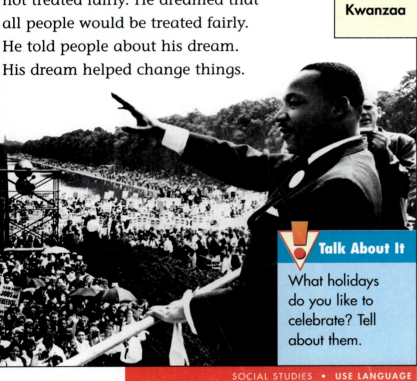

Word Bank

Chinese New Year

Christmas

Cinco de Mayo

Hanukkah

Kwanzaa

Talk About It

What holidays do you like to celebrate? Tell about them.

Language Awareness

Vocabulary: Ordinal Numbers

ACTIVITY BOOK

Ask four children to come forward and help them form a line facing one way. Then say, *I see (child's name). He (She) is first.* Continue using the same pattern to name the child who is second, third, fourth, and fifth. Then ask the class *Who is first? Who is second?, third? fourth? fifth?* Next, list the ordinal terms on the chalkboard. Call another group of children to come forward, one at a time, naming who should come first, second, and so on as you identify each ordinal term on the chalkboard. Have children use page 95 in the Activity Book for more practice.

Assess

Children should be able to

- tell something about Thanksgiving Day
- tell something about Martin Luther King Day

LOOK**AHEAD**

In the next section, children will find holidays marked on a calendar.

Mixed Ability
Body Language and Gestures

TPR

Have children pantomime various facial expressions, body movements, and gestures people use with friends at different holiday celebrations. Suggest various movements by using commands such as, *Wave hello.*

Multicultural Connection
Holidays

Tell children that the seven-day African-American holiday Kwanzaa begins on December 26. Although Kwanzaa is based on the traditional African festival of the harvest, it was developed in the U.S. in 1966. Then ask voulunteers to tell about holidays from other countries.

QuickCheck

Ordinal Numbers

Check whether all children are forming ordinal numbers correctly. Help those who need practice form the ordinal numbers *first, second, third,* and *fourth, and fifth.* Point out that the first three ordinal numbers are irregular.

Connect

Activate Prior Knowledge
Use a Calendar

Display a calendar and help children find and name today's date. Invite them to point out any holidays celebrated this month.

Develop Language and Concepts
Present pages 186 and 187.

Help children read each question, and encourage them to look at the calendar for the answer. Have children explain how they figured out each answer. Then point out the rest of the months in the Word Bank.

Have each child answer the Talk About It questions. Children should name their birthday month and name any other holidays celebrated that month.

Language Awareness

Language Functions: Questions/Answers

ACTIVITY BOOK

Point out the question phrase *how many* and the question word *which* on the page. Explain that when a sentence asks *how many*, it requires you to count a number of things. When a sentence asks *which*, it requires you to choose among things. Ask children, *How many holidays are in this month?* Then ask, *Which is your favorite holiday?* Use page 96 in the Activity Book for more practice.

A Look at the Calendar

How many holidays are marked in May? On which day is Cinco de Mayo celebrated? On which day is Memorial Day celebrated?

How many holidays are marked in June? On which day is Flag Day celebrated?

Options for Reaching All Students

Beginning
Social Studies: Birthday Graph

Read aloud the name of each month, and ask children to stand when they hear their birthday month. Tally the number of birthdays for each month and display the numbers in the form of a graph. Encourage children to talk about their birthdays.

Advanced
Social Studies: Sequencing

List the months in order on a chart and let children practice saying them in order. Then ask such questions as *What month comes two months after October?* and *What is the month before May?*

Peer Tutoring
Social Studies: Using a Calendar

Assign partners of mixed abilities. Provide partners with a current calendar. Ask one child to say a date and the other child to find it on the calendar. For a challenge, provide a list of holidays, and have children take turns finding the holidays on the calendar.

How many holidays are marked in July? On which day is Independence Day celebrated?

Which month doesn't have any holidays marked?

Word Bank

January

February

March

April

September

October

November

December

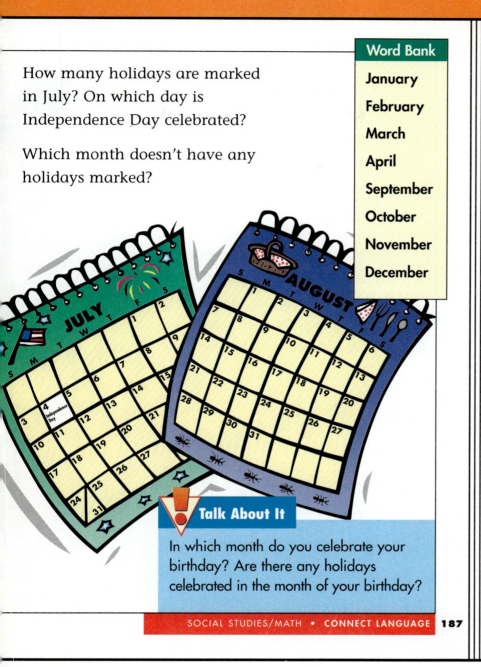

Talk About It

In which month do you celebrate your birthday? Are there any holidays celebrated in the month of your birthday?

SOCIAL STUDIES/MATH • **CONNECT LANGUAGE** **187**

Model a Strategy
Use a Calendar

Model using a calendar for information:

When I look at these pages, I see that there are many questions, but no answers. I think that I can look at the calendar to find the information I need to answer the question. For example, the first question asks, How many holidays are marked in May? When I see that the question is about May. I look for the page of the calendar that is marked May. Then I count the number of holidays shown on the May calendar. I read the next question and look on the calendar to find the answer. Calendars give me information about months, dates, days of the week, and holidays.

Assess ✔

Children should be able to

• find information on a calendar

LOOK**AHEAD**

In the next section, children will use what they have learned about holidays to read a description of one child's favorite holiday.

Mixed Ability
Language: Poem

Have children browse through a calendar and note that different months have different numbers of days in them. Then invite children to practice this poem chorally.

Thirty days has September,
April, June, and November.
All the rest have thirty-one,
Except February. It has twenty-eight.

Give each child a card and help her or him write the name of a month on the card. As you recite the poem together, ask children to hold up their card when they hear the name of the month on their card. Children holding cards for January, March, May, July, August, October, and December should hold up their cards when you say, *All the rest have thirty-one.*

Home Connection
Holidays

Invite family members to come to the class to speak about the holidays they celebrate. Encourage speakers to bring in photographs and items used for celebrations, if possible.

Connect

Activate Prior Knowledge
Brainstorm Vocabulary

Have children brainstorm names of different holidays as you list them on a chart. Then read aloud the list, asking children to raise their hand when you say the name of their favorite holiday.

Develop Language and Concepts
Present pages 188 and 189.

Read the title and invite children to examine the illustration. Have children guess which holiday they will read about.

Read the story with children. Ask them to retell in their own words how Tết is celebrated in Vietnam. Tell children that Tết, which is celebrated with a three-day festival, usually falls between the middle of January and the middle of February.

ACTIVITY BOOK
Have children work in small groups to do the Talk About It activity. They should talk about how their family celebrates a holiday and name special foods eaten on that day. Use Activity Book page 97 as a follow-up to Talk About It.

FYI Student Author
Thao Ngo wrote this story at the age of 8. Thao's school, Beech Tree Elementary, is in Falls Church, Virginia.

My Favorite Holiday

by Thao Ngo, age 8

In Vietnam, Tết is the start of a new year.

On Tết my mom gives me $2.00 in Vietnamese money.

My mom buys watermelon and cuts it up. My baby sister, my brothers, my mom, my dad, and I eat it. I like to eat watermelon. We also eat a special big cake on Tết.

188 CONNECT LANGUAGE • SOCIAL STUDIES/LITERATURE

Options for Reaching All Students

Beginning
Language: Role Playing

Let children role-play celebrating Tết. They can pretend to prepare and eat watermelon and cake.

Advanced
Language: Narrating a Factual Account

Provide a tape recorder for children to use as they discuss how their families celebrate a specific holiday. Allow time for children to listen to each other's recorded stories.

Mixed Ability
Body Language and Gestures

Have children use body language and gestures to show how they would act if they enjoyed fireworks and how they would react if they were afraid of them.

Then my mom and dad go buy firecrackers. My dog is scared of the firecrackers. He won't go outside when we light them. The best part of Têt is the firecrackers. I like them very much.

Talk About It

Tell about a holiday you celebrate with your family. What special foods do you like to eat?

Language Awareness

Grammar: Present Tense

ACTIVITY BOOK

Point out to children that the writer of "My Favorite Holiday" used many action words to tell what happens on the holiday of Têt. Write the following sentences on the chalkboard:

My mom gives me $2.

My mom buys watermelon.

We eat a special cake.

We go outside.

Have a volunteer read aloud each sentence, locate the action word, and draw a line under it. For more practice, children can use page 98 in the Activity Book.

Model a Strategy
Summarize

Model summarizing a story:

After I read this story I thought about all the important things I learned about Têt, the Vietnamese New Year festival. I remembered that Thao's family ate special treats on this holiday and that they lit fireworks. Summarizing can help me remember what I read.

Assess

Children should be able to

• summarize how Têt is celebrated

Cooperative Learning
Art: Mural

Let children form groups. Give each group a large sheet of paper and crayons. Invite children to decide together upon a favorite holiday, plan what each person will draw, and make a mural of it. Encourage children to talk about their mural with other groups.

Writer's Workshop
Write About a Holiday

Refer children to the Writer's Workshop on pages 230–236 of the Student Book. Have them write about their favorite holiday, using Thao Ngo's story as a model.

Through Moon and Stars and Night Skies

by Ann Turner
pictures by James Graham Hale

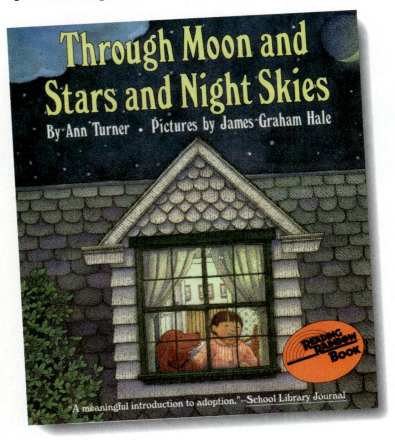

Shared Reading

1. Introduce
Display the book and read the title. Have children look at the picture on the cover. Invite them to predict what the book will be about.

2. Read
As you read aloud, be sure to allow children time to see the illustrations. This should help them understand what is happening in the story.

3. Reread
Invite children to reread the book with you. Discuss the book by asking questions such as the following:

- *How does the boy feel about meeting a poppa and momma of his own?*
- *How do you know the boy loves his new poppa and momma?*

Through Moon and Stars and Night Skies
A boy in need of a poppa and a momma travels for a day and a night to discover a new home.

Options for Reaching All Students

Beginning
Art/Language: Draw a "Snapshot"

Recall with children that the boy in the story first learned of his new home and family through "snapshots." Have children draw a "snapshot" of their family, pet, or home. Help children write about and discuss their "snapshots."

Advanced
Language: Speaking in the First Person

Discuss with children the fact that this story is written in the first person. Explain that this means that the author uses the word *I* to tell the story. This makes it sound as if the child himself is telling the story. Encourage children to tell stories about themselves in the first person.

Mixed Ability
Language: Recalling Events

Help children who remember their experiences in coming to this country tell about them. Encourage children to tell how they felt and what they saw. Also help children talk about the first encouraging thing that happened to them in this country.

Grammar: Past Tense

Have children find the verbs in the following sentences:

I needed a poppa and momma of my own.

I climbed the long steps to the plane.

But I looked and looked and saw you!

List the verbs *needed, climbed,* and *looked* on the board. Point out that the *-ed* ending shows that the action happened in the past. Have children work in groups to find other regular past tense forms in the story. Encourage volunteers to write these sentences on the board. Ask each group to write five sentences each using one or more of the past tense verbs on the board.

Model a Strategy

Take Notes

Model using a story sequence chart to take notes:

When I read this story, I want to make sure I know what took place. A Story Sequence Chart helps me take notes. I think about and write what happened at the beginning, middle, and end of the story. In the beginning of this story, the boy has only the pictures of his new home to tell him what his future will be like. In the middle of the story, the boy meets his new parents. At the end of the story, the boy realizes that he loves his new home. Can you think of other ways to take notes?

Response Activities

Discuss Feelings

Encourage children to discuss how the boy felt before meeting his new momma and poppa. Then have children tell how the boy felt after meeting his new parents.

List Good Things

The boy in the story is happy at the end of the story because he loves his new momma and poppa and his new surroundings. Encourage children to name things that they enjoy about their lives. List their responses on the board.

Look at Picture Details

To help children understand what is happening in the story, encourage them to look carefully at the pictures. Let children tell about details in the pictures that aren't included in the text.

Cooperative Learning

Language: Thinking and Writing

Let children form small groups to discuss ways that they can make someone who is new to this country feel at home. Help the groups make a list of suggestions. When the lists are complete, let the groups share, edit, and revise their lists. As a follow-up activity, encourage children to write letters offering advice to real or imaginary friends moving to a new country.

Multicultural Connection

Social Studies: Customs

Invite children to locate and mark their native countries on a world map. Encourage children to tell about how life was different in their native countries. Also have children tell about things that are the same in both cultures.

Connect

Activate Prior Knowledge
Review Vocabulary

Review the names of holidays children know. Write the holiday names on a chart. Ask volunteers to sing songs that are sung for holidays in their native countries.

Develop Language and Concepts
Present page 190.

BLUE TAPE

Read aloud the song title and lyrics. Then play Side 2 of the Blue Tape several times and encourage children to join in singing.

Have children complete the Write About It activity.

Language Awareness

Vocabulary: Onomatopoeia

Call children's attention to the sound of the bells in the poem: *Bim, Bom, Bim, Bom!* Ask children why they think these words are used to describe the sound of bells. Children should respond that the words are used because they sound like bells ringing. Then write *ding dong* on the board and teach it to children. Ask them what words are used in their first language to designate bells ringing. Have children think of other examples of words used to represent sounds.

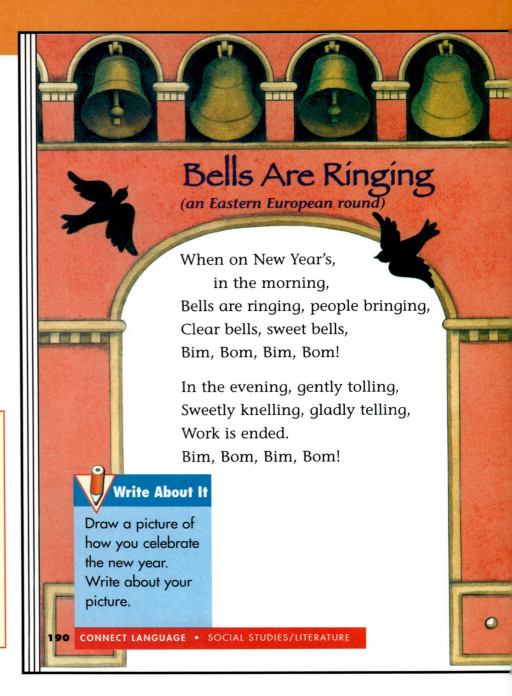

Bells Are Ringing
(an Eastern European round)

When on New Year's,
 in the morning,
Bells are ringing, people bringing,
Clear bells, sweet bells,
Bim, Bom, Bim, Bom!

In the evening, gently tolling,
Sweetly knelling, gladly telling,
Work is ended.
Bim, Bom, Bim, Bom!

Write About It

Draw a picture of how you celebrate the new year. Write about your picture.

190 CONNECT LANGUAGE • SOCIAL STUDIES/LITERATURE

Options for Reaching All Students

Beginning
Social Studies: New Year's Day

Have children bring in a photo or draw a picture to describe how their family celebrates the new year. Encourage children to talk with one another about their photos and pictures.

Advanced
Writing: Song Variations

Have children write and illustrate alternate versions of the song, substituting different holiday names.

Multicultural Connection
New Year's Around The World

In India, the new year's holiday is called Divali. It comes after the monsoon season in October or November. Ask children to share information they have about New Year's celebrations in other parts of the world.

Tell what you learned.

1. Work with a partner. Make a map that shows early Spanish settlements.

2. Act out a scene from early America. Show one way the Indians helped the Pilgrims after their first hard winter.

3. Draw a picture to show how you celebrate one holiday. Write about your picture. Share your picture with a classmate.

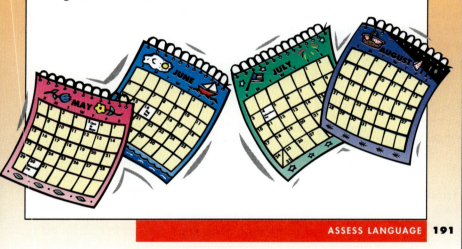

Assess ✓

Activity 1: Have children make their map on a separate piece of paper. Evaluate the accuracy and completeness of the map.

Activity 2: Evaluate whether children understand how the American Indians helped the Pilgrims.

Activity 3: Check that children draw a picture of a holiday celebration. Let children talk about holidays they celebrate.

Have children complete the Chapter Self-Assessment, Blackline Master 31. Have them choose products for their portfolios. Add results of any rubrics, checklists, self-assessments, or portfolio assessments, Blackline Masters 2–18.

Listening Assessment

 BLACKLINE MASTER

Make sure that each child has a copy of Blackline Master 83 and blue and red crayons. Play Side 2 of the Cream Tape several times stopping the tape to allow children to respond.

TAPESCRIPT

 CREAM TAPE

Listen carefully and follow the directions. Look at the calendar for January. Find New Year's Day. Draw a blue circle on the calendar around that day. (pause) Now find Martin Luther King Day. Draw a red circle around that day.

Options for Assessment

Vocabulary Assessment

 ACTIVITY BOOK
Use Activity Book page 99 to assess children's knowledge of chapter vocabulary.

Writing Assessment

Have children make personal picture books in which they illustrate and write about the holidays they celebrate.

Language Assessment

 BLACKLINE MASTER
Use Blackline Master 82 in the Teacher's Resource Book.

Standardized Test Practice

 ACTIVITY BOOK
Use pages 70 and 71 in the Activity Book. Answers: People in Egypt made a calendar with about 365 days in a year and about 30 days in a month; People from long ago and today have learned the same things about time.

Wrap-Up

Activities

Time Capsule

Explain to children the purpose of a time capsule. Talk about what a person finding things in a time capsule might learn about the past. Ask children to think about what things they might want to put in a time capsule for people in the future to learn about their lives now. Invite children to bring in small items, or draw pictures of items, to put in a time capsule. A small plastic container that can be sealed can serve as the time capsule. Write the date on the outside of the container. As each object is placed inside, talk about what people in the future might learn from it. With the school's permission, bury the time capsule on school grounds.

Comparison Drawings

Have children fold papers into three columns. Help children label each column with these heads: *My Clothing, My Food, My Home.* Then ask children to draw the clothing they like to wear, a favorite meal, and a picture of where they live. Give children another piece of paper labeled with the same headings to take home for a family member to complete in the same way. Tell children to ask the person to complete the paper to show his or her clothing, food, and home at age seven. Have children compare the completed drawings.

Phases of the Moon Chart

Encourage children to look at the moon through a window or go outdoors with an adult family member to observe it. Remind children to do this every few nights during the month. Each time they observe the moon, have them draw a picture of what the moon looked like and date the drawing. If the moon is obscured by clouds, encourage them to try observing it on the next night. Compare drawings in class and talk about why the moon looks different at different times of the month. Provide children with nonfiction books that can be used to help explain this phenomenon.

Discussing the Theme

Have children work in groups of two or three to discuss their progress during this unit about how time changes. Choose from the following activities that will demonstrate to them how much they have learned and how useful that information is.

- Make a list of holidays children know. Have children suggest words they know that will help them talk about holidays and list them on a chart.
- Invite children to tell what they know about day and night.
- Encourage them to discuss how time is measured.
- Invite children to tell what they know about the sun and the moon.
- Ask children to name words they know that will help them in science class when they talk about the sun, the earth, the moon, and the stars.
- Encourage children to role play a conversation in which they ask each other about their favorite holidays and why that particular holiday is special.

Sharing the Module Project

Use an invitation form, Blackline Master 32 or 33, to invite family members to school to see the classroom calendar.

Have children practice chanting the names of the months of the year together. Begin your presentation of the calendar with the chant and invite the audience to join in.

Allow each group of children to tell about the calendar month they completed. Encourage them to talk about the holidays that take place that month.

Ask volunteers to present one of the demonstrations previously used in class to show how the earth and sun move causing night and day.

To offer simple refreshments, have the children serve small slices of pumpkin pie. Put up a sign that children can read to their families: *Pumpkin pie is served on Thanksgiving. Thanksgiving is one of the holidays we studied.*

Signs of Success!

Duplicate a copy of this checklist for each child.

Name: _____

Refer to the checklist below for a quick determination of how a child is progressing toward transitioning out of ESL instruction.

Objectives:

- ☐ Names things in the sky.
- ☐ Tells what causes night and day.
- ☐ Tells about the sun and moon.
- ☐ Tells why a calendar is important.

- ☐ Names holidays celebrated in the U.S.
- ☐ Tells about the first people in North America.
- ☐ Tells about early Spanish settlers.
- ☐ Tells about Pilgrims.

Language Awareness

Understands/Uses:

- ☐ homophones
- ☐ compound words
- ☐ time expressions
- ☐ verbs—present/past tense
- ☐ comparatives

- ☐ onomatopoeia
- ☐ description
- ☐ ordinal numbers
- ☐ questions/answers
- ☐ similes

Hears/Pronounces/Reads:

- ☐ pattern and rhyme

Learning Strategies:

- ☐ Uses a diagram.
- ☐ Generalizes.
- ☐ Predicts content.
- ☐ Makes comparisons.
- ☐ Uses context.

- ☐ Uses prior knowledge.
- ☐ Understands chronology.
- ☐ Uses a calendar.
- ☐ Summarizes.

Comments

_____

_____

Planning Guide

CHAPTER 11

Where We Find Water

Objectives

Name sources of water.

Tell how some bodies of water differ.

Find bodies of water on a map.

Tell what happens when there is too much or too little water.

Tell how water can be saved.

Vocabulary Focus

Things water is used for, such as *drinking, fishing, swimming, washing.*

Bodies of water, such as *pond, lake, river, ocean.*

Directions, *east, north, south, west.*

Words to talk about too little or too much water, such as *dry, flood, wet.*

Lesson	Content Focus	Language Awareness Objectives	Learning Strategies
Preview pages 192–193 Tell what you know.			
Present pages 194–195 Bodies of Water	Social Studies	**Grammar** Adjectives	Use context clues.
Practice pages 196–197 Where are bodies of water in the United States?	Social Studies	**Spelling** Capitalization	Use a map.
Practice pages 198–199 Do people have enough water?	Social Studies	**Vocabulary** Expressions of Amount	Visualize.
Connect pages 200–201 What happens if there is not enough rain? Saving Water	Social Studies/ Science	**Phonics** Long *a*	
Connect pages 202–213 Brave Dog	Social Studies/ Literature	**Phonics** Short *u* **Grammar** Possessives **Vocabulary** Informal Expressions	Preview a story. Recognize cause and effect. Paraphrase/retell.
Connect page 214 "Sitting in the Sand"	Social Studies/ Literature	**Phonics** Short *i*/Long *i*	
Assess page 215 Tell what you learned.			

CHAPTER 12

Water and the Weather

Objectives

Tell how rain makes people feel.

Tell about clouds.

Tell where rain comes from.

Tell about water vapor.

Tell about the water cycle.

Vocabulary Focus

Weather words, such as *cloudy, drizzle, lightning, storm, windy.*

Words for telling about water vapor, such as *cooled, dries, changed.*

Words for discussing the water cycle, such as *falls, rises, clouds, water vapor.*

Lesson	Content Focus	Language Awareness Objectives	Learning Strategies
Preview pages 216–217 Tell what you know.			
Present pages 218–219 Clouds in the Sky	Science	**Vocabulary** Related Words	Check inferences.
Practice pages 220–221 Water in the Air	Science	**Grammar** Forming Questions	Self-assess.
Practice pages 222–223 The Water Cycle You can make a cloud.	Science	**Grammar** Prepositional Phrases	Preview directions.
Connect pages 224–225 How much rain?	Science/Math	**Grammar** Comparatives	Solve problems.
Connect pages 226–227 Marmaduke "Wash and Dry" Water Cartoons	Science/ Literature	**Spelling** Punctuation	
Connect page 228 "Raindrops"	Science/ Literature	**Vocabulary** Compound Words	
Assess page 229 Tell what you learned.			

Resources

Chapter 11

Support Materials

PICTURE CARDS
Numbers 6, 30, 58, 59

ACTIVITY BOOK
Pages 102–111

VIDEO
Unit 6, Water All Around Us

PURPLE TAPE
Side 1
Brave Dog, pages T202–T213

PURPLE TAPE
Side 2
"Sitting in the Sand," page T214

Little Celebrations Library

Mr. Sun and Mr. Sea by Andrea Butler, ScottForesman, 1993.

Water by Ann Morris, ScottForesman, 1993.

Assessment Materials

CREAM TAPE
Side 2
Listening Assessment, page T215

BLACKLINE MASTER
Language Assessment, page 90
Listening Assessment, page 91

Newcomer Book A

Survival Book for absolute beginners. For overview, see pages xxviii–xxxi.

For Extended Reading

D.W. All Wet by Marc Brown, Little, Brown and Company, 1988.

D.W. doesn't think getting wet is much fun, until she finds herself in the water at the beach.

Level: Beginning

Magic Beach by Alison Lester, Little, Brown and Company, 1990.

A story-poem about people having fun as they do all sorts of activities in this special place.

Level: Advanced

River Parade by Alexandra Day, Viking, 1990.

A little boy brings his three favorite toys along for a boat ride on the river. When the toys, and eventually the boy himself, end up in the water, he finds that swimming is not such a scary thing after all.

Level: Average

Splash by Ann Jonas, Greenwillow, 1995.

Readers can help a young girl keep track of how many animals are splashing around in her backyard pond.

Level: Beginning

To Bathe a Boa by C. Imbior Kudrna, Carolrhoda Books, 1986.

When a little boy wants to give his pet boa a bath, the battle of wills threatens to get down and dirty.

Level: Average

Related Technology

Discover the Wonder: Grade 2, ScottForesman Science, 1996.

Explore various water habitats among others in Module A, Living Things; Topic 4, Habitats.

Chapter 12

Support Materials

PICTURE CARDS
Number 24

ACTIVITY BOOK
Pages 112–121

VIDEO
Unit 6, Water All Around Us

PURPLE TAPE
Side 2
"Rain on the Green Grass," page T217
"Raindrops," page T228

Shared Reading Collection

Down by the Bay by Henrick Drescher, CelebrationPress, 1996.

Little Celebrations Library

Covers by Nikki Giovanni, ScottForesman, 1993.

Ocean by the Lake by Antonella Parisi, CelebrationPress, 1996.

Assessment Materials

CREAM TAPE
Side 2
Listening Assessment, page T229

BLACKLINE MASTER
Language Assessment, page 92
Listening Assessment, page 93

For Extended Reading

A Child's Book of Seasons by Satomi Ichikawa, Parents' Magazine Press, 1975.

This book takes children on a poetic tour through the seasons, including spring showers, summer heat, autumn harvest, and winter snow.

Level: Average

Rain Talk by Mary Serfozo, McElderry, 1990.

A young girl enjoys the sound of raindrops falling on her umbrella, the roof, the highway.

Level: Beginning

Small Cloud by Ariane, Dutton, 1984.

Children learn about the rain cycle as they follow the story of Small Cloud, daughter of Singing River and Big Sun.

Level: Average

Water's Way by Lisa Westberg Peters, Arcade Publishing, 1991.

Tony can't wait to get out and play in the snow with his new sled. He looks anxiously out his window at the changing weather and sees clouds form in the sky and rain begin to fall. But when it grows colder, snow and ice crystals form. Time to go out and play!

Level: Advanced

What Will the Weather Be Like Today? by Paul Rogers, Greenwillow Books, 1989.

At dawn, various animals speculate what the weather will be like that day.

Level: Beginning

Related Technology

Sammy's Science House, Edmark, 1994.
Visit the Weather Machine.

Project

Water Conservation

This optional project can be completed over the next two chapters. See the Unit Wrap-Up, page T229a, for more ideas on sharing the project with family members.

What You'll Need

Collect the following items for the water conservation program:

Art Materials:
- large pieces of paper
- crayons or markers

Other Materials:
- measuring cup

Beginning the Project

Tell children that they will be working on a classroom water conservation project for the next few weeks. Ask children to tell what they know about water conservation. Brainstorm a list of ways in which water is wasted.

Home Involvement

Send Letter Home, Blackline Masters 84–89, to families to let them know what their child will be studying and to solicit their cooperation in the water conservation project.

Investigating Wasted Water

Use the list of brainstormed ways water is wasted to help children choose an area to investigate. Have children form water conservation groups for areas such as, brushing teeth, finding dripping faucets, washing dishes, and saving water outside.

Brushing Teeth
- Ask the group to discuss ways to use less water while brushing teeth.
- Encourage discussion of the topic with family members.
- In class, ask volunteers to pantomime turning the faucet on and off while brushing their teeth.
- Have children draw pictures and write messages about saving water while brushing teeth.

Finding Dripping Faucets

- Ask children to search for dripping faucets in their homes and at school.
- If they find a dripping water faucet, have them measure how much water is wasted in five minutes.
- Have children report drips to parents or to the school office telling how much water is wasted by the dripping faucet.

Washing Dishes

- Let children in the group talk about how they can save water while doing dishes.
- Have children discuss with their families a plan for saving water while washing dishes.
- Encourage children to pantomime how to save water while washing dishes.
- Ask children to draw pictures and write messages about saving water while washing dishes.

Saving Water Outside

- Ask children to list ways that water is used outside, such as watering lawns and washing cars.
- Encourage children to discuss with their families ways of saving water outside.
- Ask children to draw pictures and write messages about saving water outside.

Daily Discussion

Take a few minutes each day for a general classroom discussion about water conservation. Let children practice vocabulary learned in conjunction with this project. At the end of the unit, have children summarize ways to conserve water. See page T229a for ideas about sharing the water conservation project with families and friends when the unit is completed.

Activity Book

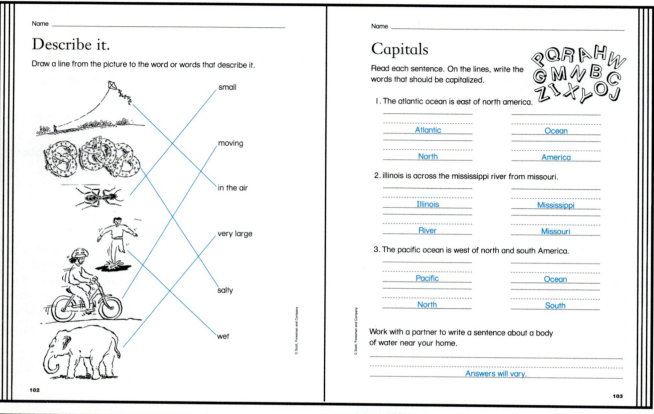

Name _____

Describe it.

Draw a line from the picture to the word or words that describe it.

- small
- moving
- in the air
- very large
- salty
- wet

102

Name _____

Capitals

Read each sentence. On the lines, write the words that should be capitalized.

PQRAHW GMNBC ZIXYOJ

1. The atlantic ocean is east of north america.

Atlantic   Ocean

North   America

2. illinois is across the mississippi river from missouri.

Illinois   Mississippi

River   Missouri

3. The pacific ocean is west of north and south America.

Pacific   Ocean

North   South

Work with a partner to write a sentence about a body of water near your home.

Answers will vary.

103

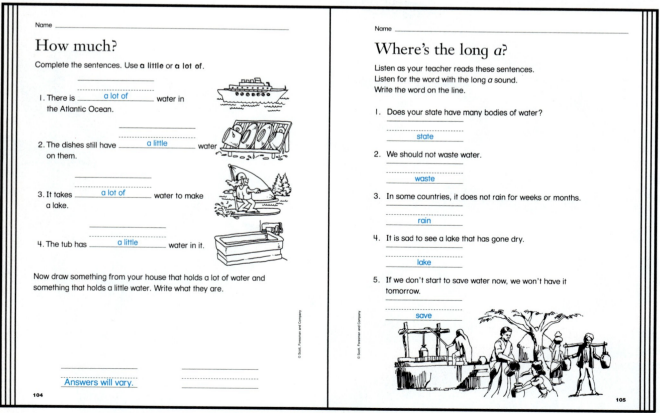

Name _____

How much?

Complete the sentences. Use **a little** or **a lot of**.

1. There is ___a lot of___ water in the Atlantic Ocean.

2. The dishes still have ___a little___ water on them.

3. It takes ___a lot of___ water to make a lake.

4. The tub has ___a little___ water in it.

Now draw something from your house that holds a lot of water and something that holds a little water. Write what they are.

Answers will vary.

104

Name _____

Where's the long *a*?

Listen as your teacher reads these sentences.
Listen for the word with the long *a* sound.
Write the word on the line.

1. Does your state have many bodies of water?

state

2. We should not waste water.

waste

3. In some countries, it does not rain for weeks or months.

rain

4. It is sad to see a lake that has gone dry.

lake

5. If we don't start to save water now, we won't have it tomorrow.

save

105

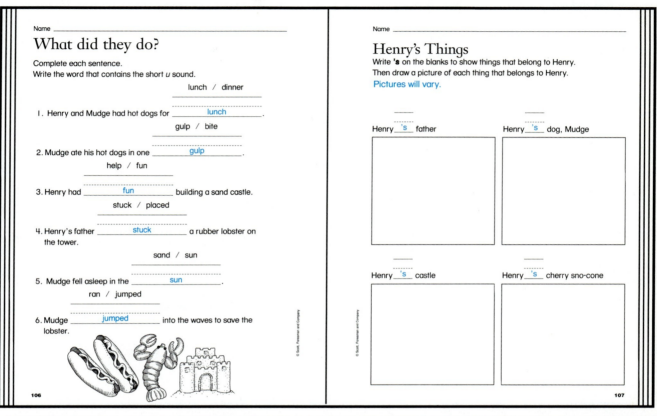

What did they do?

Complete each sentence.
Write the word that contains the short *u* sound.

lunch / dinner

1. Henry and Mudge had hot dogs for _____ lunch _____ .

gulp / bite

2. Mudge ate his hot dogs in one _____ gulp _____ .

help / fun

3. Henry had _____ fun _____ building a sand castle.

stuck / placed

4. Henry's father _____ stuck _____ a rubber lobster on the tower.

sand / sun

5. Mudge fell asleep in the _____ sun _____ .

ran / jumped

6. Mudge _____ jumped _____ into the waves to save the lobster.

106

Henry's Things

Write **'s** on the blanks to show things that belong to Henry.
Then draw a picture of each thing that belongs to Henry.
Pictures will vary.

Henry __'s__ father

Henry __'s__ dog, Mudge

Henry __'s__ castle

Henry __'s__ cherry sno-cone

107

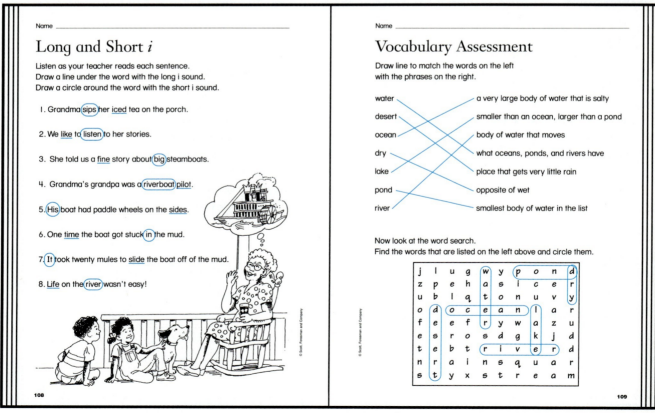

Long and Short *i*

Listen as your teacher reads each sentence.
Draw a line under the word with the long i sound.
Draw a circle around the word with the short i sound.

1. Grandma (sips) her <u>iced</u> tea on the porch.

2. We <u>like</u> to (listen) to her stories.

3. She told us a <u>fine</u> story about (big) steamboats.

4. Grandma's grandpa was a (riverboat) <u>pilot</u>.

5. (His) boat had paddle wheels on the <u>sides</u>.

6. One <u>time</u> the boat got stuck (in) the mud.

7. (It) took twenty mules to <u>slide</u> the boat off of the mud.

8. <u>Life</u> on the (river) wasn't easy!

108

Vocabulary Assessment

Draw line to match the words on the left
with the phrases on the right.

water — a very large body of water that is salty

desert — smaller than an ocean, larger than a pond

ocean — body of water that moves

dry — what oceans, ponds, and rivers have

lake — place that gets very little rain

pond — opposite of wet

river — smallest body of water in the list

Now look at the word search.
Find the words that are listed on the left above and circle them.

j	l	u	g	w	y	p	o	n	d
z	p	e	h	a	s	i	c	e	r
u	b	l	q	t	o	n	u	v	y
o	d	o	c	e	a	n	l	a	r
f	e	e	f	r	y	w	a	z	u
e	s	r	o	s	d	g	k	j	d
t	e	b	t	r	i	v	e	r	d
n	r	a	i	n	s	q	u	a	r
s	t	y	x	s	t	r	e	a	m

109

Activity Book

Chapter 12

Stormy Weather

Complete the sentences that tell about weather.
Use the words from the box.

| rainbow | drizzle | storm | puddles | clouds |

First, _____clouds_____ form in the sky.

Next, the rain comes down in a light _____drizzle_____.

Then the rain comes down harder, and a _____storm_____ begins.

The hard rain makes _____puddles_____ on the sidewalk.

Finally, the rain stops and a _____rainbow_____ comes out.

112

Rainy Day

Use the words in the box to label the things that help
keep the boy dry.
Then color the picture.

| raincoat | umbrella | boots |

umbrella

raincoat

boots

113

Weather Words

Write the correct word for each sentence.

| cloud | cloudy | wind | windy | rain | rainy |

We won't see the sun all day. It will be a _____cloudy_____ day.

Take your umbrella. The day will be _____rainy_____ too.

The flag waves in the _____wind_____.

We need a _____windy_____ day to fly my big kite.

One white _____cloud_____ floats in the sky.

Our poor garden needs _____rain_____ soon.

114

What a Question

Add a period to the end of each sentence that tells something.
Add a question mark to the end of each sentence that asks a question.
Circle the word that told you the sentence asks a question.

1. (What) do you see on the cup __?__

2. Water in the air is called water vapor _____.

3. Cool water vapor in the air changes to drops of water _____.

4. (What) does a puddle look like after the rain __?__

5. (How) does a puddle look after it has been in the sun __?__

6. I think it will rain today _____.

7. (Where) did you fill the cup with ice water __?__

115

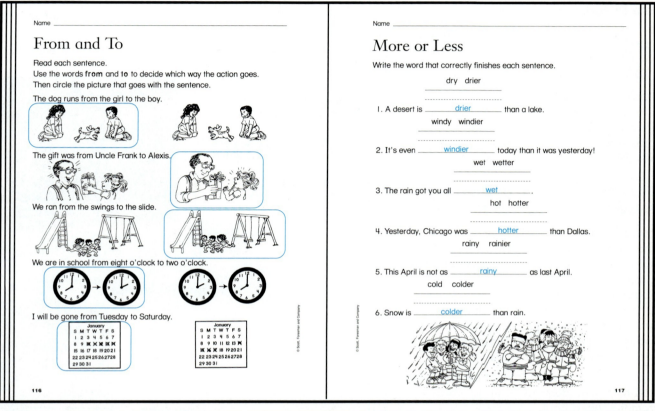

From and To

Read each sentence.
Use the words **from** and **to** to decide which way the action goes.
Then circle the picture that goes with the sentence.

The dog runs from the girl to the boy.

The gift was from Uncle Frank to Alexis.

We ran from the swings to the slide.

We are in school from eight o'clock to two o'clock.

I will be gone from Tuesday to Saturday.

116

More or Less

Write the word that correctly finishes each sentence.

dry   drier

1. A desert is _____drier_____ than a lake.

windy   windier

2. It's even _____windier_____ today than it was yesterday!

wet   wetter

3. The rain got you all _____wet_____.

hot   hotter

4. Yesterday, Chicago was _____hotter_____ than Dallas.

rainy   rainier

5. This April is not as _____rainy_____ as last April.

cold   colder

6. Snow is _____colder_____ than rain.

117

Water, Water, Everywhere

Think of four different ways you use water.
Write them on the lines. Answers will vary.

1.

2.

3.

4.

Write about a funny thing that happened when you
or someone you know were using water.

Now draw a picture of what you just wrote about.

118

Vocabulary Assessment

Match each picture with the word that describes it.

inch

bath

rainbow

water

sun

raindrop

119

Preview

Activate Prior Knowledge
Use Pictures

PICTURE CARDS

Show water pictures from magazines and the Picture Cards boat, fish, river, and sailboat to start the discussion of "where we find water." Ask children to describe the pictures and say what the pictures have in common. Elicit from children that all the pictures show water. Use Picture Cards 6, 30, 58, 59.

Develop Language and Concepts
Present pages 192 and 193.

Remind children that what they already know about water is important. Read the questions in Tell What You Know using the pictures shown above and the pictures on pages 192 and 193 as prompts. Write a list on the board. Then invite children to brainstorm other ways that people use water. Ask children what strategies they used to answer the questions.

Then invite children to look at each picture and help them describe it, using words from the Word Bank.

Help children discuss why water is important to our daily lives. Let children speculate about the source of the water that they use.

With the class, answer the questions in Think About It. Then have groups of two or three share answers.

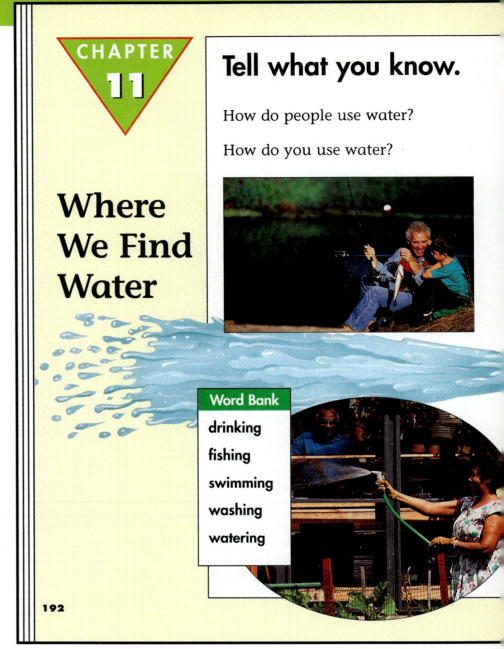

CHAPTER 11

Where We Find Water

192

Tell what you know.

How do people use water?

How do you use water?

Word Bank
- drinking
- fishing
- swimming
- washing
- watering

Options for Reaching All Students

Beginning
Language: Words and Pictures

Write the words from the Word Bank on a chart and read them aloud. On a sheet of paper, have children illustrate how water is used in relation to one of the words. Help children write about and label their picture with the correct Word Bank word.

Advanced
Language: Storytelling

Have children pretend they are an animal or plant that lives in or near water. Let children tell what kind of animal or plant they are, where the water is, and what adventure they have in the water.

Mixed Ability
Video: Water All Around Us

VIDEO

Show children the video to help build background knowledge on the unit theme. You may also choose to use the video in other ways that are appropriate during the unit.

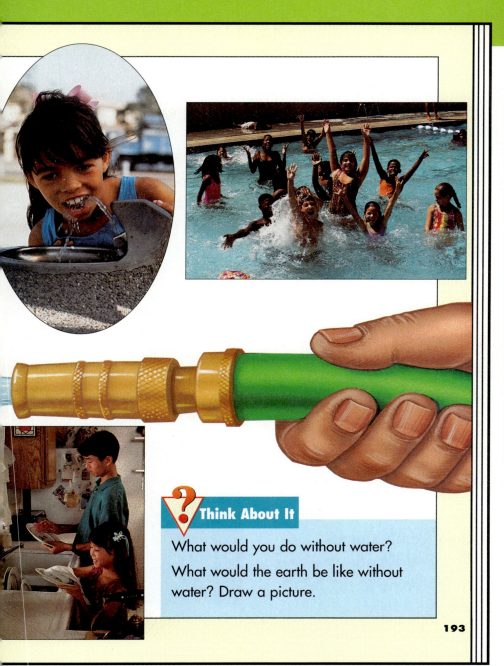

In this chapter, children will learn the language connected with water and its uses, as well as what happens when there is not enough water. Children will also study water conservation.

Use pages 192 and 193 to assess children's knowledge of water and its uses.

Water is found in ponds, lakes, rivers, and oceans.

The United States has many bodies of water.

Where We Find Water

Some people live where there is little water, and others live where there is alot.

Saving water is important.

? Think About It

What would you do without water?

What would the earth be like without water? Draw a picture.

193

Cooperative Learning

Art/Language: Drawing and Speaking

Have children work in groups of four or five. Provide each group with a piece of art paper and crayons and have them draw a real or imaginary place where they might see water. Then let children describe to the rest of the class the place they have drawn.

Little Celebrations

Water

This story shows different ways in which people use water.

Level: Beginning

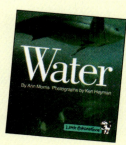

Water

By Ann Morris Photographs by Ken Heyman

Present

Activate Prior Knowledge
Make an Idea Web

BLACKLINE MASTER

Find out what children know about where water is located. Place the word *water* in the middle of an idea web and ask children to name places where water is found in nature. Use the Web on Blackline Master 20 in the Teacher's Resource Book. Add to the web as the lesson continues.

Develop Language and Concepts
Present pages 194 and 195.

Read the information with children. Pause at each illustration so children can examine it and answer the question. Encourage children to talk about their experiences with ponds, lakes, rivers, or oceans.

Language Awareness

Grammar: Adjectives

ACTIVITY BOOK

Write the following on the board: *small body of water, large body of water, salty water, moving water.* Explain that writers use describing words to tell about a person, place, or thing. Read the first phrase aloud and ask children to tell what the word *small* describes. Follow the same procedure for *large, salty,* and *moving.* For practice, use page 102 in the Activity Book.

Bodies of Water

Where can you find water?

You can find water in a **pond**. A pond is a small body of water. What are these people doing at this pond?

You can find water in a **lake**.
A lake is a body of water that is larger than a pond.
What are these people doing in this lake?

194 LEARN LANGUAGE • SOCIAL STUDIES

Options for Reaching All Students

Beginning
Art: Collage

Have children cut out photographs or illustrations of bodies of water from magazines. Let them sort the pictures into categories: ponds, lakes, rivers, oceans. In groups, have children make a collage showing each of these bodies of water.

Advanced
Social Studies: Using a Globe

Have children work in groups of five. Have each group use a globe to ask and answer questions such as these:

- What ocean do you cross to get from the U.S. to Poland?
- What ocean do you cross to get from the U.S. to Thailand?

Home Connection
Water Around the World

Have children ask their family members about the bodies of water in their native countries. Children can share the information with the rest of the class.

You can find water in a **river.**
A river is a body of moving water.
What are these people doing on
this river?

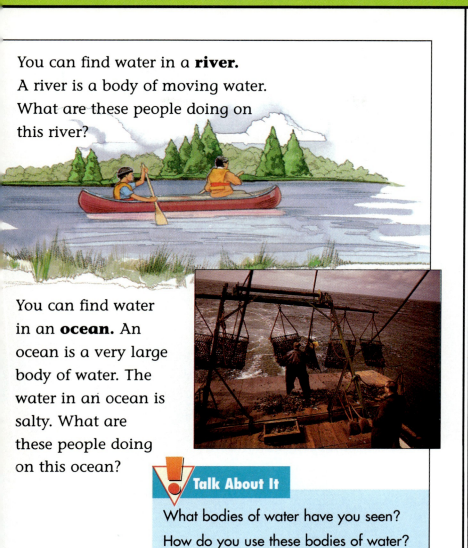

You can find water
in an **ocean.** An
ocean is a very large
body of water. The
water in an ocean is
salty. What are
these people doing
on this ocean?

 Talk About It

What bodies of water have you seen?
How do you use these bodies of water?

Practice

Activate Prior Knowledge
Finding Your Way

Ask children how someone finds a place he or she has never been. Write their responses on the board. If they do not mention a map, suggest it yourself.

Develop Language and Concepts
Present pages 196 and 197.

Help children read the title question and the words in the Word Bank. Relate the direction words to their location on the compass rose. Help them say that on a map, up is north, down is south, right is east, and left is west. Have children name places on the map that are north, south, east, and west.

Help children work in pairs to answer the questions. With the class, review each item. Then ask a volunteer to explain how the class arrived at its answer.

With the class, answer the questions in Talk About It. Then have children work in groups of three to share their answers.

Model a Strategy
Use a Map

Model using a map to get information:

For activity 2, I am asked to list two states that are on the Pacific Ocean. I will look very carefully on the map for the Pacific Ocean.

(Continued on page T197)

Where are bodies of water in the United States?

Word Bank

east

north

south

west

The United States

196 USE LANGUAGE • SOCIAL STUDIES

Options for Reaching All Students

Beginning
Social Studies: Using a Compass

TPR
Bring a compass to class and show children how the compass needle always points north. Help children use the compass to locate the four directions in the classroom. Label the walls to indicate direction. Then ask children to take turns giving and following commands to walk in specific directions.

Advanced
Social Studies: Geography

Assign children partners. Challenge them to find and list ten bodies of water shown on the map on pages 196 and 197. Suggest they include names of oceans, rivers, and lakes. Remind children when they write to begin names of places with capital letters. Have partner pairs compare their lists with other partners and add to their lists.

Home Connection
Social Studies: Finding Locations

Have children enlist the aid of family members to find postcards, photos, or magazine clippings that show bodies of water. Ask children to bring these items to class. Help children find the bodies of water on a map or a globe.

Study the map with a partner.

North

East

South

1. Think about where you live. Write the direction you would go to see the Atlantic Ocean.

2. List 2 states that are on the Pacific Ocean.

3. List 3 states along the Mississippi River.

Talk About It

Which body of water is nearest your home?

What bodies of water are in your native country?

When I find the Pacific Ocean, I will look for the names of states that touch the ocean. I see that Washington, Oregon, and California touch the ocean. I will write the names of two of those states. I can check the spelling of each state name by looking at the map.

Language Awareness

Spelling: Capitalization

ACTIVITY BOOK Ask children to look at the capitalized words on pages 196 and 197. They should notice that names of places, such as the United States and the Atlantic Ocean, are capitalized. Tell children that the names that identify a specific location should be capitalized. For practice, use page 103 in the Activity Book.

Assess ✔

Children should be able to

- understand the concept of north, south, east, and west on a map
- find bodies of water on a map

LOOK AHEAD ➡

In the next section, children will learn about water surpluses and shortages.

QuickCheck

Multiple-Meaning Words

Check whether all children understand that the phrase *bodies of water* in the title refers to separate portions of water. Help children understand that this meaning of the word *bodies* is different from the definition that means "the whole of a person or animal."

Little Celebrations

Mr. Sun and Mr. Sea

The story retells an African legend of why the sun is in the sky.

Level: Average

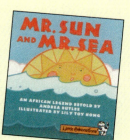

Multicultural Connection

Trips Around the World

Have children work in groups to plan an imaginary trip to a place where they can be near a body of water. Encourage them to look at maps and use information that group members know to help them decide. Encourage them to create an itinerary of things they would do. Have them do a presentation for the class in which they promote the chosen place.

T197

Practice

Activate Prior Knowledge
Make a Weather Calendar

Talk about the weather where you live. Does it rain a lot? Does it rain at a certain time of year? Have children make a weather calendar.

Develop Language and Concepts
Present pages 198 and 199.

Invite children to compare the photograph on page 198 with the photograph on page 199. Ask children to tell which photo was taken where there is a lot of water. Then ask children to tell which photo was taken where there is little water.

Read the pages with children. Encourage them to conjecture how the people live with the amount of water they have.

For page 199, help children read the words in the Word Bank. Introduce the word *desert* and write it on the board. Let children look at the illustration of the desert and describe what a desert is like.

Model a Strategy
Visualize

Model visualizing for comprehension:

When I look at the illustrations while reading the text, I remember what places that have a lot of water look like and what places that have little water look like. The pictures in my head help me understand what I read.

Do people have enough water?

Some people live where there is a lot of water.

Options for Reaching All Students

Beginning
Art: Water Painting

Let children paint a place where there is a lot of water. Encourage children to talk and write about their pictures.

Advanced
Science: Weather

Have children go to the library to discover how moisture in the air turns to snow. Let children draw a picture of the process, then let them explain the picture to others.

Cooperative Learning
Language: Storytelling

Let children form small groups to create a nonsense story about a time when there was too much rain. Have each group decide which members will tell their story to the class.

Child A: *One time there was so much rain, I went swimming in the front yard.*

Child B: *There was so much rain, a big fish knocked on our door.*

Some people live where there is little water.

Word Bank

dry

flood

wet

 Write About It

Tell about a time when you saw too much rain or too little rain.

What happens when there is too much rain?

Language Awareness

Vocabulary: Expressions of Amount—little, a lot (of)

ACTIVITY BOOK

Start with a meaning of *little* that children have already learned: *small*. Explain that *little* can also mean "not much." *Little* is the opposite of *a lot (of)*. Use a weather calendar to talk about *a little/a lot of* rain, snow, or sunshine. Have children use page 104 in the Activity Book.

Assess

Use responses to Write About It for assessment. Children should be able to

- tell about a time when they saw too much or too little rain
- tell what happens when there is too much rain

LOOK **AHEAD**

In the next section, children will discover what happens when there is not enough rain.

Mixed Ability
The Eensy Weensy Spider

Sing "The Eensy Weensy Spider" and show children how to do hand movements to the song. Repeat the song until children are singing confidently.

The eensy weensy spider
Went up the water spout.
Down came the rain
And washed the spider out.

Out came the sun
And dried up all the rain.
And the eensy weensy spider
Went up the spout again.

Home Connection
Water in Homelands

Have children ask family members whether their homeland has a lot of water or a little water. Encourage them to inquire about how the amount of water affected their way of life. Have children share with classmates the information they collect.

Connect

Activate Prior Knowledge
Brainstorm Vocabulary

Help children understand how important water is. Ask them to list everything they know of that needs water to live.

Develop Language and Concepts
Present page 200.

Have children compare the two photographs of the lake. Children should mention that one photograph shows the lake much drier than the other does. Let children speculate why a lake dries up.

Read the page with children. Invite them to explain why the cornstalks might be drooping.

What happens if there is not enough rain?

In some places it does not rain for days, weeks, or months.

If this happens, lakes and rivers may dry up. Plants may not get the water they need to grow. Animals may not have plants to eat. People may not have the water they need.

200 CONNECT LANGUAGE • SOCIAL STUDIES/SCIENCE

Options for Reaching All Students

Beginning
Art: Water-Use Pictures

Have children draw a picture of themselves using water. For example, they may draw a picture of themselves brushing their teeth or drinking water. Elicit from children how they can conserve water.

Advanced
Language: Research

Have children find picture books in the library about the desert. Encourage children to learn about desert plant and animal life. Have them share what they learn with classmates.

Cooperative Language Experience
Field Trip

Take children on a walk outdoors after a period of a little or a lot of rain. You may want to visit a place where you can view a body of water or plants and flowers. Encourage children to talk about their observations. As a class, write a language experience story.

Saving Water

Things You Need

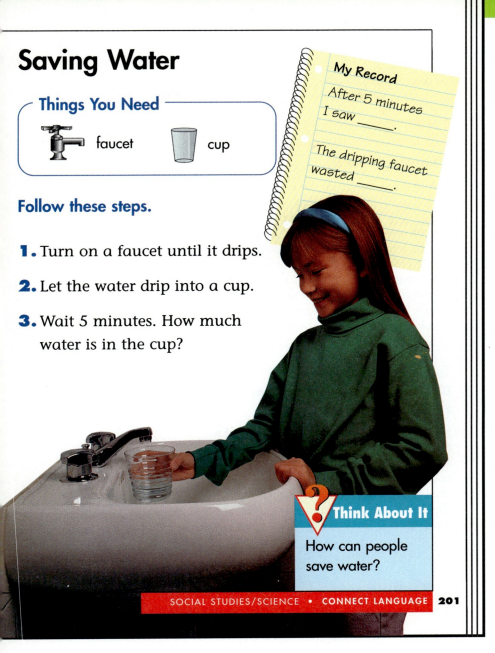

faucet

cup

Follow these steps.

1. Turn on a faucet until it drips.

2. Let the water drip into a cup.

3. Wait 5 minutes. How much water is in the cup?

My Record

After 5 minutes I saw _____.

The dripping faucet wasted _____.

Think About It

How can people save water?

Develop Language and Concepts
Present page 201.

Read the activity with children. Children can perform the activity individually or in groups. Have them repeat the instructions aloud before they begin the activity. Have children use My Record on page 201 in the Student Book as a model for recording results. (If you do not have access to a faucet, invite children do this activity at home.)

With the class, brainstorm answers to the Think About It question. During the brainstorming session with children, mention that they should not drink less water as a means of conserving water.

FYI
The average person in the United States uses over 170 gallons of water a day.

Assess ✓
Children should be able to

- tell how a lack of rain affects animals, plants, and people
- tell what they learned from the activity

LOOK AHEAD

Next, children will read a story about how a family has fun at the beach.

Cooperative Learning
Science: Water Conservation

Help children look for dripping faucets at school. Have children form small goups. Let each group write a letter to the principal describing the drips and expressing the class's concern about conserving water.

Mixed Ability
Math: Calculations

Using the activity, have children measure how much water dripped into the cup. Then help them figure out how much water would collect in an hour, and in a day.

Connect

Activate Prior Knowledge

Use Pictures to Predict

Have children look at the pictures in the story. Ask questions such as these:

- Who do you think this story is going to be about?
- Where do you think the story will take place?

Encourage children to talk about the sights they would see and the sounds they would hear on a beach.

Introduce the Selection

Help children find and read the title of the story and the names of the author and illustrator.

Read the Selection

 Read the story with children several times. Then encourage them to listen to Side 1 of the Purple Tape as often as they like. Use the suggested activities appropriate to meet children's needs.

Model a Strategy

Preview a Story

Model previewing a story before reading.

Before I read this story, I look at the title, "Brave Dog." I know by the title that this story will be about a dog. When I look at the pictures, I see a dog. I know that this dog will probably do something brave. Previewing a story helps me know what to expect as I read.

Language Awareness

Phonics: Short u

Write these words on the chalkboard: *lunch, Mudge, ketchup, yuck, stuck, gulp, rubber, up, jumped.* Point to and say the words emphasizing the short *u* sound. Have children repeat the words after you. Encourage children to find these words in the story and to read the sentence in which each word appears. Use Activity Book page 106 for more practice.

Teachable Moment

Distinguish Between Realism and Fantasy

Have children retell what has happened in the story. Ask children to tell whether this story tells about make-believe things that could never really happen or whether is tells about something that could be true. Children should report that so far the story tells about incidents that could really happen.

Options for Reaching All Students

Beginning

Language: Main Idea

Have children use crayons to draw a picture showing the most important ideas in the story. Invite children to explain their pictures.

Advanced

Language: Research

Let children go to the library to find out more about beaches. They may be interested in finding out about the animal life that lives in tidewater areas or they may want to find out more about what causes tides. Encourage children to share their information with others.

Mixed Ability

Critical Thinking: Compare and Contrast

Have children fold a piece of paper in three parts. Have them draw Henry's hot dog, Henry's father's hot dog, and Mudge's hot dogs. Encourage children to compare and contrast the toppings in the three drawings. Ask children to discuss the toppings they put on their foods.

Brave Dog

Story by
Cynthia Rylant

Pictures by
Suçie Stevenson

For lunch,
Henry and Mudge
and Henry's father
walked to a hot dog stand.

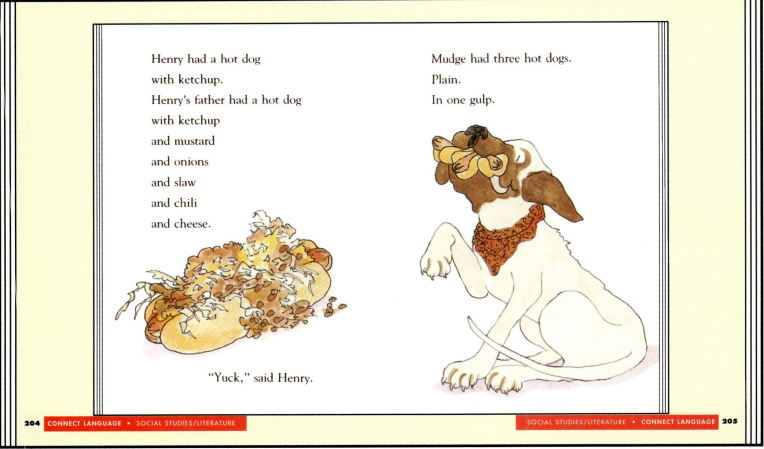

Henry had a hot dog
with ketchup.
Henry's father had a hot dog
with ketchup
and mustard
and onions
and slaw
and chili
and cheese.

"Yuck," said Henry.

Mudge had three hot dogs.
Plain.
In one gulp.

Connect

Develop Language and Concepts

Call children's attention to pages 206–207. Help children reread the information about building a sand castle. Invite those who have made sand castles on the beach to tell about the experience. Children may want to use the chalkboard to draw a rough picture of a sand castle they have made. Encourage children to tell what happens to sand castles when water washes over them.

Model a Strategy

Recognize Cause and Effect

Model recognizing cause and effect in a story.

When I read that a giant wave washes over the sand castle, I can guess that the wave will wash the sand castle away. I can also guess that the rubber lobster on the sand castle will get washed into the ocean. When I put together cause and effect ideas, I understand what I am reading better.

Teachable Moment

Predict Outcomes

Before turning the page, have children predict what will happen after Henry's father cries, "Save that lobster!" After reading the end of the story, encourage children to discuss whether their predictions were right.

Options for Reaching All Students

Beginning

Language: Choral Reading

Assign children to four groups. Help each of the groups take turns reading a page from the book. Let the class as a whole read the last page.

Advanced

Language: Personal Word Bank

Have children choose five words from the story to put into their personal word bank. They should write the word on the front of an index card and illustrate it or write a context sentence for it on the back of the card. Have children work in pairs to share their cards.

Home Connection

Historic Buildings

Point out that the sand castle in this story is a model of a kind of ancient building found in parts of the world. Have children ask family members about the kinds of ancient structures found in their homeland—castles, pyramids, temples, or the like. Encourage children to share information they learn.

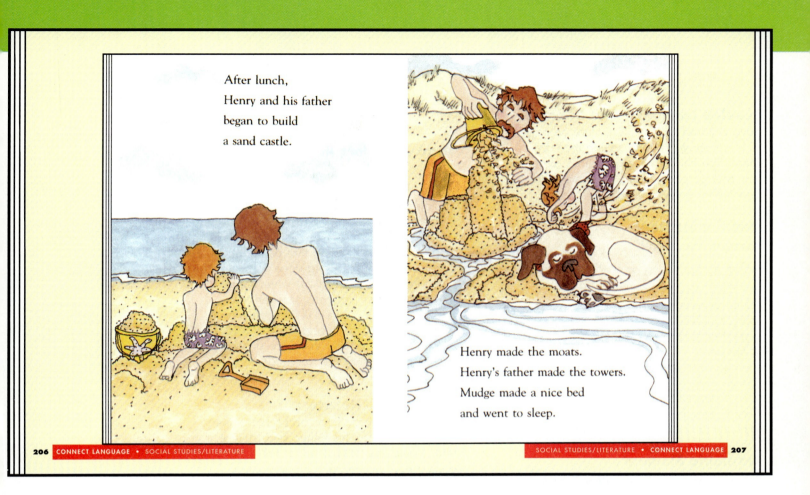

After lunch,
Henry and his father
began to build
a sand castle.

Henry made the moats.
Henry's father made the towers.
Mudge made a nice bed
and went to sleep.

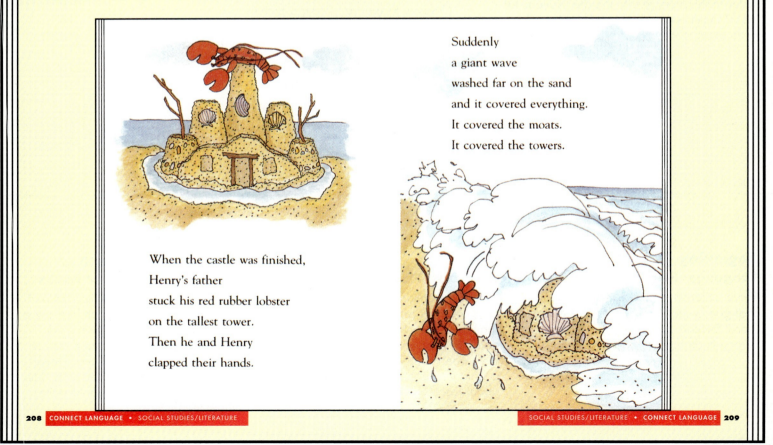

When the castle was finished,
Henry's father
stuck his red rubber lobster
on the tallest tower.
Then he and Henry
clapped their hands.

Suddenly
a giant wave
washed far on the sand
and it covered everything.
It covered the moats.
It covered the towers.

Connect

Develop Language and Concepts

Have children look at the picture on page 212 that shows Mudge saving the lobster. Encourage children to give details about how Mudge plunges into the water and rescues the lobster with his teeth.

Model a Strategy

Paraphrase/Retell

Model paraphrasing or retelling a story.

Now that I have finished the story I want to see if I understand what happens in the story. So I tell it to myself. Let's see, in this story, Henry, Henry's father, and Mudge are at the beach. Henry and Henry's father build a sand castle and put a red rubber lobster on top of the castle. When a wave threatens to wash the lobster out to sea, Mudge rescues it. Paraphrasing or retelling a story helps me remember what I've read.

Teachable Moment

Story Elements: Character Traits

Encourage children to describe each character in this story. Write the descriptions for each character on the board. Have children explain why Mudge is called brave.

Respond to Literature

Personal Response: If you had been at the beach with Henry, his father, and Mudge, what would you have liked to do?

Critical Response: Look back through the story. Make a list of what happens that shows the order in which it happened.

Creative Response: Draw a picture of a hot dog or another food just the way you like it. Tell a friend what is on your food.

Options for Reaching All Students

Beginning

Language: Retelling

Have children point out the illustration that goes with their favorite part of the story. Encourage children to tell what happens during this part of the story.

Advanced

Language: Point of View

Encourage children to retell the story from Mudge's point of view. Children should tell how Mudge feels about going to the beach, about how he feels when Henry and his father build a sand castle, and how Mudge feels about rescuing the lobster.

Cooperative Learning

Art/Language: Animal Books

Have children form small groups and make books. Have each child draw a picture of a real or imaginary pet. Then encourage children to describe their drawings to their group. Have group members work together to determine traits for each animal to write below the pictures.

It covered Mudge, who woke up.

"Oops," said Henry.

"Save that lobster!"
cried Henry's father.
The water was pulling it
out to sea.

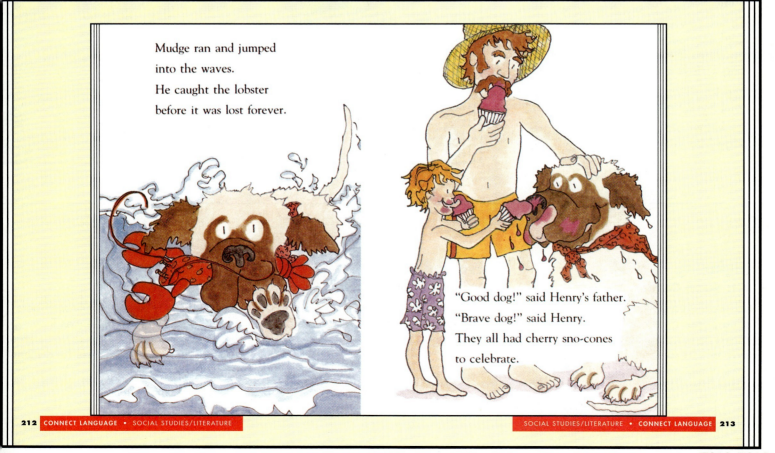

Mudge ran and jumped
into the waves.
He caught the lobster
before it was lost forever.

"Good dog!" said Henry's father.
"Brave dog!" said Henry.
They all had cherry sno-cones
to celebrate.

Connect

Activate Prior Knowledge

Demonstrate Vocabulary

Prepare a large bowl of water. Have children cup their hands and dip water from the bowl. Ask them to tell about when they might have used the scooping motion.

Develop Language and Concepts

Present page 214.

Read aloud the title of the poem, the author's name, and the verse itself. Then play Side 2 of the Purple Tape several times and invite children to join in saying the poem. Encourage children to make hand movements while saying the poem with the tape.

Help children with Think About It.

Sitting in the Sand

by Karla Kuskin

Sitting in the sand and the sea
    comes up
So you put your hands together
And you use them like a cup
And you dip them in the water
With a scooping kind of motion
And before the sea goes out again
You have a sip of ocean.

? Think About It

Would you want to sip the ocean? Why not?

214 **CONNECT LANGUAGE** • SOCIAL STUDIES/LITERATURE

Options for Reaching All Students

Beginning

Art: Sand Castles

Have children build a sand castle, using paper cups and plastic food containers to mold the sand. If you don't have access to sand, children can draw a picture of a sand castle they would like to build.

Advanced

Writing: Poems

Have children write a short poem about spending the day at the beach or a lake.

Home Connection

Fun in the Water

Ask children to talk to family members about pleasurable experiences they have had in the water. Invite volunteers to share with the class these fond memories.

Tell what you learned.

1. Work with a group. Make two lists. Then share your lists with other groups.

Ways We Use Water	Ways We Save Water
_____	_____
_____	_____
_____	_____

2. Work with a friend. Use a map of the United States. Choose a place you and your friend would like to visit that is near the Atlantic or Pacific Ocean. Trace the path you would follow. Which direction would you go?

3. Tell something that Henry and Mudge did. What would you like to do at the beach?

ASSESS LANGUAGE **215**

Assess

Activity 1 Have children work in small groups. Have each group write its answers on a separate piece of paper. Evaluate on number and accuracy of responses.

Activity 2 Have children work in pairs. See if children understand how to trace a path from one place to another and say the direction.

Activity 3 Check that children tell about something Henry and Mudge did, as well as something they'd like to do at the beach.

Have children complete the Chapter Self-Assessment, Blackline Master 31. Have them choose products to place in their portfolios. Add the results of any rubrics, checklists, self-assessments, or portfolio assessments, Blackline Masters 2–18.

Listening Assessment

BLACKLINE MASTER

Make sure that each child has a copy of Blackline Master 91 and a pencil. Play Side 2 of the Cream Tape several times stopping the tape to allow children to write. Have children listen to the dictation and write what they hear.

TAPESCRIPT

CREAM TAPE

Listen carefully. Write what you hear on the lines.

Some people live where there is a lot of water. (pause) Some people live where there is little water. (pause) In some places it does not rain for days, weeks, or months.

Vocabulary Assessment

ACTIVITY BOOK

Use page 109 in the Activity Book to assess chapter vocabulary.

Writing Assessment

Have children make personal picture books in which they illustrate and write about water.

Language Assessment

BLACKLINE MASTER

Use Blackline Master 90 in the Teacher's Resource Book.

Standardized Test Practice

ACTIVITY BOOK

Use pages 110 and 111 in the Activity Book. Answers: Ocean water is salty; Salt water fish are big.

Preview

Activate Prior Knowledge
Use Realia

Start discussion of "water and the weather" by opening an umbrella and standing under it as if it were raining. Stick your hand out and feel the "rain." Pretend you are walking and describe the rain and the water on the ground. Let children take turns using the umbrella.

Develop Language and Concepts
Present pages 216 and 217.

 Read the questions. Encourage children to talk about how rain makes people feel. Use the illustrations as a stimulus.

Read the poem to children. Then play Side 2 of the Purple Tape several times and encourage children to join in saying the poem.

 Read the words in the Word Bank with children. Help them find examples of each of the words in the illustrations. Use page 112 in the Activity Book.

Do the Talk About It activity with children. Model an answer by saying, *I enjoy the rain when I hear it pitter-patter against the windows of my house.*

 Use Activity Book page 113 to develop vocabulary for rain gear.

CHAPTER 12

Water and the Weather

Tell what you know.

How does rain make people feel?

How does rain make you feel?

216

Options for Reaching All Students

Beginning
Social Studies: Dressing for Rain

Provide rain gear and ask a volunteer to put on a raincoat, rain hat, rubber boots, and carry an umbrella. Help children name each article of clothing and tell how it keeps them dry. Also help children discuss why it is a good idea to keep clothing dry.

Advanced
Language: Writing

Help children write their own short poem about the rain. Write rhyming words that might be helpful on a chart: *rain, drain, plain; wet, pet, get, let, met; sun, fun.*

Mixed Ability
Science: Measuring Precipitation

Before a storm, have someone place an empty can in an open area outside. When the storm has stopped, retrieve the can and help children mark the can to show the amount of rainfall. Do the same at the next rainfall and compare amounts.

Rain on the green grass,
And rain on the tree,
Rain on the housetop,
But not on me.

Word Bank

clouds

drizzle

puddle

rainbow

storm

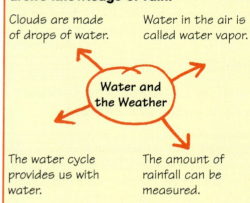

Talk About It

Tell about a time when you enjoyed rain.

217

KEY CONCEPTS

In this chapter, children will learn language connected with water. Children also will investigate water in the air and the makeup of clouds.

Use pages 216 and 217 to assess children's knowledge of rain.

Clouds are made of drops of water.

Water in the air is called water vapor.

Water and the Weather

The water cycle provides us with water.

The amount of rainfall can be measured.

FYI What Makes Weather?
Moisture is one of the four major components of weather. The others are air pressure, wind, and temperature.

Home Connection
When It Rains

Talk with children about different kinds of rainstorms. Point out that some storms are just a light drizzle, while other storms have hard rain, thunder, and lightning. Have children ask family members to tell what kinds of storms they remember from their native countries and what, if any, special names they have. Ask children to share the information in class.

Peer Tutoring
Language: Word Meaning

Have pairs of mixed abilities work together to make word cards for feelings: happy, sad, afraid, angry, and so on. Then ask one of them to act out a feeling and the other to find the card that names the emotion.

Present

Activate Prior Knowledge
Observe Clouds

Let children look out the window or take them outside to look at clouds. Encourage them to describe the shape and color of the clouds they see. Have them photograph the clouds on different days.

Develop Language and Concepts
Present pages 218 and 219.

Have children look at the different clouds. Encourage them to talk about how the clouds are different. Then introduce the words in the Word Bank. Help children use Word Bank words to describe the illustrations.

Read the information with children. Help them find the illustration that matches each piece of information.

Language Awareness

Vocabulary: Related Words

ACTIVITY BOOK

Call attention to the word *cloudy* in the Word Bank. Then write this sentence on the board: *On a cloudy day, I see many clouds in the sky.*

Point out that the words *cloudy* and *clouds* are related. Use the same procedure for talking about the words *wind* and *windy*, and *rain* and *rainy*. Use page 114 in the Activity Book.

Clouds in the Sky

Sometimes there are white clouds in the sky.

Sometimes there are dark clouds in the sky.

When there are dark clouds in the sky, it may rain.

218 LEARN LANGUAGE • SCIENCE

Options for Reaching All Students

Beginning
Science: Making Clouds

Provide mirrors and allow children to breathe on them. Children should notice the moisture clouding the mirror. Identify the moisture as drops of water, the same as are found in clouds. Ask for ideas about other places where drops of water form, such as on windows, from a boiling pot of water, or on mirrors after a bath or shower.

Advanced
Language: Using Imagination

Invite children to think about clouds. Then ask, *Do the shapes of the clouds remind you of anything?* Model a response by saying, *I saw a cloud that looked like a fluffy cat.* Have children name things clouds look like. Then have them make up a sentence or two to tell a story about the objects they name.

Peer Tutoring
Language: Speaking

Have children of mixed abilities form pairs. Let one partner tell all he or she knows about rain clouds. Let the other think of additional information. Keeping the textbook open should help children complete the activity.

Clouds are made of drops of water. It rains when drops of water from the clouds fall to the ground.

Word Bank

lightning

thunder

cloudy

gray

windy

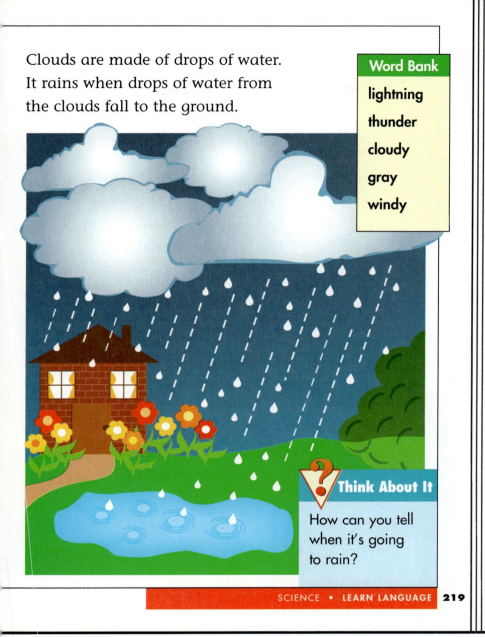

 Think About It

How can you tell when it's going to rain?

Model a Strategy
Check Inferences

Model checking inferences:

When I read the sentence When there are dark clouds in the sky, it may rain, this tells me that dark clouds may cause rain, so I read further to see if I am right. Then I see that the sentences tell me that clouds are made of drops of water and that it rains when drops of water fall to the ground. By checking my thinking, I know that I have understood what I read. Have you used this strategy too?

Assess

Use responses to Think About It for assessment. Children should be able to

- describe or draw what it looks like when it's going to rain
- tell what clouds are made of
- tell how rain happens

 LOOK AHEAD

In the next section, children will find out about water that is present in air.

Mixed Ability
Art: Cotton Clouds

Let children experiment tearing apart cotton balls and gluing them on blue or gray construction paper to represent different clouds. Help children label their art with words, such as *Cloudy Day* or *Clouds in the Sky*.

Cooperative Learning
Share a Poem

Read the poem several times and encourage children to join in. Then ask them to work in groups to plan a presentation of the poem that involves every group member. Plans might include art, choral reading, pantomime, or the like. Groups should rehearse their presentations several times before doing it for the class.

Clouds

White sheep, white sheep
On a blue hill.
When the wind stops
You all stand still.
When the wind blows
You walk away slow.
White sheep, white sheep,
Where do you go?

—Christina G. Rossetti

Practice

Activate Prior Knowledge
Feel Condensation

Put a cold carton of milk or a can of soda on a table, so that condensation forms on the outside. Invite children to feel the container. Help them describe what they feel and talk about what caused the moisture.

Develop Language and Concepts
Present pages 220 and 221.

Read the activity with children. Have them work alone or in groups. Before they begin, have them retell the steps they need to do for the activity. Then read the explanation of what happened with children.

Encourage children to answer the questions on page 221.

Do Think About It together. Help children explain where water goes as wet hair dries.

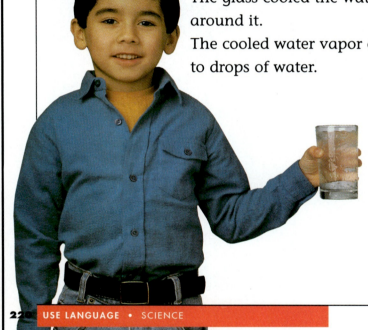

Water in the Air

Fill a glass with ice water.
Wait 5 minutes.
What do you see?

The drops of water on the glass came from water in the air.
You cannot see this water in the air.
It is called **water vapor.**

The glass cooled the water vapor around it.
The cooled water vapor changed to drops of water.

220   **USE LANGUAGE • SCIENCE**

Options for Reaching All Students

Beginning
Science: Label a Diagram

Prepare labels for the following words: *ice water, glass, air, water vapor, drops of water*. Draw a picture to show an ice-filled glass with drops of water forming on the outside. Help volunteers label the picture. Discuss each label as the child attaches it to the diagram.

Advanced
Science: Evaporation

Write *evaporate* on the board using a wet sponge. Ask children to watch as the word disappears. Lead children to conclude that the water changed to water vapor, that is, it evaporated. Make available a timer and write other words. Ask children to time how long it takes for each word to disappear, record the time, and then compare times.

Mixed Ability
Language: Vocabulary

Tell children that when water dries and goes back into the air, we say it *evaporates*. Write the word on a chart. Tell children that the words *vapor* and *evaporate* are related. Point out the word *vapor* inside the word *evaporate*.

Have you seen a puddle after
it rains?

How does the puddle look?

How does the puddle look after the
sun has been out for a while?

The water in the puddle dries up.

The water goes into the air.

Think About It

When your hair
is wet, it dries
after a while.
Where does the
water go?

Model a Strategy
Self-Assess

Model explaining a process you have read about:

After I read about how water vapor in the air changes to water that I can actually feel on the outside of a glass, I explain the process to myself in my own words to see if I understand it. In my head, I say The water on the outside of the glass came from water vapor that I can't see in the air. When the water vapor touched the glass, it cooled and changed to little drops of water. I know that if I can explain this process to myself, I understand it. Do you ever explain something to yourself after you read?

Assess ✓
Children should be able to

- explain the experiment in their own words
- tell how the sun can dry up a puddle

LOOK AHEAD

In the next section, children will use the vocabulary they have developed to learn about the water cycle.

Cooperative Language Experience
Visit a Dry Cleaner

Arrange for children to visit a dry cleaner near the school. Have the dry cleaner explain why air in a dry cleaning shop is often humid and how dry cleaners use steam in their work.

As a class, write a language experience story about the trip. Children can draw pictures about what they saw.

QuickCheck

Check to find whether all children can form a question using the question word *how*. Have those who need practice take turns forming questions that begin with *How*. Suggest beginnings such as *How many, How does,* and *How can.*

Practice

Activate Prior Knowledge
Brainstorm Concepts

Ask for volunteers to tell what they have learned about clouds. As they speak, draw a cloud full of raindrops on chart paper. Draw rain falling under the cloud.

Develop Language and Concepts
Present page 222.

Help children read page 222. Let them study the diagram of the water cycle. Encourage them to trace the path of the water in the water cycle with fingers. Tell children *cycle* is related to *circle* and point out the circular path in the diagram.

Language Awareness

Grammar: Prepositional Phrases—*from the, to the*

ACTIVITY BOOK

Write these sentences on the board and read them aloud.
Rain falls from the clouds.

Water vapor goes to the clouds.

Ask a volunteer to underline the words that tell where the rain falls from. Then ask a volunteer to underline the words that tell where water vapor goes. Extend the activity using other sentences that include *from the* or *to the*. For practice, children can use page 116 in the Activity Book.

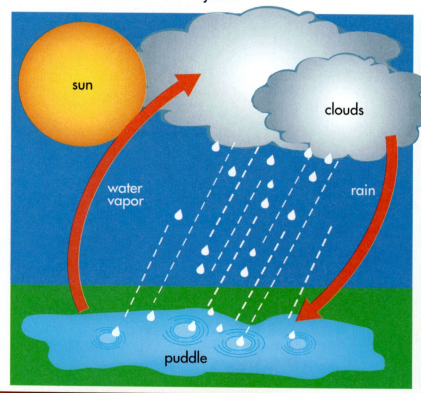

The Water Cycle

Water falls from clouds to the earth.

Then it rises from the earth to form new clouds.

This is called the **water cycle.**

sun

clouds

water vapor

rain

puddle

Options for Reaching All Students

Beginning
Art: Making a Mural

Have children work in groups. Give each group a sheet of drawing paper and crayons. Have each group draw their own water cycle. Help children explain the water cycle they have drawn.

Advanced
Language: Word Definitions

Help children develop a class definition for *water vapor.* Let children use their dictionary to see examples of the format in which dictionary definitions are written. Help children write their definition in large letters and display the definitions on a bulletin board.

Mixed Ability
Science: Evaporation

To demonstrate how water evaporates to form clouds on a hot day, pour a measured amount of water into a pan. Put the pan on a hot plate, making sure children are a safe distance away. After the water has been boiling for about 15 minutes, let it cool. Measure the amount of water again. Help children explain where the missing water has gone.

You can make a cloud.

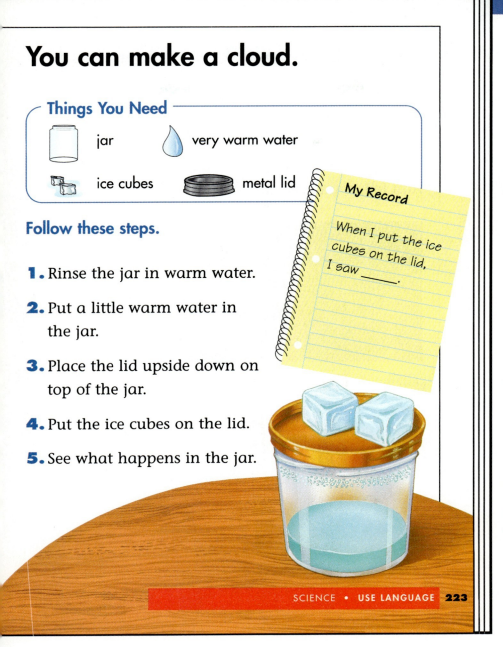

Things You Need

- jar
- very warm water
- ice cubes
- metal lid

Follow these steps.

1. Rinse the jar in warm water.

2. Put a little warm water in the jar.

3. Place the lid upside down on top of the jar.

4. Put the ice cubes on the lid.

5. See what happens in the jar.

My Record

When I put the ice cubes on the lid, I saw _____.

Connect

Activate Prior Knowledge

Review Vocabulary

Invite children to talk about how much rain falls in your area. Let children examine the rain gauges on the pages. Encourage them to guess how much rain or snow fell during the most recent storm in your area. Check newspapers for the real figures for local precipitation to share with the class.

Develop Language and Concepts

Present pages 224 and 225.

Help children read each problem separately and examine the rain gauges that go with the problem. Invite children who know how to solve each problem to write a number sentence for the problem. Then have them explain how they solved the problem.

Language Awareness

Grammar: Comparatives

ACTIVITY BOOK

Ask children whether Maria or Kim lives in a drier place. Write *drier* on a chart. Have children tell how they know Maria lives in a drier place. Then ask which person lives in a wetter place. Write the word *wetter* on the chart. Children should see that Kim lives in a wetter place. Have children brainstorm other words that compare. Write these words on a chart. Use page 117 in the Activity Book for more practice.

How much rain?

In Kim's city by the ocean, it rained 4 inches one week, 4 inches the second week, and 1 inch during the third week. How much rain fell in three weeks?

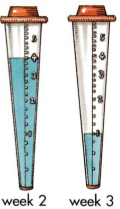

week 1   week 2   week 3

Options for Reaching All Students

Beginning

Math: Keeping a Chart

Help children keep a chart to graph the rain or snow that falls in your area. Show children how to read weather charts in the newspaper.

Advanced

Critical Thinking: Comparing and Contrasting

Invite children to compare the rainfall where they live to the rainfall where the girls in the story problems live. Then show children the weather section from a national daily newspaper and let them compare and contrast their weather with the weather in other parts of the country.

Home Connection

Science: Geography and Weather

Invite children's parents to the classroom to speak about the rainfall in their native countries. Encourage parents to bring in pictures to illustrate their talks.

In Maria's desert city, it rained 1 inch in the fall, 1 inch in the winter, and 4 inches in the spring. It did not rain in the summer. How much rain fell this year?

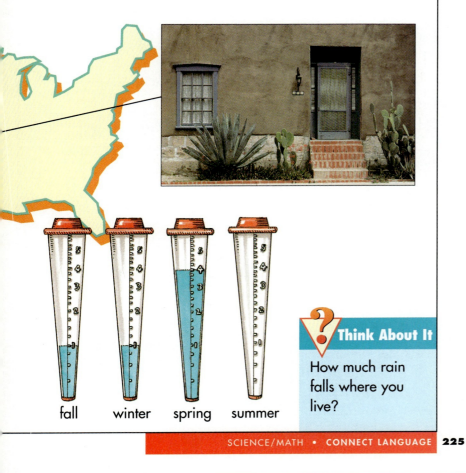

fall   winter   spring   summer

 Think About It

How much rain falls where you live?

Model a Strategy
Solve Problems

Model solving problems:

I read these problems very carefully because I want to come up with the right answer. After I read a problem the first time, I ask myself Do I need to add or subtract? Because the problems ask me how much rain fell in all, I know I must add the numbers. So I read the problem over again and add the numbers to get the total.

Assess

Use responses to Think About It for assessment. Children should be able to

- explain how they solved the problems on the pages
- describe how much rain falls in their area

LOOK **AHEAD**

In the next section, children will use the vocabulary they have developed to read a Marmaduke cartoon strip.

Cooperative Learning
Math: Story Problems

Have children form groups of four or five. Let each group make up a story problem similar to the problems in the book. Help children write their problems. Have each group read their problem to others in the class. Help the others write a number sentence to solve the problem. Encourage children to "read" their number sentences.

Little Celebrations
Ocean by the Lake

This book tells about the Shedd Aquarium in Chicago and how the animals are cared for there.

Level: Advanced

Connect

Activate Prior Knowledge
Use Pictures

Show children the Picture Card of the dog. Ask them to identify the picture and tell things they know about dogs. Then ask children to tell about their experiences bathing a dog. Use Picture Card 24.

Develop Language and Concepts
Present pages 226.

Invite children to look at the pictures and help them read the cartoon. Ask children who in the story was supposed to get a bath. Children should say Marmaduke was supposed to get a bath. Ask children who *really* got a bath. Children should say that Phil, Marmaduke's owner, is the one who really got a bath.

Help children focus on several elements that make the cartoon funny when they answer the question in Think About It.

226 CONNECT LANGUAGE • SCIENCE/LITERATURE

Options for Reaching All Students

Beginning
Language: Pantomiming

Encourage groups of children to pantomime what happens in the comic strip. Let one child be Phil, one child be Phil's wife, and one child be Marmaduke.

Advanced
Multicultural Awareness

Ask children to tell family members about the Maraduke "Wash and Dry" cartoon they read. Ask them to find out from family members in what ways funny stories are shared in their homeland. Have children report what they learned to classmates.

Mixed Ability
Language: Imagining

Have children think about what would happen if they owned a dog like Marmaduke. How would they bathe Marmaduke? What would they do with Marmaduke to have fun? Encourage children to draw a picture of something they would do with Marmaduke. Invite children to explain their pictures to others in the group.

Water Cartoons

Think about times when you use water.

Did something funny happen as you washed dishes?

Did something funny happen as you took a bath?

Did something funny happen when you went swimming?

Did something funny happen as you walked in the rain?

Write About It

Work with a partner. Make a list of times when you use water. Then together make up a cartoon about water.

Spelling: Punctuation

Have children look at the punctuation in the comic strip. Ask children if they notice anything unusual about the punctuation. Children should notice that punctuation in comic strips is somewhat different from punctuation in normal use. Point out the use of exclamation marks instead of periods to show strong feeling. Point out the use of an ellipsis (...) to show that some words are missing.

Develop Language and Concepts
Present page 227.

Read aloud the title on page 227 and ask children what they think "Water Cartoons" might be. Then read the page together, pausing to allow children to give examples to answer each question.

Assign partners and read through the directions for the Write About It activity. Have children use Activity Book page 118 as a worksheet to develop their cartoons.

Assess

Children should be able to

- look at the cartoon and retell what happened in their own words
- make a cartoon about water

Cooperative Learning
Brainstorming

Let children form groups and brainstorm outdoor washing activities such as washing pets, cars, or windows. Let each child in a group draw a different washing activity. Then have children tape their pictures on a large piece of butcher paper. Help children discuss their collage.

Writer's Workshop
Write About Marmaduke

Refer children to the Writer's Workshop on pages 230–236 of the Student Book. Have them write about a short adventure they could have with Marmaduke.

T227

Down by the Bay

**A traditional song
illustrated by Henrick Drescher**

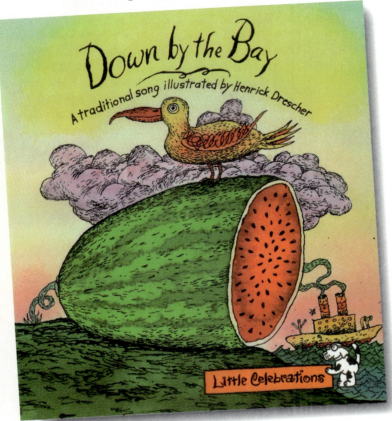

Down by the Bay
Wondrous, whimsical things can be found in a
visit down by the bay.

Shared Reading

1. Introduce
Display the book and read the title with
children. Ask, *Have any of you ever been
to a bay? What was it like?* Invite children
to share their experiences at a bay or other
body of water and to predict what they
think the book will be about.

2. Read
As you read aloud, emphasize the rhymes
in the song. Invite children to join in reading the words *down by the bay.*

3. Reread
Invite children to reread the book with you.
Discuss the book by asking questions such
as the following:

- What do you think is the silliest thing to
  see down by the bay?

- Is this story real or make-believe? How
  can you tell?

Options for Reaching All Students

Beginning
**Critical Thinking: Comparing
and Contrasting**

Encourage children to draw a picture
of their favorite scene from *Down by
the Bay.* Elicit from them why the picture they chose is their favorite. Let children compare and contrast their pictures. Help children write comparative
sentences.

Advanced
Language: Using References

Provide children with easy nonfiction
materials. Encourage them to research
and take notes on the animal and
plant life that can be found in or near
a real bay. Let them report their findings to others. Invite them to tell which
books were the most helpful and why.

Cooperative Language Experience
Field Trip

Encourage children to name what they
see down by the bay on page 16.
They should see a snake eating cake,
a pig in a wig, a bat with a hat, a
snail on a pail, a goat in a boat, a
monkey riding a donkey, and a mouse
on a house. Take the class to a body
of water where they can observe animals and people. Ask children to draw

Phonics: Rhyming Words

Have children name the rhyming words in the story. List the words as children name them.

grow	go
bear	hair
bee	knee
moose	goose
whale	tale
say	bay
fish	dish
see	tree

Encourage children to make up new sentences using each rhyming pair. It may be useful to point out that some words that rhyme do not have the same spelling pattern.

Model a Strategy

Distinguish Real from Make-Believe

Model distinguishing between real and make-believe:

When I read this book and look at the pictures, I realize the book tells about things that couldn't really happen but are fun to think about. That's how I know that what the song tells about is make-believe.

Response Activities

Perform a Choral Reading

Have children form two or more groups. Have each group read one left- and right-hand page, emphasizing the phrase *down by the bay*. Have everyone join in on the last page.

Matching Animals to Activities

Let children leaf through the book and name each animal. After they name the animal, encourage children to describe it and tell what it is doing.

Add Additional Animals

Have children work in groups to create a new book about other animals doing actions *down by the bay* or by another body of water of their choosing. Invite volunteers from each group to read their book aloud to the class.

a picture of something they saw. Have children display their pictures as prompts for a language experience story. As a class, write a language experience story patterned on *Down by the Bay*.

Cooperative Learning

Language: Rhyming Words

Have children form groups and brainstorm a list of animals such as *dog, cat, rat, bug, crow, sheep*. Let each group pick one of the animals and think of a rhyming word that tells about the animal. Then ask them to illustrate their rhyme. Have a volunteer from each group present their rhyme and illustration to the class.

Mixed Ability

Language: Asking Questions

Have children work in pairs. Ask each pair to pick an animal from the story and think of a question about the animal. For example they could ask, *What was the fish doing down by the bay?* Another pair could answer, *The fish was sailing in a dish*. Each pair that answers correctly gets to ask a question.

Connect

Activate Prior Knowledge

Brainstorm Vocabulary

Invite children to look at the illustration and make up words that describe what raindrops sound like as they hit the ground. Write their suggestions on the board.

Develop Language and Concepts

Present page 228.

PURPLE TAPE Read through "Raindrops" with children. Make sure they understand that *patter pat, patter pat* refers to the sound of rain. Talk about why the grass and flowers will be fresh and bright. Play Side 2 of the Purple Tape several times and encourage children to sing along.

TPR To help children do the Try It Out, use TPR to teach them to use their hands and arms to act out what the rain does.

Language Awareness

Vocabulary: Compound Words

Remind children that a compound word is made up of two smaller words. Write the following compound words on the board: *rainbow, raincoat, raindrop, rainfall, rainstorm.* Read aloud the words and have children repeat them after you. Have a volunteer underline with different-colored chalk each of the two words that form each compound.

Raindrops
by Clara Belle Baker

Patter pat, patter pat,
What a gentle sound is that!
Patter pat, patter pat,
Hear the raindrops tap!

Now the grass and flow'rs will be
Fresh and bright for you to see!
Patter, pat, patter pat,
Hear the raindrops tap!

Try It Out

Sing the song. Use hand and arm motions to act out what the rain does.

228 CONNECT LANGUAGE • SCIENCE/LITERATURE

Options for Reaching All Students

Beginning
Language: Memory Game

Have children compose a cumulative sentence naming things that raindrops water, with each child repeating the list and adding an item.

Child A: The raindrops tap on grass, flowers, and trees.

Child B: The raindrops tap on grass, flowers, trees, and birds.

Advanced
Writing: Song Variations

Have children write and illustrate an alternate version of the song, with different sounds for the rain and different plants that the raindrops make fresh and bright.

Multicultural Connection
Weather Poems and Songs

Invite children to bring in poems or songs from their native countries that tell about rain or other kinds of weather to share with their classmates. Perhaps children can teach their classmates the words.

Tell what you learned.

CHAPTER 12

1. Make a chart. Tell what the weather will probably be.

Clouds	Weather
white clouds	
dark clouds	

2. Work with a group. Make a mural of the water cycle. Tell about it.

3. Work with some friends. Draw a picture together to show what is happening in "Raindrops." Then sing the song or take turns telling about it.

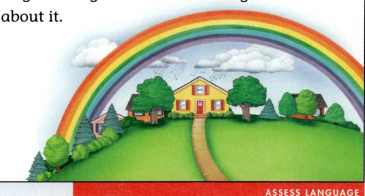

ASSESS LANGUAGE **229**

Assess ✓

Activity 1 Have children write their answers on a separate piece of paper. Evaluate the number and accuracy of responses.

Activity 2 Evaluate whether children understand the water cycle.

Activity 3 Check that children draw raindrops falling on grass and flowers.

Have children complete the Chapter Self-Assessment, Blackline Master 93. Have them choose products to place in their portfolios. Add the results of any rubrics, checklists, self-assessments, or portfolio assessments, Blackline Masters 2–18.

Listening Assessment

BLACKLINE MASTER Make sure that each child has a copy of Blackline Master 58 and crayons or markers. Play Side 2 of the Cream Tape several times stopping the tape to allow children to draw.

TAPESCRIPT

CREAM TAPE Listen carefully. Follow the directions.

You can show the water cycle. Draw rain falling from the cloud into the lake. (pause) Draw an arrow from the cloud to the lake. (pause) Draw another cloud in the sky to show where the water stays before it comes down again. (pause) Then draw an arrow from the lake to the sky to show the water rising from the lake to form new clouds.

Options for Assessment

Vocabulary Assessment

ACTIVITY BOOK Use Activity Book page 119 to assess vocabulary.

Writing Assessment

Have children make personal picture books in which they illustrate and write about water and the weather.

Language Assessment

BLACKLINE MASTER Use Blackline Master 92 in the Teacher's Resource Book.

Standardized Test Practice

ACTIVITY BOOK Use pages 120 and 121 in the Activity Book. Answers: more than 40, 8 hours, 15.

Wrap-Up

Activities

We Save Water Book

Collect any drawings that children made to show ways of conserving water. Help them organize the pictures into a book entitled *We Save Water.* If anyone has ideas for water conservation that are not pictured, encourage them to add a picture to the book. Have children take turns talking about their pictures and telling what they learned.

Water Around the World

Have children ask family members for help in preparing a word card for the word *water* in their native language. Invite children to ask family members to tell about how water was collected and used when they were growing up, as well as current practices used in their native countries. In school, collect the cards and mark them with the name of each language and country. Display the cards and point out any similarities in languages. Have children hold up their own cards and tell what they learned about water in their homeland.

Fun in All Weather

Have children form groups to think about things to do for fun in various kinds of weather. Have each group choose a kind of weather—rainy, windy, or snowy, for example. Then have them brainstorm activities that are fun to do in that kind of weather. They can decorate a box with pictures or designs to show their kind of weather and then fill it with illustrated cards showing the activities they recommend. Have each group plan and make a presentation of the ideas in their box.

Discussing the Theme

Have children work in groups of two or three to discuss their progress during this unit Water All Around Us. Choose from the following activities that will demonstrate to them how much they have learned and how useful that information is.

- Write words children have learned on 3″ x 5″ cards. Have children take turns saying the words and, if possible, drawing pictures to show what the words mean.

- Have groups discuss situations in which the words they learned will be useful. For example, words related to water can be used in science class and in discussing the weather with family and friends. Words related to bodies of water can be used in discussing maps, scenery, or planning a trip.

- Let children role play various situations in which their new vocabulary can be used. For example, children can take turns pretending to be caught in a sudden storm, to be a weather forecaster predicting the next day's weather, or to be playing in snow.

Sharing the Module Project

Use the invitation form, Blackline Master 32 or 33, to invite family members to see the water conservation program.

Set up the classroom so that each of the four groups has a station. Make sure children have rehearsed what they will say at each station.

As visitors walk in, let them visit each station and listen to children at that station tell about what they have learned.

Decorate the room with interesting projects completed during the Water All Around Us unit. Be sure that children's names are on their projects so that family members can see the work of their child.

For simple refreshments, have children offer guests ice water in paper cups. You might also have hot water and tea bags available for adults to make a cup of tea. Put up a sign that children can read to their families: *Water is important. We drink water to stay healthy.*

Signs of Success!

Duplicate a copy of this checklist for each child.

Name: _____

Refer to the checklist below for a quick determination of how a child is progressing toward transitioning out of ESL instruction.

Objectives:

- ☐ Tells how some bodies of water differ.
- ☐ Finds bodies of water on a map.
- ☐ Understands what happens when there is too much or too little water.
- ☐ Tells how water can be saved.
- ☐ Tells about clouds.
- ☐ Tells about water vapor.
- ☐ Tells about the water cycle.

Language Awareness

Understands/Uses:

- ☐ adjectives/comparatives
- ☐ capitalization/punctuation
- ☐ expressions of amount
- ☐ possessives
- ☐ related words
- ☐ forming questions
- ☐ prepositional phrases
- ☐ informal expressions

Hears/Pronounces/Reads:

- ☐ long *a*
- ☐ short *i*/long *i*
- ☐ short *u*

Learning Strategies:

- ☐ Uses context clues.
- ☐ Uses a map.
- ☐ Visualizes.
- ☐ Previews a story.
- ☐ Recognizes cause and effect.
- ☐ Paraphrases/retells.
- ☐ Checks inferences.
- ☐ Self-assesses.
- ☐ Previews directions.
- ☐ Solves problems.

Comments

_____

_____

Writer's Workshop

Follow these steps to be a good writer.

❶ Prewriting

Choose a topic.
Write your ideas.

Animals

fish
bird
bear
cat
woodchuck
turtle
spider

Organize your ideas.

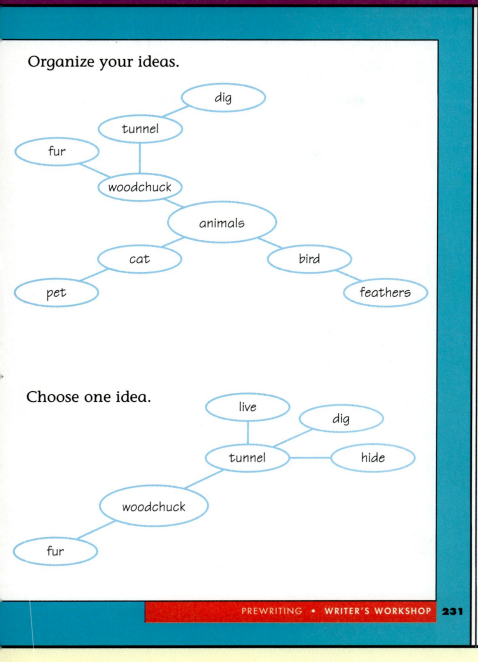

Choose one idea.

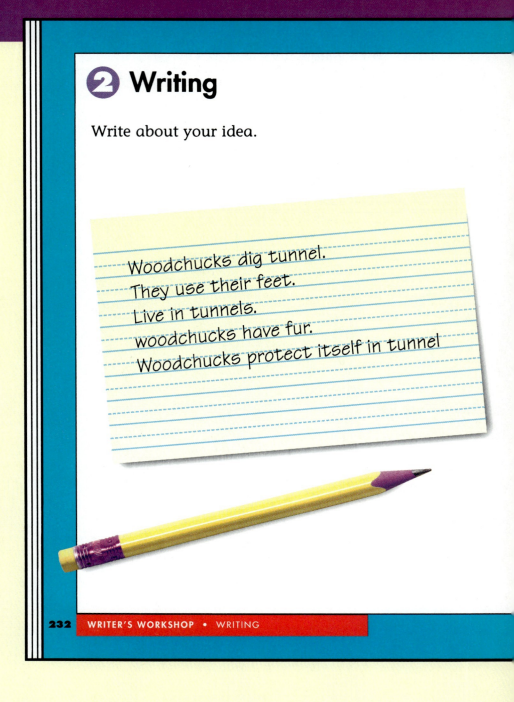

② Writing

Write about your idea.

Woodchucks dig tunnel.
They use their feet.
Live in tunnels.
woodchucks have fur.
Woodchucks protect itself in tunnel

❸ Revising

Read your story.

Can you make it better?

Can a friend help you make it better?

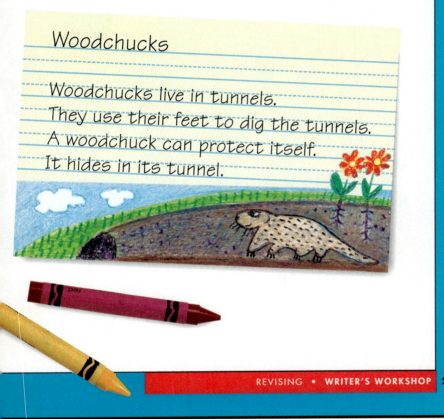

Woodchucks

Woodchucks live in tunnels.
They use their feet to dig the tunnels.
A woodchuck can protect itself.
It hides in its tunnel.

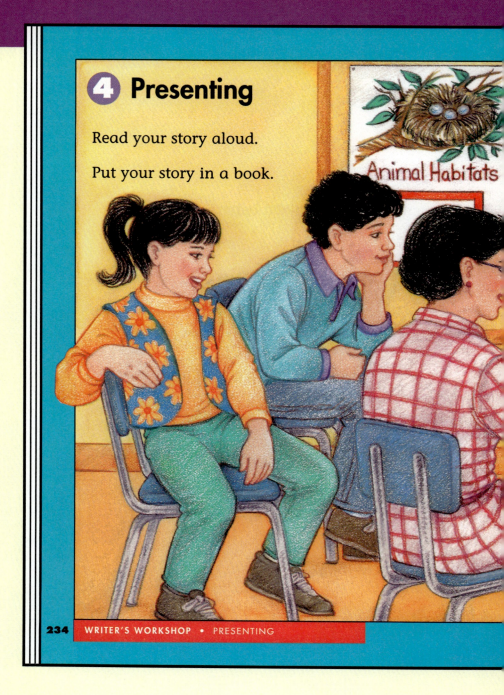

4 Presenting

Read your story aloud.

Put your story in a book.

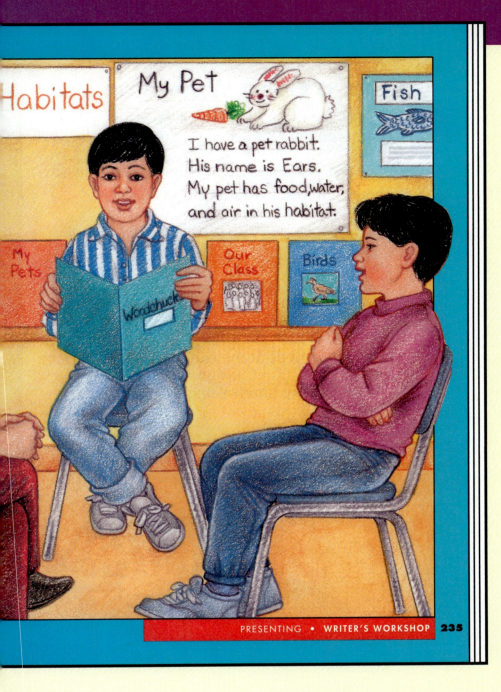

Habitats

My Pet

I have a pet rabbit.
His name is Ears.
My pet has food, water,
and air in his habitat.

Fish

My Pets

Our Class

Birds

Woodchuck

What a Good Writer Can Do

- I can plan before I write.

- I can write about things I know. I can write about animals, my family, and myself.

- I can write stories with a beginning, a middle, and an end.

- I can ask others to read my work.

- I can write in complete sentences.

- I can put periods at the ends of sentences.

- I can make my handwriting easy to read.

ScottForesman

Scope and Sequence

Chapter	Objectives	Content Focus	Language Awareness Objectives	Learning Strategies
1 Families	Tell who is in a family; tell what families do; tell how families change.	social studies, science, literature	plurals, pronouns, present tense, capital letters, initial *f*, color words	Use what you know; predict content.
2 Growing and Changing	Tell new things children can do as they grow; tell how children and animals grow and change.	social studies, science, literature	adjectives that mean "more," plurals, prepositions *in* and *on*, color words, proper nouns, offering to do something, typographical devices	Use picture clues; use pictures to get meaning; recognize main idea; draw conclusions.
3 At School	Tell how children get to school; tell what's seen at school; name rules; tell what's done at school.	social studies, math, literature	pronouns—*I* and *we*, days of the week, question words, *many*, contractions, initial *m*, initial *c* /k/, initial *d*, greetings	Use pictures; recognize patterns; understand a process; paraphrase/retell.
4 Learning	Name some things done alone and some things done in a group; name things practiced at school; tell how children feel at school; tell what's learned in school.	social studies, health, literature	infinitives, verbs, verb— *can*, pronouns, multiple meanings— *like*, *if*	Understand cause and effect; recognize repetition.
5 Neighbors	Tell where people live; tell what neighbors are; tell what a community is; tell how maps help people.	social studies, math, literature	question words, initial *n*, capitalization, opposites, initial *p*, words for noises, position words, initial *s*, initial *r*, rhyming words	Use a map; use brainstorming; use what you know; make inferences; draw conclusions.
6 Animals and Their Homes	Name places where animals live; name animals that live in trees, in ponds, and in fields; name animals that can be pets; tell how to care for pets.	science, math, literature	prepositional phrases, initial *t*, verbs, number and verbs, initial *w*, names for animal babies, future tense, initial *h*	Reread; use pictures; visualize word problems; make predictions based on prior knowledge.
7 How You Can Feel Safe	Name places where safety is important; name people who help keep others safe; name rules that help people stay safe.	health, math, literature	word families, verbs + *-er*, multiple meanings, rules, initial soft *g*, short *i*, word order, question mark, exclamation mark	Use what you know; compare and contrast; use predicting; use selective attention; recognize reality and fantasy; make predictions.

Chapter		Objectives	Content Focus	Language Awareness Objectives	Learning Strategies
8	How You Can Feel Healthy	Tell benefits of exercising; name ways to keep clean and healthy; name foods that assist growth and good health.	health, math, literature	adjectives with -y, pronoun *they*, antonyms, count vs. noncount nouns, days of the week, period, short *a*, expressing gratitude	Use picture cards; use a chart; use finding the total; make predictions based on prior knowledge.
9	Using Our Senses	Tell how to take care of the eyes and ears; tell how to make high and low sounds; tell what body part is used for each sense.	health, science, literature	verbs, antonyms, plural forms, giving instructions, capital letters, short *o*, multiple meanings—*went*, places in a house, past tense	Use imagining; recognize cause and effect; make predictions; recognize reality and fantasy; draw conclusions.
10	How We See and Hear	Compare how people and animals see; compare how people and animals hear; compare things seen and heard.	science, math, literature	expression *very well*, capitalization and punctuation, numerals and number words, questions and answers, short *u*, rhyming words	Use prior knowledge; follow directions.
11	The Four Seasons	Name the four seasons; name the months of the year; tell how the weather changes from season to season; tell what seasonal things people do; tell how people dress for the weather.	science, social studies, literature	phrases, root words, consonant blend *cl*, capitalization/punctuation, adjectives, contractions	Predict content; get information; understand that numbers show sequence; compare and contrast.
12	Trees	Tell ways people can save and protect trees; tell ways people use trees; tell why people and animals need trees.	social studies, science, literature	long *a*, period and question mark, opposites, verbs, pronoun—*they*, color words, superlatives, adjectives of size—*small/long/wide*	Use pictures for meaning; visualize; use planning; understand type conventions; use context clues.

SCOPE AND SEQUENCE 2

Chapter		Objectives	Content Focus	Language Awareness Objectives	Learning Strategies
1	People and Places	Name different kinds of groups; tell what different groups do; name places in the community; tell what people do in each place; name states in the U.S.; begin recognizing animal groups and their places.	social studies, science, literature	present tense; sentence patterns; capitalization; irregular plurals; rhyming words with long *a, e,* and *i;* informal English expression *OK;* statements showing approval	Use picture details; read maps; use pictures for meaning; recognize fact and fantasy; summarize.
2	Animals and Their Habitats	Name animals and some of their attributes; understand what animals need from their habitats.	science, math, literature	subject/verb agreement, short *a,* explaining choices, comparatives, similes, rhyme	Use pictures for meaning; understand patterns; understand main idea; count how many; remember details.
3	How People Work	Name community workers; tell how workers help us; name workplaces; tell what people's "needs" are; tell the difference between *needs* and *wants;* tell what animals' needs are.	social studies, science, literature	verbs, related words, words *needs* and *wants,* contractions, rhyme	Use pictures for meaning; use title to predict; note repeated words; find a way to classify; use what you know.
4	What Animals Do	Tell ways animals work; tell how animals protect themselves; tell how protective coloration works.	science, math, literature	subject/verb agreement; consonant blends *sm, sk,* and *spr;* giving directions; punctuation; contractions; verbs; describing; rhyme	Recognize main idea; recognize sentence patterns; follow directions; understand specialized language; use prior knowledge; use pictures to get meaning; summarize.
5	How We Have Fun	Name toys and games; name ways to play alone and to play with friends; tell how to get exercise while playing; name ways that exercise is good for you; tell what parts of the body are used with different exercises.	health, math, literature	final consonant *s /z/,* long *i,* number and present progressive tense, irregular past tense, future tense, pronouns, contractions, addressing family members and friends	Visualize; use imagery; recognize cause and effect; use pictures for meaning.
6	How Things Move	Tell what things can be pushed or pulled; understand *force;* tell what magnets do; tell about play involving pushing and pulling.	science, social studies, literature	consonant blend *tr,* adjectives, prepositions, present progressive, future tense, imperatives	Use picture clues; ask questions for information; use word structure; use context clues.

Chapter	Objectives	Content Focus	Language Awareness Objectives	Learning Strategies
7 **Plants We Eat**	Name the parts of plants; tell what each part of a plant does; name plants we eat; tell which parts of plants we eat; name grains and foods made from grains.	science, social studies, literature	consonant blends *st* and *str, a few* and *a lot (of)*, count vs. noncount nouns, passive expressions; sentence patterns, nouns and verbs; long *o* spelled *ow* and *oa*	Use pictures for meaning; see that numerals show sequence; find a way to classify; locate patterns; understand a process; summarize.
8 **Where We Buy Food**	Tell where fruits and vegetables are grown; tell where foods are purchased; tell which foods can be purchased in which places; name kinds of restaurants.	social studies, math, literature	phrases, capitalization, making requests, numerals and number words, possessives, pronouns	Preview text; monitor meaning; plan to read orally; use pictures and text; use context clues.
9 **Night and Day**	Name things in the sky; tell what causes night and day; tell about the sun; tell about the moon; tell why a calendar is important.	science, social studies, literature	homophones, compound words, expressing time, irregular past tense, comparatives, similes, describing, pattern and rhyme	Use a diagram; generalize; predict; make comparisons; use context; use prior knowledge.
10 **Long Ago and Today**	Tell about the first people in North America; tell about Spanish settlers of North America; tell about Pilgrims; name U.S. holidays.	social studies, math, literature	telling why, time expressions, ordinal numbers, questions and answer, present tense, onomatopoeia	Understand chronology; use a calendar; summarize.
11 **Where We Find Water**	Name sources of water; tell how some bodies of water differ; find bodies of water on a map; tell what happens when there is too much or too little water; tell how water can be saved.	social studies, science, literature	adjectives, capitalization, expressions of amount, long *a*, short *u*, possessives, informal expressions, short and long *i*	Use context clues; use a map; visualize; preview a story; recognize cause and effect; paraphrase/retell.
12 **Water and the Weather**	Tell how rain makes people feel; tell about clouds; tell where rain comes from; tell about water vapor; tell about the water cycle.	science, math, literature	related words, forming questions, prepositional phrases, comparatives, punctuation, compound words	Check inferences; self-assess; preview directions; solve problems.

Chapter	Objectives	Content Focus	Language Awareness Objectives	Learning Strategies
1 **The Farm and the City**	Tell what farmers do; identify products that come from a farm; tell how wheat is grown; read a thermometer.	social studies, science, literature	singular and plural nouns, subject-verb agreement—*is/are*, simple present tense, recognize commands, /p/ and /b/	Use time expressions; follow directions; recognize patterns in English.
2 **Life in the City**	Tell about a community; name services and goods in a city; solve math story problems; name parts of a city; name state capitols; name the five food groups.	social studies, math, health, literature	sentence structure, consonant sounds /g/ and /k/, capitalization of proper nouns, numbers as words, slang/informal English, extending an invitation, present progressive tense	Reread; use a map; read a chart; recognize opinions; type conventions; draw conclusions.
3 **How You Use Light**	Name lights used in the past and today; read a time line of lights; tell uses of lights in a community; explain how people use their eyes to see.	social studies, science literature	words in a series, time words, *when* and *where*, the sound of long *i*, contractions, rhyme	Recognize time and sequence; use a time line; visualize; use a diagram.
4 **What Light Can Do**	Tell what light can and cannot move through; identify what makes light bend and bounce back; use a prism to see rainbow colors; put on a shadow play.	science, social studies, literature	*some, all,* or *none;* prepositions of location *on, in, under;* commands; nouns as adjectives; communicating with sounds; expressing the same idea with different expressions; plurals of words ending in -y; alliteration	Explain a process; use pictures for meaning; paraphrase; use different expressions with the same meaning.
5 **How You Make Sound**	Tell how sound is made; demonstrate vibrations; tell how sounds are different; name musical instruments from around the world.	science, social studies, literature	the *v* sound, *can* and *can't*, adjectives, the pronoun *it*, past tense, long *a* and short *a*, rhyme, onomatopoeia	Record information; recognize sentence patterns; use type conventions; understand specialized vocabulary.
6 **How You Use Sound**	Tell how you hear sound; name parts of the ear; tell how ears help animals survive; find out how well you hear; name inventions in communication.	science, social studies, literature	the sound of *ear*, singular/plural agreement—*has/have, you* as understood subject in commands, *can* + verb + complement, *so . . . that*, long *o* and short *o*	Read a diagram; set a purpose for reading; recognize main idea; distinguish between fact and opinion.
7 **Plants, Animals, and Climate**	Describe the climate of deserts and forests; tell how a cactus can live in the desert; tell how animals live in a forest; tell how veterinarians help animals.	science, social studies, literature	*some* or *other;* adjectives; long *e;* pronouns *he, she, they; many, most, some* and *all, they* and *them; once, twice;* words for the senses	Compare and contrast; use a Venn diagram; use picture captions; reread sentences.

Chapter	Objectives	Content Focus	Language Awareness Objectives	Learning Strategies
8 **Weather and People**	Tell how weather affects the way people live; tell how people dress for the weather; identify climates in various parts of the world; tell how to stay healthy in hot weather; tell how to stay healthy in cold weather.	social studies, health, literature	antonyms; infinitives of purpose; consonant blends *sl, pl, cl;* commands; similies; quantity expressions	Recognize cause—effect relationships; recognize main idea; use a map key; use pictures for meaning.
9 **What Shelters Are Made Of**	Name materials used to build homes; tell how people found building materials long ago; tell how homes changed over time; name steps in building a beaver lodge.	social studies, science, literature	beginning and ending consonant sounds *st* and *ch, house* or *home,* past tense verbs ending in *t,* sequence words, short *i* and long *i,* identify a sentence and punctuation, parenthetical expressions	Recognize a pattern; read a time line; use numbers; learn information.
10 **How Shelters Are Built**	Name tools and materials and tell how they are used; tell how bricks and glass are made; name simple machines; name shapes in houses.	science, math, literature	forms of *build, /ks/,* subject-verb agreement *is* and *are,* show possibility—*can be,* phrases that tell *where* and *when*	Reread to understand; understand a process; use pictures for meaning.
11 **Changing the Earth**	Tell how people affect the environment; tell about a local habitat; tell how children can save a rain forest; name endangered or extinct animals write a letter to an environmental group.	science, social studies, literature	special singular and plural nouns, consonant blends—*str* and *thr,* context and picture clues, *when* clauses, making requests, possessive adjectives	Set a purpose for reading; use pictures to follow directions; use context clues; take notes.
12 **Pollution**	Name causes of water pollution; name ways to prevent water pollution; tell how to find out how clean the air is; tell how recycling works; name things that can be recycled; tell what people can do to prevent pollution.	science, social studies, literature	gerunds, sounds /h/ and /j/, conjunctions—*and,* verbs with *up, was going to,* prepositions—*under, above,* adverbs of degree—*very, too*	Paraphrase; draw conclusions; recognize language patterns; recognize supporting details; use prior knowledge to predict.

Chapter	Objectives	Content Focus	Language Awareness Objectives	Learning Strategies
1 **The American West Today**	Name the states and landforms in the West; name crops farmers grow in the West; describe ranching, fishing, and mining in the West.	social studies, science, literature	singular and plural nouns; verbs; /m/ and /n/; simple present tense; place an order; antonyms	Use a map key; recognize a pattern; read money amounts.
2 **Settling the West**	Explain why people went west; describe the trip west; tell what settlers took with them; talk about the Oregon Trail; talk about the dangers and benefits of prairie fires.	social studies, science, literature	*want* + infinitive; household items; /w/; habitual *would*; quotation marks; recount past activities; exclamations; metaphors	Set a purpose for reading; visualize; use pictures for meaning; recognize a personal title.
3 **You Are a Living Thing!**	Explain that all living things are made of cells; describe how cells grow; tell why living things need energy; demonstrate that yeast is a living thing; tell how people communicate.	science, social studies, literature	/k/ and /s/ spelled *c*; simple present vs. present progressive tense; questions with *what* and *how*; onomatopoeia; describe activities with other people; using *cannot*	Use pictures for meaning; classify to understand; use chronology to understand.
4 **Living in Your Ecosystem**	Define an ecosystem; explain how an ecosystem works; make an ecosystem; use bat facts to solve math problems.	science, math, literature	compare with *as* + adjective + *as*; conjunctions *when* and *as*; diphthong /oi/; *how many* and *how much*; prepositions of location; noun phrases with *who*; express obligation	Use labels to understand; prepare for an activity; use pictures for word meaning; visualize a relationship.
5 **The First Americans**	Name some American Indian shelters and the resources used to build them; identify the parts of a buffalo and how they were used; describe American Indian crafts; tell what an archaeologist does; name some materials that are good insulators.	social studies, science, literature	pronoun *they*; sentence patterns with *use . . . for*; present perfect tense; sequence words *first, second, third, last*; deductions with *must be*; /j/; fraction words	Classify information; use numerals for sequence; predict content; use context clues; visualize story details.
6 **The Aztec Indians**	Name some crops that Aztec farmers grew; describe Aztec arts and crafts; name foods that come from the Aztecs; explain how the Aztec calendar worked.	social studies, math, literature	past tense verbs; consonant blend *st*; expressing preference; *before* and *after*; adverbs; *I am . . .*	Use context clues; set a purpose for reading; paraphrase.

Chapter	Objectives	Content Focus	Language Awareness Objectives	Learning Strategies
7 **You Are What You Eat!**	Explain that people need food for energy; describe a balanced diet; describe a food pyramid; tell where foods grow.	health, social studies, literature	compare past abilities to present abilities with *can/couldn't;* expressing people's needs; *yes/no* questions with *did;* adverbs *well* and *poorly;* /ü/ and /yü/; /fr/	Use graphics for information.
8 **Let's Eat!**	Use a diagram to explain digestion; tell what saliva does; explain why people feel hungry; describe how people learned about vitamins.	science, social studies, literature	words for parts of the body; *when* clauses; *yes/no* questions with *do/does;* /v/ and /b/; express obligation; prepositional phrases; foreign words; *I like* + noun vs. *I like* + infinitive	Understand specialized vocabulary; use phonetic spellings; use pictures for meaning; read to find information.
9 **Life in the Rain Forest**	Tell where rain forests grow; name types of species that live in a rain forest; describe a food chain in a rain forest; tell the history of rubber.	science, social studies, literature	prepositions *above, below, along, through;* give examples with *such as;* pronoun referents; /l/ and /r/; comparisons; frequency expressions; present and past tenses	Identify main idea; use pictures for meaning; use a map key; use punctuation to read.
10 **Using Our Forests**	Tell why people need trees; explain why people need rain forests; find rain forest products; describe a rain forest scientist; tell how people are trying to save the rain forests.	social studies, science, literature	consonant blends *gr* and *tr;* past tense of irregular verbs; possibility—*might;* present progressive tense; use *please*	Use graphics to compare; use prior knowledge.
11 **Regions of Our Country**	Identify directions on a map; name regions of the U.S.; read a map; make a map; recognize state symbols.	social studies, science, literature	form plurals; capitalization of proper nouns; /sh/; expressions of amount *some, most, each, a lot of;* polite requests; rhyme scheme	Use sources of information; recognize patterns.
12 **State Histories**	Tell events in the history of California; read a time line; read a population bar graph; read a population line graph.	social studies, math, literature	ordinal numbers; irregular past-tense verbs; prefix—*re;* comparatives and superlatives; digraph *th;* express wants; /kw/; contractions	Read time lines; use prior knowledge; read a line graph; use pictures for meaning; understand author's point of view.

Chapter	Objectives	Content Focus	Language Awareness Objectives	Learning Strategies
1 **The Science of Sound**	Tell what sound is; tell how people hear; make and use an ear trumpet; read a decibel graph.	science, math, literature	The *v* sound, singular and plural nouns, action words as directions, comparatives, rhyming sounds, the long *o* sound	Recognize cause and effect; use a graph; use pictures to predict.
2 **Uses of Sound**	Make sounds of different pitch; tell how musical instruments make sound; make a musical instrument; name events people celebrate with music.	science, social studies, literature	superlatives; passive voice expressions; count vs. non-count nouns; the sound /ng/ in the final position; time expressions; suffixes *-er, -ist;* idioms	Use a graph; use classification; work cooperatively; use pictures for meaning; use intonation.
3 **The Earth Is Not Flat!**	Tell why the Indies were important; identify Columbus and describe his voyage; tell about the meeting of Columbus and the Taino people; explain how a compass works.	social studies, science, literature	use language for buying, selling, and trading; past tense verbs; word origins; digraphs in the final position, *-sh, -th;* verb tenses; asking questions; expressions of frequency	Use pictures for meaning; visualize; make inferences; make a model to understand meaning.
4 **The Aztecs and the Spaniards**	Describe the Aztec city of Tenochtitlán; explain how Cortés conquered the Aztecs; name the parts of a horse; make an Aztec sun god mask.	social studies, science, literature	prepositions *in, on;* saying dates; /ėr/ sound spelled *er, ir, ear, or;* making general statements; verbs in directions; rhythm and rhyme	Identify main idea; use patterns; understand a process.
5 **Precious Water**	Explain differences between fresh water and salt water; tell why living things need water; name ways people use water; do an experiment with salty water.	social studies, science, literature	capitalization of proper nouns; infinitives; use of *as;* the pronoun *it;* /y/ in *Yaya* vs. /j/ in *magical;* the sound /v/; clauses with *that*	Find a topic sentence; read on to get meaning; recognize supporting details; record observations; summarize.
6 **The Forms of Water**	Name the forms of water; explain the water cycle; do a water cycle experiment; describe water sources in the Sahara Desert.	science, social studies, literature	Sounds for *s,* the *-tion* ending, long vowel sounds, simple present tense for presenting facts; asking questions	Use pictures for meaning; use context to get meaning; follow directions; use imagery to understand poetry.
7 **Coming to America**	Name countries from which settlers came; tell why setters came to America; tell about a journey to America; describe a beaver.	social studies, science, literature	time expressions; short *a,* long *a;* past progressive tense; describing; transportation words; *there is, there are*	Visualize story details; formulate opinions; summarize.

Chapter	Objectives	Content Focus	Language Awareness Objectives	Learning Strategies
8 Life in the Colonies	Tell something about Jamestown; become familiar with the names of the thirteen colonies; tell something about the New England, Middle, and Southern Colonies; read a graph on tobacco exports.	social studies, math, literature	infinitives; names of languages; past tense of irregular verbs; comparisons— *more, less;* compound sentences; comparisons—*as* + adjective + *as;* short *i* and long *i*	Recognize cause and effect; use a Venn Diagram; read a bar graph; make predictions; use context clues; paraphrasing.
9 What Do You Read?	Tell why people read; name materials people read; identify the parts of a front page; identify the sections of a newspaper; use word clues to solve story problems.	language arts, math, literature	infinitives; letter-sound correspondence—*f, ph, th;* report information; clauses with *that;* use of *do;* make exclamations	Use pictures to answer questions; read story problems; decode unfamiliar words.
10 What Makes a Good Story?	Define setting, characters, and plot; read a plot diagram; write a plot diagram; tell about storytelling around the world.	language arts, social studies, literature	subject/verb agreement—*is, are;* present tense verbs; question marks; the sound *s* spelled *c;* idioms; consonant digraph—*sh;* contractions; expressing approval and disapproval; rhyming words	Recall the plot; make a plot diagram; skim and scan; use pictures for meaning; ask questions to understand word meanings.
11 Problems with England	Tell that America's thirteen colonies belonged to England; explain why some colonists were angry with England; describe what happened at the Boston Tea Party; write and solve a sales tax problem.	social studies, math, literature	*only/many,* idioms, irregular past tense, the short *e* sound, sound words, indefinite pronouns and adverbs, the present perfect tense, long and short *i*	Draw conclusions; take notes; recognize point of view; follow directions.
12 The War for Independence	Identify Thomas Jefferson as the writer of the Declaration of Independence; identify George Washington and describe conditions at Valley Forge; tell what happened at the Battle of Yorktown; use capital letters; name important beliefs in the Declaration of Independence.	social studies, language arts, literature	pronouns—*they, he, it;* describe conditions; sounds *or* and *ar;* capitalization of proper nouns; adjective/pronoun—*these*	Summarize; use a time line; generalize; read on to get meaning.

SCOPE AND SEQUENCE 6

Chapter	Objectives	Content Focus	Language Awareness Objectives	Learning Strategies
1 **Digging Up Fossils**	Describe dinosaurs; tell how scientists learn about dinosaurs; tell when dinosaurs lived; compare old and new ideas about dinosaurs.	science, art, literature	plurals; the idiom *turn into*; *before* and *after*; consonant *p*; consonant blends *pl* and *pr*; past tense of *to be*; antonyms; conjunctions *or* and *and*; synonyms	Use headings; recognize patterns; read a chart; use action words in directions; find details; remember details.
2 **Digging Up Ancient Objects**	Name ancient Egyptian artifacts; tell how archeologists learn about the past; tell about ancient Egyptian burial; tell about King Tut's tomb; tell about hieroglyphics.	social studies, language arts, reading, literature	letters *f* and *ph*; past tense; expressions *years old/years ago*; numbers; quantity words *all/most/many/several*; rhyme	Use diagrams for meaning; keep track of chronology.
3 **Types of Fitness**	Name various types of physical fitness; describe steps one must take to be fit; identify body parts; understand and use commands in exercises; make a fitness plan; talk about games played around the world.	health, social studies, literature	*when* clauses; number words; gerunds; present tense; initial consonants *b* and *f*; contractions	Rehearse steps; read a chart; use reference resources; use techniques to memorize.
4 **Olympic Challenges**	Describe the history of the Olympic Games; explain how the modern games differ from the ancient Olympics; name various Olympic events; identify skills Olympic athletes need; explain the nature of Greek myths.	social studies, math, literature	irregular past tense; expression *such as*; ordinal numbers; superlatives; subject pronouns; real conditional sentences; regular past tense; punctuation rules	Use a map; categorize information; predict before and during reading.
5 **Life Underwater**	Name the areas of the ocean; name the things found in the ocean; compare the areas of the ocean; tell why things float; name the oceans of the world.	science social studies, literature	comparatives with *-er*; adjectives —position and agreement; articles *a* and *an*; expressions *surrounds/ is surrounded by*; antonyms; irregular past tense verbs long *e*; vowel digraphs *ea/ee*	Identify main topics; follow order in an experiment; use dialogue to evaluate character; use pictures for meaning.
6 **Taking Care of the Ocean**	Tell how people use the ocean; tell how people pollute the ocean; name some solutions to pollution; tell how students can help the environment; tell about aquaculture.	social studies, science, reading, literature	questions with *how*; answers with *by* + *-ing*; *stop/start* + *-ing*; expressions *less* and *more*; consonant digraph *sh*; *wh-* questions in the past tense; consonant *s*	Use a graphic organizer; find information in a newspaper article.

Chapter	Objectives	Content Focus	Language Awareness Objectives	Learning Strategies
7 **The Roman Empire**	Tell how the ancient Romans built their empire; describe the ancient Romans as builders; discuss the nature of Roman law; identify Latin words in English; discuss contributions of the ancient Romans.	social studies, language, reading, art	regular and irregular past tense; the verb *be* + adjective; hard and soft *c;* prefixes; amounts and container words; plurals	Read a map key; find the topic sentence; use prior knowledge; follow a recipe.
8 **Volcanoes in History**	Describe the eruption of Mount Vesuvius; discuss what archaeologists learned from Pompeii; tell what a volcano is; retell an ancient Roman myth.	social studies, science, literature	verbs and infinitives; passive verbs; consonant blends and digraphs with *s;* capitalization of proper nouns; discourse connectors; prepositional phrases of direction; regular and irregular past tense; letter *v*	Make personal connections; summarize to remember information; use a graphic organizer; visualize a story.
9 **What Makes Things Move?**	Explain why objects move; identify everyday activities that use motion; experiment with friction and gravity; explain why things move and why they stop.	science, math, literature	present tense; shape words; comparisons with *-er;* superlatives with *-est;* quotation marks for dialogue; action words; rhyming words with different spellings	Predict, monitor one's work; use context clues to find meaning.
10 **Physics of Roller Coasters**	Explain how a roller coaster works; experiment with the forces that make a roller coaster run; learn about synonyms and the use of a thesaurus.	science, math, reading, literature	words that show a sequence; expressions with *up;* conditional sentences; math words for averaging; express excitement; synonyms and antonyms; slang	Visualize; how to read a chart; understand words with multiple meanings; use word groups to remember new words.
11 **Handling Stress**	Describe some of the physical effects of stress; identify situations that cause stress; name ways to deal with stress; discuss school and differences among schools attended.	health, language arts, reading, literature	may; *have to;* end punctuation; giving advice; greetings and introductions; infinitives; telling "why"; stating rules; comparisons *good/better/best*	Paraphrase/retell; solve a problem; state main idea; identify with characters; compare and contrast.
12 **Getting Information**	Describe sources of information; tell how to use an encyclopedia as a reference tool; describe information found in magazines and newspapers; use graphic organizers to connect information.	study skills, language, reading, literature	appositives; quotation marks; questions and answers; colon; *wh-* questions; cognates	Understand chronology; understand magazine articles; consider the source; use graphic organizers; read on to get meaning.

Chapter	Objectives	Content Focus	Language Awareness Objectives	Learning Strategies
1 Immigration Then and Now	Give reasons why people immigrate; tell about the first settlers in North America; name the early English and Spanish settlements in the United States; tell where later immigrants to the United States came from.	social studies, literature, math	infinitive answers to *why* questions; past tense; expression *such as*; verbs *increase/decrease*; dialogue; action verbs; expressions *there was/there were*; short *a*	Make a time line; read large numbers; visualize the story.
2 Gifts from Many Lands	Tell how immigrants have brought their culture to the US; tell how people borrow customs and language from other groups; describe how different ethnic groups celebrate; identify place names from other cultures.	social studies, language arts, reading, literature	information questions; *when* clauses; words for nationalities ending in *-ese* and *-an*; capitalization; imperatives; vowel digraphs *oo* and *ou*	Use cognates; use paragraphs to follow meaning.
3 How the Eyes Work	Identify parts of the eye and how they work together; explain how pictures are formed and transmitted to the brain; compare human eyes to those of bees; learn idioms about eyes and seeing.	science, language arts, literature	position words; present tense: third person singular; hard and soft *c*; gerunds; negative present tense; greetings and farewells	Read science vocabulary; use a diagram to get meaning; follow steps compare and contrast.
4 Looking at Colors	Name different kinds of radiant energy; describe how light is comprised of different colors with different wavelengths; explain where rainbows come from; tell how artists use color to affect the viewer's mood.	science, art, literature	the conjunction *but*; present perfect tense; position of adjectives; *all/most/many/some/several/few*; past tense; *sh, sl,* and *sp*; words that describe sequence; *like* used for comparison	Scan text to predict content; read a scientific process; use diagrams to visualize; identify values; understand italics.
5 Life in the Middle Ages	Name classes of people during the Middle Ages; describe life in a castle; explain how a boy became a knight; tell about the legend of King Arthur.	social studies, health, literature, art	negative past tense; pronouns; gerunds; frequency adverbs; antonyms; sentence structure; future expressions; possessive forms	Recognize patterns in text; use reader's tips; make inferences; analyze a legend.
6 Trade in the Middle Ages	Describe how people traveled in the Middle Ages; tell how towns grew during the Middle Ages; identify products Europeans imported and exported during the Middle Ages; explain how the Black Death spread through Europe.	social studies, health, literature	names of occupations ending in *-er*; verbs + infinitives; past perfect tense; irregular past tense verbs ending in *-aught* and *-ought*; giving reasons with *because* and *so that*	Track cause and effect; use maps; revise predictions and self-correct; understand the use of italics.

Chapter	Objectives	Content Focus	Language Awareness Objectives	Learning Strategies
7 **Reading Stories**	Tell about types of reading materials; identify story elements; tell about story genres; tell how scientists test ideas.	language arts, science, literature	question words; irregular plurals; *may/might; yes/no* questions; use of italics for emphasis; interjections; long *e:* vowel digraphs *ie/ea;* contractions	Use an idea web; identify genres; use pictures to get meaning; identify story elements; identify a fantasy.
8 **Writing Stories**	Tell about languages and alphabets; tell about the parts of a dictionary; name types of writing; tell about different kinds of writers; write about yourself.	language arts, careers, reading literature	capitalization of place names, languages, nationalities, and book titles; words with multiple meanings; common punctuation; verbs that express necessity; words that describe people; long *o:* vowel digraphs *ow, oa*	Look up words in a dictionary; prepare to write.
9 **Mysteries in History**	Tell about the Inca civilization in South America; describe the end of the Inca civilization; tell about the historical site of Machu Picchu; describe various features of the Andes Mountains.	social studies, science, literature	position of adjectives; passive voice; cause and effect with *so* and *since;* comparatives and superlatives with *-er* and *-est;* real conditionals; expressing opinions; present and past tense; express likes and dislikes	Keep track of main ideas; use maps; use selective attention; take notes on main ideas.
10 **How Science Solves Mysteries**	Describe the process scientists use to solve mysteries; explain hypotheses scientists have about whales' songs; tell about the mystery of Loch Ness.	science, math, reading, literature	*why* questions; digraphs *ch* and *tch;* cause and effect; math vocabulary; connecting words *however* and *but;* sensory words	Paraphrase; read math problems; follow arguments.
11 **Desert Life**	Describe conditions found in the desert; name deserts of the world; tell how plants, animals, and people survive in the desert; name animals that live in the desert.	science, social studies, literature	adjectives ending in *-y;* present tense; ordinal numbers, prepositions of time; *because* clauses; negatives; intensifiers; long *a*	Identify main and supporting ideas; use information to understand characters' feelings; visualize.
12 **Water in the Desert**	Describe how plants and animals adapt to lack of water and to sudden rainfalls; explain how cities, towns, and farms get water; identify ways to conserve water; describe other solutions to the water shortage problem.	science, math, reading, literature	present tense: third person singular and negative; appositives; transitions; questions about amounts; *start/stop* + gerund; vowel digraphs *aw* and *al*	Read diagrams; guess word meanings; use context clues.

Chapter	Objectives	Content Focus	Language Awareness Objectives	Learning Strategies
1 Growing Up	Name physical characteristics family members share; describe the growth of boys and girls between ages 9 and 15; tell how heredity influences growth; name foods from the different food groups.	health, math, reading, literature	comparatives; present tense *has/have* and *is/are*; plural forms; possessive adjectives; superlatives; opposites	Understand key words; use a chart; understand directions.
2 Life Cycles of Plants	Name the parts of a plant; name the four main parts of a flower; describe the life cycle of a plant; tell how plants and animals are interdependent; identify parts of plants that people can eat.	science, math, literature, reading	words that describe; initial consonant *p*; consonant blends *pl* and *pr*; count and noncount nouns; position words; capitalization of place names; expressing intention with *going to* or *will*; past tense; punctuation	Use pictures for meaning; follow a sequence; make inferences; recognize cause and effect; visualize story details.
3 Changing Weather	Name kinds of weather; tell what makes weather change; tell how we know that air has weight; tell what causes storms; use weather idioms and sayings.	science, language arts, literature	conjunctions *and* and *or*; imperatives; present tense; adjectives that end in *-y*; *he/she/they*; past tense; *ou* and *ow*	Follow directions; track cause and effect; infer word meaning; understand story elements; read on to get meaning.
4 Predicting the Weather	Name the ways we get information about weather; tell about meteorologists; tell about the tools meteorologists use; tell who uses weather forecasts; read a weather map.	science, math, reading, literature	future with *will*; the expression *use (it) to*; clauses with *so* to express purpose; *there is/there are*; future with *going to*; the letter *l*; long *a*	Use a graphic organizer; understand specialized vocabulary; recognize text organization; use a map key.
5 The United States Before the Civil War	Describe the prewar economies of the North and the South; tell about slavery and the abolitionist movement; talk about Harriet Tubman and the Underground Railroad.	social studies, math, reading, literature	words that contrast; passive voice; italics for titles; expressions for comparison; past tense; contractions	Recognize supporting details; use encyclopedias; understand textbook explanations.
6 War Between North and South	Tell how people were affected by the war; describe the results of the war; name the leaders and some famous people of the war; tell how the songs of the era describe the times; tell how literature describes the war.	social studies, music, literature	use commas in numbers; stating opinions; occupation words ending in *-er* and *-ist*; future tenses with *will* and *going to*; action words; words that paint pictures; position words; prefix *un-*	Understand chronology and biographies; understand characters' feelings; summarize events.

Chapter	Objectives	Content Focus	Language Awareness Objectives	Learning Strategies
7 **The Sun**	Describe the solar system; explain why space appears to be black; tell how ancient peoples interpreted the universe; cite some literary examples that were inspired by the Sun and moon.	science, social studies, literature	prepositions of position; words for big; *little* vs. *few*; nationalities ending in *-ese* and *-an*; homonyms; synonyms	Read a diagram.
8 **The Planets**	Describe different physical characteristics of the planets; describe some major events in the history of space exploration; name idioms that relate to space.	science, math, literature, language arts	present tense to state general facts; comparatives; dates; *before* and *after*; unreal conditions; words that describe; ordinal numbers; superlatives; idioms	Use charts to make comparisons; read a time line.
9 **Settling the West**	Tell how, why, and when immigrants and and other settlers moved to the West; describe a prairie home and life there in the late 1800s; recognize problems caused by increased contact between settlers and Indians.	social studies, science, literature	capitalization of place names; the suffix *-less*; passive voice; amount words *many/few/little*; quotation marks with unattributed dialogue; negatives; long *o*	Use maps in textbooks; scan; use previously learned information; use a dictionary to increase vocabulary.
10 **Industry Changed the Nation**	Describe the Industrial Revolution; identify some U.S. industrial leaders and inventors; tell about the causes and effects of the reform movement; describe the life of Andrew Carnegie; sing songs of the Industrial Revolution.	social studies, math, literature	expressions of time; appositives; phrase *because of*; question formation; recognize unreal conditions; rhyming words; making requests	Read on to get meaning; use a time line; predict content; compare and contrast.
11 **Citizenship**	Describe the requirements for becoming a naturalized citizen and the meaning of good citizenship; tell about the Statue of Liberty, Ellis Island, and immigration experiences there.	social studies, math, reading, literature	*by* + gerund; answers to *how* questions; expressions with *must* and *have to*; spelling rules for gerunds; present perfect tense; silent letters in words; words with double *ss*; use of *would*; words that rhyme	Use a Venn diagram; understand the use of bulleted text.
12 **Government**	Describe the U.S. as a democracy; name the three branches of government; discuss the Constitution and some key amendments; list some views on the meaning of the U.S.	social studies, math, literature	*or* to signal appositives or explanations; colons; two-word verbs with *out*; present perfect tense with *since*; speech fillers; consonant blends	Understand text organization; use charts to get meaning; use a time line.

NOTES

NOTES

NOTES

NOTES

NOTES